MORTAL ENGINES

The Science of Performance
and the Dehumanization of Sport

John M. Hoberman

THE FREE PRESS
A Division of Macmillan, Inc.
NEW YORK
Maxwell Macmillan Canada
TORONTO
Maxwell Macmillan International
NEW YORK   OXFORD   SINGAPORE   SYDNEY

The Free Press
A Division of Macmillan, Inc.
866 Third Avenue, New York, N.Y. 10022

Maxwell Macmillan Canada, Inc.
1200 Eglinton Avenue East
Suite 200
Don Mills, Ontario M3C 3N1

Macmillan, Inc. is part of the Maxwell Communication Group of Companies.

Printed in the United States of America

printing number
1   2   3   4   5   6   7   8   9   10

Library of Congress Cataloging-in-Publication Data

Hoberman, John M. (John Milton)
    Mortal engines: the science of performance and the dehumanization of sport
    John M. Hoberman.
        p.   cm.
    ISBN 0-02-914765-4
    1. Sports sciences.   2. Sports—Physiological aspects.   3. Doping
in sports.   I. Title.
RC1235.H63   1992
613.7'11—dc20   92-7245
                                                                        CIP

To my parents

Contents

Preface

The history of scientific interest in athletic performance is an untold story. It is a story of how scientists have tried to find the sources of human speed, strength, and endurance, and how some of them have attempted to boost the human organism beyond its known limits. Scientific interest in these problems is of recent origin. A century ago the idea of devising medical or psychological techniques to improve an athlete's performance was a novelty. Although it is hard for us to imagine, the pioneering physiologists of a hundred years ago had only just begun to investigate human athletic potential. It did not occur to them to produce Olympic medal-winners. For these investigators sport served the ends of scientific research rather than the other way around.

For the past century high-performance sport has been a vast, loosely coordinated experiment upon the human organism. The first unstated aim of this great project has been to investigate how the human mind and body react to stress. Its second aim has been to adapt the athlete's mind and body to greater and greater degrees of stress. Athletic training, after all, is the pursuit of stress in order to prepare the athlete for the even greater ordeals of competition.

Today's attempts by teams of athletes, trainers, doctors, and scientists to produce record-breaking performances have the quality of an obsession. The widespread use of drugs to boost athletic performances is only the most publicized symptom of this global mania to produce "world-class" athletes, which is as excessive in China as it is in Germany or the United States, as newly fashionable in Morocco as it is in Kenya. This book, then, is the story of this obsessive quest to find the limits of human athletic potential: how it began, how it grew, and where it may take us in the future. Surprising as it may sound, most of this story has never been told before.

Because this book describes an obsessional and often corrupt subculture within the world of sport, it should begin with the author's confession of his own vulnerability to its temptations. I have spent twenty of my forty-seven years as a runner of modest ability. My interest in the history of attempts to surpass human limits is, therefore, highly personal. It derives both from my having exceeded previous limits as well as from many painful encounters with limits that have proven to be permanent. The precise nature of these limits remains mysterious to this day.

Many years ago when I was running faster than I ever have, I was presented with an opportunity to buy a can of chemical powder that would make me stronger and faster. Whether I paused to reflect if this was licit or illicit behavior for an athlete, I cannot remember. In fact, I jumped at this chance to acquire a chemical advantage, paying more money than I could really afford. The fact that the can contained nothing more than powdered amino acids, the building blocks of ordinary protein, is beside the point. The real meaning of this episode was the intoxicating feeling—still unique to my experience—that I might actually become capable of unprecedented performances. This was a "peak experience" I have never forgotten, and it has partially tempered my own judgments of athletes who take drugs in secret to outperform their competitors. I do not think they should, but I can understand something about why they do.

Perhaps the most mysterious dimension of the high-performance athlete is the willingness to take medical risks for the purpose of surpassing previous limits. I marveled at this perversity until the day I realized that writing this book was damaging my eyesight. "It doesn't matter," said a voice in my head. "It will have been worth it."

Acknowledgments

M any colleagues and friends have contributed to the making of this book by providing information, reading chapter drafts, or by offering their support. I would like to thank in particular Katie Arens, Charles Bearden, Robert Edelman, Peter Hess, Arnd Krüger, Robert Malina, Thomas H. Murray, Robert A. Nye, Clark T. Sawin, M.D., Janet Swaffar, Jan and Terry Todd, John M. Weinstock, Walter D. Wetzels, and Charles Yesalis. My editor, Adam Bellow, understood the importance of the story told herein from the beginning and supported me unswervingly for three years. The editorial work of Charles Flowers resulted in countless improvements to the manuscript. I am grateful to the University Research Institute of the University of Texas at Austin for its generous support of my research at a crucial phase. Finally, I am grateful to my wife, Louisa, for putting up with the two years of obsessional writing that made this book possible.

1

In the Penal Colony
Sport and the Great Experiment

"Great sport begins where good health ends."

—Bertolt Brecht

The Death of Birgit Dressel

By the time Birgit Dressel was admitted to the Urological Clinic at the University of Mainz medical center on April 9, 1987, she was in agony. The terrible pain that radiated throughout her torso had already resisted a series of powerful analgesic drugs prescribed by a platoon of medical experts. A new team of specialists could find no urological disorder. The twenty-six-year-old West German heptathlete was next taken to emergency surgery, where four surgeons concluded that her suffering was not caused by any sports-related injury. By now Dressel's fingernails were turning blue, and a white crust had formed on her lips. The attending neurosurgeon began to suspect she had been poisoned. She was rushed to an intensive care unit and attached to an artificial respirator. But despite the accumulated efforts of more than two dozen medical specialists, her death was only hours away. Only the autopsy would reveal the inflammation of the spinal cord that had caused her untreatable pain. So ended the ugliest chapter to date in the history of West German sports medicine.[1]

1

The death of Birgit Dressel shook the West German sports medical establishment and its hundreds of athletic clients, many of whom assumed that her death had resulted from her use of the vast array of drugs and other fortifying substances police found in her living quarters.[2] While Dressel's father described her as a victim of the pharmaceutical industry, this charge absolves too many people who share responsibility for her drug abuse, not least the athlete herself. Over several years preceding her death, Dressel had permitted her primary sports physician, the notorious Armin Klümper,[3] to inject her at least four hundred times with dozens of substances, including proteins known to be immunologically hazardous. In addition to these treatments from a man known as "The Needle Doctor," she had given herself injections and oral doses of various drugs, including an anabolic steroid (Megagrisevit) which she had received anonymously in the mail. The trainer-lover with whom she lived had doubtless encouraged and monitored her performance-enhancing drug regimen. It is probable that the fatal chemistry of her death was somehow catalyzed by a series of injections that had been initiated when she had to break off training due to a recurrence of pain in her lower spinal region. Precisely how the promiscuous polypharmacy of her athletic regimen spiraled out of control will never be known.

The Birgit Dressel affair offers a comprehensive portrait of modern high-performance sport in miniature. The cast of characters is complete: the ambitious athlete and her trainer-companion, both hoping to escape from their cramped attic apartment into the brightly illuminated world of international stardom; the sports officials who take the necessity of illicit drug use for granted and therefore tolerate or even encourage the use of performance-enhancing drugs; and the physician whose need to associate with famous athletes rendered him unfit to distinguish between maintaining the body's health and boosting its performance with medically reckless procedures.

It is now widely understood that high-performance sport is a medically hazardous activity. Birgit Dressel was only one of many modern athletes who have taken medical risks and suffered serious and even fatal consequences—and not just from drug use alone. Indeed, the damage her body had incurred prior to her death included intervertebral disc injuries, fusion of the vertebrae, a pelvic dislocation, pathological degeneration of both kneecaps, and inflamed joints. Dozens of athletes, professional cyclists in particular, have died from overdoses of stimulants and other performance-boosting substances.[4] In the course of 1987 and 1988 alone, eighteen Dutch and Belgian cyclists, including one woman, died for unknown reasons. It is widely assumed that some or all of them were taking superdoses of artificially produced erythropoetin, a natural hormone that stimulates the formation of red blood cells, thereby increasing oxygen transport to the muscles.[5] An underground report claiming a high death rate among Soviet Olympic athletes surfaced just prior to the 1984 Los Angeles Olympic Games. "The list, it is claimed, was compiled with the participation of Soviet athletes, many of whom fear for their own life-expectancy as a result of training procedures."[6] The German biochemist Manfred Donike, the world's most prominent drug-detection specialist, has stated that legalizing anabolic steroids (and thereby increasing their use) would lead to hundreds of deaths among overly ambitious athletes.[7]

Most of the medical damage caused by high-performance athletic training and drug use is not fatal. But the risks and discomforts are real. The variety of circumstances in which elite athletes find themselves can be described as a continuous spectrum involving various degrees of pressure from trainers, sports federations, and even governments. At one end is the consenting adult who lives free of official pressures to overtrain or take drugs, while at the other end of the spectrum is the child-athlete who is pressured into a punishing training regimen and perhaps fed anabolic steroids without his own or his parents' knowledge. The Soviet hammer-thrower Yuri Sedykh, to take one example, belongs somewhere between these two extremes. Sedykh once told a journalist how much he looked forward to "detoxifying" his body in the periods between major competitions—a clear reference to the illegal hormone treatments required by the Soviet trainers and officials who managed his career prior to the collapse of communism in the Soviet Union and Eastern Europe.[8] The disintegration of Communist authority in these societies has released a flood of information about official government involvement in the medical mistreatment of athletes. As Rolf Donath, director of the Central Institute for Sports Medical Service in Kreischa, formerly East Germany, confessed in 1990: "We have simply destroyed many sports by subjecting the athletes to ruinous training in defiance of the basic laws of physiology."[9] Lothar Pickenhain, a cofounder of the famous Research Institute for Physical Culture and Sport in Leipzig, has reported gymnasts in training who suffered accidents leading to paralysis and even death.[10] Similar abuses on a smaller scale have occurred in West Germany, ranging from covert doping schemes to training regimens that have lead to cardiac, renal, and other medical problems. In one case unknown to the public, one of West Germany's leading female athletes spent eleven months in a medical clinic being treated for anorexia.[11] At the same time, however, West German athletes have always enjoyed a degree of personal autonomy denied to their East German counterparts. When a team physician ordered the professional soccer star Uli Hoeness to submit to a knee operation, the latter objected: "This is something no one can require of me, because it is an assault on my personality."[12]

While the medical risks taken by athletes are sometimes imposed on them, others make wholly voluntary decisions to accept virtually any hazards in pursuit of performance gains. For all of these people the most dangerous temptations derive from the underground drug culture that has developed in the world of high-performance sport since the 1960s—a pharmacological wonderland of exotic substances, swirling rumors, black-market drug dealing, anonymous and privately circulated doping handbooks, and constant uncertainty about what is actually being injected and ingested. There are anabolic steroids and testosterone, along with drugs (probenecid and epitestosterone) that allegedly "mask" their presence in the body; stimulants like amphetamines, caffeine, and strychnine; an artificial human growth hormone that is alleged to promote muscle growth; beta-blocker drugs used by marksmen and biathletes to slow breathing and heart rates; and both erythropoetin and "blood doping" transfusions to increase the red blood cell count in endurance athletes. The most bizarre reports of physiological manipulations concern pregnancy doping, whereby an athlete becomes pregnant for the express purpose of inducing hormonal changes that boost athletic performance.[13] While these reports are unsubstantiated, the fact that they have circulated widely in medical and athletic circles suggests that the rumor mill, like doping itself, is out of control.

"A Gigantic Biological Experiment"

Startling as it may seem that many athletes are willing to risk their health and even their lives in the pursuit of records and victories, the entire enterprise of elite sport is best understood as a recent chapter in the history of applied medical research into human biological development. Olympic sport, as one prominent German sports physician has said, has been nothing less than "a gigantic biological experiment carried out on the human organism" over the past hundred years.[14] Our purpose here is to illuminate the largely unknown story of "scientific" sport—its origins, phases, current predicament, and uncertain future in a time of momentous biotechnological innovations that may conceivably be applied to the development of athletes in the future. The genetic engineering of athletes, for example, could be the next logical step for the sports sciences.

The ambition to boost athletic performance in a scientific manner is a fairly recent development.[15] Scientific interest in the physiological and psychological dimensions of athletic performance first appeared among the biologists and anthropologists of nineteenth-century Europe, accelerating sharply during the 1890s. But the investigation of human athletic potential was never a primary goal of those who studied the human organism at this time. Thus when the great German physiologist Emil du Bois-Reymond published a pioneering essay in 1881 on the science of "exercising" the entire range of human faculties, he treated the idea of producing superior athletes like runners and jumpers as a hypothetical afterthought.[16] Indeed, Germany's first track-and-field meet was held only the year before du Bois-Reymond's essay appeared.[17]

Quantified sports performances—excluding those of seventeenth-, eighteenth-, and nineteenth-century racehorses[18]—became an institutional feature of the Euro-American cultural landscape only during the later nineteenth century;[19] and it was only toward the end of the century that physiological thinking began to be applied to athletic performance in the scientific literature of Germany, France, England, and the United States.[20] Anthropological and physiological assessments of the human organism during this period were cultural symptoms of an Age of Calibration—a mania for measurement that continues unabated to this day. For example, scientific interest in quantifying muscular energy—a requirement of any future sport science—developed along with a general trend toward regarding the entire human body as a legitimate object of scientific study. Such new devices as the dynamometer (for measuring muscular strength), the sphygmograph (for recording the pulse), the pneumatometer (for measuring exhaled air), and the ergograph (for measuring muscular work) served mainstream physiology and were eventually applied to sports physiology as well.

At the same time, we must see these experiments in their nineteenth-century context. For, difficult as it is for us to escape the perspective of a "postindustrial" civilization obsessed with extreme muscularity and record performances, it is important to remember that a century ago the high-performance athlete was still a curiosity and not a charismatic figure at the center of huge commercial enterprises like the Olympic Games. Sport at the turn of the century occupied a very humble position within a much broader range of physical performances such as manual labor and military service. Emil du Bois-Reymond's previous mentioned neurological theory of "exercise" was applied not merely to athletes but also to mechanics, glassblowers, surgeons, draftsmen, watchmakers, and even the "highly developed musculature" of the great Russian pianist Anton Rubenstein.[21] The scientific marginality of sport during this period, and the general lack of interest in boosting (as opposed to investigating) athletic performance, has a quaintly premodern quality that ought to stimulate our curiosity. And the modest cultural status of sport at this time reminds us that early sports medicine was only one part of a much large investigation of human potential—mental and physical—that was accelerating dramatically at the end of the nineteenth century. It is thus no accident that the appearance of sports physiology coincided with that of intelligence testing; or that in 1893 the father of the IQ test, Alfred Binet, noted in a study of high-performance chess players that "the first rank player must bring to tournament games physical vigor and almost unlimited endurance."[22]

German scientists in particular worked to produce a new biological science of man, while seldom foreseeing its future role in exploring the foundations of athletic performance. Yet the linkage often occurred quite naturally. A pioneering physiologist like Nathan Zuntz (born in 1847), for example, did not put horses on his laboratory treadmill in order to promote the fortunes of Germany's athletes. But his research on the energy consumption of the mammalian organism did stimulate his interest in the physiology of the marching soldier, the alpinist, the high-altitude balloonist, and the (sportive) cyclist,[23] on whom his son Leo Zuntz also did important work.[24] Research on the overall physiological effects of many potentially energizing substances, including caffeine, alcohol, cocaine, and strychnine, was well underway at this time; it followed that by the 1870s medical observation of athletes had begun in England. This was an era of versatile and interdisciplinary scientists. Unfettered by the more precise biochemical knowledge of the future, they produced ambitious (if often erroneous) theories about the functioning of the human organism. It is not surprising that their interest in human beings as physical and psychological specimens led gradually to attempts to measure, and possibly improve, athletic performance within limits that were still unknown.

What we call sports medicine began as an avocation of a small number of sports-minded physicians who were often athletes themselves. Early physiological interest in sport, like interest in the various systems of gymnastics exercises, was also of potential political significance. After their disastrous defeat in the Franco-Prussian War of 1870–71, the role of sport in producing military readiness figured prominently in French thinking about national revival and a future challenge to German preeminence in Europe.[25] Similarly, the Crimean and Boer wars prompted the British to test the physical abilities of large numbers of men.[26] More precisely, this political dimension of nineteenth-century biology was directed less at military fitness than at the overall health and reproductive capacity of the "race," in the sense of a national community. In Britain, for example, the debate over "national efficiency" targeted the physical state of the industrial worker. In the same vein, the French physician Philippe Tissié, an important early sports scientist, recommended mass sport as a public health measure.

Tissié was also interested in examining elite athletes under stress. This did not require a military or nationalistic rationale, since he felt that scientific curiosity provided an entirely adequate motive, even as he worried about the potential impact of such curiosity on the future of sport. In fact, anxieties about the effects of athletic stress were common in the late nineteenth century. Archibald Maclaren's Training in Theory and Practice, a British handbook written 1874, offers a typically premodern (that is, inherently cautious) definition of "training" that is clearly incompatible with our modern training regimens: "to put the body with extreme and exceptional care under the influence of all the agents which promote its health and strength, in order to enable it to meet the extreme and exceptional demands upon its energies." Reflecting the temper of the times, a contemporary reviewer of Maclaren's book[27] found "the essence" of this passage in the phrase "extreme and exceptional care," in contrast to our own emphasis on braving physiological dangers to improve performance. Maclaren himself noted wryly that university oarsmen of this period enjoyed a reputation for physiological daring they knew they did not deserve[28]—an early example of how the public imagination creates its own romantic fantasies about high-performance athletes. In contrast with these gentlemanly rowers, the modern athlete accepts the physiological hazards of training as a professional risk.

Maclaren was bent on demystifying the alleged dangers of athletic sports, not on emphasizing medical risks of athletic stress. But Tissié was not so sanguine. In fact, his portrait of contemporary high-performance sport is both more alarmed and more prophetic than that of his British colleague. In 1896, two years after his pioneering medical observations of a record setting cyclist (see Chapter 3), Tissié reported that "intensive training" could produce a wide range of psychopathological symptoms including hysteria, hallucinations, and phobias.[29] By 1919 he was calling high-performance sport a kind of illness and warning that athletes could die from its effects. He even struck a blow at the cherished notion that athletic training prepared a man to go to war. On the contrary, Tissié argued, many athletic champions and record-breakers—even boxers—had failed the test of combat,[30] and he was joined in this view by a number of contemporaries (see Chapter 5).[31] In short, Tissié understood that the ambitious athlete had become an experimental subject who faced unknown medical dangers in the years ahead.

But scientific interest in sport did not focus exclusively on what later came to be called the "pathological physiology" of the athlete. As we have already seen, the scientists who turned their attention to athletic physiology during the late nineteenth and early twentieth centuries did so not to produce athletic wonders but to measure and otherwise explore the biological wonders presented by the high-performance athlete of this era. It was a time, one scientist of the age wrote, when phenomena once considered mere curiosities or freaks of nature called out for scientific investigation.[32] The appearance of the term *dynamogenesis* during the 1890s (see Chapter 3) signaled a new sense of human potential for which the athlete had not yet become the prominent symbol so conspicuous in the pictorial advertising of our own time. Thus in 1898 the American psychologist Norman Triplett presented his experiments on the psychology of competition among racing cyclists as "a study of dynamogenic stimulation."[33] Triplett's application of a term first used by French physiologists[34] to describe the psychological component of athletic competition was very much in the spirit of the times, since even the early sports physiologists understood that psychological functioning was an irreducible dimension of athletic performance (see Chapter 5). How, then, did contemporary scientists see the athlete as a biological phenomenon? What did they hope to learn from studying him? And how did "athletic potential" in a scientific sense emerge from these investigations?

Working at the Psychological Laboratory at Indiana University, Norman Triplett had studied the voluminous racing data provided by the Racing Board of the League of American Wheelmen so as to compare the emotional dynamics of competitive races with those run against the clock. "In presenting these records," he wrote, "it is with the feeling that they have almost the force of a scientific experiment."[35] This feeling was shared by other investigators in Europe and the United States during the 1890s, primarily physiologists and physicians who found the cyclist a convenient experimental subject.[36] The popularity of the bicycle soared during the last decade of the century, and this new device became on both sides of the Atlantic a symbol of technological progress and the man-machine relationship. Throughout the 1890s *Scientific American* published periodic articles on the development of cycling. The sport's first world championship was held in 1895, and the public began to acquire a taste for quantitatively measured feats and the accelerating pursuit of new record performances.[37]

This new awareness of the potential dynamism of the human organism occurred at a time when Darwinian thinking about the evolutionary process had become a powerful force in Western culture.[38] Small wonder that the notoriously eccentric French playwright Alfred Jarry, a famous bicycle buff of the fin de siècle, "described the bicycle as an 'external skeleton' which allowed mankind to outstrip the processes of biological evolution."[39] Only a generation earlier, a more static view of human athletic potential was the norm. "The blacksmith's arm," an American physician wrote in 1883, "cannot grow beyond a certain limit. The cricketer's quickness cannot be increased beyond this inexorable point. . . . This limit is fixed at different points in each man in regard to his various powers, but there is a limit beyond which you cannot go in any direction in each faculty and organ." This limit, in turn, was nothing less than "a law of Nature."[40] Indeed, the last decades of the nineteenth century saw an important struggle between these two opposed theories of human potential: an older doctrine of natural limits and the new doctrine of expanding biological limits.[41] The new experimental approach to high-performance athletics was one expression of the expansive interpretation of human capacities.

Yet even those involved in the experimental approach to athletics still showed little interest in boosting performance. The Austrian physiologist Oskar Zoth, perhaps the first athlete in history to inject himself with a hormonal substance (see Chapter 4), studied the pedaling motion of the cyclist as a problem in muscle physiology without mentioning the possibility of improving performance.[42] The *Scientific American* reports of the 1890s emphasized the mechanical development of the bicycle rather than the physiology of the rider.[43] A German report of 1901 on the nutritional needs of the athlete in "training"—a new word for this scientist—addressed sport only to study the bioenergetics of the human "machine."[44] In 1903 an American physiologist found a scientific rationale for the sprinter's "warming up" procedure but said nothing about faster sprinting.[45] In short, the primary interest of these scientists was to discover the natural laws that regulated the functioning of the body. If they did not express an interest in applying science to the boosting of athletic performance it was in part because the scientific mysteries they found in the world of high-performance sport were already exciting enough. In addition, as we have seen, there was a great deal of medical concern about the physiological dangers of athletic overexertion. In 1892, for example, the British medical journal *The Lancet* reported on the fearful consequences of one of the "long and sleepless" bicycle rides that were coming into fashion. Tormented by episodes of vomiting, one exhausted rider "lost the power of his senses, and for some miles tugged on as if he were blind, tearing away, in fact, in a kind of trance, his higher nervous centers paralyzed and his body retaining its life and mere animal power." Such efforts, this author wrote, were "dangerous up to the verge of insanity," and they did not encourage contemporary observers to dream of extending the limits of an already overtaxed organism. Despite the many references to the "human machine" that appear around the turn of the century, this image should not be interpreted too literally. "Man is not an engine of iron and steel," this physician wrote; "he is constructed for other and nobler purposes than mere engine labor."[46] Interest in improving the "vital engine" focused instead on the racehorse which, unlike human beings, could be bred in a systematic fashion (see Chapter 8).[47] The extraordinary human jumper or lifter, on the other hand, was regarded as a wonder of nature more at home in the circus arena than on the stadium floor.[48]

A combined emphasis on this scientific puzzle-solving and the physiological stress that worried Tissié appears as late as the 1920s in the work of a major scientist, the British physiologist A. V. Hill. Only a few years after winning the 1922 Nobel Prize for Physiology or

Medicine for his work on the production of heat in muscle fibers, he was at Cornell University studying athletes, and sprinters in particular, in order to analyze athletic performance as a larger-scale scientific problem. "This application to human muscular exercise is perhaps a digression," Hill had stated earlier in his Nobel Lecture, "but I feel rather an interesting one. It shows that the purely academic study of the frog's muscle may be applied to the extremely important practical case of muscular exercise in man: it explains many of the well-known phenomena of athletics."[49] Several years later Hill wrote that "matters of very great scientific interest can be found in the performances of that extraordinary machine, the human athlete."[50]

To this Nobel laureate, the human athlete was extraordinary for two reasons. First, he was capable of repeatedly producing consistent performances. Second, and more dramatic, were the effects of what Hill called "severe exercise"—a type of behavior that, under various names, had been emerging as a scientific category since the 1890s and whose alleged dangers we have mentioned. "The magnitude of the bodily changes involved in severe exercise is such that it is difficult at first to appreciate their importance," Hill wrote in 1926.[51] A man running one hundred yards at top speed "does enough mechanical work to lift his body 85 yards into the air—about one third the height of the Woolworth Building in New York City."[52] In the last analysis, however, and despite all its physiological sophistication, Hill's approach to athletic performance was not so different from the turn-of-the-century idea that the high-performance athlete was a wonder of nature—a marvelous phenomenon that did not require improvement.

This lack of interest in boosting performance was related to Hill's understanding of the physiological limits of the human or animal body. "There is a resistance, increasing with the speed, inherent in the muscle-substance itself," he wrote in 1927. "This acts as an automatic brake, preventing an animal from moving too quickly and so developing such high speeds in his limbs that they would be apt to break under their own inertial stresses." The prospect of tampering with this mechanism—this "physico-chemical system carefully adjusted by nature to the greatest speed at which it is expedient for an animal to move"—did not appeal to Hill, who was fascinated instead by the intricacy of the mechanism itself.[53] In short, we see again that athletic performance was of genuine interest to scientists long before athletes began to demand that science improve their performances.

The theory and practice of making stronger and faster athletes

developed, not in the laboratories of the fin de siècle, but among
contemporary athletes and their trainers. The (sometimes medically
supervised) doping practices of the late nineteenth century (see Chapter
4) were pioneering efforts in this area. In fact, this period was
notable for its generally innocent and uninhibited attitude toward
such experimentation. In 1912, for example, a French scientist describing
a long-distance bicycle race mentions without any unfavorable
comment the champagne that, along with the encouragement of
their trainers, had kept the riders going during the last half-hour of
their ordeal.[54] The spirit of these collective experiments is captured
in a 1908 document announcing that a Mr. Leonard Hill, a Fellow of
the Royal Society and a lecturer in physiology at the London Hospital,
"has been making some tests of the effect of oxygen on athletes."
After breathing pure oxygen for two or three minutes, his two subjects
had allegedly found new speed and stamina. The physiologist
intended to carry out four other experiments: to test a world-record
breaker in this manner, to test the effects of sending long-distance
runners through an oxygen-filled awning on each lap around the track,
to discover whether it was advantageous to stop during a race to
breathe oxygen, and to test the effect of oxygen on racehorses. The
skeptical and slightly cynical tone taken by the unknown writer of this
report—titled "The Gas 'Dope' "—suggests that the doping issue was
not yet a serious concern within the world of track and field:

> Are we getting back to the old "gunpowdering" days? Or are we to
> have a return to the superstitious times when the [famous trainer] poor
> "Choppy" Warburton practically mesmerised the cyclists under his
> care by persuading them that a little phial which he carried carefully
> about with him there contained a potent drug, the taking of which
> meant, oh, ever so much more pace than the man had previously
> possessed? Of what, think ye, was that drug composed? Of water, and
> not so good water at that, bearing in mind the time it remained in the
> bottle. But the men firmly believed it did them good, and other trainers
> would have given anything for "Choppy's dope." Gunpowder was
> a great "incentive" in the long ago, and not every man readily got over
> the habit, while hypodermic injections of strychnine have been popular
> for many a long day.[55]

In fact, the collaborations between cyclists and their trainers
were not always so lighthearted. In December 1893, at Madison
Square Garden, during an event described as "the greatest six-day
bicycle race ever held in the world," the German rider who finished

second supposedly showed a lack of "ambition and courage, and it was with difficulty that he was kept on the track by his friends and trainers."[56] More than any other athletic events of the time, the six-day races were de facto experiments investigating the physiology of stress. The advent of the racing bicycle during the 1890s came at the end of a century that had seen many experiments designed to measure the effects of (sometimes fatal) stress on animals, and in this sense the six-day riders were carrying on a tradition. Stress, trauma, and death—the extreme outcomes of sportive exertion—had been studied by many physiologists before doctors began to wonder about the medical consequences of extreme athletic effort. These inadvertent human sacrifices belong to an experimental tradition that in the nineteenth century included the daring operations performed by some doctors on themselves, as well as experiments on living animals known as vivisection. This pursuit of biological secrets showed a tolerance for the inflicting of suffering that eventually provoked widespread outrage in the form of antivivisection crusades, especially in England. Our own acquired indifference to the medical problems of elite athletes can be traced back to this experimental ethos. The death of Birgit Dressel—and the deaths of many athletes during this century—can be understood as "experiments" that went terribly wrong. Indeed, the emotional distance that separates the sporting public from the physiological ordeals of its heroes and heroines confirms that the high-performance athlete is widely viewed, consciously or unconsciously, as an experimental subject whose sufferings are a natural part of the drama of sport.

It is no exaggeration to say that nineteenth-century physiology was largely built on a vast number of animal experiments.[57] The sufferings and exertions of the creatures that were mutilated, drugged, electrified, run on treadmills, and decapitated by vivisectionist science made it unnecessary to subject human beings to similar experiences. With animal subjects the scientist could even experiment with pain itself. When the prominent French physiologist Charles-Edouard Brown-Séquard tried to locate the physiological site of pain, as reported in 1849, he virtually destroyed the brains of dogs and rabbits that shrieked and struggled violently, even while apparently in deep comas. He preferred hogs to dogs, he said, because they cried out more easily.[58] This attitude toward the physiological investigation of pain anticipates not only the ethos of Nazi medical experiments, but also some far less reprehensible research carried out in 1910 on the relationship between pain and fatigue. In this case, reflecting the growing interest in sport, it was "a [French] cyclist of average strength" who played the role of experimental subject.[59]

French physiologists also had occasional access to involuntary human subjects. Brown-Séquard performed experiments on headless corpses fresh from the guillotine.[60] In 1885 his colleagues Regnard and Loye were able to explore even farther into physiological terra incognita, since "thanks to the extreme kindness of the authorities of the city of Troyes, we find here conditions for experimentation and observation which have never before been granted to physicians." Having posed the question of whether consciousness persists after the separation of head and torso, they had been favored by the city fathers with an invitation to a decapitation. The clinical sangfroid of the pair, who actually rode with their experimental subject in the death carriage, is most impressive. Their first examination occurred less than a minute after the prisoner's head was severed.[61]

Vivisectionist science employed other established methods of studying traumatic death. Animals or humans could be put to death—or simply die—of decapitation, freezing, overheating, electrocution, or asphyxiation, the aim being to reveal similarities or dissimilarities between various modes of death. Paul Loye, for example, reported that the head of a dog lopped off by a guillotinelike device demonstrated movements "analogous to those presented by an asphyxiated animal."[62] Similarly, Charles Richet described strychnine poisoning as a form of death by asphyxiation.[63] One scientist could argue that death by cold was not a form of asphyxiation,[64] while another could claim that oxygen deprivation and carbon dioxide poisoning were actually two different forms of asphyxiation.[65] In all of these cases, the study of traumatic death served as a window through which the physiologist hoped to gain an understanding of basic life processes.

The suffering of experimental animals and condemned men does not seem to have been a moral issue for these scientists, some of whom also experimented on themselves. Investigating death by heat, the French scientist Bonnal found that the "physiological perturbations" caused by slowly heating up human beings (all of whom survived) could be tracked precisely, while those of animals could not—a lucky finding for the many animals such experiments would otherwise have consumed. Demonstrating a fine sense of chivalry along with his adherence to the long and honorable tradition of self-experimentation, Bonnal elected "to experiment on myself when it was a matter of very high temperatures [135° F]."[66]

Bonnal's experiment reappears in the sports physiology of the French physician Philippe Tissié, who compared the record-breaking cyclist he studied to an experimental subject another investigator had enclosed in a metal box, which was then placed in a steam bath. Like this overheated subject, Tissié's rider had subsisted on a liquid diet and lost considerable weight through perspiring.[67] By comparing liquid intake and excretion, the two investigators hoped to explain the bioenergetics of the "human machine" when it was in a traumatized state.

Like today's high-performance sports medicine, the trauma experiments of this period aimed at nothing less than finding the physiological limits of the living organism. But the ambitious experiments of a century ago also typify the last stage of laboratory physiology in which scientists routinely studied the human organism in a holistic fashion. (Today's popularized sports psychology offers a holistic approach to the mind and body of the elite athlete that also reproduces both the ambition and scientific naïveté of this period [see Chapter 5].) But despite its naïveté, the physiology of this period produced exciting, if often misguided, ideas about the human organism, including the still mysterious connections between physiological and psychological functioning. In a study published in 1903, for example, the physiologists Vaschide and Vurpas set out to establish nothing less than "genuine laws [which] should be applicable to the problem of the physiology of death." But this territory proved to be a twilight zone in which theory went blind. "To a greater degree than applies to any other biological problem," they wrote, "the vital phenomena follow here laws which are capricious and difficult to pin down." Such experiments, these investigators realized, meant confronting the emotions of their subjects, including those who, "timid by nature . . . have been moved by the fear of death, an emotion which has a physiognomy entirely its own from a psychological standpoint."[68]

In their meditation on the physiology of death Vaschide and Vurpas captured both the intellectual ambition and the pathos of the nineteenth-century experimental ethos:

> In all of these cases, we have scrupulously observed the subjects throughout the course of their illnesses; we have been present to witness all of the psychological and biological modifications which distinguished the courses and successive stages of their conditions; step by step, minute by minute we have followed these sick people in their agony, we have carefully noted their spasms, their slightest movements, their final gestures.[69]

But Vaschide's subjects were not always passive victims. His diverse interests included, for example, a quasi-athletic phenomenon he called "neuro-muscular force" and its extraordinary eruption "in the death-agony"[70] of people who fought desperately to stay alive, suggesting a causal link between pathology and a concealed reservoir of strength within the human organism. Similarly, other researchers often credited epileptics with a capacity for unusual feats of strength. This important association between abnormal physiology and prodigious strength is only one example of late nineteenth-century physiologists' interest in the relationship of unusual physiological and psychological states to extraordinary physical and mental performances. (Our own view of the elite athlete who tolerates extreme physiological states as a matter of course represents a modification of this interest in human limits and capacities. The Tour de France cycling race, for example, is an "inhuman" physical challenge that athletes have made tolerable by taking drugs. Many riders, according to one German sports physician, take 2,000 milligrams of a certain drug just to get over Mont Ventoux.)[71] Over the past century extreme athletic experiences like the Tour have lost some of their exotic quality as the abnormal stresses experienced by athletes have come to be accepted by athletes and their public as the normal cost of competing at this level.

As far back as 1896 the inhuman potential latent in this sort of clinical objectivity became the subject of H. G. Wells's medical horror story *The Island of Dr. Moreau*. The British protagonist, an inventive and pitiless surgeon who creates semihuman beasts, bears an unmistakably French name to suggest the special horrors of vivisection across the English Channel. Like Mary Shelley's Victor Frankenstein, this renegade presides over his own "work-shop of filthy creation," remaining fiercely indifferent to the terrible pain he inflicts. By contrast, the narrator of the novel, whom Moreau had rescued at sea, embodies the civilized conscience of his age: "Could it be possible, I thought, that such a thing as the vivisection of men was possible?" Wells's answer is that the prevailing ethos of physiological research did make such experiments theoretically possible, since Moreau's obscene innovations were no more than logical extrapolations of nineteenth-century vivisectionist science and its search for the laws of the organism. In fact, from our point of view, Moreau is a prescient witness of things to come:

> You begin to see that it is a possible thing to transplant tissue from one
> part of an animal to another, or from one animal to another, to alter its

chemical reactions and methods of growth, to modify the articulations of its limbs, and indeed to change it in its most intimate structure. And yet this extraordinary branch of knowledge has never been sought as an end, and systematically, by modern investigators, until I took it up!

The mad surgeon's scientific imagination makes him our contemporary. His purpose—"to find out the extreme limit of plasticity in a living shape"—is both ahead of its time yet perfectly consistent with the experimental biology of his day. His interest in the alteration of "chemical reactions and methods of growth" anticipates with some precision, at a time when fantasies about superathletes scarcely existed, the more advanced ambitions of modern sports medicine. But Moreau's visions bear comparison with our own fantasies about athletes. In our own age of organ transplants and genetic engineering, Moreau's scientific program cannot really shock us. It is rather Wells's neo-gothic exploitation of the moral problem of pain, and the blasphemous union of man and beast, that appear to put Moreau beyond the pale. The novelist diabolizes experimental physiology by creating a monomaniac whose indifference to suffering is a caricature of the intellectually stimulated, but emotionally impassive, bedside manner of the respectable Dr. Vaschide. Even so, Moreau is less of an extremist than he seems. "The study of Nature makes a man at last as remorseless as Nature," he tells the appalled narrator, and the history of vivisectionist science suggests he is right.[72]

"The vivisection of men" was to be efficiently accomplished on the battlefields of Europe.[73] The systematic development of military medicine began during the Franco-Prussian War of 1870, and by the end of the First World War modern ordnance had inflicted every conceivable trauma upon the human mind and body, opening up a myriad of scientific opportunities. As one physiologist wrote in 1921:

> The war created a vast, and yet extremely haphazard laboratory in which lesions of the human central and peripheral nervous systems were inflicted at almost every conceivable point. Such patients as survived formed material for the study of any defects which existed in their nervous mechanism as the result of a lesion, the location of which in a large number of instances was exactly known. In this respect, then, we are dealing with a well-recognized method, which has heretofore been carried out experimentally upon animals, now applied through the agency of war to human beings.[74]

History thus created a physiological laboratory analogous to the "work-shop" of Dr. Moreau but without limits. It was discovered that scratching a man's foot could empty his bladder, and that men with wholly severed spinal cords could be sexually stimulated to the point of ejaculation. What is more, wounded soldiers proved "infinitely superior" as patients to the aging, broken-down or dim-witted aphasics who had been available as experimental subjects before the wounded soldiers arrived. Like healthy athletes, the military men had been in prime condition; like injured athletes, they were curious about their medical problems and prospects for recovery, and were thus in a mood to cooperate.[75] The history of scientized sport has confirmed the sense of this comparison, and it is not surprising that the only published report on the death of Birgit Dressel described many high-performance athletes as "an army of cripples and premature invalids."[76] From a medical as well as political standpoint, high-performance sport can seem like the continuation of war by peaceful means.

We should not, of course, exaggerate the similarities that have made soldiers and athletes physiologically comparable populations over the past century. For one thing, the hazards of sport are voluntary in a way the dangers of military life are not. But the subculture of high-performance sport does depend upon a military-style mobilization of social and scientific resources and of the human organism itself. It is no accident that this sort of effort has been most compatible with the totalitarian rule of Marxist-Leninists (see Chapter 6). The former East German state, for example, pursued a general "militarizing of thought"[77] at the same time it developed the most efficiently scientific sport culture in history. This ideal of social and athletic mobilization—a form of totalitarian ambition—should alert us to the hidden agenda that scientific sport pursues regardless of its political context. Sport at this level is a kind of monomania, and elite athletes have shown little interest in the moral and intellectual challenges that typically threaten the power of dictatorships.

Athletes have experimented with drugs for over a century. Scientific supervision of such pharmacological trials has been extensive but limited by ethical concerns about sportsmanship and medical risks. To understand the relationship between drugs, athletes, and medical workers we have to ask why many athletes have been willing and eager to take performance-enhancing substances in violation of the international rules that proscribe them, and why they are willing to take the attendant medical risks. These athletes have, in effect, volunteered themselves as subjects for illicit versions of clinical trials. Most "experiments" of this kind in the West have involved black-market drugs with "supervision" by the athletes themselves. In the former East Germany, experiments with anabolic steroids were carried out with cold-blooded efficiency by highly trained scientists.

Virtually all such episodes qualify as informal experiments, since there is no legitimate source of reliable data about the likely effects, and the less predictable side-effects, of allegedly performance-enhancing drugs. At least some scientists now believe that current restrictions on research into steroids should be removed so that the medical establishment can more credibly address the consequences of their use.[78] In addition, the possible performance-enhancing effects of caffeine, which has been studied for a century, remain unconfirmed.[79] Indeed, this gap between what (little) these drugs are known to do and what they are commonly assumed to do is one of the least noted aspects of the current drug crisis in sport. As we shall see, this discrepancy fits into a tradition of scientific romanticism about drugs in general as well as their supposed capacity to unleash the hidden potential of the human organism.

This fundamental relationship between high-performance sport and the experimental tradition of Western science has been obscured by the notoriety of drug use in sport. Sport and medicine have, in fact, developed a symbiotic relationship during the twentieth century. Medical scientists have wanted to study acute reactions and training-induced adaptations to the athletic regimen in order to expand their knowledge of the human organism, while athletes and trainers have expected these researchers to evaluate aptitudes of individual athletes and the effects of specific training methods.[80] Training, after all, is the pursuit of physiological stress, and the consequences of such stress can require medical attention.

This mutual fascination, and the common interests that bind these subcultures together, was already evident a century ago in the bicycle, which can be ridden either to demonstrate performance or— when fitted out as an ergometer—to measure it. Experimentation and performance are, then, inherently related dimensions of human effort, whether mental or physical. This virtual identity of scientific and sportive ambition suggests that sports medical experimentation is, in principle, as irreversible as other advancing biotechnologies such as organ transplantation or genetic engineering. Thus, it is the inseparability of sportive training from the scientific ambitions of our civilization—not the availability of drugs—that has produced the current crisis of high-performance sport.

As we have already seen, the emergence of sports medicine at the turn of the century was in part a response to concerns about the physiological stress experienced by such athletes as champion cyclists. Even though the "extreme" physiological states encountered by the most advanced sportsmen then were rather benign by modern standards, contemporary observers felt that sportive stress was an unknown territory best explored with caution. Their successors, of course, have increasing reason for concern. In recent years such prominent sports physicians as Wildor Hollmann, Heinz Liesen, and Alois Mader have warned that high-performance sport has now pushed the human organism into what Hollmann has called "the biological border zone."[81] He has argued that the highest possible levels of oxygen uptake and muscular acidity have already been measured in certain world-class athletes, and that these physiological norms cannot be exceeded in human beings.[82] Liesen has spoken of "extreme stimuli" and observed that the body of the elite athlete is simply not comparable to that of a normal person.[83] In 1977 Mader wrote that high-performance sport was already subjecting "the biological structures of the human being" to maximum levels of stress and adaptational challenges.[84] That such cautionary observations have had no discernible impact on the practice of elite sport suggests once again that the progressive logic inherent in sportive effort at this level will keep on unfolding until it is restrained by larger social forces outside the sport subculture itself. The grand experiment will continue until it comes into direct conflict with more important cultural norms bearing on the integrity of the human organism and our fears about transforming it.

Sports medical experimentation has been characterized by conflict as well as collaboration between sports physicians and their athlete-clients. When doping was an established but officially secret policy in East Germany, young athletes were sometimes drugged without their knowledge or that of their parents, older athletes often understood what was going on and accepted their "medication," and some trainers and athletes who did not want to dope felt they could not refuse orders from above. One West German runner, Mark Henrich, now looks back in amazement at the performance of his lifetime and assumes that only drugs could have caused the strange ringing in his ears and the inexplicable absence of exhaustion during the last stage of his 400-meter race.[85] This is an example of how doping can literally confuse an athlete's sense of self. He awakens to the uncanny possibility that his greatest feat may well have been an experiment performed by an unseen hand. This threat to the integrity of the person is undoubtedly a primary source of our instinctive resistance to the experimental procedure we call doping.

Yet experiments on athletes eventually confront that irreducible willfulness that drives the elite performer. When doctors asked the West German runner Gaby Bussmann to wear an electrocardiographic device in training, she refused on the grounds that it was incapable of recording the experience of maximum stress. What is more, maximum stress was a physiological state she never wanted to experience again.[86] In this case, the human complexity of the athlete defeated the experimental ambition of the scientists. In short, the rigors of sport transcend the stress of controlled experimentation, because no experimental situation can simulate the stress of competition. One wonders how long such obstacles to progress will remain.

The Bioethics of High-performance Sport

The fusion of sport and science has transformed the generally accepted meaning of "sportsmanship." Traditionally, the rules of sportsmanship governed relations between athletes whose athletic abilities were less important than their honorable intentions, whose muscles counted less than their motives. The nineteenth-century "gentleman" did not approach athletic training with the single-mindedness of the contemporary lower-class "professional," who might even take drugs. This ethos of honorable self-restraint is by no means extinct, but it has lost ground to the modern fixation on performance and productivity that has come to supercede the ideal of fair play. In fact, the performance principle has virtually supplanted the ideal of "sportsmanlike" self-restraint in the prevailing ethos of elite sport.

This ideal of sportsmanship honored the self-restraint of the athlete who refused to seize an unfair advantage. Performance-enhancing drugs have subverted this ideal in two distinct ways. First, many athletes have abandoned self-restraint in this regard, resulting in a crisis of *conduct*, such as Ben Johnson's disgrace as a "cheater." Second, the scientization of the athlete, either through drugs or other techniques, also involves a crisis of *identity*. What sort of human being is competing? To what extent can the emotional experience of competition be truly shared with an athlete who has transformed himself, not only physicially but also psychologically, with drugs? On this level Ben Johnson revealed himself to be a modern reincarnation of Victor Frankenstein's artificial man. This new, and more profound,

violation involves, not merely the transformation of the athlete's possibilities within the game, but the psychobiological transformation of
the athlete himself. Given his status as a charismatic role-model, the
athlete can now influence our idea of what a human being can and
ought to be.

Once the athlete has abandoned self-restraint, drug testing becomes the sole guarantor of the "integrity" of sport. Indeed, the
crucial role drug testing plays in legitimizing world-class sport has
transformed the world's leading expert on drug-testing technology,
Dr. Manfred Donike, into an Olympic celebrity whose global authority is a consummate symbol of the scientizing of sport. This physiological monitoring of the athlete is both invasive and validating, since
violating the "biological privacy" of the athlete is what permits his or
her certification as a "clean" competitor. At this point the athlete has
become equivalent to a biological organism. The integrity of the body
has replaced the integrity of the person. And the "human factor" has
been lost in the technological game of certifying the integrity of the
athlete's body, hence the lack of concern about invading his "biological privacy." The athlete's body demonstrates its authenticity in the
form of a chemical assay, while the athlete's character—his capacity
for honesty, for honorable conduct—is discounted as unreliable. In
summary, the human presence of the athlete has been diluted by the
scientific ritual of purification.[87]

This kind of analysis of the scientized athlete is rarely articulated
publicly, yet our culture's ethical doubts about sport are already
evident in certain familiar themes and images. Media reports portray
many extraordinary athletes—often not without reason—as the
vaguely unnatural products of physiological wizardry and pharmacological enhancement. These stories make the world of high-
performance sport a mythical subculture, where science commingles
with romance as athletes, scientists, and training techniques take on
an aura of the uncanny. Our anxieties about these mythic people and
procedures are well-founded, because they concern nothing less than
what we call human nature and how it may be transformed in the
future.

Among the many commentaries inspired by the Ben Johnson
scandal was an analysis in *The Times* of London by an English priest,
Monsignor Michael Sharkey, who is also an official of the Congrega-
tion for Catholic Education in the Vatican. As a Roman Catholic
theologian, Monsignor Sharkey understood all too clearly what is at
stake in experiments that attempt to transform the human organism.

He pointed out the disconcerting possibility of genetically crafted athletes and Bionic Games. He also put his finger on a peculiar dynamic of the scientific age that bears on the future of biotechnology. Our society, he wrote, "seems to proceed in the fatalistic thought that whatever is scientifically possible will one day be scientifically realized,"[88] that every act of the scientific imagination is inevitably a prophecy of things to come.

But what is scientifically possible? And how do we even begin to imagine what such possibilities might be? One graphic answer appeared as a starkly nightmarish illustration accompanying Monsignor Sharkey's essay. It is a pen-and-ink rendering of a sprinter plunging forward, its mechanical viscera revealed, its body trailing severed wires, a disintegrating robotic humanoid exposing its terrible secret to the world—Victor Frankenstein's artificial monster reborn as an artificial athlete.

In fact, *The Times*'s choice of this eviscerated biomechanical man to represent the scientifically developed athlete was to some extent appropriate; but it was also misleading because it inaccurately caricatures the intact (if doped) human organism as a synthetic mechanism. The idea of creating mechanical men was popular during the eighteenth century. As late as her 1817 Preface to *Frankenstein*, Mary Shelley wrote that "some of the physiological writers of Germany" had endorsed her synthetic creature "as not of impossible occurrence."[89] But this myth lost its scientific authority as European physiology developed during the nineteenth century. Decades later, German physiology developed a very different (and far more accurate) model of the "human engine" based on the law of the conersation of energy. The real question, then, is why the Frankenstein myth has survived the scientific developments that discredit it and remained the dominant myth of human transformation.

The Frankenstein myth is the most scientifically ambitious, the most Promethean myth of its kind. The modern imagination has a tendency to believe in the eventual fulfillment of extreme scientific possibilities, because we imagine that the power of science is unlimited. At the same time, Frankenstein's creature has maintained its hold on our imagination because Western culture is haunted by the ability of science to transform human identity itself. The story is essentially a blasphemous myth of creation, and that is why it is related in an important way to the furor over the Ben Johnson affair.

The hysteria caused by history's greatest doping scandal resulted in part from an indistinct but compelling fear felt by many people that

Johnson had engaged in a secret and unauthorized experiment that threatened human identity as we know it.[90] The element of secrecy in particular was essential for establishing the mythic proportions of Johnson's betrayal. Analogous experiments involving drugs, organ transplants, artificial blood, and more have become a staple of science reporting in modern societies, but there is a crucial difference in that these cases are presented in a kind of public forum and often include interpretations by professional ethicists. Lacking this kind of legitimacy, the experiment carried out on Johnson by his handlers was consigned by the media to something like that "workshop of filthy creation" in which Frankenstein committed this sin for the first time. "Who shall conceive the horrors of my secret toil as I dabbled among the unhallowed damps of the grave or tortured the living animal to animate the lifeless clay?" In this state of concealment he had "disturbed, with profane fingers, the tremendous secrets of the human frame."[91] Secrecy is an essential part of the transgression, since the unholy flourishes in darkness.

That Victor Frankenstein's anxieties have survived into the age of modern science is of great importance, because we are on the threshold of unprecedented biotechnological interventions into the human organism.[92] But we should not overestimate either the power of these inhibitions or the dread that signals their presence. For Mary Shelley's tale is not one of unmitigated horror; instead, it mirrors our own ambivalence about the power of scientific inquiry and what "pursuing nature to her hiding-place" makes possible, including a wealth of exciting and beneficial discoveries. "The image of Frankenstein in his laboratory is not only of an unnatural act, but also one of an heroic dream," as one literary scholar has noted.[93] Before his disgrace Ben Johnson was a unique symbol of the biological heroism elite athletes represent, a new kind of Prometheus. The problem for modern civilization is to determine where biological heroism ends and biological fraud begins.

Frankenstein's humanoid is a modern figure because he is artificial. He is also premodern, however, in that he is neither a performer nor proud of himself as an imposing physical specimen. In fact, the monster's heroic stature was the undesired result of Frankenstein's limitations as a surgeon: "As the minuteness of the parts formed a great hindrance to my speed, I resolved, contrary to my first intention, to make the being of gigantic stature, that is to say, about eight feet in height, and proportionately large."[94] This is a statuesque figure rather than a dynamic one, premodern rather than modern.

For this reason, the Frankenstein story is a myth of spectacular creation rather than a myth of spectacular performance. Yet all such fantasies that dream of human transformations imply undreamed-of performances as well.

Nowhere have the philosophical implications of high-performance sport been examined more deeply than in West Germany. On November 16, 1985, the president of the Federal Republic, Richard von Weizsäcker, addressed a meeting of the West German National Olympic Committee on the subject of modern sport and its entanglement in a bioethical dilemma, and sounded a warning. He began by noting, first, the fantastic success of modern sport as a form of culture and, second, the "inner law" of sport, which he identified with the Olympic motto *Citius, altius, fortius:* faster, higher, stronger. "This constant comparative process," he argued, "constitutes the dynamism and the fascination of sport. It is an expression of the dynamic character of Western civilization which, through science and technology, has given shape to world civilization as we know it." The fundamental law of this civilization is the performance principle, he said, linking it in turn to the idea of virtually endless progress. In the same way, the charisma of sport grows out of its promise of limitless performances, and here is where the trouble begins.

Von Weizsäcker noted that, whereas technological devices can be limitlessly transformed, the human body cannot be. The temptation to treat the body as if it were a machine comes into conflict with our most deeply rooted ideas about human identity, and the result of this conflict is a reckoning with the idea of human limits. "That the specific limits which have been set by nature itself should not be exceeded is beyond doubt. What remains in question is precisely how these limits are to be defined." He warned that in some circles the temptation to exceed these limits has become overwhelming. "The danger that specific body types will be developed for specific sport disciplines is no longer a matter of science fiction; for this reason we can already see on the horizon the danger that specific athletic types will be bred by means of more or less concealed or even genetic manipulations."

The solution von Weizsäcker proposed for this difficult situation is "a clear and binding ethics of sport" resulting from a kind of self-interrogation. Sport "will be able to preserve its humanizing influence and contribute to human dignity only if, as it develops, it resists this pressure, if it recognizes its own inner laws, if it sees and accepts these limits. . . . Its worldwide success does not release sport from the obligation to examine its own deepest premises. On the contrary, it is precisely this almost limitless success which forces sport to reflect both on its premises and its limits."[95]

The von Weizsäcker statement was virtually unique in that a high public official had characterized the most troubling ethical problem for sport as an anthropological problem bearing on human identity. But for all its eloquence and wisdom, this analysis begs the crucial question of "natural" limits, just as it overestimates the capacity of the high-performance sport establishment to examine, let alone revise, "its own deepest premises." In particular, the idea that there are "natural" limits to human functioning and athletic achievement, and thus "natural" limits on performance-enhancing techniques, has been challenged by proponents of a more libertarian approach to drugs and other ergogenic aids.

In fact, the idea of "natural" limits is to some degree a social construct: Within certain parameters, there is much variability that subverts fixed categories.[96] Some observers have exploited this variability to argue that currently illicit drugs like anabolic steroids cannot be distinguished in principle from accepted performance-enhancing techniques like electric muscle stimulation (EMS) or electromassage,[97] and that doubts about steroids "appear to be based more on vague, moralistic feelings than on rational analysis."[98] "Our ethical and moral rules," a Swedish strength coach said in 1984, "have maintained that one must not administer anything to the body. But I view the hormonal substances as a progressive development comparable to the use of fiberglass poles by vaulters."[99] Whether or not one agrees with these arguments, they perform a valuable function by exposing the emotional foundations of certain cultural values; for example, our feelings about drugs, their invisible but seemingly magical presence within the body, and their associations with intoxication surely influence our "ethical" deliberations about the use of such substances within the idealized world of sport. But despite the value of these arguments, they are flawed by naïveté about the pathological consequences of steroid use and about the social dynamics of steroid abuse both inside and outside elite sport circles (see Chapter 7). They also employ an imprecise kind of analogical reasoning that demands scrutiny.

Such apologias for the use of steroids in sport usually employ a relativizing strategy that situates these compounds within larger categories of performance-enhancing aids.[100] For example, drugs are said to represent only one "technology" among others used by athletes. Why, then, should one technique be banned while others are allowed? A rebuttal must show why some techniques violate the essence of sport while others do not. One way to draw this line is to distinguish between what the athlete consumes internally (drugs and nutrients) and what remains external (ointments, wraps, braces, etc). But this distinction fails, in turn, when we differentiate between allegedly performance-enhancing (and, therefore, illicit) drugs and (presumably innocent) substances like vitamins and sugar, with caffeine serving as a borderline case (too great a caffeine concentration in the body is now a violation of the doping rules).[101] And the ambiguous status of caffeine now requires a further distinction between this stimulant, which affects the nervous system, and the substances called anabolic steroids that affect hormonal levels. This distinction in turn requires a coherent definition of "doping."

But the history of doping (see Chapter 4) illustrates clearly how difficult it has been to define this concept in a wholly consistent manner. The difficulties involved in distinguishing between the "natural" and the "unnatural," the "nutrient" and the "stimulant," the "regenerative" and the "performance-enhancing" have bedeviled Western sport for most of a century, reflecting deeper uncertainties about the essential nature of the human organism. In the process, this debate has illuminated a number of interesting medical and physiological issues. Today the most urgent problem is to determine whether anabolic steroids, the most notorious and widespread ergogenic drugs, are uniquely dangerous to the ethos of sport. The medical and psychological hazards of steroid use suggest that indeed they are, not least because of the ways these performance-boosting drugs affect the very *identity* of the athlete.

Those who put all performance-enhancing bioactive drugs into a single category overlook crucial distinctions that have to do with the biological and cultural significance of specific substances or procedures. For example, steroids, like all hormonal derivatives, are unique because they affect the human endocrinological system, which is the physiological basis of gender and sexual functioning. This is an unusually intimate modification of the athlete, particularly in the case of women. It is well known that steroids modify female physiology, anatomy, and sexual drive, and that they can cause irreversible masculinizing of the female organism, including clitoral enlargement, a deepened voice, and baldness.[102] The symbolic import of such modifications exceeds whatever symbolic meaning is attached to the use of caffeine, amphetamines, beta-blockers, or other substances believed to improve athletic performance. The athletic trainer who assures the steroid-enlarged shotputter that she is still a desirable woman attempts to compensate for these effects.[103] Another example of unusual cultural significance is blood doping, which involves reinfusing a hemoglobin-rich blood fraction into the athlete prior to competition. Even the use of one's own blood cannot cancel out the combination of technology and infusion that mimics the Frankenstein procedure and thereby raises the question of who or what this athlete actually is. Finally, the use of hypnosis in sport (see Chapter 5) has raised objections based upon a similar concern about the (questionable) identity of the athlete. While it is true that other substances and methods also modify the athlete, these three techniques express a heightened level of scientific ambition aimed at modifying human functioning and identity. They are properly controversial because they symbolize scientific ambition out of control.

The idea that scientific ambition must be "controlled" is not, of course, universally accepted—whence the "anthropological" dimension of boosting human performance. If the conservative ideal is that sport be pursued by essentially unmodified human beings, then its progressive alternative is a romantic Prometheanism that dreams of human transformations and demands unrestricted access to the drugs that might catalyze such metamorphoses. One proponent of such drug use in sport has written of "an essentially conservative attitude" that "presupposes a relative fixity in the human condition as opposed to an evolving transformation of what we are." This author, in fact, predicts transformations over the next century that will make current forms of athletics obsolete.[104] For whereas high-performance sport has always been an experimental field of human activity, it has now become an experimental theater in which the drama of human self-transformation, however veiled by old pieties and inhibitions, is displayed for all to see.

The bioethical crisis of high-performance sport today can be traced back to developments within nineteenth-century physiology that dissolved a traditional distinction between the "normal" and the "pathological" states of the human organism. The dissolution of this boundary implied both a new and provocative idea of disease and an altered sense of what was physiologically normal. Disease came to be seen as a kind of experiment, and pathological processes as research tools devised by nature itself.[105] This new definition of disease legitimated the pursuit of the pathological for scientific—and, eventually, sportive—ends.

A century ago, as we have seen, the pathological consequences of strenuous athletic training were already evident to the early sports physicians who worked with the elite athletes of that era. Apprehension about the physiological effects of sportive overexertion was widespread among European physicians. In 1892 a contributor to the *British Medical Journal* warned against "the frequent repetition of severe muscular effort" and, especially, "the practice of cycling against time," described as "a particularly pernicious practice." But a question remained as to whether the hypertrophy of the left ventricle observed in the hearts of "trained athletes" was "to be regarded as *physiological* or *pathological*" [emphasis added].[106]

The same distinction appears in a 1908 German medical dissertation on the Olympic athlete of this period, which calls competitive cycling "a very dangerous experiment." The nature of the stress inflicted on the kidneys by athletic exertion makes it difficult, he says, "to draw a clear distinction between physiological and pathological states" of the organ. He and other physicians, he reports, were now seeing in their practices "professional sportsmen who frequently contract arteriosclerosis and wind up invalids or dead at relatively early ages"—overambitious athletes who took on the status of patients. At one point the author of this study, Arthur Mallwitz, had opposed a 130-mile endurance march—a quasi-sportive event initiated just after the turn of the century—as "medically irresponsible."[107] Five years later the German physiologist Albu proposed lower and upper age limits (of eighteen and thirty years) for intensive physical training.[108] Such judgments belong to the early phase of bioethical concern about high-performance sport, during which the athlete became a medical risk-taker toward whom the physician began to feel an ethical obligation.

The most dramatic symptom of physiological danger was a syndrome Albu called "collapse," a condition he had observed in participants in a long-distance march: total exhaustion, cold sweat, a barely detectable pulse, blue lips, and cold hands. What is more, a similar trauma affected the best sprinters finishing races of only 400 or 800 meters.[109] It is easy to imagine the impression these prostrated bodies and distorted faces must have made on the physicians of this era, as well as the emotional hurdles that stood in the way of accepting athletic collapse as a part of "normal" human functioning. By 1913 Albu did understand that the stricken appearance of the exhausted athlete could be deceiving, but it was also clear that high-performance athletics required a medical ethics to balance the athlete's right of self-expression against the physician's duty to preserve him from the temptation to exceed his own physiological limits. Today this dilemma has become an integral part of modern sports medicine.

Mallwitz, Albu, and their contemporaries decided that the most "modern" way to deal with the "pathological physiology" of the athlete was to acknowledge the pathology and accept it as the price of high-performance athletics. By 1919 the pioneering French sports physician Philippe Tissié could bluntly assert that: "The athlete is a sick person [un malade]." His truly modern claim was that "sportive fatigue produces a kind of experimental disease in the healthy man," "a brief experimental illness on the level of cellular physiology"[110] that manifests itself as a rise in body temperature and even as a degree of immune deficiency—an intuition modern sports physiologists have confirmed.[111]

As we shall see (in Chapter 3), Tissié was no apologist for the physiological hazards of sport; on the contrary, with more prescience than his contemporaries, he understood that the increasingly powerful performance principle would put athletes at medical risk. Yet Tissié himself made his own small contribution to erasing the boundary between physiology and pathology. His distinction between the "experimental" and "pathological" disorders caused by sport relativized the idea of illness itself by presenting less severe disorders as temporary, and apparently justifiable, experiments. But if "pathological physiology" could be regarded as a form of sports medical research, then ethical thinking about the risks of sport now had to compete with the claims of scientific curiosity about the performance limits of the human organism. The resulting unequal contest between restraint and ambition continues to this day. Indeed, it is difficult to imagine what medical tragedies might be shocking enough to reverse the ascendancy of scientific ambition in the arena of sport.

For one thing, our own idea of the intrusion of the pathological into sport is not what it was for early sport physicians like Mallwitz and Tissié. They feared the pathological because it meant injury, disease, or even perhaps the death of the athlete. Although these health issues are more acute than ever today, they have receded into the background because the nature of our apprehension has fundamentally changed. Over the past century the demand for high performance has transformed what medical common sense calls the "pathological" into a "normal" state of affairs for many world-class athletes. Influenced in part by a century of popular science fiction, we now confront our visceral fear of transgressing the "natural" limits of the human organism in order to create a race of athletic freaks. Our fear is rooted in the intuition that, since there is no natural limit to such transformations, we alone are responsible for prohibiting or legitimating them. The physician's responsibility to his athlete-patient now appears less important than the scientist's responsibility to the human race as a whole. Medical ethics in this sense involves, not the health of the individual, but the nature of the species, and must therefore deal now with our sense of what is physiologically possible.

As the medical ethicist Joseph Fletcher wrote in 1974, "one of the most searching and basic issues to take shape in modern times is whether life is a process or something already given and essentially complete." Fletcher, a progressive evolutionist who proclaims the biological revolution in science "a quantum leap in human change," argues that any system of medical ethics is a product of the historical period that formulates it and not a transcendent code of principles. "Our situation," he writes, "is Promethean."[112] But Promethean ambition does not have to mean unlimited "improvements" in every human organ or sphere of endeavor. Fletcher would promote the goal of reducing human suffering, not boosting athletic performance.

Our problem, he says, is that it is notoriously difficult to channel either scientific ambition or its eventual applications to human life. "In science-based affairs," Fletcher notes, "especially those of a biological kind of medicine, the hypothetical quickly becomes the actual."[113] Sport has long functioned as a kind of scientific theater in this regard by providing medical science—and sport's mass audience—with tangible evidence of "actual" human capacities. Late nineteenth-century physiologists, for example, regarded muscle functioning as indispensable scientific evidence of otherwise invisible metabolic processes. Muscle action was nothing less than a quantifiable biological phenomenon that permitted scientists to peer into the hitherto unknown world of energy relationships within the organism itself. This fusion of muscular performance and experimental science has become part of the modern imagination and a powerful influence on our attitude toward sport. Having acquired the legitimacy of scientific experimentation, the pursuit of high performance has become largely immune to the cultural criticism that might restrain it. Having legitimated high-performance sport as a kind of experiment, scientific civilization finds itself unable to formulate ethical arguments that would constrain sport and also, by implication, its own ethos of unlimited inquiry.

The ethical implications of biological discoveries change along with the societies that practice science and imagine its potential applications. Back in 1895, for example, a contributor to *Nature* reported an interesting discovery. "It is possible by certain kinds of gland-feeding," he wrote, "to increase the stature of dwarfed persons very rapidly. . . . Experiments in feeding animals and men with the pituitary body are now in progress."[114] Focused on the goal of rescuing dwarfs from their unhappy condition, this author did not make the conceptual leap that, less than a century later, came naturally to some American parents who began asking pediatricians to administer human growth hormone (hGH) to their children to make them into more imposing athletes, thereby creating a new ethical dilemma for physicians. In 1895 the subculture of high-performance sport was still in its nascent state; athletic ambition lacked the cultural prestige that has made parents willing to experiment on their own children. Along with other current developments, the threat of pediatric abuse of hGH confirms that the bioethical crisis of sport is a crisis of human engineering in which our concept of human nature itself is at stake.

2

Darwin's Athletes
The "Savage" and "Civilized" Body

Darwin's Athletes

Two decades after winning gold medals in the 100- and 200-meter dashes at the 1972 Munich Olympic Games, Valery Borzov, now minister of sport for the Ukraine, admitted that he felt his victories were tarnished. The absence of the black American sprinters, disqualified for having arrived late for their trial heat, was "regrettable," he said, since "black runners have a natural gift" because of certain anatomical traits: Their bone and muscle structures give them an advantage over competitors of other races. These were men who would have challenged him. Ironically, Borzov himself had been known in his prime as the "computer" or "test-tube" sprinter. A finely tuned product of Communist sports science, he was known for his perfect technique—a precision that enabled him to match the "natural" black athletes who represent a mysterious challenge to the sports physiologists of the industrialized world.[1]

The dramatic ascendancy of black runners over the past twenty-five years has stimulated much commentary on the racial biology of athletic superiority, a subject that has attracted scientific interest for at least a century. The all-black 100-meter dash finals at the 1991 Seoul Olympic Games and 1991 World Track-and-Field Championships, along with the disqualification of the steroid-assisted Ben

33

Johnson, have provoked wide discussion of the theory of black athletic superiority. In a racially mixed society with a large black population like the United States, this type of speculation is a sensitive subject. Such theories are often (and sometimes unfairly) condemned as racially bigoted. In Western societies with few black citizens, sports figures and journalists tend to be less inhibited about discussing racial differences. For example, Björn Ekblom, an internationally known exercise physiologist, told the readers of one Stockholm newspaper in 1988 that blacks might have longer heel-bones—"a little difference that could explain the superiority of black runners in recent years."[2]

The increasing dominance of black runners in recent years provoked one West German sports journalist in 1988 to offer his readers what amounted to a half-ironic lament on the twilight of Caucasian athleticism. Sports experts, he said, owe the public an explanation of why Western sports medicine has been unable to keep white athletes competitive with their black counterparts. His own theory exemplifies the contradictory racial imagination at work, ascribing to black African champions both "a legendary hardness" and the ability to draw on "an inner state of relaxation that is part of their primeval inheritance from Mother Africa."[3] The emergence of black African soccer stars during the World Cup year of 1990 provoked similar comments about the "natural" superiority of the black athlete and his inevitable domination of a sport invented by imperial England.[4] The novelty of the situation, says a fatalistic German coach, "is that now we are the exotics."[5]

Scientific speculation about what we would call the athletic potential of non-Western races has been a part of physical anthropology for almost two centuries. Recent claims that black athletes have greater numbers of "fast-twitch" muscle fibers than whites[6] represent a modern version of more fanciful ideas about racial differences that have appeared since the European age of exploration in the fifteenth century. The European "ethnology" of the nineteenth century, which sought to produce a comprehensive portrait of the human organism that included a full inventory of its various capacities, recorded many observations on the physical strength, endurance, and quasi-athletic skills of Australian aborigines, black Africans, American Indians, Eskimos, and other geographically remote peoples. The assessment of racially specific athletic aptitudes thus belongs to a tradition that is, as we have seen, by no means extinct.

Scientific curiosity alone, however, cannot account for the long history of this research, usually carried out by rank amateurs, or the judgments about racial differences that result from such inquiries. For one thing, the colonial context in which these ethnological observations were made profoundly influenced how and why "savage" peoples were studied. The knowledge obtained became an adjunct of administrative power, a politically strategic science of human habits and traits.[7] On the other hand, it would be naive to overlook the straightforward intellectual curiosity so abundantly evident in the reports brought back by the motley band of European travelers who spread across the globe during the age of European expansion. For example, a "Manual of Ethnological Inquiry," published in London in 1854, suggested that travelers record the physical dimensions, head shapes, odors, pain thresholds, and "dances and games exhibiting agility, strength, or skill of peoples encountered in far-flung parts of the world."[8] Some modern counterparts of these inquiring travelers are the track-and-field coaches who go to East Africa to find raw talent that can be refined on American college campuses or in other affluent societies.[9]

This curiosity also extended in the nineteenth century to the many racial and ethnic groups of Europe. While the explorer-anthropologists of this period were primarily interested in the anatomical and physiological traits of more remote "primitive" subjects, a self-described "anthropologist" like the prolific John Beddoe, a physician and Fellow of the Royal Society, could take the same ethnological approach to such European exotics as the Bulgarians, about whom relatively little was known in London. He could even point to apparent physical similarities between these Balkan peoples and the primitives of Africa and aboriginal Australia,[10] thereby attaching a stigma to the lower classes of Europe. In other words, it was possible to do "field work" at home or abroad, among the "savage" blacks of other continents or among the "degraded" whites of the civilized world, including the "crackers" of the American South.[11]

Nor was the anthropological examination of Europeans limited to the lower orders. In France and England during the nineteenth century ideas about "temperament" or "constitution" coalesced into a theory of human types that amounted to an intraracial physical anthropology Europeans could apply to themselves. This was, in effect, a domestic reenactment of the anthropological expeditions that had taken European observers and their calibrated instruments to the far ends of the earth in pursuit of human variety and the opportunity to construct a hierarchy of racial types.

This constitutional theory was rooted in ideas about the rela-

tionship between physique and character that can be traced back to
Hippocrates' theory of temperaments, which contrasted a long thin
body type with a short and stocky one.[12] Such speculative typologies
respond to a deeply rooted curiosity about the deeper meaning of
human appearance. Since the late eighteenth century, however, they
have often degenerated into pseudoscientific folklore and stereotypes
of the bodies and temperaments of various racial groups. In 1828 a
French physician named Rostan published a classic example of this
kind of characterology, proposing three fundamental human types: a
type digestif, a *type cérébral,* and—precursor of things to come—a
type musculaire. All would reappear essentially intact during the
1920s in the enormously influential constitutional theory of the German psychiatrist Ernst Kretschmer.

The idea of a sportive type was latent in all characterologies of
this sort. In 1850 the French army doctor Michel Lévy divided men
into "sanguine," "nervous," and "lymphatic" types. Within the sanguine type, characterized by a striking degree of muscular development, he distinguished an "athletic temperament" as a subcategory.[13]
Twenty years later, the British physician John C. Murray agreed that
sanguine temperaments were "strong, athletic, ardent in their passions."[14] By the time Kretschmer was popularizing constitutional theory after the Great War, German sports physicians were attempting
to match specific athletic abilities with Kretschmerian body types (see
Chapter 5).

A century before, the age of imperialism had coincided with the
burgeoning interest of European scientists in measuring and testing
the mental and physical resources of the human organism. Investigation of protoathletic potential was only one part of this comprehensive inventory of human abilities. The aim was not to recruit athletic
talent in the modern sense. Even the term "athletic," whether used
by a Frenchman or an Englishman, referred not to sportive ability
but to the "constitutional" strength and vitality of the individual in a
most basic sense. In the colonial context, assessments by European
observers of their "primitive" subjects reflected the one-sided nature
of this comparative project: The men from Paris, London, and Berlin
were the scientists, while the indigenous populations of Africa, Australia, and Polynesia provided an endless stream of interesting subjects. Even so, these unequal interactions tended to be more complex
than the anticolonialist might assume. Although Caucasian superiority was an unquestioned assumption of the ethnologists' cultural chauvinism, they felt an interesting ambivalence toward the physically

impressive "savage" they could simultaneously admire and patronize. This ambivalence has reappeared in our culture's emotionally conflicted relationship with the black athletic champion and the related interest in probing the physiological mysteries of his supernormal body.[15]

In the colonial context, this ambivalence toward the physical capacities of the racial alien expressed itself as a conflict between the Caucasian observer's racial narcissism and his psychological need to find in the "primitive" an idealized male type, an athletic version of the "noble savage." In fact, this impulse to romanticize the vitality of primitives could extend even to their women, who were credited with the ability to recover from childbirth much faster than their "refined" European counterparts.[16] Thus the German anthropologist Theodor Waitz, while praising the "unexampled endurance" of the "aboriginal North Americans," praises also their women "who, in order not to give birth to cowards, sustain the labours of parturition with the same firmness, retiring to the forests when their time approaches"—[17]an ordeal we moderns might call high-performance childbirth.[18] It was only natural that such observations of primitive aptitudes encouraged interracial comparisons and in turn provoked European anxieties about the role of physical strength, endurance, and skills in constructing the racial hierarchy of mankind.

Comparative ranking of the physical abilities of the different races could serve as a method for comparing the cultural vitality of different peoples. In his little treatise *The Observation of Savage Peoples*, written in 1800, Joseph-Marie Degérando points out that the anthropologist-explorer is an indispensable inquirer into the physical capacities of primitive peoples: "We shall be given more positive information of the physical strength of the individual savage. You will discover what burdens he is capable of lifting, carrying, or dragging; what are his most successful muscular movements; how quickly he can run; how far he can travel without rest; how good he is at swimming; what physical exercises he ordinarily undertakes; you will observe how he climbs trees, crosses ditches, climbs rocks, and so on."[19] Only a little later, the amateur anthropologist François Péron, armed with a dynamometer to measure physical strength, managed to join an expedition to Australia. According to Waitz, Péron "was the first who performed experiments with the dynamometer and in wrestling."[20] The physiological mystery Péron aimed to resolve was: "Does civilization vary inversely with strength?" Having utterly bungled the application of this instrument to his subjects—getting accurate readings from these primitive devices was difficult enough in the most skilled hands—he concluded that it did not: Muscular force seemed to result from a higher level of civilization, not from its primitive antithesis.[21]

Péron was not alone in finding data to vindicate his biases. The ethnological literature of the nineteenth century makes it clear that Europeans had an emotional stake in the data produced by their experiments. An apparent result of this emotional investment was rankings that typically flattered either national or racial vanity. A Frenchman who published his dynamometer rankings in 1827 came up with data that placed his compatriots at the top and Australian aborigines at the bottom of his list; in 1840 a British colleague found Englishmen to be the strongest and Tasmanian aborigines the weakest participants in his survey. It is true that such results were not accepted by all European ethnologists. Waitz, for example, recommended "caution in coming to any conclusion from such experiments [with dynamometers], as they can only be decisive when performed on individuals of the same nature and the same practice in physical efforts."[22] In 1910, the American psychologist R. S. Woodworth speculated "that all our tests, founded as they are on material which is familiar to us, will be more or less unfair to peoples of very different cultures and modes of life."[23] But an awareness of such testing problems does not frequently occur in the ethnological literature of this period, suggesting that a great deal of work on primitive peoples had failed to take this crucial anthropological insight into account.

The primary question was whether or not the advance of civilization brought physical "degeneration" in its wake. Theories of cultural decline assumed that comparative anthropological data were relevant to the racial dynamics of world history; the dynamometer or a set of lifting weights thus offered a seductively quantitative index to vitality in more than one sense of the word. When the physician A. S. Thomson announced triumphantly in 1854 that it was "obvious that in physical strength the English are far superior to the New Zealanders" of aboriginal origin, his finding was considered significant because it appeared to refute the degeneration thesis:

> To those who delight in thinking that the world is degenerating, and that men were stronger in olden time, before trade and civilization had changed the manners and customs of men, the foregoing facts may prove interesting, for here we observe the New Zealanders, a race just emerging from the darkest savage state, and we find that in physical

strength they are much inferior to men drawn from a country where machinery and civilization had produced changes in the manner and habits of the people to an extent unknown among other civilized races.[24]

But despite its obvious appeal to the imperial mentality, this kind of physiological chauvinism did not prevail. Contrary evidence from other traveling ethnologists, the persuasive logic of the degeneration theory (which saw the European races in decline), and the appeal of the athletically noble savage presented a powerful challenge to the doctrine of Caucasian physical supremacy. While many of the ethnographers' comparative observations found Europeans to be stronger and hardier than the primitive peoples they were studying, other comparative assessments acknowledged the superior strength, skills, or endurance of the racial aliens. The native Indians of Vancouver Island "all swim well, and as divers cannot be beaten."[25] Eskimos are "powerfully built, long bodied, exhibiting great strength in lifting weights."[26] The aborigines of central Queensland handle their boomerangs with "a skill unattainable by a white man."[27] A New York physician reported that the "red men" of North America "draw a bow to the full length of the arm that I could hardly bend to a foot and a half," and the Indians "endure more fatigue, and go without eating for a longer period, than a white man can do."[28] Such comparisons could even match modern Europeans against their stone-age ancestors, who were credited with "a much greater bodily recuperative capacity than their more highly developed civilised successors."[29] When they were presented as physical paragons, these portraits of nineteenth-century noble savages tended to mitigate the racial chauvinism of the ethnographers and encourage the idea of the family of man.[30]

Eventually, however, the superior physique of the primitive became reinterpreted as a sign of inferiority. The Victorian educator Frederick William Farrar ascribed the "keen senses, and singularly powerful physique" of "the pure-blooded negro" to "his salient animality." Physical superiority became insignificant because the important "mental faculties seem to be deficient in all the dark races."[31] This inverse relationship between brains and brawn had traditionally been invoked in the comparison of man and beast. As one British traveler to southern Africa wrote in the 1820s: "Can we view animals of immense bulk and strength, either flying from man, or submitting to his domination, without acknowledging at once that their timidity or submission forms a part of that wise plan, predetermined by the deity, for giving supreme power to him who is physically the weakest of all?"[32]

The belief that muscularity and high intelligence are incompatible traits was one of the anthropological truisms of the nineteenth century. The Victorian critic Leslie Stephen wondered how an "athletic giant" like Tennyson could have written his great poetry, but left it to the physiologists to determine whether "there is any real incompatibility between athlete vigour and delicacy of nervous organization."[33] In any event, physiologists were not the real arbiters of this debate. Rather, Victorian anthropologists, obsessed with hoary Darwinian images of man's brutish antecedents (and their degenerate modern counterparts, such as cretins, blacks, and women), pursued the brain-versus-brawn idea to its logical conclusions.

Charles Darwin, in fact, had led the way. The relative physical weakness of the human organism is one of his themes in *The Descent of Man,* published in 1871. By the latter part of the nineteenth century, this bodily deficiency could be interpreted in three ways: as a sign of degeneration or refinement or both. Ethnologists speculating about the softening effects of civilization on Europeans had to confront the possibility that contemporary "savages" were physically superior to "civilized" whites. According to Dr. George Harley of the Royal Society, man's "evolution from a state of barbarism into one of *bien séance* and refinement" had exercised "a direct deteriorating influence on his animal vitality."[34] Darwin had emphasized the benefits of this trade-off. "The slight corporeal strength of man, his little speed, his want of natural weapons, &c., are more than counterbalanced, firstly by his intellectual powers . . . and secondly by his social qualities." He makes it abundantly clear that muscular strength alone was of limited evolutionary value. A highly intelligent organism like man could, for example, increase his own strength in a nonevolutionary way by fashioning tools. What is more, civilization promoted "the better development of the body. This may be inferred from civilised men having been found, wherever compared, to be physically stronger than savages. They appear to have equal powers of endurance, as has been proved in many adventurous expeditions."[35] While Darwin's attitude of confident physiological superiority was common enough among his social and intellectual peers, it was frequently challenged, as we have seen, by contrary evidence from other European observers. Writing several years before Darwin, the German anthropologist Theodor Waitz refers to a report that "the Englishmen excel the aborigines of North

America in short races, but are beaten by them in long distances"—
an early example of what may be called athletic anthropology.[36]

Living before the modern era of athletic ambition, early physiologists and anthropological observers felt no urge to look for the
biological foundations of athletic performance. Nevertheless, Darwin
knew an accomplished athlete when he saw one, even if he did not
analyze such a performer in sportive terms. "To throw a stone with as
true an aim as can a Fuegian in defending himself," Darwin writes,
"or in killing birds, requires the most consummate perfection in the
correlated action of the muscles of the hand, arm, and shoulder, not
to mention a fine sense of touch."[37] Had he lived a century later,
Darwin might have rhapsodized over the skills of major-league base-
ball players. It is also conceivable that a more sports-minded Darwin
might have compared the marksman from remote Tierra del Fuego to
a contemporary athlete like W. G. Grace, the legendary cricket player
considered "without question the greatest Victorian sporting hero."[38]
But where we might see athletic perfection, Darwin saw instead a
perfect prototype of "athletic" ability that he appreciated for its utilitarian value. "In throwing a stone or spear, and in many other actions," he continues, "a man must stand firmly on his feet; and this
again demands the perfect coadaptation of numerous muscles." He
does not include sportive movements among the "many other actions" that require perfect coordination. "To chip a flint into the
rudest tool, or to form a barbed spear or hook from a bone, demands
the use of a perfect hand."[39] Twenty years later, a brief article in
Nature quoted the ancient Mexican chronicles of Tezozomoc, "who,
in describing the drill of the soldiers, relates 'how their chiefs ordered
them out in canoes to practise throwing spears at flying ducks before
engaging the enemy in warfare.' "[40] Here, too, the writer saw no
reason to relate this "athletic" behavior to sport.

The Descent of Man does contain an embryonic sportive anthropology, despite Darwin's disinterest in the subject. In addition to the
perfectly coordinated Fuegian, there is the dexterous, seal-catching
Eskimo: "But in this case it is mental aptitude, quite as much as
bodily structure, which appears to be inherited." Darwin also quotes
a report that "from continually breathing a highly rarified atmosphere
[the Quechua Indians of Peru] have acquired chests and lungs of
extraordinary dimensions. The cells, also, of the lungs are larger and
more numerous than in Europeans."[41] Darwin's emphasis on the
anatomical consequences of "altitude training" is typical of nineteenth-century physical anthropology. Because he was unaware of the

physiological implications of increased "vital capacity," Darwin's early foray into high-altitude exercise physiology ignored the athletic significance of his observation. Within the next two generations, however, physiologists could study the high-altitude metabolism of mountain-climbers[42] and describe aviation physiology as a branch of sports medicine.[43]

Darwin did not envision breeding a superior athletic type. In fact, his attitude toward selective breeding appears to have been ambivalent. In *The Descent of Man,* he seems to be caught between a cynical contempt for efforts to preserve the weak and the Christian mercy he eventually endorses. Unlike savages, he says, we civilized men "do our utmost to check the process of elimination; we build asylums for the imbecile, the maimed, and the sick; we institute poor-laws; and our medical men exert their utmost skill to save the life of every one to the last moment. . . . Thus the weak members of civilised societies propagate their kind." The consequences of this humane largesse, he says, are "highly injurious to the race of man," for "excepting in the case of man himself, hardly any one is so ignorant as to allow his worst animals to breed." Yet allowing the worst humans to breed is a moral necessity, since to do otherwise would result in a "deterioration in the noblest part of our nature."[44]

The breeding of men, Darwin says, "has not been controlled, either through methodical or unconscious selection." The interesting exception is "the well-known case of the Prussian grenadiers" whose tall wives gave birth to tall children.[45] ("Jewish eugenics," as one author pointed out in 1916, forbids this type of selective breeding, as the rabbis advised "that an extremely tall man should not marry an extremely tall woman, lest the children be awkwardly tall.")[46] Darwin sided with the rabbis on practical grounds, since "[i]n the case of corporeal structures, it is the selection of the slightly better-endowed and the elimination of the slightly less well-endowed individuals, and not the preservation of the strongly-marked rare anomalies, that leads to the advancement of a species."[47] The whole idea of breeding "rare anomalies" to be athletic types—a staple of our own speculations about the future of sport—was simply beyond Darwin's imagination.[48]

The idea that mental ability and physical strength are antithetical traits is implicit in Darwin's model of human evolution. While he refused to guess whether man had evolved from the smaller chimpanzee or the larger gorilla, he readily conceded that physical inferiority was a small price to pay for the powers of the human mind. This "law of compensation," in fact, worked to the benefit of mankind. After all, even "one of the puniest races, namely, the Bushmen . . . in Southern Africa" and "the dwarfed Esquimaux of the Arctic regions" could survive nicely in dangerous environments thanks to their ingenuity.[49] And it was by dint of intelligence and character, not brawn, that the British became rulers of an empire on which the sun never set.

But not all of Darwin's contemporaries were willing to accept this notion of an inverse relationship between mind and muscle. Male vanity was not served by assuming that the cultured classes were physically inferior; and, given the prominent role of masculine self-regard in the imperialist mentality, it is not surprising that the mind/muscle dichotomy was challenged by some of the notable minds of the epoch. Darwin's robust cousin, Francis Galton—a brilliant polymath, explorer, and the founder of eugenics—challenged the "law of compensation" inherent in evolutionary theory. In *Hereditary Genius* (1892), he attacked "a prevalent belief. . . that men of genius are unhealthy, puny beings—all brains and no muscle—weak-sighted, and generally of poor constitutions. I think most of my readers would be surprised at the stature and physical frames of the heroes of history, who fill my pages, if they could be assembled together in a hall." And he concludes with a phrase that reveals his curiously primitive temperament:[50] "A collection of living magnates in various branches of intellectual achievement is always a feast to my eyes; being, as they are, such massive, vigorous, capable-looking animals."[51]

Galton's praise of "such massive animals" incautiously revealed an indelicate identification with some of the more brutish creatures on the evolutionary ladder. This attitude reflected more than just Galton's own eccentricity. The sociologist Herbert Spencer had declared that "to be a nation of healthy animals is the first condition of national prosperity," adding that only a mastery of "the elements of practical physiology" would secure "the physical vigour of our imperial race."[52] Comparing Europeans and Asians, the ethnologist John Crawfurd wrote in 1867: "The European is a larger animal, possessing more bodily strength, with a great capacity for enduring toil."[53] This urge to identify himself with "natural" creatures is a sign of the "civilized" European's conflicted feelings about biological vigor at this time. Was animal strength a sign of vitality or evidence of arrested development? Galton and others, for whom physical strength and vitality were important characteristics of the "imperial race,"saw sport as an important instrument of character formation. The key role of "the British Imperial spirit of sport"[54] was widely acknowledged by many, including some scientists. Writing in 1903, the prominent eugenicist Karl Pearson claimed that "the athletic are considerably more intelligent than the non-athletic" and that the athletic boy "should make a better soldier than the non-athletic."[55] The message was clear: The superior European combined fine physical traits with a virile force of character seldom to be found among the savage races.[56]

The racial vanity of the imperialistic European (or the American commentator on black slaves) included a specifically male vanity. Some ethnographers who observed primitive peoples felt obliged to compare themselves in certain respects to their subjects, and their implicitly competitive attitude was often revealed by their comments on the appearance (or lack) of "manly" traits among the "savages." While the inability of Africans to pull the strings of English long-bows[57] might confirm the physical superiority of Caucasian males, "character," though less tangible, was a more crucial dimension of superiority. In other words, European racial narcissism competed with a European longing to find ideal human types among the primitives.

This ambivalence produced a wide range of assessments of primitive masculinity, including some verbal portraits in which physical and characterological qualities dissolve and combine into a seamless whole. Thus Sir Edward Parry describes two young Eskimo men as "handsome and prepossessing, and their limbs well formed and muscular; qualities which, combined with their activity and manliness, rendered them, to speak like a naturalist, perhaps as fine specimens of the human race as almost any country could produce."[58] A more extreme form of "manliness" forced Darwin to acknowledge a toughness of character he could only esteem: "The American savage voluntarily submits without a groan to the most horrid tortures to prove and strengthen his fortitude and courage; and we cannot help admiring him."[59]

Such appreciations of primitive manhood were counterbalanced by efforts to delineate sharply between white and black masculinity. Just after the American Civil War, the surgeon in charge of the General Hospital for Coloured Troops at New Orleans described his clients as "*at present*, too animal to have moral courage or endurance,"[60] suggesting that military "morale" is a male product of cultural evolution quite beyond the experiential range of "savages." But this view required an explanation for the battlefield courage of certain primitive groups. One British ethnographer solved this problem by dismissing "the surprising courage and apparent utter recklessness of life" of the Andaman Islanders as the product of ignorance and implies that these overconfident warriors are really natural cowards: "All is regarded as fair in war, and cunning and treachery are considered worthy of commendation; in short, the high type of courage common among most civilised, and a few savage, nations appears to be totally lacking among the Andamanese."[61] The "high type of courage" was, in short, a race-linked virtue exclusive to the Caucasian male. This trait has survived as a stereotypical marker for all masculine performances that require an aptitude for leadership. Stereotypes of this kind frustrated the career ambitions of black American military men even after the partial integration of American fighting forces during the Second World War.[62] A similar stereotype continues to deny equal opportunity to blacks who want to play quarterback in the National Football League, since this position requires quick thinking and leadership skills. The persistence of these stereotypes shows that it is important for us to look into the cultural origins of the idea that black and white masculinities differ.

Darwinism prepared the way for the contemporary view of the physical prodigy and its racial meaning. The split between mind and muscle clearly implied a link between athleticism and primitive human types. This idea would not immediately prevail, however, because one version of the strong and well-proportioned male body retained its ancient prestige and appeal: the classical Greek model of athletic muscularity. It would persist to the end of the nineteenth century and beyond, inspiring among others Baron Pierre de Coubertin, founder of the modern Olympic Games. To nineteenth-century ethnographers, the ancient Greek model was a panracial physical ideal. The legendary Mohican of James Fenimore Cooper—"slim and athletic, of Grecian proportions"[63]—sprang from this tradition. Similarly, well-built South Sea islanders were typically described by European travelers as "herculean" and "symmetrical" figures.[64] But the most influential Hercules-like body to achieve prominence within Western culture belongs to Tarzan, the Euro-African fantasy figure who is "muscled as the best of the ancient Roman gladiators must have been muscled, and yet with the soft and sinuous curves of a Greek god"[65]—a triumphant embodiment of classical aesthetics set against the racial wilderness of the African jungle.

The enormous popularity of the Tarzan myth—and, more recently, of Sylvester Stallone's "Rocky" and "Rambo" films—illustrate the important psychological role that physical prowess continues to play in relations between the white Euro-Americans and formerly colonial peoples of color. These contemporary celebrations of Caucasian manhood recall the racial comparisons made by nineteenth-century ethnographers. One writer, conceding that "the Andamanese greatly surpass the majority of Europeans" in swimming, qualifies this praise by adding that "it is probable that, in competition with an experienced English swimmer, their best man would be distanced in the first few hundred yards"[66]—only one example of a Eurocentric athletic chauvinism now threatened by the achievements of many world-class black athletes. Indeed, Caucasian anxiety about measuring up to African athletic norms was already evident in a sports medical text published in 1922. Noting the high-jumping feats of Watusis as well as shorter "plantation Negroes" in German East Africa, the prominent German physician Ferdinand Hueppe asked rhetorically, and perhaps plaintively: "What, then, will be left of our world records?"[67]

Edgar Rice Burroughs's *Tarzan of the Apes* (1914) and its many sequels gave Europeans and Americans a heroic fantasy that exempts the Caucasian from the consequences of natural selection and its "law of compensation." By creating a Caucasian physical prodigy who is able to rule the jungle with strength and intelligence, Burroughs disarms the specter of white physical inferiority that is often implicit in the myth of the "noble savage." His achievement, then, was to create a racial myth that reconciled white racial narcissism with the unsettling implications of evolutionary theory as it was understood early in the twentieth century.

The Tarzan story is a racial fable because it asserts the power of good genes—the white racial heritage—to nullify the effects of a "savage" black environment; for in this story Africa's supreme warrior-athlete is a European aristocrat. The orphaned son of an English lord, Tarzan is raised from infancy by African great apes. The result, his divided nature, is the dynamic core of the fable: "Tarzan of the Apes had a man's figure and a man's brain, but he was an ape by training and environment." His "African" physiology is made clear: "His survival had depended upon acuteness of eyesight, hearing, smell, touch, and taste far more than upon the more slowly developed organ of reason." So, too, is the connection between animality and tribal Africa. He is "a mighty muscled animal" possessing a "wondrous agility and speed" comparable to the "incredible swiftness" of the black African.[68]

As a white who is both noble and savage, Tarzan is a fantasy vehicle through whom the European can come to terms with a disturbing African physicality. But he also unsettles the European, since he is an idealized figure who illustrates the deficiencies of all lesser Caucasian males who have been spoiled by civilization. Burroughs forces "civilized" Englishmen to taste a measure of male humiliation in confronting this "perfect type of the strongly masculine." He also makes it clear that Tarzan is a superathletic figure far superior to the sportsmen of Europe. His future wife, Jane Porter, points out that he "as far transcends our trained athletes and 'strong men' as they surpass a day-old babe."[69]

Who were these trained physical specimens of a century ago? Decades before Tarzan appeared, one ethnologist had already held up the "trained athlete" as more than a physiological match for the "savage." "Civilised athletes" who have undergone "a course of training," said Dr. George Harley, can reach "the highest state of physical perfection a human being can attain to . . . a super-recuperative bodily vitality" which is "far beyond that of the standard of either the savage, or of the civilised typical man living in a rude state."[70] The idea that training (or drugs) can give the white athlete an advantage over "naturally" gifted black competitors has reappeared in recent years. This modern version of Harley's theory sees sports medicine and sports psychology as techniques that compensate for the presumed physiological deficiencies of the Caucasian athlete.[71]

The persistence of the Tarzan myth—and our own bodybuilding cult—tend to obscure the fact that not every "herculean" model is an athletic type. Fin de siècle physiology recognized herculean pathologies as well, identifying them not as primitive traits but as physiological abnormalities. On June 1, 1892, for example, the Medical Society of Berlin convened to discuss an interesting series of clinical anomalies. Following the exhibition of an infantile tumor and a distorted face, Dr. Hans Virchow, son of the great pathologist Rudolf, introduced the most visibly dramatic of the assembled patients—a herculean male who had been presented to the society some years before by Rudolf Virchow himself.

This impressively muscled individual, Dr. Virchow's audience soon learned, was anything but a picture of health. The powerful thorax concealed a severely impaired breathing apparatus, while the sheer muscle mass of the body limited its natural movements. Worst of all were respiratory seizures that often made this *Muskelmensch* feel he was about to collapse. But such symptoms were then beyond medical remedy. A Dr. Fränkel had examined the man's larynx, taking refuge in the loosely descriptive term "laryngeal vertigo," and made a vague reference to neurasthenia. A Dr. Remak had observed that such patients were unusually reactive to the stimulus of an electric shock.

From the perspective of a society obsessed with muscularity and athletic performance, the clinical reception of this anonymous "muscle-man" appears both peculiar and naive. It is odd to see the physique of a potential international celebrity presented as a freak of nature. But a century ago muscularity did not have the prestige it has acquired from almost a century of Olympic fanfare. This Hercules was presented as a damaged human being, not as a potential hero of sport. As Virchow noted to his colleagues, the only "athletic" feature of this human specimen was a bulging chest that scarcely let him breathe. The complexity of his muscles prevented his examiners from measuring the strength of any one of them, but this was reported without undue disappointment.[72] The German physicians were not, after all, interested in his athletic potential.

Skepticism about the physiological implications of muscularity also appeared in the context of research on "fatigue," the term used for a mysterious and hydra-headed phenomenon that was one of the major preoccupations of European science for the half-century between 1880 and 1930.[73] For example, on December 18, 1893, a military physician named Dr. Coustan submitted for the Bellion Prize competition of the French Academy of Sciences a two-hundred-page volume titled *On Fatigue and its Relationship to the Etiology of Military Illnesses*. The author noted that a Roman consul, cited by Livy, had observed that heat, exhaustion, hunger and thirst—only a few of the multiple faces of the nineteenth-century scourge "fatigue"—had broken down the Gauls, "despite their impressive stature and physical strength."[74] Here was classical testimony that muscular bodies alone did not necessarily stand up to the physiological ravages of forced marches and exposure to the elements. Even the eugenicist Francis Galton, no admirer of England's "weakly and misshapen individuals," wrote in 1883 that it was "by no means the most shapely or the biggest personages who endure hardship the best. Some very shabby-looking men have extraordinary stamina."[75]

By the late nineteenth century, physicians and physiologists associated unusual muscular development with physical problems or weakness for several reasons, not all of them well founded. For example, the Berlin physicians assumed rather than demonstrated scientifically that the heroic chest of Hans Virchow's *Muskelmensch* had caused his respiratory problems. Similarly, the great German phys-

iologist Emil du Bois-Reymond cited in 1881 the ancient Greek critique of disproportionate muscular development and referred to "the
Hercules Farnèse" (a contemporary giant) and the famous child of
nature Caspar Hauser as pathetic specimens who were unable even to
walk. Du Bois-Reymond argued (correctly) that "the exercising of the
body is not only, as superficial observers have wrongly believed, an
exercising of the muscles, but is as much or even more an exercising
of the gray matter of the nervous system."[76] For du Bois-Reymond,
these muscle-bound giants were neurologically retarded defectives.
But nothing he wrote indicates that the great scientist had anything
more than the vaguest notion of what he was talking about.

A better understood malady at this time was the phenomenon
known as "giantism," a collection of disorders that reinforced the
association between pathology and "herculean" stature. Dr. Pierre
Marie of Paris had received a series of women patients "seeking relief
from a persistent headache, and mentioning incidentally that their
faces, bodies, hands, and feet had altered so much in recent years that
their best-known friends failed to recognise them."[77] In his classic
description of this disorder in 1886, Dr. Marie called it "acromegaly."
In 1892 the Italian pathologist Roberto Massolongo showed that acromegalics were victims of their hyperactive pituitary glands and "not
simply freaks," as *Nature* put it in 1895.[78] But all "giants" were not
necessarily acromegalics. A young man might be an acromegalic of
normal stature, "or he may become—although this is rarely the
case—a giant in stature and yet may not assume acromegalic features."[79] (For a better understanding of this condition, note that the
professional wrestler "André the Giant" is an acromegalic.) In either
case, this condition made life miserable for its unfortunate victim. As
the influential but pseudoscientific Italian criminologist Cesare Lombroso wrote in 1898, giants "pay a heavy ransom for their stature in
sterility and relative muscular and mental weakness."[80]

Other scientists felt a kind of romantic wonder in the presence of
these biological marvels—not surprising given the role of the giant in
legends and folktales. Dr. Arthur Keith's description in 1919 of one
growth disorder in children reveals just this sort of ambivalence toward
the physiological prodigy: "The sexual organs become rapidly mature,
and through the framework of childhood burst all the features of sexual
maturity—the full chest, muscularity of limbs, bass voice, bearded
face, and hairy body—a miniature Hercules—a miracle of transformation in body and brain." He even makes a connection between the development of the athlete and acromegaly: "Such a power of co-

ordinated response on the part of all the organs of the body to meet the
need of athletic training," he says, "presupposes a co-ordinating mechanism."[81] But like many scientists before him, Keith shows no interest
in using an unusual physiological condition—in this case a hormonal
abnormality—to produce a superior athlete.

In fact, the turn-of-the-century period produced very few fantasies about supernormal athleticism involving abnormally large people or anyone else. The young giants in H. G. Wells's 1904 science
fiction, *The Food of the Gods*, have no relation to sport. A British
anatomist's account in 1909 of "The Bristol Giant" of the late eighteenth century—like contemporary ethnological portraits of "savages"—dwells almost exclusively on his proportions rather than his
potential as a strongman. An account of 1785 refers to the "athletic
make" of this giant, who measured several inches under nine feet in
height. But at this time, and for most of the next century, this term
signified not dynamic physical ability but only a muscled and statuesque appearance. Rescued from a debtors' prison, the Bristol Giant
led a decent life as an exhibited freak of nature until his death at the
age of forty-six in 1806, his physical strength having remained un-
tested. Even a century later, the scientist who reviewed the extant
data on this physical prodigy for the Royal Anthropological Society
did not appraise him as a potential athlete.[82] Such anomalies of nature
were not yet regarded as the raw material for athletic ambition.

To the first generations raised on Darwin's theory of evolution
and its preoccupation with primitive life forms, the coarse features of
the acromegalic were a throwback to the apes.[83] Such doubts about
the very humanity of the physical prodigy echoed the core of evolutionary dogma, which over and over again contrasts the powerful
body of the beast with the mental refinement of man. Because this
dogma has reverberated through our culture for more than a century,
powerfully linking physical strength with arrested development, even
benign speculations about the superiority of the black athlete can be
transformed into an unintentionally racist discourse. As a society,
therefore, we continue to look at the issue of racial aptitudes in sport
through nineteenth-century eyes.

Sport and Racial Physiology

Racial comparisons and speculations about racial differences prolifer-
ated during the nineteenth century. The "ethnologists" of this period

sought, and often claimed to find, a variety of anatomical and physiological differences between the races, with special emphasis on distinguishing Caucasians from Negroes. Darwin himself took careful note of racial differences; "it would be an endless task to specify the numerous points of structural difference," he wrote.[84] Physical comparisons between Europeans and non-Europeans emphasized anatomical measurements, and especially the dimensions of the cranium, rather than the dynamic abilities we associate with sport. For economic reasons, Europeans did assess the work potential of colonial races; thus a report on "Eastern Coolie Labour" read to the Anthropological Institute of Great Britain and Ireland in 1874 notes "the strong dissimilarities in the capacity and aptitude for certain work which exist among different peoples under almost the same conditions."[85] A later report on a tribe native to Chile adopts a more overtly racist attitude: "Although from his robust frame it would be supposed that the Araucano was extremely muscular, his bodily strength and stamina are inferior to those of European extraction or the halfbreeds. This has been proved over and over again, both in the army and on the farm."[86] This kind of physiological utilitarianism prepared the way for the racial physiology of sport that appears around the turn of the century.

Certain physiological traits associated with athletic aptitude involve the nervous system, and a classic criterion of racial difference during the nineteenth century was an individual's perceived tolerance of pain.[87] The almost invariable conclusions drawn from many anthropological observations was that "savages" were less sensitive to pain than Europeans, an assessment that made its own contribution to the subhuman image of the primitive that circulated as common intellectual currency during this period. In *The Observation of Savage Peoples*, Joseph-Marie Degérando calls on explorers to "tell us whether the Savages endure suffering with calm, courage, and patience; whether the source of their endurance is in apathy of character, in an ignorance of the future which admits no fear of the duration of pain, or in some reflective concept like a kind of glory and vanity in the peaceful endurance of suffering, as among the Savages of America."[88] Degérando's first impulse, like some other judges of "primitive" courage, was to trivialize the legendary stoicism of the American "Savages," to construe it as a deficiency rather than as a virtue. Darwin's response to these performances, as we have seen, was more chivalric, confessing admiration for the "American savage" with whom Darwin identified as a fellow male subject to a code of honor whose terms a European could respect.[89]

A relative immunity to pain became a marker for what Cynthia
Eagle Russett has called "all those groups outside the charmed circle
of Caucasian male adulthood—children, women, and the lower
races."[90] The criminologist Lombroso ascribed insensibility to pain to
the criminal, the epileptic, the idiot, the madman, and the savage,[91]
and others added women to the list.[92] When Lombroso described the
famous intellectual D'Alembert as "insensible to the sufferings of a
surgical operation,"[93] his purpose was to demonstrate, not courage,
but rather the pathological and freakish nature of genius. In short,
insensitivity to pain was a physiological criterion with which one
could turn a heterogeneous collection of "deviant" types into a single
inferior category, and this became common during the latter part of
the nineteenth century. Thus the anatomist Carl Vogt put the female,
the Negro, the "infantile European," and apelike creatures in the
same abnormal class as if this were a matter of course.[94] While association with these lower forms of human life made it difficult to think
of the primitive as a biologically noble savage, the alleged insensitivity to pain did suggest an unusual fitness for a sport like boxing.

This pseudophysiology of pain served to deny the outsider the
fully human status implied by a highly developed nervous system.
Thus, in his "Remarks on the Physical Constitution of the Arabs"
delivered to the French Academy of Sciences in 1838, a M. Larrey
claimed that, despite their outward "physical perfection," Arabs possessed a nervous system "composed of nerves which are denser than
those usually found in European peoples."[95] This idea also appears in
the medical literature of mid-nineteenth century America. One physician had allegedly proved by dissection that the nerves of the Negro
"were larger in proportion than in the white man." And, according to
an article published in the *American Journal of Medical Science* in
1846, Negro women were supposedly less prone to hysteria during
childbirth because "they failed to receive from their nervous systems
impressions which would seriously affect a more delicate organization"[96]—yet another example of "high-performance" childbirth
among the primitives.

This comparative racial physiology plays a conspicuous role in
the Tarzan myth. The black African is credited with an "incredible
swiftness" of foot and an ability to fit an arrow to a bow "with almost
unthinkable quickness."[97] Eventually, physiological speculations of
this kind were applied to the question of athletic aptitude, with physical anthropologists leading the way. "No one who follows sporting
news," the prominent anthropologist E. A. Hooton wrote in 1941,

can fail to be impressed with the apparent supremacy of Negroes in certain types of contest—notably, sprinting, middle-distance running, high- and broad-jumping, boxing. Here there would seem to be certain advantages in body build, reaction time, or other morphological and functional characters which are factors in Negro success. This subject has not been explored and I cannot develop here the possibilities of Negroid variations which may be involved.[98]

Similar ideas about special Negro aptitudes included an anatomical advantage combined with a neurological one. The German anatomist Carl Vogt, although he did not find the Negro to possess a superior athletic physique, claimed that his neck and cranium gave him a distinct combative advantage: "There is a certain resemblance in the form of the neck to that of the gorilla, to which the remarkable development of the cervical muscles, combined with the shortness and curvature of this part, gives something of the aspect of a bull's neck. . . . and it is for this reason that he, like a ram, uses his hard skull in a fight." This kind of toughness, says Vogt, "affords a glimmer of the ape beneath the human envelope."[99] As we shall see, speculations of this kind fueled the idea that Negroes possessed a special aptitude for boxing.

In the American South, the stereotype of Negro physical hardiness played an important desensitizing role in the mentality of the slave culture. "It was especially the day-to-day business of commercial slavery which placed a premium on the Negro's purely physical qualities," as one historian has written. "New slaves off the ships were described as 'well-fleshed,' 'strong-limbed,' 'lusty,' 'sickly,' 'robust,' 'healthy,' 'scrawny,' 'unblemished.' "[100] What is more, the alleged toughness of the black slave was converted into a precursor of the legend of the superendowed black prizefighter:

> The comforting notion that slaves did not suffer, even from flagrant mistreatment, was given expression by a Southern lady novelist in 1860. She not only argued that Negroes could not be overworked but claimed that it was physically impossible for a master to knock a slave "senseless to the ground"—as he was so often knocked in abolitionist writings—because the Negro skull was so thick that such an effort would bruise or break a white man's fist.[101]

A century earlier, Captain Cook, the English explorer of the South Seas, had reported that the Tonga Islanders were better boxers and wrestlers than his crewmen,[102] but this encounter did not be-

come a part of Western racial mythology. The special pugilistic aptitude of the Negro is a theme that dates instead from the late
nineteenth century. The idea that the Negro skull is especially suited
to the hazards of boxing appears as late as 1948 in the writings[103] of
the prominent Swiss sports physician Wilhelm Knoll, a Nazi sympathizer[104] whose fixation on racial differences made him a paradigm of
the right-wing anthropological thinker.

The neurological argument for the superiority of the Negro boxer
was based on the implicit racist logic of the "law of compensation."
This organismic economy principle, as we have seen, made brains
and brawn antithetical traits. One protoathletic variation on this
theme portrayed the primitive as a kind of robot. Joseph Jastrow, who
in 1900 assumed the presidency of the American Psychological Association, had "argued [in 1892] that 'lowly organized creatures,' among
whom he included the 'inferior races,' were 'guided almost entirely
by reflex actions.' "[105] And reflex actions are crucial to the success of
many athletes, including boxers.

In 1895 a more elaborated theory of the fighting Negro automaton appeared in *The Psychological Review*. The American psychologist R. Meade Bache claimed that the Negro's "reaction time"—a
measure of the elapsed time between stimulus and response—is faster
than that of the white. But he also argued that this advantage is of
very limited value to the Negro race, since fast reaction times represent an inferior kind of aptitude: "The popular notion that the more
highly organized a human being is, the quicker ought to be the response to stimuli, is true only of the sphere of higher thought, not at
all of that of auditory, visual, or tactile impressions, which invite
secondary reflex action"—and success in sport. The intellectual is
doomed to pugilistic inferiority, therefore, because "in proportion to
intellectual advancement, there should be, through the law of compensation, a waning in the efficiency of the automatism of the individual"[106] and, therefore, his ability to deliver (and elude) quick
punches.

While Bache regarded "the relative automatic quickness of the
negro" as a straightforward sign of racial inferiority, he understood
that racial pride prevented many whites from acknowledging even
this sort of Negro superiority. He notes that

> there are several negroes and mulattoes at the present day in the ring
> whose excellence is scarcely approached, some of whom have cheer-
> fully encountered opponents of much greater size and weight for the

privilege of being able to prove their skill. When additionally it is considered that the negro has in pugilism the advantage over the white in length of arm and thickness of skull, it ought to be easily seen that, with equal opportunity, were prejudice not so strongly against him, he would be regarded as the boxer *par excellence* of the world.[107]

Dehumanizing the black "automaton" while exalting his physical skills, Bache provides yet another example of Western ambivalence toward the biology of the racial alien. In a similar vein, the influential German anthropologist Theodor Waitz wrote in 1859: "The great vital energy of savage, compared with civilized nations, is shown by the relatively greater healing power of nature (vis medicatrix naturæ) possessed by the former. The experiments made in this respect extend to all races." These "experiments" are described in a series of gruesome second-hand accounts featuring castrations and other bodily mutilations and the unenviable "recoveries" that followed. And "savages" displayed greater athletic aptitude, as well. Waitz fills page after page with accounts of the extraordinary physical endurance of the "aboriginal North Americans," of Arab camel drivers and Bushmen, of Peruvian Indians, of African tribesmen who outrun zebras and others who keep up with giraffes.[108]

But there is a crucial difference between the primitive who carves out an existence on the wind-swept plains and the athlete who tests himself on the artificial surface of the stadium. Conspicuous by its absence in Waitz's diverse collection of physical performances is the standardized, measured, and recorded activity we call sport. It is true that Waitz did intuit the need for something resembling the universal athletic standards of the Olympic movement in order to facilitate racial comparisons; but the point of such standards would have been scientific rather than sportive. While properly skeptical about cross-cultural dynamometer tests, Waitz endorsed the idea of "experiments to be performed in running, spear-throwing, etc., to form a judgment of the proportion of bodily strength in different nations."[109] Such tests would have been "experiments," however, rather than "athletic" events.

More than a century later, contemporary Western interest in the physical potential of "primitive" bodies can take the form either of scientific curiosity, or fantasies about latter-day noble savages, or be a synthesis of both.[110] Writing in 1990 about the prodigiously successful runners of East Africa, one American journalist observed: "Sport is a pale shadow of the competitive life that has gone on

forever across this high, fierce, first continent. Is it any wonder that
frail European varieties feel threatened?"[111] This is a consummately
Darwinian vision ("competitive life," "first continent," "frail European varieties") of race and physical aptitude, but cleansed of the
overtly racist judgments so common in comparable commentaries
that appeared well into this century. Indeed, the striking feature of
this essay is the forced coexistence of Darwinian categories and the
deemphasis of racial biology. Yet here, too, the nineteenth-century
imagination is still at work, romanticizing human potential while trac-
ing its sources to a primeval vitality the white race cannot hope to
match.

To nineteenth-century scientists, the legendary feats of African
savannah-dwellers and Peruvian highlanders suggested the existence
of exotic, unfathomed human physiologies, comparable to exotic cus-
toms or ceremonies beyond the understanding of European ethnologists. The exotic was both attractive and frightening, since it could
offer visions of miraculous human possibilities or raise the specter of
darker ones. But not all exotic physiologies were to be found on
distant continents. Exotics were also to be found at home in the alien
world of the lower classes, whose unusual physiques or muscularity
could be associated with abnormality and pathology.

The world of pathology defined by the educated establishments
of England, France, and Germany included biologically deviant Caucasians and, in particular, lower-class Caucasians. Inferior types were
also found in the more exotic corners of Europe, and they were
frequently equated with the primitives of other continents. One of
these exotic places was Ireland, where, as one Englishman wrote in
1869, "an approximation to an absolutely negroid type has been occasionally detected by keen observers."[112] In *The Descent of Man*,
Darwin himself biologized and criminalized the status of the lower
orders: "Thus the reckless, degraded, and often vicious members of
society, tend to increase at a quicker rate than the provident and
generally virtuous members. Or as Mr. Greg puts the case: 'The
careless, squalid, unaspiring Irishman multiplies like rabbits.' "[113] In
the case of the Irish, the fusion of class and "race," reinforced by
images derived from the theory of evolution, inspired English and
American cartoonists to depict Irishmen as apes.[114]

In Italy, Cesare Lombroso developed a theory of "criminal stigmata" that played a major role in fusing the pathological variations of
class, race, and biological status into a single category of disgrace. He
defined the criminal as a separate (and atavistic) species, *homo deli-*

quens, whose face and body clearly bore the signs, or stigmata, of his disorder, and compared his cranial measurements with those of Hottentots and Bushmen. Lombroso's doctrine was widely accepted as a natural extension of Darwinism. Stephen Jay Gould has pointed out that Lombroso's promiscuous use of the term "epileptic" had fateful consequences for thousands of epileptics who "became a major target of eugenical schemes in part because Lombroso had explicated their illness as a mark of moral degeneracy."[115]

Lombroso was not the first anthropologically minded European to seek out experimental material among the vulgar classes. Early in the nineteenth century, Franz Joseph Gall, one of the founders of phrenology, the "science" of determining character by measuring head shapes, had assembled in his apartment a motley group "taken from the very lowest classes" and then proceeded to inspect these figurative savages: "I arranged them in two lines and, having carefully examined their heads, found that those of the troublemakers [*querelleurs*] were larger behind the ears than those of the more tranquil types."[116]

This physical anthropology of the lower classes survived well into the twentieth century, and eventually some practitioners came to regard the muscular body type as one criterion for identifying the criminal type. Lombroso did not find a correlation between muscular strength and athleticism: "Contrary to what might be expected, tests by means of the dynamometer show that criminals do not usually possess an extraordinary degree of strength." Yet he also refers repeatedly to the violent (and potentially criminal) consequences of epileptic seizures, "paroxysms of rage or ferocious and brutal impulses (devouring animals alive), . . . strange muscular contortions or terrible spasms."[117] In 1912 the French Academy of Sciences heard two reports from researchers who claimed to have correlated muscularity with criminality, thanks to documents furnished them by the Parisian Prefecture of Police. A majority of French killers, they say, are of large stature and belong primarily to the *type musculaire*, meaning "long and sturdy limbs, a normal chest, and a square or rectangular face." These authors refer as well to "the *pathological* importance of the problems associated with 'gigantism' and 'acromegaly,' and to the noxious effects of internal secretions." These researchers aimed to diagnose, not to excuse, these malefactors. Society, they made clear, has a right "to pursue the struggle against these dangerous individuals in every possible way."[118]

Other Parisians of modest origins were tested for their "reaction time," like the many non-Caucasian "savages" whose physiological functions had been measured by intrepid explorers.[119] One Louis Lapicque—who had departed with the yacht *Sémiramis* to study the reaction times of Andaman Islanders in 1893—concluded back home in 1901 that "97% of the manual laborers of Paris closely resemble the Negritos"—a racial group of diminutive stature who inhabit certain islands of the Malay archipelago. What is more, says Lapicque, some of his Parisians proved to be physiologically comparable to a hospitalized group of Hindu convicts.[120] Such episodes make it clear that physical anthropology could be pursued either at home or abroad.

By the end of the nineteenth century, this interest in European "savages" among the lower orders fastened upon the violent, even sadistic, potential of the athletic type, which had become an interesting subtheme of evolutionary theory. Even before *The Origin of Species* appeared in 1859, and before the concept of the performance-oriented athlete had really taken shape, the French military doctor Michel Lévy, invoking the law of compensation, had observed that a dynamic and muscular physique usually excluded a cultivated sensibility. Calling up one of the stereotypes formed during centuries of Franco-German enmity, Lévy refers to "these massive constitutions of which northern Europe offers so many examples." Like non-Caucasian "savages," Lévy wrote, these impassive Nordics were almost immune to pain,[121] implying that they were therefore all the more willing to inflict it on others.

Eventually, this domestically applied physical anthropology made it possible to see the sportsman as a deviant physical and characterological type, and here too Darwinian imagery provided a sinister backdrop to contemporary developments. In 1870 a character in Wilkie Collins's novel *Man and Wife* had declared: "There is far too much glorification in England, just now, of the mere physical qualities which the Englishman shares with the savage and the brute. . . . Read the popular books; attend the popular amusements—and you will find at the bottom of them all a lessening regard for the gentler graces of civilized life, and a growing admiration for the virtues of the aboriginal Britons!"[122] In *Culture and Anarchy*, the great poet and essayist Matthew Arnold deplored the exaggerated pursuit of "British muscularity"[123] by the upper crust of British society, seeing this trend as a sign of cultural decline.

Darwinian images facilitated the linking of athleticism and primitivism. The philosopher John Dewey pointed to a "hunting psychosis or mental type"—a throwback to an earlier hunting stage of civilization[124] that was clearly incompatible with modern civilization. But it was the American cultural critic Thorstein Veblen who applied this kind of thinking to sport in *The Theory of the Leisure Class* (1899), interpreting "the predatory temperament" as a sportive one. Males who reach maturity, he says, "ordinarily pass through a temporary archaic phase corresponding to the permanent spiritual level of the fighting and sporting men" who—"punctilious gentleman of leisure" and "swaggering delinquent" alike—show "marks of an arrested spiritual development." Sporting activities present an opportunity for "histrionic" displays that Veblen regards as inane and unredeemed by any useful function. Veblen succinctly dismisses "the sporting character" as "a rehabilitation of the early barbarian temperament."[125] The athlete, he suggests, is a lower human type than the rest of us.

Veblen's "swaggering delinquent" recalls the criminal *homo delinquens* of Lombroso, who also portrayed the man of action as an athletic type comparable to Veblen's athletic barbarian. "The colonisation of wild regions," Lombroso says, "and all professions (motoring, cycling, acrobatic and circus feats) which demand audacity, activity, love of adventure, and intense efforts followed by long periods of repose are eminently suited to criminals. There are cases on record in which young men have actually become thieves and even murderers in order to gain sufficient means to become comedians or professional cyclists."[126] In short, Lombroso foresaw the protean character of the modern man of action—athlete, stuntman, mercenary, psychopath. And it was the professional cyclist—Lombroso's potential murderer—who became the notorious athlete drug-abuser of the turn of the century.

Whereas Matthew Arnold criticized a cult of the body among the privileged classes, it was the lower-classes, as we have seen, who provided more conventional opportunities for the sort of fieldwork that could be done on native grounds. Less frequently, the physical traits of the social classes were compared. In his "Contributions to the Pathological Physiology of Sport," written in 1913, the German physiologist A. Albu looked briefly at the sportive preferences—and body-types—of the upper and lower classes. Albu noted first that in many working-class families "a methodical development of the body" through heavy labor was, as he delicately phrases it, "traditional." "In these circles wrestling is regarded as a sign of unusual muscular strength and is therefore a preferred sporting activity." This preference, he believed, accounted for the almost total lack of interest in wrestling on the part of "the so-called better circles." But Albu also

argued tenaciously against the idea that the bodies of professional
men were naturally inferior to those of the workers. The middle class
does not participate in "heavy" sports like wrestling, he says, "not on
account of fewer natural attributes, but because practice and the
development of latent powers had been neglected."[127] By the time
Albu wrote, a similar argument had frequently appeared in Central
European Zionist publications bent on correcting the "physical inferiority" of the Jews.[128] Physical fitness was now firmly established as
a desirable racial trait among Zionist "self-critics" who accepted much
of the anti-Semitic critique of the Jew's inferior physical condition.

But not all German physiologists regarded the lower orders with
Albu's objectivity. Adolf Basler's *Introduction to Racial and Social
Physiology* still served up in 1924 the full panoply of anatomical and
physiological observations we associate with nineteenth-century
physical anthropology and its expeditions to the far-flung corners of
the earth. Basler's racial physiology examines and compares body
odors, vital capacity, hand strength, visual and auditory acuity, mu-
sicality, and reaction time, even noting the resistance to heat of African spermatozoa. But Basler reserves his special disgust for the
dregs of German society—the "criminals, whores, pimps, lazy bums."
"This human scum," he says, "we call the proletariat," which he
describes as "the sewer into which all those who are useless or harmful to society descend." Small wonder that Basler attempts to portray
this human refuse as racially alien to his own kind: "The proletarians,"
he says, "resemble the primitive peoples more closely than they do
the other social classes of their own nation."[129]

For the history of the idea of the athlete, it is interesting that
Basler makes a certain kind of athleticism his primary criterion of
"racial" difference:

> I have already mentioned that the Negroes carry the heaviest burdens
> on the run over hill and dale, paying no regard to their physical lim-
> itations and causing extreme damage to their hearts through such over-
> exertion. The same can be observed in Germany among the
> proletarians. On their bicycles these people set a pace as if they were
> racing in competitions. You can see them transporting the heaviest
> burdens on their bicycles at high speed, often entire trees, evading
> every obstacle with the greatest skill, and without the slightest concern
> for the dangers posed to their own lives or health."[130]

Basler's loathing of the degraded classes led him to demonize
this sort of masculine energy. Writing a generation or more after

Lombroso, Basler should have seen that his own society was already encouraging the restless and physically dynamic male to seize upon a range of legitimate opportunities: athlete, aviator, alpinist, and more. Nor did he foresee that the prestige of this sort of athletic extremism was destined to grow throughout the twentieth century.

As we will see in the next chapter, this cult of the athlete developed along with scientific interest in extreme physiological states. In addition, the rise of the black athlete during our own century has given racial physiology another lease on life. The romanticizing of the African champion in particular has served to link exotic physiological states with the racial alien and his alleged biological advantages. The increasing importance of sport has therefore acted to reawaken the curiosity about racial differences that is so evident in the ethnological literature of the nineteenth century.

This curiosity about racial exotics has coexisted with anxieties about the physical fitness of the white race and the anthropological significance of athletic aptitude. In this sense the modern athlete can be understood as Western civilization's most celebrated response to the challenge of the physically impressive "savage." At the same time, and as Lombroso understood, the athlete belongs to a larger collection of male action figures: the explorer, the soldier, the alpinist, the astronaut, and more, and each is a kind of sportsman. Having climbed one of the highest peaks in the Cameroon mountains, the explorer Richard Burton said: "To be first in such matters is everything, to be second nothing"[131]—Olympic ambition even before the games had been revived. Burton's uncompromising standard incarnates the ethos of performance that eventually shaped high-performance sport as we know it: to be first, no matter how. The scientific project that served this soaring ambition was the physiology of supreme human effort that flourished at the end of the century.

3

Prophets of Performance
The Birth of Sports Physiology

Sport and the Range of Performance Types

Over the past century, high-performance sport has become the most popular dramatic representation of human achievement. Even in an age of space travel, the athlete is a more charismatic figure than the astronaut, although it is the latter who endures the more demanding training regimen and who makes history in a way no athlete can hope to emulate. But the current prominence of athletic performance as a symbolic representation or celebration of human performance in a wider sense did not exist during the nineteenth century. In an age when magazine and television advertising routinely equates athletic performance with the powerful and efficient functioning of machines and corporate organizations, the novelty of sport's preeminence is difficult to appreciate. But finding out why modern civilization has conferred a special status on the athlete is a problem worth solving.

The rise of sport as a distinct and celebrated type of performance may be related to the technologizing of other physical accomplishments, such as geographical exploration and military service which—as styles of (male) action—have not captured the modern public imagination the way polar expeditions and cavalry charges did around the turn of the century. It is tempting to conclude that sport has achieved its global popularity in part by presenting the athlete as an autonomous performer who appears to be independent of technological support systems and devices that amplify human effort.[1] The value of the dynamic-athletic body for advertising technological products would then be based, paradoxically, on the fact that technology has thus far failed to integrate the athlete's body into its own schemes (automobiles, airplanes, etc.) on a large scale. A hundred years ago, however, the human body was not viewed from this postindustrial perspective.

While seeking the origins of the modern idea of performance, we should keep in mind that the ultimate source of human performance is inherently ambiguous. The exploration of human potential includes assessments of inherited ability as well as strategies for transforming the organism by means of "training" or other techniques such as the use of drugs. Over the past century, and as the biological sciences have advanced, the scientific approach to athletic performance has shifted emphasis away from the study of innate aptitudes toward the investigation of performance-enhancing strategies. Even so, the aptitude testing of the past century has ranged across the entire spectrum of mental and physical abilities. In a word, our interest in athletics does not make us any less interested in the intelligence testing, which, by the way, emerged in Europe at the same time as sports physiology. Indeed, they are two facets of a single cultural process.

By the standards of our technological and sports-obsessed age, the last decades of the nineteenth and the early decades of the twentieth centuries were a premodern world in terms of physiological investigations of human performance. Dynamic athleticism was a peripheral preoccupation rather than the self-evident ideal it has become for many people in widely varying cultures across the globe.[2] What we call "sportive" aptitudes and efforts were viewed in the context of a plethora of human faculties and performances, all of which could be studied to yield clues about the nature of the human mind and body. This is the period during which a true science of performance, applied to both humans and animals, came into being. During this early phase of performance physiology, the long-distance walker (or "pedestrian") and the marching soldier were of equal scientific interest.[3] Scientists who attempted to measure the muscular strength of crayfish claws, for example, were participating in a much vaster project that was now drawing a diverse population of living organisms into the standardized universe of performance norms and potential strategies for extending their limits. But there was little interest at this time in determining the limits of athletic performance.

Still in an early state of development, sport lacked that power over the public imagination that would later give rise to so many pseudo-scientific fantasies about boosting human performance.

The marginality of sport at this time and the multidimensionality of the performance concept are exemplified by a lecture ("On Exercise") delivered to an audience of German army doctors in 1881. The speaker was Emil du Bois-Reymond, one of the major physiologists of the nineteenth century. His approach to "exercise," or what, depending on the context, we might call "training" or "practice," employed a psychophysical model embraced by so many other physiologists of this period. Exercise, he said, is usually misunderstood as "the frequent repetition of a more or less complicated physical effort in conjunction with the intelligence or a specific mental effort with the aim of bringing about an improvement [in performance]." Du Bois-Reymond claimed this approach was superficial because it overlooked the neurological character of exercise physiology. In fact, he suggested, gymnastics, fencing, swimming, horseback riding, dancing, and skating—all were "exercises of the central nervous system, of the brain, and of the spinal cord." "Muscular gymnastics," he said, was actually "neurological gymnastics."[4]

Du Bois-Reymond argued further that the full range of human performances called upon capacities that are more than "neurological" in the narrow sense. Billiards, tightrope walking, equestrian sport, the rapid descent of a steep cliff—such performances demanded, not just motor nerves, but also "the system of sensory nerves and the psychological functions that can and should be exercised" themselves. His list of trainable human capacities is very diverse: our senses for music, distances, colors, and time, or the faculty of memory developed by a champion chess player or by a botanist who had memorized twenty thousand kinds of plants. The accomplished pianist and the wine-taster, too, were performers in their own ways. This expansive concept of performance returns us to the problem posed by its mysteriously entangled components: native ability and "trained" talent. Writing at the dawn of the Age of Performance, du Bois-Reymond did not even attempt to determine where one ended and the other began. Consequently, he mentions only in passing the idea that developing athletes might be an "ultimate goal."[5]

Performance in the modern sense can be defined specifically as any mental or physical effort that is subjected to psychological or physiological measurement or assessment. Technological devices now become the ultimate witnesses of performance. At the turn of the century, new instruments for monitoring the human body created a new category of physiological microperformances, making it possible for a physiological variable to set its own kind of "record." In 1902, for example, a Swiss physiologist who ascended in a balloon to a height of 4,000 meters announced that his blood cell count had probably reached the highest level ever seen in a human being.[6] This and many other experiments performed around the turn of the century were contributions to a massive, uncoordinated, yet ultimately coherent project aimed at finding the limits of human physiology. It is at this historical juncture that scientists began to subject themselves to a self-conscious fashion to the kinds of stress levels they had long inflicted on vivisected animals.

Fin de siècle physiologists were interested in many kinds of performances, and they now realized that it was possible to make physiological assessments of an entire range of performance types. Scientific curiosity prompted experimenters to make physiological assessments of human experiences that involved stress but were very different from conventional sportive competitions. For example, the development of one physiological instrument transformed the act of lying to an interrogator into a kind of competitive performance. This scientific dimension of lying can be traced back to 1875, when two French physiologists devised a "polygraphe" (or "sphygmographe") to record the pulse rates of dogs while different drugs were administered to the immobilized animals.[7] Several decades later, the sphygmomanometer, a related instrument for measuring arterial blood pressure, was being used to detect human emotions. During the First World War, an American scientist used this apparatus to conduct research on identifying human emotions including deceit, while another American physiologist produced results that seemed to "indicate that blood-pressure determinations can be used as a mild variety of the 'third degree' for detecting falsehood."[8] An experimental psychology textbook published in 1938 discusses the usefulness of blood pressure, breathing patterns, and free association tests for detecting lies.[9] In this technological environment, the "performance" dimension of lying is not only the subject's effort to outwit his interrogator but also the act of physiological monitoring itself. It is a short step from this sort of monitoring to the psychophysiological assessment of the athlete through biofeedback techniques or other sports medical testing procedures of the present day.

Scientists also began to study the human organism in more physically dynamic situations. In 1907, for example, the French Academy of Sciences heard a report on the physiological effects of riding in an automobile, an experience that was viewed as a kind of medical adventure.[10] What were the effects of wind and velocity on the skin, sense organs, breathing passages, circulation, digestive organs, and the nervous system? Here, too, was an opportunity to do a red blood cell count under extreme conditions. And here, too, in conformity with nineteenth-century medical tradition, the investigator could conduct an experiment on himself.[11]

Singing is another type of performance that can be analyzed with the physiological idiom we have come to associate with athletic achievement. The British philosopher Herbert Spencer pointed out a century ago that "the act of singing" transforms "[m]ental excitement" into "muscular energy."[12] More specifically, we find in 1886 the French physiologist Piltan discussing singing in essentially "athletic" terms: strength, fatigue, and technique. He even goes so far as to define singing as "respiratory gymnastics."[13] Forty years later, Adolf Loewy, an important German physiologist who did pioneering work on high-altitude respiration, published a study of the energy requirements of a variety of musical activities, including singing, trumpet-playing, drumming, and conducting. Loewy put some of his subjects in a "respiration chamber" in order to measure their carbon dioxide production and attached others to an oral breathing apparatus (already being used in experiments on athletes) to measure their expiratory frequency, depth, and volume. His measurements carried out on singers required that the breathing hose be replaced by a military gas mask. Loewy equated singing, judged as physiological effort, with physical labor and marching.[14]

It is symptomatic of this period that physiologists like Loewy and Nathan Zuntz studied a range of performance types. But this typology is only one of several that illustrate the breadth of the performance concept at this time and its inseparability from physiological criteria. In 1887 a German physician had used a sphygmograph and other rudimentary instruments to study the range of physiological stresses presented by rowing, caffeine, and coitus.[15] In 1901 the French physician Philippe Tissié presented courage itself as a phenomenon offering its own spectrum of types.[16] In 1926 the German physician August Bier discussed a range of activity-types (professor, hunter, etc.) supposedly affected by fatigue substances.[17] The psychophysiological measure known as "reaction time" developed during the nineteenth century among precision-conscious astronomers and was later applied to World War One machine-gunners,[18] machinists,[19] taxicab drivers,[20] and athletes.[21] All of these examples show that a range of performances can "share" a physiological norm. But the larger point is that advances in the physiological monitoring of the human organism both created and were absorbed into our concepts of aptitude and performance. And the technologizing of the performance concept only increased its appeal. It is therefore not surprising that by 1939 a German physiologist was proposing to integrate performance capacity as a fundamental element of character into the very concept of human "constitution."[22]

This dynamic view of the human organism originated in the scientific optimism of the fin de siècle, which flourished before the physiological and psychological limits of humans and animals gradually came into better focus. Scientific naïveté also produced some pseudoscientific ideas about human potential. H. G. Wells's 1904 pharmacological fantasy *The Food of the Gods*, featuring a superhuman race of young giants grown on drugs, is one example of this kind of thinking. In short, by the end of the nineteenth century, both psychology and physiology could romanticize mental and physical potential in a credibly "scientific" fashion.

Many of the romantic fantasies that resulted concerned animals, perhaps because it was easier to project supernormal capacities onto nonhuman creatures (whom one could not know like other people) than to imagine superhuman versions of friends and neighbors. The most romantic scientific problem of animal physiology was avian flight. Contemporary racial mythology based on travelers' accounts of keen-eyed savages and Indians who could run for hundreds of miles had its counterpart in the legendary performances of migratory birds. Yet here, too, scientific method contested with the power of fantasy. Armed with the law of the conservation of energy[23] and current laboratory techniques, a physiologist could demonstrate that the metabolic efficiency of a bird was the same as that of a man or a horse and that flying creatures operated within the same physiological constraints as other animals.[24] "All recent observations," a German scientist wrote in 1910, "have shown that the heights attained during avian flight have been greatly exaggerated." At the first International Aeronautical Exposition held in Frankfurt in 1909, a map of the world showing the maximal migratory routes of birds was displayed to the pioneers of European aviation—a last testimony to avian physiology by the men whose machines would eventually surpass their animal predecessors.[25]

This approach to animal aptitudes caused some resentment

among more sober-minded colleagues. In 1903, for example, two French physiologists complained that the study of animal intelligence had become "a perpetual eulogy of animals," having succumbed to "the well-nigh universal tendency in human nature to find the marvelous wherever it can."[26] Reports of horses that could read and do arithmetic calculations caused much excitement before they were disproved by less credulous investigators.[27]

Nineteenth-century biology also produced a more subtle, and potentially perverse, romantic doctrine that has actually been absorbed into the ethos of high-performance sport. Early scientific observers of high-performance athletics already understood that sport meant subjecting the human organism to artificially induced stress and even illness.[28] The "modern" way to deal with what these men called the "pathological physiology" of the athlete has been to acknowledge the pathology and accept it as the price of performance. This dissolution of the qualitative boundary between the normal and pathological[29] has had far-reaching effects within the world of elite sport. Any informed observer of this subculture will be aware that the demand for higher performance has transformed what medical common sense calls the "pathological" into a "normal" routine.

The performance-oriented physiology of the turn of the century period was a last attempt on the part of biological scientists to understand the human organism in its totality before laboratory specialization narrowed and fragmented the focus of physiological research. Like Darwin himself, scientists like Charles-Edouard Brown-Séquard, Étienne-Jules Marey, Philippe Tissié, and Francis Galton tended to be intellectually omnivorous rather than specialists. This orientation prompted them to range across traditional disciplinary lines and adopt the more inclusive approaches to human functioning that appear less and less frequently in general scientific journals like *Nature* or the *Revue Scientifique* or *Die Naturwissenschaften* after the First World War.

Their ambition was to understand the human body as a kind of machine. For behind the nineteenth-century ideal of efficient work "lies the constant goal to which the period was constantly drawn— production, greater production at any price. The human body is studied to discover how far it can be transformed into a mechanism."[30] This functional-biological interpretation of the science of this period affirms a familiar maxim: that knowledge is power. Perhaps, says the medical historian Georges Canguilhem, "human physiology is always more or less applied physiology, physiology of work, of sport, of leisure, of life at high altitudes, etc., that is, the biological study of man in cultural situations which generate varied aggressions."[31] We should appreciate the ingenuity of the early performance physiologists, who followed men and their "varied aggressions" up mountains, into respiration chambers, laboratories, chess salons, and the earliest airplanes and automobiles, and onto battlefields, bicycle tracks, and marching courses. And we should not underestimate their practical ambition. "These studies," the physiologist E.-J. Marey wrote of his chronophotographic experiments, "have been conducted with regard to their practical application, either for the amelioration of the condition of the soldier or for the improvement of the methods of physical education."[32] The men who pursued the human organism into all of these venues and more made up what we may call the Physiological International.

A Cosmopolitan Science: "The Physiological International"

At an international congress held at Cambridge University in August 1898, the French physiologist Étienne-Jules Marey commented proudly on the international dimension of his scientific discipline. "The rapid progress Physiology has made in our era is the work of a virtual legion of researchers spread across the entire globe," he said. "It seems that the diverse nationalities of the men who practice our science is one condition of its progress, each nation contributing to the common effort its special aptitudes and particular genius."[33]

In fact, Marey's assessment of the international community of physiologists was generously diplomatic; Germans, in particular, and Frenchmen like himself had dominated physiological research throughout the nineteenth century. Yet despite the conspicuous predominance of these two nationalities, the fin de siècle community of physiologists appears to have been more or less immune to disruptive international rivalries. One prominent example of this internationalism was Charles-Edouard Brown-Séquard (1817–94), the physiologist and neurologist, who moved constantly between Paris and the Anglo-American world—London, Dublin, Philadelphia, New York, Boston—crossing the Atlantic more than sixty times over half a century.[34] The estrangements and mutual recriminations that divided German and French scientists during the Great War were yet to come.[35] It was thus only natural, for example, that a French military man like V.

Legros, in his preface to the French translation of Angelo Mosso's book on *The Physical Education of Youth* (1895), should praise the great Italian fatigue researcher—at home in the laboratories of Leipzig and Cambridge as well as his own in Turin—for "his cosmopolitan way of life, which serves as a model for the scientist of our era." The "flag of physiology,"[36] as Legros phased it, displayed the unofficial colors of a pan-European scientific union, and this despite the fact that physiological research was being applied to the physical training and equipping of armies.[37] (For example, as one of many studies related to marching fatigue, two German scientists performed anatomical measurements on frozen corpses to determine the optimal way to load up an infantryman with his gear.)[38]

This cosmopolitan bonhomie was confined to the Euro-American world, with no pretence being made to integrate non-white peoples into the scientific family. The evidence suggests that the physiologists of this era shared at least some of the assumptions about racial differences that played a major role in the work of their anthropological contemporaries, even as they viewed their European neighbors as cultural and intellectual equals. (It is probably no accident that Philippe Tissié's trip to Japan in 1907 came shortly after Japanese military prowess had demolished the Russians in the war of 1905, thereby earning these racial aliens the respect of many Europeans.)[39] This racial self-consciousness played an important role in scientific thinking about human differences. Performance physiology and physical anthropology overlapped during this period, since assigning physical or perceptual aptitudes to specific racial groups presupposed biological differences distinguishing whites from the members of other races.

A prime exemplar of this pan-European fraternity and its racial outlook can be found in the profoundly judgmental, race-conscious anthropologist and physiologist Francis Galton. Galton's approach to the "much underrated Bushmen of South Africa" typifies the frank ambivalence toward racial differences that was so common at this time. "They are no doubt deficient in the natural instincts necessary to civilisation," Galton writes, "for they detest a regular life, they are inveterate thieves, and are incapable of withstanding the temptation of strong drink." But he is too much the scientist not to give credit where credit is due. His admiration for their remarkable drawings, born of "the gift of carrying a picture in the mind's eye," appears to be genuine.[40] Though Galton was a typical racist of his time, his respect for measurable performance—which sometimes bordered on the fanatical—permitted him to transcend certain parochialisms and become in this sense our contemporary. For our world of high-performance sport is founded on precisely the same triumph of scientism over nativism; whatever their doubts about other races, the great majority of today's sport fans appreciate sheer performance and suppress their prejudices—however temporarily—in the process.

The need for such supranational objectivity—one of the fundamental tenets of modern science—was already evident to nineteenth-century scientists. "Linguistic diversity," Marey declared in his address at Cambridge, "is certainly an obstacle to collective work," but he also noted that "the graphical method, a kind of universal language which obeys very simple laws," offered physiology a golden opportunity to circumvent linguistic barriers. Marey's "graphical" techniques permitted physiologists to monitor and record on rotating smoked drums or paper strips such specific physiological variables as blood pressure, heartbeat, and muscle movements. Moreover, since the "curve traced by a phenomenon is its natural, clear, and concise expression," Marey suggested, "we may expect to see physiological studies, in a great many cases, reduced to curves which are supplemented by explanatory captions." Unless the precision and standardization of physiological measurements were achieved, Marey warned, an enormous amount of scientific work would be wasted.[41]

Three years later, Francis Galton issued a similar declaration: "The replacement in all scientific work by numerical values, in the place of vague adjectives, is a gain of first-class importance,"[42] he wrote. These endorsements of this technological imperative came from men whose personalities appear to have been very different. Marey's writings suggest a gentle, generous, even selfless temperament, while Galton's aggressive self-confidence is so seamless and unselfconscious as actually to mitigate his natural arrogance. Both men, however, were profoundly committed to applying scientific methods to human physiology. This involved reductionist approaches, including an emphasis on measurable capacities and performances that Galton sometimes took to comic extremes.

The Physiological International of this period included many important scientists not portrayed in this chapter. Angelo Mosso, Adolf Loewy, and Nathan Zuntz also exemplified in their careers the scientific versatility that characterized the work of Brown-Séquard, Tissié, and Marey that we will examine, not to mention Galton's polymathic energy and achievements. By 1914, however, intellectual appetites within this scientific community had already begun to nar-

row, if only because more precise knowledge had made certain kinds
of wide-ranging speculation unnecessary. The theory of "hormones"
that appeared in the early years of the twentieth century, for example, replaced Brown-Séquard's mistaken theory about the effects of
testicular extracts. Yet, as we shall see, Brown-Séquard turned out to
be right in a larger sense, precisely because he was willing to think
publicly about the human organism in a boldly speculative way.

The Father of Steroids: Brown-Séquard and
the Male Hormone

On June 1, 1889, the distinguished physiologist Charles-Edouard
Brown-Séquard, then seventy-two, told a startled audience[43] at the
Société de Biologie in Paris that he had recently succeeded in dras-
tically reversing the effects of his own physical decline over the past
quarter-century by injecting himself with a liquid extract derived
from the testicles of a dog and a guinea pig. In a report published later
that year, Brown-Séquard noted that, twenty years earlier, he had
proposed injecting the sperm of a healthy animal into the veins of an
old man to produce greater vitality. Now he had confirmed the scientific wisdom of this theory by performing the experiment upon
himself. The injections had increased his physical strength and his
intellectual energy, relieved his constipation, and even lengthened
the arc of his urine. "I carried out this experiment," he wrote, "with
the conviction that I would thereby bring about a significant increase
in the effectiveness of the nerve centers and, in particular, the spinal
cord." These expectations were more than realized, and the result
was a "radical change" in both the physiological and psychological
functioning of an aging man.[44]

Brown-Séquard's predisposition to believe in these astonishing
results was rooted both in his own scientific temperament and in the
belief systems that shaped his scientific assumptions. As for his personality, throughout his forty years as an experimental scientist,
Brown-Séquard had been given to bold (and sometimes mistaken)
physiological speculations. Several years after his death in 1894 he
was described by a colleague as a man who "proceeded rather by
intuitions, based upon the execution of incomplete experiments,
which appeared still more unsatisfactory because of the extreme complexity of physiological problems."[45] Yet the same stubbornness that
produced false theories about epilepsy, the effects of lesions on the

nervous system, and the inheritance of acquired characteristics also led to major discoveries about the nervous and circulatory systems.[46]

Brown-Séquard's interest in the stimulating potential of injections had been evident as early as 1851, when he injected his own blood into the body of a decapitated prisoner, thereby demonstrating its capacity to relieve muscular rigidity in the human corpse.[47] Several years later he used oxygen-rich blood to animate the eyes and facial muscles in the head of a decapitated dog, although he refused to perform the same experiment on the severed head of an executed criminal.[48] By 1869 he was proposing injections of "healthy animal sperm" to invigorate old men. As we shall see, the later experiments toward which this idea pointed led Brown-Séquard to draw some ambitious conclusions about the bioenergetics of the human organism.

Brown-Séquard's belief in the regenerative power of testicular extracts was based on current ideas about the biological significance of the testes. By the end of the nineteenth century, but before the advent of modern scientific endocrinology, European science had developed a physiology of sex that incorporated an invidious comparison between male and female biologies, assigning an innate active principle to the former and an innate passivity to the latter. Cynthia Eagle Russett has summed up Darwin's contribution to this dichotomous biology as follows: "When all was said and done, woman was an overgrown ovum, about whose nature nothing more need be known. Time might go by, nations rise and fall, she would remain true to the constancy, sympathy, and patience of the egg awaiting in joyful expectation the dynamic embrace of the sperm."[49] Clearly, this view of gender differences implied a sexual politics that assigned the more powerful role to the bearer of the more dynamic sexual cells.

Brown-Séquard's belief in the powers of *liqueur testiculaire* conformed to this model by assigning a higher biological energy to the male fluid while treating the female organism as a beneficiary of male glandular products. He also assumed, like so many of his contemporaries, that loss of semen caused a loss of physical strength and a squandering of "nervous" energy.[50] Brown-Séquard had no doubts about the role of the testicles in producing "a true man [*un véritable mâle*]" or in the essential value of semen retention for the "spermatic economy" of the male organism. The "state of spermatic abundance," he wrote, was nothing less than the source of the "dynamogenic power" (or *dynamogénie*) he ascribed to his testicular extracts.[51] A man's physical and intellectual strength went up or down depending upon the state of this precious reservoir of energy. What is more, this male energy could now be made available to women in both natural and artificial forms.

The original theory of the spermatic economy, and its related ideas about male and female biologies, appeared at the end of the eighteenth century in France. "Man's deep voice, his musculature, beard, ruddy complexion, his courage and magnanimity were all manifestations of this vital force. Female qualities, or absence of qualities, if you will, were the consequence of women's lack of this vivifying fluid."[52] In conformity with this model, Brown-Séquard believed in the energizing effect of coitus on the female. In fact, he appeared to have found experimental confirmation of this effect, since the vagina was in a position, as he put it, to absorb at least as much fluid as he had been injecting into his patients,[53] and he assumed that both human semen and male animal extracts contained the crucial "dynamogenic" factor. A century later (in 1990), two Swiss cardiologists conducted an experiment to test the sportive consequences of sexual relations on athletic fitness. Men who had just had intercourse were subjected to a battery of tests, including endurance exercises on a bicycle ergometer, to measure the effects of postcoital fatigue on athletic performance. The doctors' recommendation: at least ten hours between sex and competition.[54]

The development of testicular extract now it made possible to administer this "dynamogenic" factor to women in an artificial form. This advance made possible a medical scenario, reported by Brown-Séquard, that reads like science fiction. In this case a Dr. Kahn had injected testicular extract into a pregnant woman suffering from locomotor ataxia. Even after six months of pregnancy, the movements of the fetus inside her womb had been scarcely perceptible. Yet after less than a month of treatment the injections had to be stopped, Brown-Séquard says, because the sheer force of the fetal kicking had become too painful for the mother to endure. At delivery this "vivified" child weighed a full eleven pounds and was, needless to say, *un enfant du sexe masculin.*[55]

Brown-Séquard's initial reports to the Société de Biologie had postulated an ovarian extract capable of affecting women much as testicular extract affected men. A year later he reported that, following his pioneering example, a Parisian midwife had injected herself with an extract derived from the ovaries of guinea pigs. Another experiment using ovarian extracts from rabbits was carried out by one Mrs. Augusta Brown, an American physician attached to the Faculty of Medicine in Paris. Among the many patients who supposedly benefited from these treatments was a woman who regained her ability to sing. In the last analysis, however, Brown-Séquard would not accept that the sexes are biological equals. Ovarian extract, he wrote, "acts like testicular extract, but with less force," and the correct procedure was to administer male fluids only to men and women alike.[56]

Brown-Séquard was not one of the sports-minded members of the Physiological International, but his association of a "dynamogenic" biological factor with masculine biology in general, and physical strength in particular, makes him the authentic father of our thinking about anabolic steroids and their alleged effects. He correctly assumed that "internal secretions" function as physiological regulators independent of the nervous system, an insight that makes him a pioneer of endocrinology. But the integration of a concept of sportive high-performance into Brown-Séquard's thinking was unlikely, if not impossible, by the time of his controversial experiments around the year 1890, if only because so few people were thinking in those terms. In 1892, for example, Brown-Séquard reported the case of an army sergeant who was suffering from an allegedly incurable locomotor ataxia. Testicular extract injections, by this account, restored him to the point where he was able to engage in twenty fencing matches in a single day.[57] But even though this restoration of virile capacities undoubtedly occupied a special place in Brown-Séquard's heart, there was no compelling reason for him to celebrate this therapeutic outcome anymore than that of the woman who had recovered her beautiful singing voice. Popular culture had not yet come to celebrate athletic performance above all others within the entire range of performance types.

"Dynamogenics," the core concept of Brown-Séquard's theory of *liqueur testiculaire*, was essentially an unexplained manifestation of biological energy within the nervous system. The most significant aspect of this term as a cultural construct was its clear allusion to energy; but it also had a vague, almost incantatory tone that raised suspicions among the less credulous. Ten years after Brown-Séquard's death in 1894, a French physician was still complaining about the "abuse" of the term "dynamogenic action" to account for increased muscular strength.[58] Brown-Séquard himself was convinced that *dynamogénie* was not produced by the spermatozoa themselves. He reasoned that because these *animalcules* could not pass through the Pasteur filter used for straining the extract they could not be absorbed by the body to play a physiological role other than that of fertilization.

Like the late nineteenth-century term for stimulant [*excito-moteur*], the word *dynamogénie* reminds us that Brown-Séquard's thinking about biological systems was based on contemporary ideas about biological energy but also incorporated important themes from the world of machines that were proliferating around him. Yet despite this touch of modernity, there are moments when Brown-Séquard sounds like a sorcerer poised over a bubbling pot of mysterious brew. "What is essential," he writes, "is that the animal be young, vigorous and healthy, that the testicles be taken from a living being or one which has just been killed, and finally that the injection be made within an hour or two of the animal's death."[59] An unmistakable odor of animal sacrifice and superstition hangs in the air. But this was by no means the last time that the modern and the primitive would commingle in speculations about the boosting of human performance.

The Mysteries of Movement: E.-J. Marey and Photochronography

Étienne-Jules Marey (1830–1904) is one of the forgotten innovators[60] whose ingenious devices created the world of twentieth-century experience as we know it. But, as one historian has pointed out: "Like most of the great nineteenth-century scientists, Marey was not interested in the market value of his ideas."[61] It was left to more practical thinkers like Thomas Edison to immortalize themselves in the form of standard technological devices. For science, according to Marey himself, "has also other functions; it gives a lofty satisfaction to the mind by causing us to comprehend the marvelous harmonies of nature."[62]

Yet it would be misleading to portray Marey as an otherworldly figure, divorced from the technological consequences of his work, even if he elected to leave the applied science to others. "Certain minds," he wrote in 1894, "value science only for its practical application." Yet it was easy for him to demonstrate that the work carried out at his Physiological Station in Paris served practical ends. Physicians, military physiologists, gymnastics instructors, artists, artisans, farmers—all could profit from what Marey's studies of human and animal motion revealed: that movements could be "frozen" in time and thereby analyzed, leading to an understanding of how they could be made precise and efficient.[63]

Marey's definition of the physiologist's role was thus dramatically different from that of his predecessors. It is, he says, "to devise all kinds of strategems" to capture the movements of an organism.[64] "Movement, movement in all its form—in the blood stream, in the stimulated muscle, in the gait of the horse, in aquatic animals and molluscs, in the flights of insects and birds—was the ever-returning burden of Marey's research," writes one observer.[65] But his study of movement involved more than just an aesthetic appreciation of nature's diverse wonders. Marey is the prototype of the performance physiologist because of his contributions to our understanding of the role played by motion in the work performed by an organism.

Marey's obsession with movement made him the world's first *visualizing* physiologist, and his infatuation with graphical records of movement made him impatient with verbal depictions of flowing phenomena. "Language," he wrote toward the end of his life,

> is as slow and obscure a method of expressing the duration and sequence of events as the graphic method is lucid and easy to understand. As a matter of fact, it is the only natural mode of expressing such events; and, further, the information which this kind of record conveys is that which appeals to the eyes, usually the most reliable form in which it can be expressed.[66]

The lines and curves recorded by his devices on paper strips or his smoked drum [*tambour*] translated motion in time and space into purely spatial forms, thereby "capturing" movement for the benefit of the mind's eye. His indispensable instrument in this endeavor was the camera.

Marey's technique of "photochronography" involved taking a series of pictures at precisely equal time intervals, whether of a living being, a moving object, or a flowing substance. Viewed in sequence, these images permitted the investigator to follow movements that otherwise escaped both the eye's and the brain's vain attempts to conceptualize unaided the forms of movement. For example, using this camera along with an apparatus for recording exactly when a horse's feet touched the ground, Marey was able to answer ancient questions about equine locomotion.[67] This method was immediately applicable to some of the athletic events that would soon be contested at the 1896 Olympic Games in Athens, such as the long jump and the pole vault. "In order to render chronophotographs of movements more instructive," Marey wrote two years before the Athens games, "these images should be taken from very strong and competent athletes; for example, from the prize-winners at athletic sports. These champions will thus betray the secret of their success, perhaps unconsciously acquired, and which they would doubtless be incapable of defining themselves."[68]

Of all the major scientists of the Physiological International, Marey was the most interested in sport. As early as 1883, he had anticipated the computer-based technique that today breaks down athletic movements into discrete lines displayed on a screen for analysis in terms of their biomechanical efficiency. Like our computer-modelers, he produced stick-figure runners composed of lines corresponding to the radial bones of the athletes' limbs.[69] He also anticipated today's "force platform," a device that measures how much upward acceleration an athlete generates from a standing position. Marey called his instrument a "dynamographic platform for registering the pressure of the feet on the ground."[70]

The use of these instruments was a landmark event in the history of scientific sport. But Marey's interest in the biomechanics of sport should not be equated with the ambition of his modern counterpart, who serves a professional clientele at a time when boosting athletic performance seems to have a self-evident rationale. Marey did, however, recognize that his own physiological research implied a search for the ultimate capacities of certain organs. Discussing in 1867 the "Fifth Law" of biology, which concerned the growth and atrophy of human muscles, he acknowledged "limits [that] have not yet been ascertained in a precise manner."[71] And he did believe that planned enhancement of athletic performance was a real possibility. Combining the dynamometer and chronophotography permitted him to correlate precise movements with precisely calculated forces; maximum measured force could thus be correlated with optimally efficient movement, helping athletes to jump higher or farther.[72] Marey's physiological work thus gave a further impetus to a man-machine analogy that had been developing in European physiology for half a century. Yet despite these brilliant anticipations of future developments, Marey's consistent emphasis was on the discovery of physiological laws rather than the application of these discoveries to athletic achievement. This is a premodern dimension of this thinking. He still saw sportive performances serving physiology as experimental data, rather than the other way around. By contrast, the modern outlook sees symbolic importance in the pursuit of the record performance, thereby putting physiology in the service of sport.

Marey's devotion to pure science, and the selfless, almost ethereal persona he projects in his writings, set him in a scientific Age of

Innocence. And yet there is a curious tension between Marey's scientific rapture and his work, its implications, and its sponsors. For concealed within this premodern career is the germ of Marey's modern successor: the harnessed scientific brain who serves a powerful institution and is subservient to its aims. In this regard, it is significant that the ground on which Marey's research facilities stood was a gift to him from the French minister of war, "who was interested in my experiments on the gaits of men and horses."[73] Such were the origins of the Physiological Station, which included a circular running and walking track measuring 500 meters in circumference. The symbolism of this venue—its synthesis of athlete and soldier—prefigures the sports culture of East Germany and its unholy alliance of state bureaucrats and endocrinologists preparing athletes for the ideological equivalent of war. For Marey, too, dreamed of modifying the muscular and nervous systems. He even theorized—inspired by one of Brown-Séquard's fallacious ideas—that such modifications might be inherited by new generations. Marey assumed, for example, that "the excitation to more rapid and more energetic muscular action" had produced anatomical changes that had resulted in faster generations of racehorses.[74] It was a short step from these speculations to similar investigations of human athletes (see Chapter 8). A year after the 1900 Olympic Games in Paris, Marey reported to the Academy of Sciences on the work of a Committee on Physiology and Hygiene that had conducted studies of athletic performances at the games. While a "phonendoscope" had made it possible "to determine the volume and position of the viscera" of some athletes, his own chronophotographs had revealed the technical secrets of the champions.[75] The significance of this technology, however, far exceeds its value as a tool for the athlete (such as the U.S. champion hurdler Edwin Moses) who wants to examine his own movements with the aid of Marey's invention. Over several generations, high-speed photography has also made high-speed performances intelligible to mass audiences in the form of dramatic photographs that have become a basic feature of the sports press. Without Marey's invention, sprinting, high-jumping, and other athletic movements would offer spectators little more than an evanescent blur. As Marey understood, speed is best appreciated when it is "frozen" in time.

Marey's investigations represented the most advanced sports physiology of this period. While pharmacological experimenters groped in the dark (see Chapter 4), Marey's analyses of human movement offered a realistic method for extending human capacities. In retrospect, however, one is also struck by Marey's lack of concern about where his research might lead. It is clear, for example, that he did not see his arrangement with the French army as a Faustian bargain, and that is one of his premodern ("innocent") traits. It is all the more interesting, then, that Marey's contemporary Philippe Tissié was able to anticipate the perverse possibilities of performance physiology in a way Marey did not.

A Prophet of Sport: Philippe Tissié and the Origins of Sports Medicine

At six o'clock in the evening of June 24, 1893, in a velodrome in Bordeaux, France, a thirty-year-old racing cyclist named Stéphane climbed onto a bicycle in an attempt to break his own record in the 24-hour distance event. The previous November he had covered about 405 miles. Now, attended by the physician and sports enthusiast Philippe Tissié, Stéphane would attempt to improve on this performance.

Dr. Tissié was not in attendance as the cyclist's personal physician. Nor was he in charge of this record-breaking attempt. It was Stéphane, not the doctor, who had decided that he would drink nothing but milk as conventional nourishment during this period of extreme effort. (The management of the velodrome had even provided him with a cow.) But it was the doctor who made some pointed remarks about the physiological naïveté of this decision after Stéphane failed, by about thirty miles, to match his earlier performance. For Dr. Tissié was present, not to heal the cyclist, but to assess his bodily functions and excretions as though Stéphane were an experimental animal.

The doctor's published description of his subject shows the novelty of high-performance athletics at this time. The rider's large nostrils, Tissié noted, would facilitate the ingestion of air. In addition, Stéphane's contracted muscles were actually "hard to the touch." The fact that Tissié even made such an observation reminds us that the tightly muscled athletic body we take for granted was often seen as a wonder of nature during the nineteenth century.[76]

The postrace medical evaluation showed that Stéphane had come through his ordeal quite intact. Even after the final sprint he hardly seemed tired. Having lost thirteen pounds in twenty-four hours, he cheerfully reported that his digestion was in fine shape and he looked forward to making up the lost calories. His liver and kidneys had survived the strain without incident, his heart appeared to be in perfect condition, his breathing was normal, and his mood excellent. That night he enjoyed a deep and dreamless slumber.

Only one physiological sign pointed to the extreme dimension of this athletic experiment. Ten cubic centimeters of Stéphane's post-race urine sample was toxic enough to kill the two-pound rabbit into which it was injected. After the cyclist had rested for a day, it took more than twice this amount to prove fatal to the next rabbit. Dr. Tissié saw this toxic urine as proof that "violent" muscular exertion had catapulted the rider's body into a state of "auto-intoxication," and that athletes considering a voyage into this biological twilight zone should get a thorough medical examination before setting out into the unknown.

Born in 1852, Philippe Tissié was the most important, and certainly the most prophetic, sports physician of the fin de siècle. Like Pierre de Coubertin, founder of the modern Olympic movement (and Tissié's eventual opponent in the factionalized world of French physical culture), Tissié combined the international outlook of the scientist with the political sentiments of a patriotic Frenchman. Both men saw physical exercises in nationalist terms, not least on account of the disastrous French defeat in the Franco-Prussian war in 1871. "For a long time," he wrote two decades later, "it was believed that our tranquillity was a product of our sterility, and the foreign theater took pleasure in representing the young Frenchman as short, gaunt, and pale, wearing a thin, brown moustache, somewhat debilitated, and incapable of making any effort whatsoever."[77] To combat this sort of degeneration, Tissié initiated in 1888 the Ligue Girondine de l'Éducation Physique. He lived long enough to be named honorary president of Les Amis du Sport Universitaire in 1930.[78]

The resolve of men like Tissié, Coubertin, and a host of others[79] to regenerate France through physical culture led them, paradoxically, toward the cosmopolitanism of today's global sport establishment. The internationalist strain in their thinking, especially that of Coubertin, is abundantly evident.[80] Tissié's less programmatic internationalism is evident in remarks about the international sports competitions that had begun around the turn of the century. Eschewing racial chauvinism, Tissié congratulated the Japanese on the "anthropological advantage" represented by their relatively small stature (supposedly making them less susceptible to fatigue) and their sobriety. He also recommended the gymnastic exercises of the Swedish physical educationalist Per-Hendrik Ling on the grounds that Ling's "principles are not Swedish, but universal; they derive from the physiological, anatomical and mechanical sciences."[81] These observations may seem peripheral, but they are actually the twin foundations of today's racially egalitarian, scientifically oriented elite sport that proceeds on the assumption that all races can systematically develop high-performance athletes of generally equal ability.

Although Tissié's observations of the long-distance cyclist Stéphane made him a pioneer in the field of sports medicine, he was not an active proponent of high-performance athletics. Like his contemporaries Brown-Séquard and Marey, Tissié thought in terms of a range of performance types and investigated the human organism in the holistic fashion still possible in physiology before the age of specialization set in for good after the Great War. For example, speculating in one essay on the mechanism of pain and how it is overcome, Tissié presents the phenomenon of courage as the facilitator of performances by physicians, coastal lifeguards, and soldiers without even mentioning athletes.[82]

Tissié's intellectual range is further evident in his interest in neuromotor physiology, the relationship between the brain and the muscular system, and his dream theory of fatigue, which assigned "pathogenic" dreams a role within an energy model of dreaming, exhaustion, and oneiric catharsis. The dream that produces fatigue, Tissié says, has been a frequent theme in the scientific literature. Now he argued that fatigue was the initial cause of all dreams.[83]

Tissié's concept of fatigue, like that of his contemporaries, was as differentiated as his concept of performance: a pregnant mother, for example, was obligated to guard against physical, emotional, and toxic forms of exhaustion in order to preserve the health of her fetus. Similarly, any society interested in its own survival had to limit the types of fatigue caused by manual work, alcoholic drinks, lack of sleep, and even bad literature.[84] Here, too, Tissié's interest in the social significance of physiological research excludes any mention of sportive fatigue, despite his detailed speculations elsewhere on the subject.[85]

The paradox of Tissié's scientific career, from our standpoint, is that a man who recorded early and prescient observations on the physiological and psychological consequences of extreme athletic exertion actually disapproved of the high-performance sport of his era. But it is really our own "modern" assumptions about the relationship between research and its eventual applications that make Tissié's viewpoint seem paradoxical in the first place. Almost a century of science and technology separates us from Tissié's early work in the area of what is now called "exercise physiology," and in the course of this century the pursuit of athletic records has become one of the unquestioned norms of our popular culture. Therefore, we tend to assume that the whole point of scientific research is its application on behalf of tangible, and often measurable, gains.

It is more appropriate, however, to examine Tissié's thinking about sport in the context of his own time and its divided attitude toward a sport culture based upon a linear notion of progress like the *citius, altius, fortius* of Pierre de Coubertin, who believed that exceeding previous limits was part of the athlete's task. Indeed, Coubertin himself was ambivalent about the record-breaking performance and what it portended for human development. This ambivalence is evident in his 1909 essay "La limite du record," where he endorses the record attempt even as he acknowledges the possibly harmful effects of the specialized training such efforts require.[86] In his *Pédagogie sportive*, written in 1922, he claims that Sparta had withdrawn from the ancient Olympic Games to protest the "scientific tendency" that had begun to prevail. He also criticizes "the art of creating the human thoroughbred"—his reaction to a body-building manual that had appeared in 1908[87]—and "scientific animalism."[88] Elsewhere in his writings Coubertin offered a much more positive, and even romantic, interpretation of record-setting. But it is also fair to say that he never lost this ambivalent attitude toward the pursuit of the record performance.[89]

It is hardly surprising that a scientist like Tissié, with no personal stake in the Olympic enterprise, would share Coubertin's reservations about extreme sportive effort while rejecting his romantic interpretation of the athlete as a standard-bearer of human progress. What is more, Tissié's work with athletes brought him into contact with the "pathological physiology" of sport in a way Coubertin never experienced. Coubertin's feeling of revulsion toward the body-building narcissist—the "human thoroughbred"—was directed against his vague notion of a "Nietzschean superman"[90] rather than any firsthand knowledge of what real athletes experienced in training.

As patriotic Frenchmen, Coubertin and Tissié were bound together by a common interest in promoting health through sport. The more important difference, however, is that Tissié staunchly opposed, because of their potential medical dangers, the competitive sports that Coubertin did so much to promote. Their rivalry came to a head at a conference of the French Association for the Advancement of Science at Caen in 1894, where Tissié successfully opposed Coubertin's appeal for track-and-field events.[91] Yet while Tissié won this battle, both men lived long enough to see the founder of the modern Olympic movement win the war. Indeed, it has been Coubertin's Games, and the "gigantic biological experiment" they represent, that have confirmed the importance of Tissié's original scientific agenda. Now, a century after the clash with Coubertin at Caen and his experimental collaboration with the cyclist Stéphane, Tissié's medical concerns about extreme sportive exertion have come back into fashion along with pharmacological and psychological issues whose future importance he could not fully anticipate, even if he was aware of their significance.

Tissié was, for example, genuinely interested in the effects of chemical stimulants on athletic performance, calling them *agents dynamogènes* in the manner of Brown-Séquard.[92] But once again we must refrain from imposing our modern viewpoint on a scientist who did not automatically associate pharmacological agents with improved performance. As we shall see in Chapter 4, Tissié's views—pro and con—on the use of drugs in sport do not fit into the categories we employ in the modern debate about performance-enhancing substances, in part because at the time so little was known about their effects. His collaboration with Stéphane, "a rider who was truly interested in cooperating with my research,"[93] occurred a decade before the concept of the hormone was established in the scientific literature and four decades before the synthesis of the first anabolic steroids in the mid-1930s.

Tissié was even more interested in the psychological dimension of extreme physical exertion. His particularly acute remarks about the relationship between the athlete and his trainer-coach, as we shall see in Chapter 5, may be unique for this period. By modern standards, his ideas about the hypnotic and even psychopathological aspects of training are prescient if somewhat melodramatic. At the same time, we should recognize that this melodramatic strain in Tissié's thinking was only one aspect of his originality. Like Brown-Séquard, whose work he admired, Tissié did not hesitate to think about the human organism in a theoretically ambitious way. In addition to these important areas of interest, his use of clinical tests, his calculations of the energy metabolism of the athlete, and his bold thesis that "the athlete is a sick person" make him the commanding sports medical theorist of this period. From our vantage point, then, he appears to be a man who saw the outlines of high-performance sport early on. But we should not make the mistake of assuming that the scientist who glimpsed the contours of this world—and its dangers—would have welcomed its arrival.

A Victorian Metromaniac: Francis Galton and the Assessment of Human Performance

Francis Galton (1822–1911) is remembered today as the founder of "eugenics," the planned breeding of human beings to produce genetically "superior" stock. It is not surprising that this partial image of Galton holds sway over our historical memory. The racial doctrines of the nineteenth century, to which he contributed, prepared the ground for the racial catastrophes of our own century. It is, therefore, only natural for us to view a complex figure like Galton in a selective fashion, and to emphasize his role in popularizing a form of applied anthropology made notorious by the Nazis.

But Galton is important to our story because the eugenicist aims to maximize human or animal performance, and because this particular man's interest in measuring performance was extraordinary by any standard. His unbridled urge to measure every human capacity— what we may call his "metromania"—was a driving force behind his polymathic career as an anthropologist, psychologist, statistical theorist, and all-purpose scientific inventor. Indeed, Galton's stature as a modern figure rests more on his metromania than it does on the discredited doctrine of eugenics, though he would have wished otherwise. Describing in 1886 his scheme to breed "a vigorous and effective aristocracy," Galton wrote of "a class of men who would be so rich in hereditary gifts of ability" that they would be "at least as highly gifted by nature as could be derived by ordinary parliamentary election from the whole of the rest of the nation."[94] The important point is that Galton's confidence in the genomes of men who were "highly gifted by nature" was based, not on mere family ties, but on performance norms. "Galton was an ardent democrat," the psychologist Karl Pearson wrote, who "would have graded mankind by their natural aptitudes, and have done his best to check the reproduction of the lower grades."[95] His primary interest was the development of what Pearson called "supermen" of intellect.[96]

Galton's eugenics and metromania—generating abilities in offspring and measuring these aptitudes—were related obsessions, even if they sometimes led rather independent lives in his head. Galton wanted to assess the projected achievements of eugenics from one generation to the next by using quantitative norms. He had few doubts about the ultimate feasibility of this enterprise, because his voracious intellectual appetite was matched by a confidence that he could digest—and quantify—virtually anything he chose to investigate, including "the amount of difference that gives rise to the maximum of attractiveness between men and women" and "civic worth (however that term may be defined)."[97] In fact, wherever he looked, Galton saw opportunities for quantifying human experiences and turning them into competitions. One wonders how the contemporary medical profession reacted to his suggestion that a statistician could calculate "the curative capacities of different medical men, in numerical terms."[98]

Galton's obsession with measuring any human aptitude led him to certain experiments on himself aimed at the discovery of mental powers that were extraordinary in kind if not in power. Thus in his attempt to establish the existence of an "olfactile imagination," Galton "tried to perform mental arithmetic, not by imaginary visual symbols, or by imaginary sounds, but by imaginary smells. . . . I made a very few similar experiments with the gustatile or taste-imagination, but they were troublesome, and I did not follow them up." Galton claims that he "had progressed far enough to be able to add or subtract small sums," but that this modest result was not the real point. "I only desire to emphasise one fact which the experiment taught me, namely, the existence of a large substratum of mental work that my power of introspection failed to penetrate."[99]

Today, the search for a hidden "substratum of mental work" —untapped mental powers, as we would say—has spawned an entire psychoindustry focused on the boosting of "performance," of which "sports psychology" is only one marketable branch. We should also recognize that Galton's apparently eccentric self-experimentations, such as performing mental arithmetic by means of imaginary smells, were no more bizarre than modern research, funded by the U.S. Army, into sleep learning, biofeedback techniques, or such paranormal phenomena as extrasensory perception and psychokinesis.[100] Seen in retrospect, Galton's refusal to be restrained by the conventional parameters of human functioning—in effect, his reconceptualizing of human intellectual potential—was a real step into a future in which performance and productivity would eventually take precedence over traditional ideas about the natural limits of the human organism.

Galton's lack of interest in the sport culture of Victorian England was not unusual for a member of the intellectual class, some of whom found the new athleticism both coarsening and anti-intellectual.[101] Galton's particular lack of engagement had two aspects. First, he appears to have had no personal interest in sport as entertainment; on the contrary, he writes like an early sociological observer of these diverse popular diversions. Consider this passage from *Inquiries into Human Faculty and its Development* (1883):

> In the earlier years of this century the so-called manly sports of boxing and other feats of strength ranked high among the national amusements. A man who was successful in these became the hero of a large and demonstrative circle of admirers, and it is to be presumed that the best boxer, the best pedestrian [long-distance walker], and so forth, was the best adapted to succeed, through his natural physical gifts.[102]

This passage (and others) make it clear that Galton's real interest was not sport per se but rather the identification of a specific "natural" talent. In the Anthropometric Laboratory he set up at the International Health Exhibition of 1885, he displayed a device of potential value to boxers that measured "swiftness of blow as distinguished from force of blow." Visitors to the exhibit were invited to punch the padded end of a rod as quickly as they could, and Galton sadly noted a decline in the pugilistic skills of his countrymen: "It was a matter of surprise to myself, who was born in the days of pugilism, to find that the art of delivering a clean hit, straight from the shoulder, as required by this instrument, is nearly lost to the rising generation." Yet this was not the disappointed chauvinism of a sportive nationalist; he was much more interested in the "very pretty principle" on which his device was based.[103] In summary, Galton's "adoration of ability" compelled him to examine athletic performance as an important measure of human ability whether or not he found it intrinsically interesting.

The second dimension of Galton's lack of interest in sport, his indifference to boosting athletic performance, was even more typical of contemporary scientific attitudes. If he mentions "improved methods of training" in his *Inquiries*, it is only to help account for the discrepancy between the walking feats of the early nineteenth century and those of his own era. More important is his observation that, training techniques notwithstanding, "the athletes of the present day are more successful than those who lived some eighty years ago"[104]— evidence that the biological quality of the race may be improving. For

Galton it was the eugenic norm—not athletic performance—that really counted.

Galton's general indifference toward the pursuit of athletic performance had been anticipated by Herbert Spencer two decades earlier. In this regard, both men represent the premodern era I have already referred to. The title of Spencer's essay "Physical Education" is likely to mislead the modern reader, for whom this term is associated primarily with sports and only secondarily with public health. But for Spencer, as for Galton, these priorities were precisely reversed: hygiene was everything, and what we call sport was scarcely an afterthought. Spencer's priorities are evident in his statement that "the sportive activities to which the instincts impel, are essential to bodily welfare." He was most interested in children's dietary habits, and he advised parents to listen to the wisdom of their children's appetite for sugar and fruit. "Any work on organic chemistry shows that sugar plays an important part in the vital processes," while the "vegetable acids" in fruit are "very good tonics." He also reminded his readers that "well-fed races" tend to be "the energetic and dominant races," and that "the preservation of health is a *duty*."[105]

Spencer relied on "instinct," not human artifice, to shape a hygienic physical culture. Thus he criticizes gymnastics as "a system of factitious exercise," inflicting upon the body "formal, muscular motions" that lead to "disproportionate development." As if this were not antimodern enough, he also rejects that spirit of struggle that is at the heart of modern sport: "Competition, it is true, serves as a stimulus; but it is not a lasting stimulus, like that enjoyment which accompanies varied play." For Spencer, the real issue was finding a remedy for "the keen competition of modern life" that was already causing thousands of people to "break down" under the hectic pressures of the 1850s.[106]

There is, however, one passage in Spencer's text that may point toward the scientific cultivation of the high-performance athlete. Some fathers who neglect the systematic raising of their own offspring, he complains, may yet "attend agricultural meetings, try experiments, and engage in discussions, all with a view of discovering how to fatten prize pigs! Infinite pains will be taken to produce a racer that shall win the Derby: *none to produce a modern athlete* [emphasis added]. . . . It is time that the benefits which our sheep and oxen have for years past derived from the investigations of the laboratory, should be participated in by our children."[107] Although Spencer's vocabulary has a suggestive ring to the modern ear, we should not mistake his concerns about health for an interest in the scientific development of "our children" into record-breaking athletes. In fact, the age of systematic training for university athletes would not begin until ten years later.[108] It is unlikely that any of the admirers of this method and its newfangled apparatus understood where all of this would lead or were interested in the pursuit of the record performance. Widespread interest in such ideas still lay far in the future.

As Spencer suggests, scientific interest in quantifying and improving racing performance at this time focused on equine rather than human athletes. In England the breeding, systematic training, and timing of racehorses began as early as the seventeenth century,[109] and this is the tradition that shaped the attitudes of Spencer, Galton, and their contemporaries. The horse was one of Galton's favorite animals,[110] and the fact that his two published papers on the speed of the American trotting horse appeared as far apart in time as 1883 and 1898 suggests that he sustained his interest in equine breeding over a long period. Yet here, too, the point of these studies was less performance per se than its significance as an index of how well scientific breeding—in effect, accelerated evolution—was actually working. In 1883 Galton could report that "the rate per mile of the hundred fastest American trotting-horses has become 2 seconds faster in each successive period of 3 years, beginning with 1871, and ending with 1880; also that the relative speed of the hundred fastest horses in each year is closely the same, though their absolute speed differs."[111] Not only was there progress to report, but Galton also extrapolated his data into the future to predict the fastest performances of 1890, just as modern scientists will occasionally set themselves to predicting the world records of the future in track-and-field events. Fifteen years later, however, Galton registered his impatience with scientific progress in this area. "It is strange," he writes, "that the huge sums spent on the breeding of pedigree stock, whether of horses, cattle, or other animals, should not give rise to systematic publications of authentic records in a form suitable for scientific inquiry into the laws of heredity."[112]

Animal performance was closely tied to Galton's interest in human physical performance and, in particular, to the analogy between the physical achievements of men and beasts. He thought this analogy useful in that it served to demonstrate how the "eugenics" routinely applied to farm animals might also improve human beings. Like Spencer, he could not understand why men insisted on applying breeding principles to animals but not to themselves, and this frus-

tration led him occasionally to deal with the topical—if not yet scientific—matter of athletic performance. "No one doubts that muscle
is hereditary in horses and dogs," Galton wrote in 1870 in *Hereditary
Genius*, "but humankind are so blind to facts and so governed by
preconceptions, that I have heard it frequently asserted that muscle
is not hereditary in men. Oarsmen and wrestlers have maintained
that their heroes spring up capriciously, so I have thought it advisable
to make inquiries into the matter." Today, of course, the genetic
component of athletic performance is taken for granted even as it
resists the quantification Galton envisioned.

Training, the other component of athletic achievement, existed
only at the periphery of Galton's awareness. He mentions rowers, for
example, and

> the frequent trainings they have gone through. Mr. Watson mentions
> to me one well-known man, who has trained for an enormous number
> of races, and during the time of each training was most abstemious and
> in amazing health; then, after each trial was over, he commonly gave
> way, and without committing any great excess, remained for weeks in
> a state of fuddle. This is too often the history of these men.[113]

Here Galton glimpsed the physiological costs of high-performance
sport, sounding a warning theme that appeared in medical commentaries more frequently toward the end of the nineteenth century. But
neither training nor the "pathological physiology" of sport to which it
eventually led were ever among Galton's real concerns. For one
thing, he was aware of the genetic limits on human performance: "Let
the blacksmith labour as he will," he wrote, "he will find there are
certain feats beyond his power that are well within the strength of a
man of herculean make, even though the latter may have led a sedentary life."[114] This passage and others make it clear that Galton's
fixation on the problem of inherited abilities relegated the potential
effect of physical training to the back of his mind, effectively obscur-
ing his view of future developments in the science of human performance.

Galton thus treated sport as a secondary theme that appeared
only from time to time in conjunction with his major interests. For
example, like other nineteenth-century anthropologists, he took an
interest in the quasi-athletic performances of various "savages": "An
ingenious traveller might obtain a great number of approximate and
interesting data . . . measuring various faculties of the natives, such

as their delicacy of eyesight and hearing, their swiftness in running, their accuracy of aim with spear, arrow, boomerang, sling, gun, and so forth, either laterally or else vertically, distance of throw, stature, and much else."[115] In a more practical vein, he recommended "a system of moderate marks for physical efficiency introduced into the competitive examinations of candidates for the Army, Navy and Indian Civil Services"[116]—in other words, quasi-sportive norms introduced for a nonsportive purpose. Finally, in conjunction with his plan for an Anthropometric Laboratory, Galton "recognise[d] that dynamic tests—the functioning of the body—are far more important than static tests. He would have *agility* tested by gymnasium or athletic sports tests. Co-ordination of muscles and eye by measured skill in well-known games from racquets to billiards."[117] In short, Galton put sport in the service of science, whereas the current crisis of scientific sport derives from the fact that this relationship has been reversed since Galton wrote a century ago.

An Apostle of Energy: Wolfgang Weichardt and the Abolition of Fatigue

The scientific career of Wolfgang Weichardt, which provoked a heated if brief controversy just after the turn of the century, was forgotten many years ago. But Weichardt was an authentic forerunner of the modern sports physiologist and a pioneering representative of the scientific romanticism that has become a recurrent theme in high-performance sport. Born in 1875, he studied at the universities of Jena, Leipzig, Munich, and Berlin on his way to becoming a physiological chemist of broad interests, including medical hygiene, immunology, and the dubious research on fatigue that makes him important to our story. A striking feature of Weichardt's life is the discrepancy between his ultimate obscurity and a series of professional associations with conspicuously successful colleagues. In 1902 he was at the Pasteur Institute in Paris with the bacteriologist Elie Metchnikoff, recipient of the 1908 Nobel Prize for Medicine and Physiology. In 1904 he worked at the University of Berlin in the laboratory of Emil Hermann Fischer, the outstanding organic chemist of this period and recipient of the 1902 Nobel Prize for Chemistry. In 1909 he held a position at the Veterinary College of Berlin's Institute for Physiological Chemistry, headed by Emil Abderhalden, a Swiss physiologist who served as president of the German Academy of Sciences.[118] It is not unreasonable to assume that the heady atmosphere of Nobel Prize–winning laboratories nourished in Weichardt a thirst for recognition that fed his occasionally strident campaign to promote his "discovery" of a chemical antidote to fatigue. In 1906 Weichardt was actually granted a U.S. patent for this substance, while cooler heads at the German patent office wisely declined his application.[119]

More than once in his scientific publications Weichardt reveals a rather thin-skinned professional ego, overly sensitive to questions of scientific precedence and recognition, and he was not averse to blowing his own horn.[120] But professional ambition alone cannot account for the fact that he managed to elaborate, over many years and in highly respectable medical journals, a sensational theory of fatigue reduction that was influential for years before evaporating without a trace. He succeeded only because his work appeared during the scientific campaign against fatigue waged in many European laboratories during the half-century from 1880 to 1930.[121] The triumph of science over the terra incognita[122] of fatigue was a grand event that had long been awaited, and we may assume that it was wishful thinking that kept Weichardt's ideas afloat in the scientific literature long past their time. The coup de grace did not come until 1924, when two American physiologists demolished his theory.[123] Even as late as 1932 we find a contributor to one German medical journal cautioning readers about another of Weichardt's innovations: protein cell injections to which he had applied the dynamic term "protoplasm activation."[124]

Weichardt's theory of fatigue was based on a series of experiments supposedly demonstrating the existence of a specific "fatigue toxin," similar to a bacterial toxin, extracted from the muscle fluids of animals that had been run to exhaustion on treadmills. He reported that the injection of this alleged toxin into healthy animals caused fatigue, stupor, lowered body temperature, and sometimes even death, while the injected "muscle plasma" or "muscle juice" of unfatigued animals left other experimental animals "vigorous and lively." What is more, Weichardt claimed that a buildup of fatigue toxin led in turn to the production of a specific antitoxin capable of neutralizing its precursor. This antitoxin, he claimed, was the key to neutralizing fatigue itself.[125] In 1909 another investigator sprayed a 1 percent solution of this "antikenotoxin" into the air of a classroom and reported that the pupils' arithmetic calculations suddenly became 50 percent faster and noticeably more accurate.[126] This kind of fantasy about human performance is typical of the wishful thinking so prevalent during the scientific campaign against fatigue of this period.

Weichardt's scientific writings are filled with references to the boosting of performance (*Leistungssteigerung*). In 1904 he even suggested that his "antitoxin" be used to neutralize the fatigue of athletes and soldiers engaged in "forced marches."[127] But his casual interest in boosting such physical performances was an afterthought within the context of the more expansive concept of performance—including the mental feats of schoolchildren and, the spraying of their classrooms—which we have found to be characteristic of this period.[128] Weichardt's definition of performance pursued this phenomenon into the realm of what he called "the mysterious activity of cellular life"[129] and included a suggestive but imprecise collection of terms such as "protoplasma activation" and "omnicellular performance boosting."[130] Nevertheless, Weichardt was not a simple-minded reductionist bent on forcing the performance concept onto a single procrustean bed. He assumed that the performance capacities of different human organs were boosted in different ways, that enhancing muscular performance was distinct from enhancing that of the circulatory system, and that "boosting" the capacity of the immune system (hence our term "booster shot") was "performance" in this expanded sense of the term.[131]

Weichardt refused to ascribe enhanced performance to a "somehow different" functioning of the organs. Such a concession would have meant importing the dying doctrine of vitalism, postulating a mysterious life-force, into the area of human performance; instead, he insisted that performances are always latent in the organism, that performances can be enhanced but can never be created ex nihilo.[132]

Weichardt's scientific temperament did include—in the words of his American critics—a "proneness to accept without question favorable evidence, however intrinsically strange."[133] Yet such credulity, like that of Brown-Séquard, was inherent in the romantic age of performance, and it persists today in the form of widespread speculative assumptions about drugs and other ergogenic techniques that are reputed to enhance the performances of athletes.

Was Weichardt, in the last analysis, an important figure in the scientific history of sport? Given the disastrous impact over the past quarter-century of anabolic steroid use on the morale and reputation of high-performance sport, his casual endorsement of "fatigue antitoxin" for athletes, along with an earlier remark made by the Austrian

physiologist Oskar Zoth proposing the sportive use of testicular extracts (see Chapter 4), has a certain historic significance. At the same
time, we should recognize how Wolfgang Weichardt both is and is not
a man of our own age. His lack of interest in sport is old-fashioned by
our standards, but his romantic approach to performance—that willed
refusal to respect the limits of orthodox science—has reemerged as a
crucial element in the scientific sport culture of our own era. Like
other members of the Physiological International, Wolfgang Weichardt promoted, not sport, but a vision of the relationship between
human beings and wellsprings of biological energy that were identified with human potential itself.

The Physiological International as a Scientific Community

"Nothing conduces more to the development of science," E.-J. Marey
wrote in 1895, "than the association in the same work of men whose
knowledge and aptitudes differ."[134] It is fair to say that the five scientific careers portrayed in this chapter confirm his observation. As
representatives of an informal Physiological International, these men
constituted a thoroughly heterogeneous group whose minds ranged
widely, if sometimes incautiously, across a broad range of scientific
problems. It is also fair to say that they were "associated in the same
work," although this point requires clarification. Several of these
men, and the French in particular, were stimulated by each other's
work, and in that sense did indeed form a kind of scientific community linked by their common interest in human performance. The
exception is Wolfgang Weichardt, who operated independently and is
unique among our protagonists in having virtually disappeared from
the historical record.[135]

Of these five scientists, Philippe Tissié was the best informed
about the work of his contemporaries in the area of sport and human
performance. He was among Marey's many admirers in the scientific
community, and he appreciated what chronophotography had contributed to the study of human and animal movement.[136] He had
used Marey's pneumograph to test the respiratory condition of the
cyclist Stéphane after his 24-hour run.[137] Tissié praised Marey in
comparison with medical men who had only done a few experiments
on muscle contraction, respiration, or circulation. These dabblers, he
maintained, were simply ignorant of exercise physiology, whereas

Marey and Fernand Lagrange, a sports-minded expert on fatigue, were competent students of the physiology of athletic exercise.[138] Like Marey, Tissié had exchanged the constricted venue and foul air of the laboratory for the open space and fresh air of the running or cycling track. Instead of dead organisms, these men studied vibrantly athletic ones, preparing the way for the sports physiologist who visits his clients in the field or in the pool. Tissié was also in touch with the psychologist Alfred Binet, who praised him as a "man of action" but criticized his use of anecdotal evidence instead of controlled experiments to test the effects of physical exercise.[139]

Tissié was also an admirer of Brown-Séquard, borrowing his term *dynamogenic* to refer to a range of energizing factors, including will-power.[140] Like many of his contemporaries, Tissié was also impressed by Brown-Séquard's theory of testicular extracts, "his most beautiful discovery," in part because it offered evidence of the mind's dependence on organic processes—physiological music to a physician's ears.[141] Tissié also invoked Brown-Séquard's theory to argue that athletes should abstain from all sexual activity during training,[142] since semen-retention was an even more economical way to store up the still mysterious dynamogenic factor assumed to be present in testicular extracts. From a modern perspective, the striking point here is that, even though he believed in the potency of testicular extracts, Tissié did not call for their use as performance-enhancing agents in sport. This restraint probably resulted from three factors: his general distrust of supposedly performance-enhancing substances (like alcoholic drinks), his view of physical stress as pathogenic, and that lack of interest in mere performance-boosting that had caused the conflict with Coubertin.

Marey, too, was interested in the wide-ranging work of Brown-Séquard, but he does not appear to have been interested in the testicular extracts. On at least one occasion he showed that he was the more cautious theorist by rejecting Brown-Séquard's assumption that the biological laws governing muscle fatigue in mammals could also be applied to the electric discharges of certain fishes.[143] Elsewhere, Marey cites experiments by Brown-Séquard to support his own (Lamarckian) ideas about the hereditary transmission of modified organs, including the "more rapid and more energetic muscular action" of new breeds of racehorses.[144] The less credulous Galton, however, found Brown-Séquard's work in this area fatally flawed.[145]

Marey was a magnetic figure to make scientists of this period. It is no accident, for example, that it was in his laboratory that the researcher Piltan came to the conclusion that singing was a kind of "respiratory gymnastics."[146] Marey's work on maximally efficient walking was known in Germany,[147] Weichardt regarded him as an expert on fatigue,[148] and his chronophotography was sufficiently well known in England to inspire Galton to work on similar instruments.[149] Galton once donned a Marey pneumo-cardiograph to test it for comfort.[150] In 1888 Marey was appointed president of Paschal Grousset's newly founded Ligue Nationale de l'Éducation Physique, whose membership included Jules Verne.[151] Today Marey's work has become an integral, indeed invisible, dimension of our cultural landscape. The mechanics of movement have been demystified, even as the phenomenon of speed still fascinates us.

These interconnections between our five protagonists occurred within the context of a common scientific project we have called the investigation of performance. Because animals played a crucial—indeed, sacrificial— role in the development of physiology during the nineteenth century, scientists usually studied the physiological capacities of animals long before assessing those of human subjects, penal decapitations being the exceptions that confirmed the rule. Working within that branch of applied science the French suggestively call *zootechnie*, Marey and Galton were more interested in the high-performance equine athlete than in his far less developed human counterpart. But this period also saw the "shift to sports in which people rather than animals exerted themselves,"[152] a period during which men slowly took the baton from horses, in particular, and ran forward into a new age of physiological experimentation. This transition took decades, because scientists were not interested in boosting athletic performance beyond modest and "normal" limits.

But how interested were Galton and his contemporaries in pushing even the animal organism to its limits? The determining factors here were the limitations of the breeding science of this era and the scope of their ambition. As a proselytizing eugenist, Galton was gratified that the data about racehorses demonstrated improved performance, and he was satisfied to chart this progress and extrapolate it some years into the future. Had he lived to see it, he would surely have been delighted that the Third International Congress of Eugenics, held in New York in 1932, featured a booth devoted to "The Inheritance of Racing Capacity in the Thoroughbred Horse," including a mathematical model for determining the genetic value of any given foal and a diagram of horses' chromosomes.[153]

Not all observers of the horseracing scene, however, were willing to leave performance-boosting in the hands of breeders. By the end of the nineteenth century, the doping of racehorses—as well as jockeys, boxers, and racing cyclists—was standard operating procedure. Many horses were doped with cocaine for the purpose of inhibiting performance and thereby influencing the outcome of a bet. Horse doping was forbidden in 1903, but it was not until 1910 that an Austrian scientist developed a saliva test to detect some of the illicit substances being used. Today the doping of horses and greyhounds remains widespread in the racing industry and occurs in Olympic equine events, as well.[154]

But doping represented, then as now, an uncertain intervention in an animal's functioning. Looking back at this crucial transitional period, it is worth asking whether the scope of scientific ambition included an interest in devising breeding procedures to produce a truly high-performance horse, an equine version of Frankenstein's monster? Such a hypothetical urge to create extraordinary animals through breeding could not be fulfilled at the racetrack, where improved performance was measured in very small increments: less than one second a year for a mile run, according to Galton's calculations.[155] Actually, the urge to come up with impressive innovations for breeding animals had already expressed itself in England almost a hundred years earlier.

During the nineteenth century radical experiments were carried out on show animals rather than racing ones. As in bodybuilding today, it was the production of the body of the animal rather than a particular physical feat that constituted the "performance" meant for public display. Just after 1800 there was a consensus that "the most impressive animals were those that pushed natural limits or approached unattainable ideals."[156] The urge to create an overdeveloped and even freakish physique, like the urge to practice vivisection, was confined to the animal realm, and a reaction against this sort of gigantism set in later in the century. In *The Descent of Man*, Darwin himself discouraged the idea that "strongly-marked and rare anomalies" would lead to the advancement of a species.[157] There was, however, an "unnatural" type of performance inflicted on horses during the nineteenth century: the artificial gait called trotting. As an American observer pointed out in the early 1880s, "a breed of fast trotters" was a counterevolutionary development, an unnatural type dependent for survival on the market for racetrack gambling.[158]

In conclusion, the Physiological International witnessed, and in some ways facilitated, the birth of high-performance sport as we know

it today. Brown-Séquard virtually created our concept of hormonal
performance-enhancement (see Chapter 4). Marey proposed that the
elite athletes of his day serve as visual models whose chronophotographic images would reveal "the secret of their success." Tissié studied the physiology of the record performance and pointed out that
high-performance athletics meant driving the human organism into a
biological danger zone. Galton, too, understood that the investigation
of athletic exertion would yield scientific dividends, while the now-
forgotten Weichardt popularized the scientific campaign against
fatigue of this era and recommended his "antitoxin" as a performance-
enhancing substance for athletes.

We should keep in mind that the work of these men and their
contemporaries was not intended to promote scientific sport in our
sense of that term. The scientists of this period were preoccupied
with discovering human potential rather than initiating attempts to
modify it. Performance-enhancement meant tapping the hereditary
potential of the human or animal organism rather than artificially
manipulating the organism itself. The handful of scientists who proposed performance-boosting injections made these offhand comments
in the fine print of professional journals. They were not promulgating
the sort of program that eventually became a reality in East Germany.
This is why the radical pharmacological and surgical interventions of
the late nineteenth century usually occurred, not in scientific laboratories, but in science fiction.[159]

Because the future development of sport had not yet been determined, the physician Tissié's conflict with the Olympic enthusiast
Coubertin was of historic importance. Tissié understood that the unrestrained pursuit of performance implicit in his adversary's sportive
ethos would lead inevitably to a "pathological physiology of sport."
Coubertin, for his part, understood that Olympic sport involved such
risks but favored daring over restraint. It was the unassuming Marey
who occupied the middle ground, uninfatuated with Olympic sport
yet nevertheless engaged in his own unrelenting pursuit of the biomechanical secrets that would contribute mightily to the Olympic
cult of performance.

One fateful portent of this development was the active support
of Jules Ferry, president of the Third Republic, for the potent combination of Coubertin and Marey. "You have the epic spirit," he told
Coubertin in 1889, and it was he who secured the funds to build
Marey's Physiological Station.[160] This investment paid off in scientific
terms. Reporting for the Commission on Physiology and Hygiene,

Marey offered some prescient remarks on the study of athletics for the great Paris International Exposition of 1900. His camera, he said, could record the styles of athletes of different nationalities; it could predict a man's fitness for a particular sport; and it could reveal the secrets of athletic superiority concealed within the otherwise incomprehensible performances of certain champions. "For several have bested their rivals, not due to superior muscular strength, but on account of the skill and ingenuity they have displayed."[161] Having encouraged the most important visionary and a pioneer technician of high-performance sport, Ferry's support was thus a significant factor in the "gigantic biological experiment" launched in 1896 at the Athens Olympic Games.

4

Faster, Higher, Stronger
A History of Doping in Sport

What is Doping?

At the 1990 World Weightlifting Championship in Budapest the exhortatory banners displayed in the competition hall read "No Doping"—a curiously muted and discordant note at a competition punctuated by the grunts and screams of the lifters. But the International Weightlifting Federation (IWF) had had no choice but to join the antidrug chorus: At the previous world championship meet, every fifth athlete had been thrown out of the competition for hormonal irregularities, and the sport was facing possible expulsion from the Olympic movement. The purpose of the banners—blue letters on a pure white background—was to perform nothing less than an exorcism. For everyone present knew that it would require some form of magic—like faultless detection methods and merciless penalties—to wash anabolic steroids out of the sport. What is more, there was now reason to believe that a real crackdown, including the new "steroid profile" detection method, could work. As a result, the lifters this year were attempting weights far below what they had put up in the past, and only one athlete even tried for a world record. Perhaps this was the new face of drug-free elite sport—anxious and anticlimactic, but "clean."[1]

The concept of "doping" includes two basic themes. In colloquial usage, "doping" refers to the boosting of human performance by artificial means. In recent years, that has meant drugs in general and anabolic steroids in particular. The second, more complicated aspect of "doping" aimed at improving human performance is the presumption that it represents an illegitimate strategy. While all sports federations, including the International Olympic Committee, and virtually all sports journalists denounce doping as scandalous, many elite athletes do not regard doping as illegitimate.

This conflict, with sports bureaucrats and journalists arrayed against the athletes who practice doping and attempt to avoid detection, is the visible core of the "doping problem" in high-performance sport. For the public, this crisis takes the form of an endless game of scientific hide-and-seek in which the crucial protagonists are faceless laboratory technicians who pronounce upon the innocence or guilt of popular champions. But this technological contest between athletes who dope and the scientific detectives assigned to catch them is only the most dramatic symptom of a profound cultural ambivalence toward athletic performance that has emerged over the past century, an ambivalence in which pharmacological aids to many kinds of "performances" have come to play an integral role.

Why should pharmacological aids to athletic performance be prohibited at all? That is the primary question of the doping debate. Indeed, given the long history of mankind's involvement with chemicals that stimulate or depress the human mind and body, the scandals provoked by "doping" in sport in our own century appear to have a curiously naive quality. As the Austrian doping expert Ludwig Prokop once pointed out, "The artificial boosting of performance is an ancient dream of mankind."[2] For this very reason, it is important to understand how and why doubts about the boosting of human performance have arisen during the modern period. For the emergence of the concept of doping itself is an event of historical significance, since it represents an unprecedented kind of self-inhibition imposed upon the development of human potential.

Formulating a widely acceptable definition of doping is the basic (and unresolved) ethical problem of modern sports science, for the concept includes a scientific dimension (physiology and pharmacology), a social dimension (the selection of norms and thresholds), and a personal dimension (the values and intentions of the athlete who uses banned substances). The absence of a clear-cut definition thus derives from several factors: the continual appearance of new and potentially performance-enhancing substances or the revaluation of "traditional" doping agents; changing attitudes toward boosting athletic performances and the need for appropriate restraints; and the virtual impossibility of determining an athlete's intentions in employing a prohibited drug. For some observers, the apparently intractable nature of this problem suggests that limits on doping are senseless.[3] For others, the failure to achieve a precise definition of doping is actually less important than their intuitive certainty that appropriate limits do exist, even if they cannot be defined to the unanimous approval of all interested parties. As Sir Arthur Porritt, chairman of the British Association of Sports Medicine, put it in 1965: "To define doping is, if not impossible, at best extremely difficult, and yet everyone who takes part in competitive sport or who administers it knows exactly what it means. The definition lies not in words but in integrity of character."[4] Such insistence on the necessity of limits is of cultural significance because it assumes a need to keep the pharmacological transformation of the human organism within defined limits. In this sense, the crucial factor is not where limits are set but the fact that they are set at all.

This "intuitional" critique of doping is the foundation of the antidoping consensus that is currently enforced by institutions such as the IOC and promulgated in sports publications around the world. At the same time, it is important to recognize that this consensus is less than a century old. Unlike Old Testament taboos, which retain much of their moral force in the Western world, the moral argument against doping represents a recent (and culturally conservative) response to specific scientific discoveries within the area of human biology. As this science develops, so do our ideas about the ethics of scientific intervention into the functioning of the human organism, as in the cases of "test-tube babies" or the use of artificial organs to sustain the lives of the aged or the infirm. As "heroic" medical interventions on behalf of these patients become routine, our shared assumptions (or "intuitions") about the propriety of new medical technologies change accordingly. Now the "test-tube baby," once a nightmare of science fiction, is an accepted member of the human family. Therefore, given such rapidly changing norms within the medical establishment, which does so much to define what may and may not be done with the human organism, we may ask whether our current societal consensus on doping, and our intuitive assessment of the ethical issues involved, will not also evolve over time as medical science learns more about the effects of substances that are widely believed to enhance athletic performance. We should also recognize that the antidoping consensus of our era, like the first antidoping consensus of the 1920s, is inherently unstable. To understand the origins of its tenuous status, we need to look more closely at the idea of doping itself and at how this concept emerged over the past two centuries.

On a fundamental level, doping is best understood as a consequence of the sheer ambition to improve performance in the absence of any restraints upon this ambition. It represents, in short, an ideology of uninhibited performance, which is precisely the source of its appeal to elite athletes and the sporting public. This expansive concept of doping includes a wide range of techniques and applications, making the use of drugs in sport only one example within a much larger category of "boosted" performances. Quite apart from sports competitions, "doping" techniques have been used to enhance sexual, military, academic, musical, and labor performances.[5] Indeed, this wide range of performance types raises the important question (addressed at the end of this section) of why the boosting of athletic performance attracts special censure while comparable "doping" practices provoke no controversy at all.

The expanded concept of doping includes drugs within a diverse collection of techniques that has seen many fashions come and go over the past century. Speculation about the value of administering extra oxygen to sportsmen appears just after the turn of the century, and at the 1932 Los Angeles Olympic Games this technique became associated with Japanese victories in the swimming competitions.[6] During the "gland grafting" craze of the 1920s, which involved inserting slices of monkey testicles into (male) patients, treatments were administered to at least a few athletes as well as other celebrities such as actors and writers who were concerned about their waning creative powers.[7] In the 1920s and 1930s there was also much debate about the biological value (and ethics) of using ultraviolet light sources to irradiate (and thereby invigorate) athletes. Even psychological techniques, including too much encouragement from spectators, were sometimes referred to as a form of "doping" in the German sports medical literature during the same period.[8] Transfusions that boost an athlete's red blood cell count ("blood doping"), a technique discovered by a Swedish scientist in 1972, resulted in several scandals during the 1980s. And in 1988 there was speculation that a number of female athletes might even have become pregnant in order to benefit from hormonal changes that might improve athletic performance.[9]

It is drugs, however, that have been the most important and notorious among these various techniques for improving athletic performance. At the same time, the notoriety of drugs has been the principal obstacle to understanding why they have been used and why they will continue to be used for the foreseeable future. In this connection, it is important to recall that the early scientific investigations into potentially performance-enhancing drugs coincided with powerful temperance movements aimed at stigmatizing alcohol and tobacco as medically and socially harmful "poisons." There was, in fact, a direct link between these disreputable substances and sport during the earlier part of this century, for alcohol and nicotine were frequently discussed by trainers and scientists as stimulants that might aid athletes. But the notoriety of doping has always transcended hygienic concerns and disapproval of "sinful" stimulants like liquor and cigarettes. The critical question has been whether and where limits on performance-enhancing techniques should be set, and this question actually consists of three issues: ethical doubts about doping as an offense against the norms of sportsmanship, medical doubts about possibly harmful effects, and anthropological doubts about transforming the human organism in an "unnatural" manner. Because this book focuses primarily on the biological dimension of doping, we will concentrate on medical and anthropological concerns about drug use in sport. Our ultimate goal is to determine whether or not the doping of athletes deserves the unique stigma it has acquired since the 1920s.

We can begin by asking to what extent doping is a deviant version of traditional pharmacology. Or to phrase the question somewhat differently, to what extent has the pharmacological tradition included the boosting of human performance? The universality of drug use throughout recorded history makes it clear that the use of bioactive substances to promote healing, to create states of intoxication, and to extend human capacities is almost as "natural" to the human species as the search for food and shelter.[10] The ubiquity of drugs, and their fundamental role in human life over millennia, are of crucial significance to our inquiry, since the distinction between what is "natural" and what is "unnatural" is at the heart of the twentieth-century controversy over the use of performance-enhancing drugs in sport.

The idea of boosting athletic performance with ingested substances is at least as old as the dietary practices of ancient Greek athletes, who supposedly ate herbs, sesame seeds, dried figs, and mushrooms for this purpose.[11] Here, in a world of religious experience remote from our own, a cultic ideal of athletic excellence flourished and then became extinct. These athletes, like ours, cultivated that intensity of ambition that rules out restraint in the pursuit of performance, so perhaps the homely nature of their training diet is misleading. For there is no reason to assume that the athletes, trainers, and physicians of ancient Hellas would have rejected steroids or stimulants or any of our banned substances. If doping is defined as a willingness to use the most advanced performance-enhancing techniques, then the Greeks practiced their own version of doping. The physician Galen's criticism of "the unnatural state of athletes"[12] is a critique, not of seeds and fruit, but of an entire way of life, allegedly detrimental to the life of the mind, that included special foods as only one element of intense training. The essential difference between their world and ours is the modern idea, accepted by many elite athletes, that there are "natural" limits to the development of athletic potential.

The dichotomy between "natural" and "artificial" behavior is central to the problem of defining "doping." If human beings have an "instinctive" affinity for stimulants like caffeine, as some writers have claimed, then it becomes more difficult to define doping as an "artificial" strategy. One can also hypothesize a utilitarian "instinct" that has prompted the universal discovery and use of narcotic substances that serve basic human needs.[13] But if this appetite—which appears to promote human survival—is universal, then "doping" appears less artificial. From this standpoint, the use of drugs in sport can be rationalized as the expression of a basic human drive to stimulate the human organism beyond its normal metabolic state.

But is sport a "human need" for which drugs are necessary or appropriate? What is "sport" in relation to the physical performances promoted by societies ethnologically distinct from our own? Is it possible to speak of "doping" in the case of physical performances that are being "boosted" for other than "sportive" reasons? Only the cultural anthropologist, by interpreting extreme physical exertion within the value systems of different cultures, can provide meaningful answers to these questions. The classic comparison matches the Tarahumara Indians of northern Mexico with modern athletes who practice "sport." Over a period of from 24 to 72 hours these runners can cover distances of from 150 to 350 miles, the purpose of which is to fulfill the requirements of a fertility ritual, and there is no limit to the methods they are allowed to boost their physical endurance. Whippings with thorny branches, sexual abstinence, and ingestion of chemical substances like dried tortoise, bat blood, and peyote—which has a strychninelike effect—are traditional techniques. Yet this is certainly not doping by our definition, since these supermarathons are cultic rather than sportive performances.[14] The nature of the performance does not call forth a countervailing restraint because restraint has no function in this context: These competitions do not require physiological equity, and there is no equivalent to our fear of the scientific ambition to alter human nature. Such comparisons show why both doping and the fear of doping are cultural constructs that evolve over time. We should remember that less than a century ago European scientists were discussing pharmacological aids to athletic performance without a qualm. But when a proliferation of such studies coincided with the sports boom of the 1920s, when athletic achievement took on new significance and now became vulnerable to the threat of "manipulation," a "doping crisis" was born. A similar situation had already occurred in seventeenth-century England, but this "crisis" had resulted from the doping of equine rather than human athletes.[15] Eventually, a more determined and systematic approach to human athletic performance would produce the intractable doping problem of our own era.

We can test the legitimacy of the doping concept in two ways. First, we can use historical comparisons; up to this point we have been exploring the elastic nature of a term that has encompassed a variety of techniques and performance types—from the ultraviolet lamp to blood doping, from soldiers and aviators to athletes. As such examples proliferate, the practice of doping appears to acquire a kind of legitimacy as familiar boundaries dissolve: The athlete joins a much larger group of performers who experience physiological emergencies, while the ergogenic drug is seen as only one of many substances that have been used to energize the human organism for a wide variety of purposes. As this comparative procedure erases the traditional distinctions between "doping" and standard medical practice, it becomes more difficult to sustain the view that doping represents a deviant type of pharmacology.

The second approach recognizes that some forms of doping are illegitimate but emphasizes the many conceptual problems involved in defining what ought to be prohibited. The distinction between "natural" and "artificial" substances, for example, does not address the diversity of performance-enhancing methods or the fact that this distinction itself can be highly debatable. If coffee is a "natural" substance, then is caffeine an "artificial" one? Is the athlete's own blood a "natural" substance that can be transfused back into his body to boost his red blood cell count? Is testosterone a "natural" substance as opposed to "synthetic" anabolic steroids even if both have similar effects? Is ultraviolet radiation from a quartz lamp an "artificial" kind of light? Is pregnancy a "natural" condition if it is contracted to boost athletic performance? Such questions demonstrate that human intentions play an important role in the entire doping phenomenon. In other words, doping is both an applied science and the expression of an ambition that society wants to pursue its goals by some means and not by others. The mere fact that doping practices are defined, detected, and penalized by bureaucracies means that scientific criteria must share pride of place with purely pragmatic ones. The "politics" of doping that results is a complex interplay between what is known about ergogenic drugs and what can be done to control their use by athletes (see Chapter 7).

This "political" dimension of doping includes a number of separate problems, including the riddle of whether some drugs work at all. Does the use of an innocuous drug qualify as doping? It is very difficult to determine the efficacy of drugs, including the so-called "masking" agents[16] used to conceal the presence of steroids, with real scientific rigor. It may well be that the East German sports scientists who secretly operated the world's most advanced doping program during the 1970s and 1980s are the only ones who have actually determined the optimal doses of anabolic steroids and how to "mask" their presence in the body. Yet despite our considerable ignorance about whether and how "ergogenic" drugs affect athletic performance, the assumption that they do work is widespread. As we shall see in the next section of this chapter, this credulity and its far-reaching consequences are one legacy of the biological romanticism of the last century. Further scientific research that might advance our knowledge of these drugs is, as the East German example shows, a political issue. Like any other decision to fund controversial science, it would require negotiations among competing interest groups. It is even possible that such research might result in a decision to legalize some drugs now associated with "doping," thereby changing the very definition of illegitimate drug use.

Another practical problem is whether certain substances are accessible to athletes and whether they can be detected. (Soviet researchers once suggested that any undetectable technique like electric muscle stimulation should be permitted.)[17] A complicating factor is the ambiguous status of certain substances. For example, the classification of common nutrients as doping agents presents obvious enforcement problems. As one observer pointed out in 1939, it is a practical necessity that any discussion about nutrients focus on "special artificial foods intended for consumption immediately before or after athletic performances," such as carbohydrates or glucose,[18] but here, too, the problems of detection and enforcement are obvious. In a major commentary on the doping problem published in 1937, a Swiss physician argued for the banning of substances that were available only from a pharmacist. He also proposed that any ban that could not be enforced was both senseless and harmful, since the result would be the alienation of athletes from their physicians[19]—a fine example of the "politics" of doping. In a similar vein, a German scientist pointed out in 1930 that it was simply impractical to prohibit certain performance-enhancing techniques. He had heard, for example, that in 1928 many Olympic athletes had been irradiated with ultraviolet light, an undetectable practice. It is interesting to note that he takes the effectiveness of this treatment for granted, even if his explanation of its physiological mechanism is quite unscientific.[20]

The argument that undetectable drugs should be allowed has a certain common-sense appeal. There are, indeed, situations in which it is clearly practical neither to detect nor to enforce a ban on certain drugs. Toiling three miles above sea level, Chilean mine workers of the 1930s chewed their illegal coca leaves unimpeded by the authorities, who knew that they could not work without this stimulation.[21] One measure of how sport and work have merged into a single category today is that such expedient oversights have become a familiar part of the politics of doping in elite sport, where sports official and meet promoters have often suppressed positive drug test results.[22] But benign neglect is not a viable doping policy for athletes, who are divided about doping in a way that the Chilean miners were not. Such noninterference is also incompatible with the antidoping policy of the International Olympic Committee and other supervisory bodies that administer drug tests, if only because such a position would be a public relations disaster for these organizations. The logic of the antidoping campaign mandates instead a continuous program of scientific research that can identify and detect new drugs as soon as they are developed.

But the central ambiguity of high-performance sports medicine is the problem of distinguishing doping from therapeutic medicine. This problem of definition is particularly acute in the case of anabolic steroids, which have had important medical applications[23] for half a century and began to spread through high-performance sport in the early 1960s. But the ambiguous status of certain drug treatments was already evident to sports physicians decades before. How can we distinguish between doping and medical hygiene? A key distinction here is the difference between performance-boosting stimulation and prophylaxis or replacement therapy. For example, taking sodium phosphate tablets or drops, one scientist wrote in 1930, is not doping and must not be equated with "infamous" techniques like strychnine injections or the use of cocaine. Why? Because phosphate therapy replaces a "natural" substance that is excreted during physical exertion. Phosphate deficiency, he says, may account for the "overtraining" phenomenon that is frequently discussed in the sports medical literature of this period.[24]

In another case, at the 1928 Winter Olympic Games in St. Moritz, the Swiss sports physician Wilhelm Knoll was reported to have administered Coramin and Digifolin to exhausted skiers who came across the finish line in "a very bad condition"[25]—a clearly rehabilitative therapy rather than a performance-enhancing one. A more ambiguous case, however, is reported by a physician who served as a medical consultant to the Austrian Olympic Committee in the 1930s. "Calcio-coramin" tablets, he says, eliminated breathlessness, headaches, and dizziness in the skiers who tested this drug at high altitude in a nonsportive situation. But what about his enthusiastic recommendation that "Calcio-coramin" be used to restore a "second wind" to exhausted athletes? In fact, the author vigorously disputes the idea that this is doping; on the contrary, he claims, "Calcio-coramin" is "medically indicated" and should be prescribed for athletes as a general rule.[26] Hormone treatments to help female athletes delay menstruation prior to competition—and thereby improve their performances—appeared in the early 1930s.[27] These are only a few of the examples from the sports medical literature that show how inseparably performance-enhancement and preventive medicine are bound up in certain cases. Today's problem of anabolic steroids, perceived by the public as just another example of "drug abuse," is also haunted by the ambivalence of many sports physicians and athletes toward substances that are rehabilitative as well as muscle-building agents.

This medical ambivalence, which can only impede current attempts at doping control, is but one complication among others. Our definition of doping, and the politics of doping that results from this definition, reflect an inherently unstable consensus among several interest groups who are themselves divided within their own ranks. As an increasing number of scientists call for more systematic research into the physiological mechanisms and side-effects of anabolic steroids, we face the possibility that our image of these drugs will change. From its origins in the 1920s, the campaign against doping has always combined unrelated arguments about health and fairness in an uneasy synergistic relationship. If steroids could be made medically nonhazardous, the argument that they confer an unfair advantage would be weakened, since it would become more reasonable to stress that all athletes could use these drugs safely. At that point, the abolition of the doping concept would be closer than it ever has been before, and many elite athletes would be relieved of the burden of using drugs in secret.

Why, outside of athletics, has the doping concept hardly existed at all? In part, of course, because every modern society is a "pharmacological" society in which a whole pharmacopoeia of drugs is taken for granted. Indeed, the ubiquity of "doping" in our daily lives is overlooked to an astonishing degree by those who decry its presence in sport. Even the fertilizing of crops, as André Noret has pointed out, demonstrates our economic dependence on pharmacological means of increasing production.[28] Stimulants, tranquilizers, painkillers, sleeping pills, antihistamines, and a vast array of other drugs are noncontroversial. Why are pharmacological restrictions imposed on athletes alone?

Consider the following group of performers for whom mental and physical stress is a way of life. Their life expectancy is 22 percent under the national average. They suffer from tendinitis, muscle cramps, pinched nerves, a high incidence of mental health problems and heart attacks, and anxiety levels that threaten to cripple their performance as professionals. These people are not firemen or policemen or athletes; they are orchestral musicians, and they use "beta-blocker" drugs to control their disabling symptoms and thereby improve their performances.[29] These antianxiety drugs have been banned by the Medical Commission of the International Olympic Committee as a form of doping.[30]

How can we account for this discrepancy? What makes sport the one type of performance that is considered to be corrupted by pharmacological intervention? One might argue that an orchestral performance is not a formalized contest like a sporting event; thus the performers are not competing against each other, so deceit is not an issue. But this argument overlooks the fact that an entire field of equally doped runners who knew exactly which drugs their competitors had taken would still constitute a scandal against our mysterious yet authoritative antidoping norm. In the last analysis, then, it is not the quality of the competition but the integrity of the performance itself that is at stake. The antidoping norm appears to demand from the athlete an untainted, and therefore accurate, measure of human potential. But why is the same requirement not imposed on the orchestral musician? Indeed, one would expect "high" cultural performances to carry greater ethical significance than sportive ones. One would assume that our sense of what we are as a species is more deeply vested in the integrity of an artistic performance, such as a symphony and the enormous cultural prestige it embodies, than in the integrity of a footrace.

Perhaps this curiously selective anxiety about sportive performance derives from the very simplicity of *corporeal* display. The philosopher Gunter Gebauer has suggested that what our skeptical age demands is "the evidence of the body" and that doping tests offer "guarantees of its reality." In this sense, the body's performance—unlike performances of the mind—is reliable evidence of a human reality that does not deceive: a morsel of authenticity in an unreliable world of appearances.[31] From this perspective, the campaign against doping appears as a desperate holding action against the corruption of the last "real" performers in the world. Small wonder, then, that the "war against drugs" in sport is fought with such tenacity, even if many of the warriors in this campaign do not understand what is at stake.

Nineteenth-century Pharmacology and Doping

One famous performer who drugged his way to fabulous productivity was the great French novelist Honoré de Balzac.[32] Half a century before French scientists were attempting to analyze in their laboratories the effects of coffee, the writer was performing experiments on himself in the honorable tradition of nineteenth-century physiology. His technique was to take cold, concentrated coffee at night on an empty stomach. The results he described as follows: "The ideas surge forth like army batallions on the field of battle, and the battle begins. Memories charge ahead, their flags unfurled; the light cavalry of comparisons develops at a magnificent gallop, while the artillery of logic arrives with its retinue," etc.[33] Balzac had, in effect, confirmed an earlier observation by the great French physician and physiologist Pierre-Jean-Georges Cabanis (1757–1808), who cited the testimony of "several writers" who had called coffee "an intellectual beverage."

According to Cabanis, coffee was the drug of choice for any number
of literati, scientists and artists whose work required special efforts
from "the thinking organ."[34] This approving reference to the diverse
kinds of performers who could benefit from a drug anticipates the
attitude of the entire nineteenth century toward performance-
enhancing substances. By the turn of the next century, the idea of the
wonder drug had begun to appear in science fiction, and the use of
drugs to boost athletic performances was becoming increasingly common. Pharmacology now transcended its purely medical role and
became a realm of fantasy in which dreams of human self-
transformation could be acted out. The idea that the human organism
could be modified in a scientific fashion was a legacy of the Enlightenment of the eighteenth century. A century later, scientists had at
their disposal a pharmacopoeia that promised to make such transformations possible.

The idea that drugs might boost human performance grew out of
physiological science and its attempts to understand the nervous and
muscular systems of human beings and other organisms. Progress in
physiology led to a dynamic human biology that studied the interre-
lationship of nerves and muscles as well as their susceptibility to
pharmacological influence. At the most basic level, physiologists studied how and why organisms moved, and this required investigations
of muscular "irritability," the composition of muscle fibers, the energy sources of muscular movement, the relationship of oxygen consumption to muscular effort, and the relationship between nervous
impulses and muscular contractions.[35] The concept of the "stimulant"
developed along with this model of the dynamic organism it could
animate in mysterious ways, and here is where the possibility of
doping begins.

That the drug issue involved more than laboratory biology was
evident throughout the nineteenth century. The phenomenon of addiction made it clear that drugs like alcohol and morphine involved
social peril as well as medicinal promise, and the result was an ambivalence toward drugs that continues to affect our responses to pharmacological advances to this day. Physiologists of this period
understood that pharmacologically active substances displayed a
range of effects: They could be medicines, stimulants, depressants,
intoxicants, antiseptics, narcotics, poisons, or antagonists of other
drugs. The special promise as stimulants shown by certain drugs like
caffeine and strychnine was noted without unusual interest. We have
already seen that widespread attention to the maximizing of human

performances began only toward the end of the nineteenth century and that physiologists appear to have had no interest in boosting athletic performance. The attitude toward stimulants to be found in the rudimentary sports science of this period stresses hygiene and recuperation rather than the setting of new records. An 1873 British manual entitled *Exercise and Training* recommends, for example, "a certain quantity of alcoholic stimulant" for "the improvement of the system" or as an antidote to "that condition known as overtraining"— clearly therapeutic goals. In much the same way, digitalis, belladonna, and certain other drugs come under the category of "medical treatment" as remedies for sleeplessness or "an uneasiness difficult to describe" in the wake of "unusual exertion."[36] At this point, the distinction between instrumental and therapeutic medicine—a prerequisite for the doping concept—had not yet appeared. This age of innocence would eventually last for another generation or two until doping was recognized as a threat to the integrity of sport.

Although stimulants were of only marginal interest to the pioneering physiologists, signs of a more substantial engagement with the drug issue became evident in the early part of the century. One example of this is Balzac's "Treatise on Modern Stimulants" (1838), an eclectic, sometimes humorous, but ultimately serious meditation on the impact of five "stimulants" [*excitants*] on the "modern society" of that day. The novelist argues that alcohol, sugar, tea, coffee, and tobacco, having entered French life over the past two centuries, had changed society profoundly. The abuse of tobacco, alcohol, coffee, and opium had produced hypertrophized organs and other "grave disorders" that damage the human "machine," while the abuse of tea could sap the female libido. Drug abuse had also had incalculable social effects. The fate of a people, Balzac says, echoing eighteenth-century ideas, depends on its biological way of life [*régime*] in general and on its nutrition in particular. Nutrients can create racial aptitudes—grains produce artists—while certain stimulants have destroyed civilizations. Russia is "an autocracy built on alcohol," and the discovery of chocolate had subverted Spain's chance to restore the Roman Empire.[37]

But Balzac also knew that powerful stimulants had their beneficial uses. Coffee galvanized *les esprits moteurs*, and he believed that each dose of anhydrous coffee delivered an equivalent "dose of cerebral force"—an early quantification of mental energy that anticipates the materialist psychologies of the fin de siècle we will examine in the next chapter. While in this scientific mood, Balzac tells a story—"the truth of which has been guaranteed to me by two trustworthy people, a scientist and a politician"—that has an eerily modern quality.[38]

Three British convicts who had been sentenced to hang were offered an alternative fate by His Majesty's government. They would be spared the gallows if they agreed to participate in a subtly ghoulish experiment meant to test the relative nutritive value of chocolate, coffee, and tea. These unfortunates accepted the bargain, each drawing his substance by lot. The results of this physiological investigation were appropriately dramatic: the chocolate man died after eight months, putrescent and devoured by worms; the man who had drawn coffee lasted two years, "burned to deal as if calcified by the fires of Gommorah"; while the tea drinker died of consumption after three years, a diaphanous, virtually translucent creature.

However apocryphal Balzac's tale may be, it captures well the experimental ethos of an age of vivisection. Had not the great physiologist (and notorious vivisectionist) François Magendie sent dogs to agonizing deaths on a diet of sugar?[39] And while the element of biological fantasy foreshadows the science fictions of H. G. Wells, Balzac's story also belongs to a long tradition of fantasies about the common stimulants: Three centuries earlier the Aqua vitae called alcohol was believed to promise the rejuvenation of mankind, and for a thousand years tea had made possible the meditative endurance of Japanese monks.[40] What makes Balzac "modern" is the combination of anxiety about and infatuation with drugs that is presented in scientistic terms. The experiments on himself that appeared to have produced an awe-inspiring literary output were viewed with a fear of biological degeneration tempered by a doctrine of potentially unlimited energy. But the first stage of a physiology of performance required a more systematic inventory of the human organism and its sources of energy, and this was found in Cabanis's Reports on the Physical and Moral Aspects of Man (1802) and the physiological works that followed it later in the century.

Cabanis's treatise is a genuine precursor of the modern science of man because it includes virtually all of the elements of a true physiology of human performance. An Enlightenment optimist in regard to human development, he offered an environmentalist biology that amounted to his own version of a doctrine of human perfectibility.[41] That is, changes in an individual's daily habits could make possible so profound a transformation of the human organism that eventually the human race would be "indefinitely perfectible; after a fashion, capable of everything."[42]

Cabanis's emphasis on factors that modify the human organism makes his physiology inherently experimental. The most fundamental of these factors is "regimen," defined as "the totality of physical habits." He makes a point of expanding the scope of regimen beyond the "systematic use of food and drink" to include the air one breathes, exercise, rest, sleep, the nature of one's habitual work, and "the affections of the soul"—in short, the entire repertory of a present-day athletic trainer's concerns at a time when our idea of training did not exist. But Cabanis does describe both an "athletic regimen" and a "muscular temperament"[43] that point toward (without further resembling) our modern fixation on the development of physical abilities for sportive purposes. This doctrine of human transformation points forward to the idea of high performance. For even if Cabanis's physiology was rudimentary, we can still discern in his doctrine the ideal of unlimited productivity and the scientific approach to creating maximally productive human beings. As Martin Staum has noted, "His reflections opened up vistas of industrial psychology that were rarely explored until the twentieth century."[44]

It is not easy for us to imagine an analytical attitude toward muscular development that does not intend to put those muscles to some kind of sportive use, but that is how "the athletic temperament" was discussed in France until late in the nineteenth century. Cabanis's use of terms like "temperament" and "physical constitution" also show that he saw the robust body as more than the product of physical exercise. "Great muscular strength," he says, can result from "an inherent primitive disposition" or from "accidental changes" that are pathological in nature.[45] Nor did he ignore the potential of physical exercise to cause harm. It was Hippocrates, Cabanis correctly notes,[46] who equated extreme athletic development with illness. The athletic regimen, Cabanis says, reduces longevity and, pursued to excess, brings about a hostility to the life of the mind and a proclivity for violence. Major criminals, in fact, tend to be of a "vigorous organic structure" and notable for "the toughness of their muscle fibers."[47] Yet Cabanis's awareness of Hippocrates' view of pathological athleticism stimulated no comparable interest in an athletic revival to which his own science might be applied. A century would pass before another French physician, Philippe Tissié, offered his own Hippocratic warning against the dangers of extreme physical exertion. By this time, as we have seen, the initial fascination with high performance sport was gaining momentum, and cautionary hygienism of this kind fell on deaf ears.

Doping ultimately falls under the heading of a metaconcept that includes the entire class of substances that animate or energize the human organism—in other words, all sources of nutrition and stimulation. Cabanis may be the first scientist since the ancient Greek sports physicians to address the complete repertory of such substances in relation to the efficient functioning of the human body. His physiology of nutrition discusses the effects of different food types, of fasting, and of meat-based versus vegetarian diets. Not surprisingly, he claims that carnivorous peoples have always been superior to herbivorous types in activities, such as war, that require great energy and initiative. This protoscience of nutrition anticipates more systematic studies of vegetarianism and athletic performance that appeared a century later.[48]

Cabanis classified "stimulants" and "narcotics" as a category of substances distinct from food and (even fermented) beverages. He appears to have regarded "stimulant" as the more inclusive term, distinguishing the effects of "narcotics" from those of "pure stimulants," while acknowledging an "analogical" resemblance between them. To him narcotics are like stimulants because they both diminish sensitivity and affect the limbs through the circulatory and nervous systems. This passage is followed by a recommendation that sounds as if it might have come from the *Underground Steroid Handbook:* "In order to really increase muscular strength, narcotics should be taken in moderate doses."[49] But what do these terms actually mean? Cabanis and his readers seem to share a colloquial definition of "stimulant" so self-evident that only a handful of substances is ever mentioned. Opium is the prototype "narcotic" (and an aphrodisiac), while coffee, snake poisons, aloes, and cantharide compounds appear to be only a few of many "stimulants." Air that has been supercharged with oxygen makes all the organs of the body "more sensitive to the action of external stimulants" but is not called a stimulant itself. Liquors count as "artificial stimulants" that, in a temperate climate, are appropriate for soldiers and laborers working in stressful conditions.[50] Others would eventually replace this patchwork approach to the classification of bioactive substances with a more systematic and scientific procedure. But most of a century would pass before Rudolf Buchheim, the founder of modern pharmacology, would propose that "we translate our often obscure ideas about drug actions into an exact physiological language."[51]

Cabanis also anticipated our division of performance-enhancing substances into inorganic stimulants, for instance, opium and coffee, and others derived from the male hormone. His discussion of *la liqueur mâle* presupposes "the transformational energy of semen, a principle well established in French medicine by the end of the eighteenth century. Man's deep voice, his musculature, beard, ruddy complexion, his courage and magnanimity were all manifestations of this vital force."[52] He also speaks of "the glandular system," including the testicles and ovaries, "whose different parts communicate with each other." Almost a century before Brown-Séquard injected himself with his famous testicular extracts (see Chapter 3), Cabanis offered two observations that relate sex, stimulation, and muscular vigor. He associates the male fluid with muscular strength and adds that "narcotics" excite both sexual organs and muscle fibers.[53]

Cabanis has nothing to say on the subject of race beyond the conventional observation that the "savages" of North America were remarkably insensible to pain—a basic stereotype of nineteenth-century racial neurology (see Chapter 2). He does, however, conjoin the idea of race and pharmacology by noting a "universal" taste for stimulants that extends even into the animal realm,[54] an idea that reappears in the writing of French and British anthropologists later in the century.

Encounters between Europeans and the "primitive" races of other continents have their own place in the history of pharmacology and in the history of ideas about race and athletic aptitude (see Chapter 2). These two themes were linked by the fact that the impressive physical performances of non-Europeans were often associated with their use of stimulants. The nineteenth-century ethnologist could even regard the use of stimulants by "savage" races as a mark of civilization. In his "Ethnological Hints afforded by the Stimulants in use among Savages and among the Ancients" (1879), the Victorian anthropological writer A. W. Buckland notes that it is "among the lowest races" that "no intoxicant is known" and that the use of "simple medicinal stimulants [as distinct from true "stimulants"] would seem to be the first instinctive effort of the savage towards supplying himself with something more than mere food." The development of "fermented liquors," for example, had been made possible only by a knowledge of agriculture.[55]

But at the same time, given the backward state of pharmacology in Europe, it is not surprising that mere savages could tutor curious Europeans in herbal medicine:

The doctors of civilised Europe have been indebted to rude aborigines for many valuable medicinal discoveries, the importance of which can scarcely be over-estimated; the invaluable Peruvian bark is too well known to require notice here, but the rude Australian aborigines have recently brought a new stimulant to the notice of the medical profession, which according to the reports given, seems like to rival quinine in the future. This is the Pitbury (Duboisia), a plant chewed by the natives to give them strength and courage, the chewed portion being afterwards applied as a plaster behind the ear in order to increase the effect.[56]

Buckland's description of savage pharmacology includes examples of the wondrous feats that have traditionally been associated with drugs. The Pitbury leaves are "said to be of marvelous power as a stimulant" and are "chewed by the natives of Central Australia to invigorate themselves during long foot journeys through deserts." "With a little toasted maize and coca," says one of his sources, the Tarapaca Indians of South America "will travel for days over the most desert tracks."[57] For the Nicobar Islanders, another author reports, the chewing of betel nuts is "valuable in allaying the pangs of hunger while hunting, travelling, or otherwise engaged at a distance from home or beyond reach of provisions."[58] What is more, the European explorers who encountered these savage herbal experts could also benefit from performance-enhancing drugs of European origin. Speared by Australian aborigines in 1838, the explorer Sir George Grey continued his explorations with the help of laudanum (a tincture of opium in alcohol).[59] Gustave Le Bon, better known as the pioneering psychologist of crowds, reported in 1893 that European explorers in Africa had employed cocoa nuts in the native fashion and had confirmed their astonishing powers.[60]

Europeans thus observed the doubtless prehistoric origins of performance-enhancing pharmacology among "primitive" peoples. They should have noted similarities between this savage science of potions and their own, for at least some savage tribes associated the male sexual organs with physical performance and went to non-European extremes to get results. "As instances of transmission of properties," A. E. Crawley writes in 1895,

we may cite the idea which holds among the natives of Mowat, that the penis of great warriors slain in battle possesses "virtue," and is therefore worn by the victor to increase his strength and ferocity. In South Eastern Africa, during a protracted war, the soldiers are frequently "doctored," in order to stimulate their courage. The heart, liver and testicles of the slain enemies are made into a broth which is taken internally, to restore virility, or communicate strength to the sick.[61]

It did not occur to Crawley to point out that the recently deceased Brown-Séquard and other European scientists had been injecting a testicular broth into themselves and their patients for precisely the same reasons that "natives" had been taking it by mouth—experiments that were by now well known in British medical circles.[62] The closest Crawley comes to this insight is his statement that "there is a universal identification of manly strength with generative [sexual] power." Savage beliefs about "secretions, excretions and the like" are "universal" when they coincide with "the physiological fact patent to all mankind" regarding the relationship between semen and organismic energy.[63] But Crawley's most interesting remark refers to the African soldiers who had been "doctored" with the broth derived from internal organs, for here is a fine example of one fin de siècle observer groping toward the concept of doping outside the context of sport: Men are being altered, but there is no apparent reason to oppose this "doctoring." The sportsmanship issue that became a major aspect of the doping debate during the 1920s is absent because these are soldiers and not athletes.

The pharmacologies of Cabanis and Buckland presuppose a universal human physiology; racial and ethnic differences have been superseded by a fundamental biochemical unity of mankind, implying that drugs must act in the same ways in all bodies. But not all nineteenth-century scientists embraced this sort of cosmopolitanism. The physical anthropology of this period, heavily influenced by medical thinking about racial anatomy and physiology, still found physical differences between racial groups in general and Europeans and Africans in particular to be significant (see Chapter 2), and this emphasis on difference could even extend into the pharmacological realm. At a time when it was not unusual to believe that Negro blood and semen differed in color from the bodily fluids of whites, or that "the muscles of Chinamen, Frenchmen and negroes are very different,"[64] a racially differentiated pharmacology was entirely plausible. Antebellum physicians in the American South, for example, could not agree on whether the physiological inferiority of the slave's nervous system required larger or smaller dosages of medication.[65]

This idea of racially specific drug dosages is just one element of a more comprehensive biology of species and racial differences that developed during the latter part of the nineteenth century. The range of this comparative approach to the entire animal kingdom, and its relevance to pharmacology, are evident in a French "pathological anthropology" that appeared in 1881. While humans and insects reportedly respond in similar ways to alcohols, chloroform, and unbreathable gases, other animal species or types can react differently to the same toxic substance. Thus, two types of frog respond differently to caffeine, belladonna has no effect on certain rodents, morphine is a strong stimulant for horses, and digitalis does not affect snails. As a general rule, this author states, the less intelligent the creature on which a substance is being tested, the less effect it has.

His next step is to note analogous differences between men of different races. The muscle tissues of blacks and whites, for example, show chemical differences; whites, yellows, and blacks demonstrate racially distinct responses to alcohol; and blacks can somehow tolerate enormous doses of antimony.[66] Comparable ideas will recur later in the medical literature: The polar explorer Fridtjof Nansen reports that the Eskimos fear coffee more than alcohol since it makes them too dizzy to navigate their canoes,[67] while another author claims that a sluggish constitution makes the Germanic race invulnerable to hashish-type poisons.[68] Such notions have generally not survived the age of interracial high-performance sport, where doping scandals have engulfed black and white athletes alike, but anecdotal evidence suggests that some white athletes take steroids to compensate for a perceived racial athletic inferiority (see Chapter 2).

By the end of the nineteenth century European as well as "savage" pharmacology had at their disposal performance-enhancing substances of botanical and hormonal origin. Starting with Brown-Séquard's first experiments in 1889, European scientists could match savage virility broths with similar concoctions of their own. Although seldom associated with athletic performance, the primitive hormonal extracts were of course the wave of the future in elite sport. The rest of the experimental pharmacopoeia consisted of drugs derived from various kinds of plants, some of which had been used by people for hundreds or even thousands of years. Alcohols, coffee, tea, cocaine from coca leaves, chocolate (theobromine) from cocoa beans, theobromine (and caffeine) from kola nuts, the poison strychnine (one of the earliest athletic stimulants) from the *nux vomica* plant, nicotine from tobacco, morphine, opium, digitalis—all of these substances were investigated as aids to mental or physical performance before the turn of the century and after.

Modern pharmacological experimentation began with tests carried out on animals in the late eighteenth century,[69] and by the last decades of the nineteenth century many such experiments had been performed by French and German investigators. By 1819 François Magendie had demonstrated the convulsions produced in frogs by strychnine, isolated the year before; in 1844 his student Claude Bernard began to study the effects of the South American poison curare that had puzzled explorers and scientists for half a century. By using curare as a technique for the "physiological dissection" of frogs, Bernard showed that curare shut down motor nerves while leaving sensory nerves unaffected and thereby established that muscles could contract in the absence of a nervous stimulus.[70] Other experiments were made possible by the isolation of morphine (1817), caffeine (1819), quinine (1827), and many other bioactive substances, by the development of techniques for measuring physiological changes in animals, and by the frequent willingness of some investigators to experiment on themselves. One French physiologist reports in 1868 that a doctor who took half a gram of caffeine had begun to tremble, become nauseous and sleepy, and had watched his pulse sink from 80 to 50 beats per minute. The same physiologist had injected caffeine into frogs, guinea pigs, rabbits, dogs, and cats and measured heart, breathing, and pulse rates, but he was also interested in its human applications. It had been prescribed for migraine headaches, asthma, and typhoid fever among other afflictions. The French researcher Leven, however, presents caffeine as a performance-boosting drug. Men in caravans, we are told, had crossed deserts for weeks taking caffeine and little else, while Belgian miners at Charleroi were performing "an enormous amount of muscular work" on two liters of coffee a day.[71]

Years later, however, the tale of the Belgian miners was revealed as apocryphal in a scientific paper by a Dr. Guimaraês that tells us a great deal about how pharmacological myths appear and how late nineteenth-century physiologists went about assessing the allegedly performance-enhancing powers of a controversial drug. In 1850 the credulous witness to the "great muscular vigor" of the miners of Charleroi had written that these men were essentially subsisting on coffee plus a solid diet that would not have sustained a child. But more accurate information was provided by the director of mines, eventually reaching François Magendie himself; in fact, in addition to their coffee, the hardy miners were consuming pork, red meats, vegetables, gin, and a lot of beer. The myth of the coffee diet was based

on a misunderstanding stemming from the fact that it is a lot easier for
a miner to drink coffee than to eat a full-course meal while he is
squeezed into a mine shaft.[72] Such "misunderstandings" and other
forms of wish-fulfillment run through the history of pharmacology like
a bright red thread. As this author points out, exaggerating the powers of a cup of coffee was typical of the temper of the times. What is
more, little has changed in this regard, and grasping the psychody-
namics of this mythmaking process is essential to understanding the
modern doping problem in sport.

Having disposed of the coffee myth, Dr. Guimarâes proceeds to
a more sober estimate of what coffee can offer mankind. His aim is
to take the analysis beyond naive empiricism and inadequate theories
to the classification of this substance in terms of its physiological
mechanism. Does it regulate nutrition? Is it a "special or dynamophoric stimulant"? Is it a genuine nutrient itself? When his team
began its research on coffee in 1881, they had intended to use the
conventional methods of physiological and toxicological analysis. Hoping to find the differences indicating the physiological action of the
coffee, they meant to compare the circulation, respiration, temperature, and the urine of the same animal in its normal state and after
coffee injections. But a senior colleague pointed out that this procedure had yielded unsatisfactory data with alcohol. Their new (and
much simpler) procedure was to give water to one group of dogs,
coffee to another, and measure weight loss over time. When the
caffeinated dogs shriveled and died faster than the control group, the
scientists concluded that coffee speeds up metabolism, and that it
facilitates the consumption of nitrogenated substances, including
meat. For this reason they recommended coffee as a performance-
enhancing beverage suitable for all "active" people.[73]

Although convinced that his group had made a significant discovery,[74] Dr. Guimarâes emphasized that coffee remained a mysterious substance. It had been impossible, for example, to find any fixed
relationship between a given dose of coffee and any functional symptom related to circulation or caloric consumption. The novelist Balzac
had thought that a given dose of coffee liberated a fixed quantity of
"cerebral force," but the scientist Guimarâes knew that he could not
even correlate caffeine and calories, let alone fixed units of psychic
energy. He concluded that coffee's action in the body could not be
reduced to simple and constant relationships. "It is necessary," he
writes, "to look into the animal itself, into its individuality and those

unknown factors, for the differences that reveal themselves to direct observation."[75]

Any attempt to classify coffee also meant confronting the romantic terminology that had been applied to alleged stimulants throughout the nineteenth century. Dr. Guimarâes has no patience for fashionable jargon like "dynamophoric stimulant," "dynamogenic nutrient," and "reserve nutrient." This kind of theory-less reductionism, he complained, produces "simple formulas" that are more like incantations than scientific statements.[76] The problem was that revolutionary discoveries about biodynamics naturally gave rise to a dynamic vocabulary that suggested more than it actually described. By the twentieth century this hyperactive nomenclature had degenerated into self-parody—euphorin, neuronal, oblivion, vomicin, adastra ("to the stars").[77] But the less pretentious search for an appropriate vocabulary goes back as least as far as Cabanis's references to "pure" and "artificial" stimulants. In 1838 Balzac applied his scientistic terms not to coffee but to the *esprits moteurs* and *fluide nerveux* it supposedly animates.[78] A half-century later a contemporary of Dr. Guimarâes stated that coffee exercises a "reflex or stimulating [*excito-moteur*] power" on the spinal cord, and he speaks of "conserving" and "consuming" nutrients.[79] But none of this charged language had yet been applied to athletic stimulants.

Brown-Séquard's testicular extracts are the true prototype of the athletic wonder drug, and his favorite term for these substances was "dynamogenic." His classic paper of 1889 reporting his self-administered injections describes its effects in dramatic language. The sexually continent man between twenty and thirty-five years of age, having stored up a reservoir of physical and intellectual energy, is like a bomb about to go off. His state of "spermatic fullness" is the basis for the "dynamogenic power" of the seminal liquid.[80] "Dynamogenesis" is "a simple dynamic change, a transformation of force, which has taken place."[81] The effect of the male sexual fluid is to "dynamogenize the nervous system and above all the spinal cord."[82] A secondary effect of this vocabulary was to "dynamogenize" a large and expectant public in several European countries, as well as a number of "charlatans" ready to cash in on the ostensible promise of a rejuvenating treatment. These unscrupulous types were peddling an "elixir" and a "tonic syrup for the nervous system" purporting to be testicular extracts.[83] Brown-Séquard was profoundly irritated by these opportunistic quacks, but he does not appear to have had second thoughts about his own performance. Several years later an editorial in the *British Medical Journal* reminded Brown-Séquard that "there is in all men a natural tendency to draw general conclusions from particular instances, to seize an idea and run it to death."[84] But the scientific naïveté of the lay public could not deter a man of Brown-Séquard's temperament. At his death in 1894 he was eulogized as a grand speculator in the nineteenth-century tradition—in short, a man to whom a romantic biological idiom came naturally. So it was only natural that testicular extracts gave rise to a quasi-scientific idiom that could sometimes become more extravagant than that of the master himself. The effects of these "orchitic" extracts, one of Brown-Séquard's French colleagues wrote, was nothing less than "tonic, eutrophic and dynamogenic."[85]

The transition from this dynamic language to the actual stimulants that would boost athletic performance was greatly facilitated by the widespread popularity of the bicycle that developed during the 1890s on both sides of the Atlantic. The merging of man and bicycle offered history's first opportunity to pharmacologize the man-machine relationship—a practice that is now a century-old tradition and still going strong. But the crude hormonal substances that appeared along with the cycling craze of the nineties did not play a role in the new sport. Despite their importance as the progenitors of steroids—and their otherwise promiscuous application to a host of medical disorders during the last decade of the century—testicular extracts did not figure in the performance-boosting drug experiments carried out on cyclists that were underway in France when Brown-Séquard died in 1894.

Instead, the cycling experiments of the early 1890s employed kola nuts, alcoholic and nonalcoholic beverages, and were unimpeded by any doubts about the ethics of using performance-enhancing substances for this purpose. In 1893 Gustave Le Bon published an enthusiastic testimony to the powers of the kola nut based on the work of a Marseilles chemistry professor and Le Bon's experiments on himself. Black Africans, he said, had demonstrated the efficacy of kola nuts from time immemorial. Although the French army had performed its own promising experiments, a fossilized hierarchy had prevented the adoption of this proven energizer. And this was all the worse, since Le Bon fully expected that the next army faced by French soldiers would have discovered the properties of this drug and would be carrying a kola ration of its own. At a dose of one gram per marching hour, its combination of caffeine and theobromine would suppress fatigue and "increase and prolong the intensity of muscular contractions" in a way that caffeine alone could not. Le Bon, who had a serious interest in horses, lost any doubts he might have had about the effectiveness of kola when he tested himself while taming a particularly violent steed—"I didn't need a chemical analysis to know when I was under the influence of caffeine or kola." The new jargon for this performance-booster was "accelerating rations," although Le Bon took the trouble to warn that the extracts, syrups, tinctures, elixirs, etc. that were being marketed as kola were quite useless.[86]

The kola experiments on cyclists aimed at testing the drug rather than the rider, who in this context was nothing more than a guinea pig. The problem with the human guinea pig, however, was his vulnerability to the power of suggestion; what he believed about a drug might boost his performance more than its physiological effects, assuming that it was possible to separate the psychological and physiological dimensions in the first place. The confident Brown-Séquard, convinced of the sheer physiological potency of his extracts, had dismissed this widely discussed complication; but other investigators took a less cavalier attitude toward a methodological hurdle that continues to bedevil the testing of supposedly performance-enhancing compounds. Some athletes today, for example, who are given steroids in "blind" or "double-blind" procedures, recognize the effects of the drugs immediately, thereby subverting the objective character of the experiment.

To circumvent this problem Le Bon provided one Charles Henry with three drugs in the form of two kinds of tablets for use in "blind" cycling trials. One was chocolate-flavored, the other sugar-flavored, and Henry knew nothing about the chemical content of either. The purpose of these trial runs was to test kola, caffeine, and the combination of caffeine and theobromine against each other. Henry claimed that he had no trouble distinguishing between the effects of the chocolate-flavored and sugar-flavored tablets, nor was he surprised to learn after one trial that the chocolates contained caffeine and theobromine just like a fresh kola nut. The author of this report cautions, however, that "this powerful resource" should be used with "great moderation," and only when a special energy burst is really necessary (one potential beneficiary being the weary cyclist). The abuse of caffeine-theobromine, he says, can cause heart palpitations, cardiac irregularities, and painful renal congestion.[87] But there is still no mention of giving kola to competitive athletes.

Le Bon's paean to the kola nut also elicited a more exotic communication to the *Revue Scientifique*. This correspondent reported that he, too, had been carrying out experiments on himself and his friends with the "accelerating" kola nuts. Whether hiking, cycling, or playing tennis, he had experienced the "well-known phenomena" of renewed energy and the fading away of hunger and fatigue. His friends had experienced a range of effects: One had been nauseated by the taste of kola whether in biscuit or liquid form; another had eventually contracted a nausea that negated the energy benefit of the drug; yet another had felt absolutely nothing; while the last had found himself sexually stimulated to the point where he had to renounce kola altogether.[88]

Here we find the time-honored association of sexual energy and physical vigor. A series of "observations and experiments" had demonstrated that kola renewed energy "while stimulating the genital functions." The "analogy" with the "orchitic juice" of Brown-Séquard was only too clear: Kola stimulated the genital activity made possible by the "juice." This, our incautious author maintains, makes kola absolutely different from "the general nervous systems stimulants" like coffee, tea, and such "tonics" as strychnine and quinine. What is more, bicycle races run on tracks offered "excellent conditions for conducting experiments on the comparative effects of different substances."[89] He was apparently unaware that France's pioneering sports physician, Philippe Tissié of Bordeaux, had already carried out an experiment of this kind.

Tissié's monitoring of the elite cyclist Stéphane (Chapter 3) included an attempt to assess the usefulness of an entire series of stimulants [*excito-moteurs*]. The obstinate rider's predilection for milk, says Tissié, showed his physiological ignorance, and in the course of his twenty-four hours and some four hundred miles on the track the physician plied him with tea-and-milk, mint water, lemonade, rum, rum-and-milk, and champagne. Tissié also recorded the following data: the time into the run and the time of day when the stimulant was administered, the distance covered by the rider before taking the stimulant, the duration of the stimulant's effect, the distance covered while under the influence of the stimulant, the duration of the period of "reaction" during which the rider's physiology slumped once the effect of the stimulant had worn off. These data enabled him to draw conclusions about the relative merits of these various substances, and he even went so far as to calculate the total effect of the combined stimulants on Stéphane's performance.[90] Tissié's surprise at the conclusion—that tea, mint, and lemonade were superior to alcoholic stimulants—must be understood in the context of his feelings about alcohol in a more general sense.

Because fin de siècle physiologists like Tissié considered athletic physiology only one approach among others to the study of the human organism, it was only natural for him to place the problem of athletic stimulants within the larger field of medical pharmacology, and in this area he was consistently cautious. In an 1896 report on the treatment of fatigue in patients suffering from nervous disorders, he advised that stimulants [excito-moteurs] and "reserve nutrients" be used only with "great caution." Alcohol, quinine, kola, coca, maté, strychnine and other substances must be prescribed on a strictly individual basis, since "[a] debilitated nervous system benefits from stimulants in the manner of a very sensitive battery that is destroyed if it is over-charged."

But Tissié saves his special scorn for the powerful drinks called apéritives, a new public health hazard that provided "an illusion of strength" to fatigués whose nervous systems oscillate between depression and the artificial euphoria produced by this noxious stimulant.[91] And Tissié applied the same argument to liqueurs intended to energize the athlete. The danger was "the illusion of physical strength" provided by the stimulant that Tissié calls the agent provocateur of the nervous system. "When the strength exerted surpasses the individual's physiological reserves, the stimulant induces a pathological state by exhausting the nervous system." While cacao, coffee, tea, coca, quinine, etc. could be used with care by the athlete, "alcohol should be forbidden during training." This "water of life" [eau-de-vie], he says, is really a water of death. Like morphine and hashish, alcohol does not defeat fatigue but rather causes it.[92] Five years later, he writes that stimulants like alcohol are "imposters who promise more than they deliver."[93] By now it is clear that Tissié is addressing not merely a harmful athletic practice but a social scourge of much wider dimensions.

Tissié's attitude toward athletic stimulants appears strangely ambivalent to the modern reader accustomed to the antidrug propaganda of the sports world. For the same physician who had no reservations about urging a cyclist around the track to discover effective stimulants seems to be biased against stimulants in general. To dissolve this apparent contradiction, we must abandon our own conditioned reflexes to the idea of doping and project ourselves into Tissié's world. If he had no qualms about energizing his cyclist, it is because his experiment with Stéphane occurred before stimulants were regarded as a threat to equitable competition. It is medical prudence, not moralizing, that prompts his frequent cautionary remarks about stimulants. Indeed, his ban on alcohol is immediately followed by a recommendation that "the better beverage" for boosting performance is sugar water—a formula attested to by the great fatigue researcher Mosso himself.

The second, if less evident, dimension to Tissié's thinking about stimulants is the sheer lack of interest in boosting athletic performance so evident among the scientists of this period. Tissié did not automatically see scientific advances as opportunities for chemical interventions that would extend the limits of human performance, and this is confirmed by his remarks on the work of Brown-Séquard. What Tissié admired here was the "most beautiful discovery" that "organic juices" affected the nervous system, and he advised long-distance cyclists to put this discovery to work by remaining sexually abstinent while in training. But he never proposed that athletes be injected with testicular extracts. On the contrary, what he proposed was a passive strategy rather an active one.[94]

The idea of an active pharmacological strategy to extend human capacities, while almost entirely absent from the scientific literature, does appear in the science fiction of this period. It is clear from this and other evidence that the idea of the performance-boosting drug was achieving a certain currency, yet here too sport is not a priority. H. G. Wells's *The Food of the Gods* (1904) tells of a growth hormone-like substance that creates giants possessed of a strength so tremendous that it simply transcends human athletics; the meaning of this fanciful biochemistry turns out to be a vacuous Nietzschean cult of "strength" analogous to a doctrine of racial superiority. In a different vein, Wells's *Tono-Bungay* (1909) is a comic account of the commercial exploitation of an allegedly energizing substance sold in the form of "Tono-Bungay Lozenges" and "Tono-Bungay Chocolates":

> These we urged upon the public for their extraordinary nutritive and recuperative value in cases of fatigue and strain. We gave them posters and illustrated advertisements showing climbers hanging from marvellously vertical cliffs, cyclist champions upon the track, mounted messengers engaged in Aix-to-Ghent rides, soldiers lying out in action under a hot sun. . . . I really do believe there was an element of "kick" in the strychnine in these lozenges, especially in those made according to our earlier formula. For we altered all our formulæ—invariably weakening them enormously as sales got ahead.[95]

Wells's fictional "cyclist champions" take their modest place among a variety of real-life performers who benefit from a strychnine "kick." For by the turn of the century the stimulant properties of strychnine were well known. François Magendie's earlier experiments had found that strychnine produced an extreme sensitivity in animals,[96] and this was confirmed in greater detail by later research. A German report of 1883 notes that strychnine promoted "an extraordinary heightening of reflex action" and "an enormously stimulating effect on the respiratory center." By deepening and accelerating respiration and increasing blood pressure, this stimulant/poison was seen to promote oxidation and the elimination of chemical waste products.[97] But the imaginative possibilities offered by this potentially deadly stimulant are given short shrift in Wells's novel, which presents little more than the inside story of a commercial scam. A far more imaginative treatment of strychnine and human potential appears in the eccentric French playwright Alfred Jarry's 1902 comic-grotesque science fiction novella, *The Supermale*.

Like so many of his countrymen, Jarry became fascinated by the bicycle as a marvel of modern technology at a time when quantified records were becoming part of public consciousness. On top of this he developed a taste for the excitement of the sports festival and the frenetic atmosphere of the velodrome, where men pushed themselves and their machines to the limit, often with the aid of drugs. Two years after a world championship race for professional cyclists was established in 1895, Jarry bought himself a fancy racing machine for the considerable sum of 525 francs. Although he was seen riding in an automobile as early as 1904, this vehicle never inspired him as a literary theme;[98] it demanded too little of the human organism whose fantastic adventures are the subject of *The Supermale*.[99]

Jarry's novella offers parallel accounts of sexual and athletic performances that are equally heroic and record-breaking. His central protagonist, André Marcueil, is an ideologue of physiological energy who proclaims that "human capacities have no limits." Sexual abstinence has given young André the thick, muscular body of a gymnast, and now he feels driven to explore its potential. Scorning the use of stimulants, he demonstrates his vast physiological powers by surpassing the legendary performance of Hercules, who supposedly ravished fifty virgins in the course of a single night. All the while, André is observed by a physician who records every detail for science. At the end of the novella André dies a terrible, incandescent death in the fiery embrace of a Love Machine whose fabulous electrical energy his own organism can almost, but not quite, match. This concluding scene of Jarry's technological farce combines mordant comedy with an extravagantly overdrawn portrait of the electric chair then being used to execute criminals in the United States.

The specifically athletic part of Jarry's outrageous tale is a 10,000-mile race between a locomotive and a six-man cycling team riding a single oversized machine. The sponsor of the contest is a pharmaceutical entrepreneur, the American William Elson [= Edison?], whose aim is to promote a new "Perpetual-Motion-Food." The primary constituents of this wonder drug are strychnine and alcohol. The chemically fueled riders perform like superhumans, but in the end it is alcohol that wins the day in unexpected fashion when the ingenious entrepreneur defeats the locomotive by pouring rum into its firebox.

Jarry has borrowed liberally from the six-day cycle races of this period:

> Lasting from Monday morning to Saturday evening, these races placed extreme physical and psychological demands on the riders; consequently many of them turned to various stimulant preparations. The French used a mixture known as "Caffeine Houdes," while the Belgians sucked on sugar cubes dipped in ether. The riders' black coffee was "boosted" with extra caffeine and peppermint, and as the race progressed the mixture was spiked with increasing doses of cocaine and strychnine. Brandy was also frequently added to cups of tea. Following the sprint sequences of the race, nitroglycerine capsules were often given to the cyclists to ease breathing difficulties. The individual 6-day races were eventually replaced by two-man races, but the doping continued unabated. Since drugs such as heroin or cocaine were widely taken in these tournaments without supervision, it was perhaps likely that fatalities would occur.[100]

Jarry's story provides a more interesting look at this period than the strictly factual account given above, for he has taken the scientific analysis of human potential far beyond the model of the "human machine" so often discussed in the physiological literature of this period.[101] As one commentator notes, he has brought together in this fiction all of the major themes associated with the thermodynamics of the living organism: muscle, sex, death, energy, fuel, and the limits to its functioning.[102]

The Supermale may be a burlesque science fiction, a projection of the romantic potential of nineteenth-century biology, but it is based solidly on the contemporary scientific literature.[103] Its techno-pornographic fantasy of limitless sexual potency is only a minor innovation on the primacy of male biology that is central to the thinking of Brown-Séquard and many other investigators at this time. His mating of man and machine (and his interest in electricity) coincided with reports in a French physiology journal that scientists had used telephones to listen in on the human nervous system.[104] Indeed, it is in the second half of the nineteenth century that human and animal organisms are first hooked up to a variety of monitoring devices—instruments that in turn made possible the physiological measurements associated with record-breaking performances. Jarry's concept of sexual and athletic performance originates in the contemporary debate about "fatigue" and the energy reserves latent in the human organism. Finally, his pharmacological imagination, featuring strychnine and alcohol as doping agents, is entirely conventional. In retrospect it is clear that an exploration of the primitive hormonal substances of this period, and the associated theme of gender identity, would have been both more original and prophetic. As we shall see later in this chapter, Jarry's career as an amateur cyclist coincided with the first visions of injecting these substances into athletes.

The Doping Debate in Germany, 1920–40

The year was 1933, the occasion the annual meeting of the German Swimming Federation in Breslau. The distinguished speaker was Prof. Dr. Otto Riesser, director of the Pharmacological Institute of the University of Breslau, who had chosen to address the topic of "Doping and Doping Substances." In the course of his remarks, Dr. Riesser presented a sobering portrait of the role of drugs in the competitive sport of his day:

> The use of artificial means [to improve performance] has long been considered wholly incompatible with the spirit of sport and has therefore been condemned. Nevertheless, we all know that this rule is continually being broken, and that sportive competitions are often more a matter of doping than of training. It is highly regrettable that those who are in charge of supervising sport seem to lack the energy for the campaign against this evil, and that a lax, and fateful, attitude is spreading. Nor are the physicians without blame for this state of affairs, in part on account of their ignorance, and in part because they are

prescribing strong drugs for the purpose of doping which are not available to athletes without prescriptions."[105]

The surprising message of this admonitory lecture was the suggestion that doping actually worked. Three years earlier, speaking before a group of sports physicians in Berlin, Riesser had demystified the legendary aura of doping by explaining how difficult it was simply to understand, let alone manipulate, the physiological processes of the high-performance athlete. The sportsman looking for a competitive advantage should not expect wondrous news from him, Riesser had bluntly declared. Such athletes should instead learn something about the physiological complexities of athletic performance and stop looking for shortcuts.[106]

The debate over doping that took place in Germany between the world wars is in most ways indistinguishable from its modern counterpart, even though most of the doping substances of that era are no longer used or have ceased to be controversial. For the doping issue has never been about specific substances or techniques. The central question has always been whether we should impose limits on athletic ambition and certain methods that might serve it. The fact that anabolic steroids (testosterone was first isolated in 1935) and the drug testing of humans were unknown to the sports world of the 1920s and 1930s is significant but finally irrelevant. The crucial issue is not what to take or whether one will be caught, but whether athletes should attempt to improve performances by resorting to what one German physician of this period called "deviations from a natural way of life."[107]

Widespread condemnation of doping does not appear in Germany until after the First World War. To be sure, alcohol and tobacco—both of which are discussed in the sports medical literature—carried a special onus there as elsewhere as "immoral" intoxicants; among other opponents, the racial hygienists of the interwar period feared both of these "poisons" as threats to the German genetic pool. And in 1925 the German Association for Volkish Improvement and Genetics identified narcotics, too, as "external enemies of inheritance."[108] But moral condemnation of these seductive drugs appears only rarely in the sports medical literature,[109] which is much more concerned with determining their physiological mechanisms and potential usefulness to athletes.

This scientific attitude toward alcohol (and other drugs) is evident in "Sport and Stimulants," a 1913 article by the prominent sports physician Ferdinand Hueppe. Modern life is impossible without stimulants, Hueppe says, and the task of the physician is to replace harmful substances with more benign alternatives. Like that of Tissié twenty years earlier, Hueppe's critique of alcohol as a stimulant is purely functional—alcohol offers the athlete fewer benefits than disadvantages. Although it might give the less-trained participant in endurance events a final brief impetus toward the finish line, it can do nothing for the well-trained athlete. This wholly practical attitude toward stimulants is typical of the fin de siècle period. Hueppe's references to "doping" reveal little if any disapproval of certain agents apart from their uselessness or medical hazards. At one point, having noted that only a fool would replace alcohol with arsenic or strychnine, Hueppe does associate these poisons (as well as coca leaves, kola nuts, and caffeine) with "doping." But he also has no qualms about dispensing practical advice about stimulants, that is, if cacao beans don't perk you up, then coffee will give you "a more powerful kick."[110] Hueppe casts a wide net as he surveys the athletic pharmacopoeia—from caffeine and theobromine to meat extract and Munich beer. But this is a thoroughly benign and rather ineffective repertory of stimulants by modern standards. Widespread concern about the threat to sportsmanship posed by effective doping agents was still some years away.[111]

The relatively noncontroversial status of doping prior to the First World War coincided with a lack of scientific interest in producing high-performance athletes. Doping had, of course, been practiced for decades before 1914; the marathon champions of both the 1904 Olympic Games in St. Louis and the 1908 games in London, for example, are suspected of having taken strychnine to improve their chances.[112] But there was no science of doping such as appears during the 1920s, nor was there a sense of urgency about putting science to work in the area of sport. A treatise on "the pathological physiology of sport" published in a German medical journal in 1913, for example, typically combines a detailed scientific agenda with disinterest in, and even disapproval of, pushing athletes to outperform each other. This author had been testing athletes since 1896, the year of the first modern Olympiad, and by now he had investigated the effects of sport on the heart, kidneys, metabolism, blood pressure, and body temperature. Although *he* is very concerned about the medical dangers inherent in athletic competition, he finds that even "the most intelligent" athletes could not care less about the scientific analysis of what they are doing, although this may be because so many of them derive from the "less educated" classes. The idea that sportive competitions might induce athletes to drive their bodies to the limits of human strength is, he says, by no means inevitable—one of the least prescient comments ever made about the future of sport.[113] And there is no mention whatsoever of doping.

This investigator of sport's "pathological physiology" was clearly aware that the keenest athletes of his day were unthinkingly participating in a kind of experiment on the capacities of the human organism. But this was crude "experimentation" amounting to little more than risk taking; indeed, our physiologist found these athletes supremely unconcerned, not only about scientific analysis of their feats but even about medical precautions. Twenty years later, Otto Riesser, too, saw athletes engaged in "a large-scale experiment," except that now they were being used to assess the performance-enhancing value of alcohol.[114] Another German report (1926) told of an American doctor who, having procured the pills used by Amazonian Indians to prolong their ritual dances, fed them to unwitting athletes with "astonishing" results—yet another typically extravagant myth of this decade of doping.[115] Sports physiology had now left its age of innocence behind. For in the 1920s it was embarked upon a new experimental path requiring the collaboration of athletes, trainers, physicians, and the pharmaceutical industry.

The sports medical and physiological journals of this interwar period make it clear that the use of drugs in German sport was now widespread and widely known, but stimulants were only one part of a larger pharmaceutical market offering a wide range of products. As a Danish observer noted in 1939, "phosphates are in great demand in athletic circles, particularly in Germany, owing to extensive advertising of their beneficial properties."[116] What is more, many German physicians clearly believed that certain substances actually did improve athletic performance. The prominent sports physician Herbert Herxheimer, for example, had already claimed in 1922 that the commercial product Recresal (primary sodium phosphate) produced a detectable increase in physical fitness. More interesting than his endorsement, however, are the verbal gymnastics that follow. With the approach of the spring sports season, he says, the aspiring athlete will need his full dose of phosphates. Without mentioning the word "doping," the doctor goes on to assure his readers that this ergogenic "aid [Hilfe]" is not comparable to the many "stimulants" in use, since it merely "supports" basic physiological processes. Nevertheless, he says, the question of whether the use of phosphates was *in general* a defensible practice in sport was not one for the doctor to decide.[117]

A less restrained attitude toward the use of Recresal by athletes was evident by 1930. According to W. Poppelreuter, a professor of medicine in Bonn, wartime tests on German troops and later tests on mountain climbers had confirmed positive laboratory results. What is more, feeding this substance to horses, cows, and pigs had caused them to grow larger, look better, sweat less, work harder, give more milk, and produce higher quality litters. Poppelreuter's own experiments indicated that Recresal also improved arithmetic performance: The speed of mental calculations rose while the number of errors went down, a surprising result that contravened the more typical results from such tests. This ostensible boosting of the brain and neurologically significant glands, says Poppelreuter, is of major relevance to sport because the mental dimension of athletic performance was increasingly evident (see Chapter 5). He is adamant about the propriety of Recresal therapy, which he calls a "normal hygienic procedure" not to be equated with strychnine injections, cocaine doses, and other clear instances of "doping." In fact, Poppelreuter is bold enough to claim that sport has a pioneering role to play in the rationalizing of human nutrients, whether they are considered natural or artificial—a distinction he pointedly does not accept. In addition, he insists that harmful "doping" must be sharply distinguished from substances that "support" basic physiological processes. Although Poppelreuter assumes that "nerve poisons" like strychnine, alcohol, caffeine, cocaine, and arsenic can, in fact, boost performance in sports competitions, his first priority is an almost eugenic ambition to improve the race as a whole. As he points out, both he and the famous British physiologist J. B. S. Haldane had been taking Recresal for years, and both believed in its adoption as a universal human nutrient.[118]

While Recresal was well received,[119] other substances got mixed reviews. The main investigators who studied caffeine generally considered it an effective boosting agent. One physician assumed that caffeine boosted mental performance by widening the blood vessels of the brain and thereby increasing the rate of circulation. This effect made caffeine a useful stimulant for all sports requiring sharpened presence of mind, but many athletes mistakenly believed that it boosted physical strength in a more general sense.[120] The industrial psychologist Robert Werner Schulte, who wrote extensively about the psychological dimension of sport (see Chapter 5), knew better. He conceded the "doping effect" of caffeine while stressing the "artificially concealed consumption of nervous energy" that made it possible and the toxic effects of *Coffeinismus chronicus*.[121] Surprisingly, however, perhaps the best-known experiment carried out on any drug during this period failed to confirm the generally held view, dating from the first ergographic trials of Ugolino Mosso, that caffeine increased muscular strength. In 1921 and 1922 Herbert Herxheimer's exceptionally well-controlled experiment on forty-six subjects found that caffeine had no effect whatsoever on performance in the 100-meter dash.[122] This sobering result also called into question the usefulness of laboratory tests for assessing the effects of drugs in actual competitions (see below). And there were negative results on other drugs to report. Adrenalin did not improve the javelin throws of seven well-trained subjects, alcohol was in general disrepute, and cocaine was declared worthless.[123] Such negative results led many researchers to the conclusion that artificially boosting the performance of a trained athlete who was already at the height of his powers was simply not possible.[124] Nor can one help but notice the innocuous character of many of these allegedly ergogenic aids. Among the few substances recognized as performance-enhancers, writes the cautious Otto Riesser, are phosphates, caffeine, theobromine, and chocolate.[125] By the standards of the 1920s as well as our own, this was a tame pharmacology that could not satisfy the fantasy needs of athletes looking for substances that would transform them.

Pseudoscientific myths have a way of flourishing within the field of pharmacology. As one of these medical authors put it, people are inclined to be faithful to their "chemical talisman," exaggerating positive results and forgetting negative ones, while the imaginative interpretation of anecdotal evidence catalyzes a romantic attitude toward the powers contained in tiny tablets.[126] Nor were physicians and scientists wholly innocent in this respect. As Riesser pointed out in 1930, a large number of poorly controlled and arbitrarily evaluated experiments linking drugs and athletic performance were giving the entire field the appearance of a pseudoscience.[127] Robert Werner Schulte, who wrote enthusiastically about a "psychochemistry" that would banish "psychic deformities," endorsed the use of "minor remedies" like coffee, tea, and chocolate to reduce precompetition anxiety and thereby improve athletic performance.[128] But it appears that it was athletes who were (and remain) especially inclined to create myths about drugs. In 1924 fantastic stories about kola nuts were circulating among athletes, according to a German doctor who had seen cocaine used many times at sports events.[129] There were similarly inflated stories about a combination of cocaine and kola nuts devised in America and marketed in Germany as Dallkolat.[130] By the early 1930s pure oxygen was a faddish "doping" substance, reportedly used by six-day cyclists[131] and hyped by rumors that Japanese swimming victories at the 1932 Los Angeles Olympic Games resulted at least in part from a mysterious oxygen therapy. "My feeling," one observer wrote in 1939, "is that most athletes and sports leaders have the most fanciful and confused ideas about the meaning of 'oxygen priming.' "[132] A report that the Nobel Prize-winning physiologist A. V. Hill had boosted recovery rates with superdoses of oxygen[133] can only have encouraged such thinking. Otto Riesser, who had heard stories about "oxygen priming" by swimmers, calls this practice a clear case of illegitimate doping despite oxygen's dubious value as a stimulant.[134] For as Riesser and at least some of his colleagues understood, the intentions of the athlete who uses any questionable technique are a crucial factor in determining whether he has engaged in "doping."

The most controversial boosting technique in Germany at this time was the use of ultraviolet radiation (UV) to invigorate all or part of the athlete's body. The use of UV light to promote the cure of rickets had accelerated during the early 1920s,[135] although this is almost never mentioned in the German sporting and medical journals that published many commentaries on the effectiveness and propriety of UV treatments for athletes. The new technique was an American import, and the idea of using it on athletes arrived in Germany accompanied by encouraging stories of a familiar genre. According to one of these reports, the trainer of the Yale University rowing crew, one Edward Leader, had irradiated his oarsmen two weeks before a race against their traditional rivals from Harvard. The result was a Yale victory by a boat length and a winning crew that felt less fatigued than their defeated counterparts. What is more, America's Olympic champion sprinters Allan Woodring and Jackson Scholz (gold medals at 200 meters in 1920 and 1924, respectively) had used both UV and "high frequency currents."[136] By 1934 an eager Nazi apologist for the "invisible rays" was heralding their use as a way to strengthen the bodies of German youth, boost athletic performances, and restore the leading role of the German *Volk*.[137]

As an episode in the debate about doping, the German controversy over UV has some uniquely interesting features. For one thing, it was a scientific issue that started out as a hard-fought argument in the sports pages before being taken up by medical scientists.[138] Dr.

Karlheinz Backmund had begun his experiments on UV and physical performance out of sheer scientific curiosity, quite unaware that this was a bone of contention in the sports world.[139] UV therapy was also interesting from the standpoint of cultural history, as an example of "reactionary modernism"[140]—in this case, an archaic German fascination with sunlight combined with a technological version of the sun itself; this peculiarly Germanic form of heliophilia (*Licht-Luft-Therapie*) had already been associated with the German nudism movement of the fin de siècle and its racially charged fixation on bodily health.[141] For this reason, the sharp German debate over UV may well have expressed deeply rooted German feelings about the importance of separating what is "natural" from its "artificial" (and therefore degenerate) forms.

The other aspects of UV that made it so contentious an issue were its simultaneously intangible and magical qualities. From one point of view, UV was about as invasive and "artificial" a procedure as standing in sunlight. (Dr. Poppelreuter of Bonn had heard that UV treatments were common at the 1928 Olympic Games.)[142] But from a different perspective, UV light was the product of "technical and machine-like devices" characteristic of "hypercivilized sport" that threatened to destroy the "honorable competition" sport was meant to be.[143] What is more, German readers were told that an American sports physician named Leslie Clough was irradiating virtually all of the athletes at certain competitions.[144] How long could Germans afford to abstain from a technique their own scientists proclaimed to be effective? One physician went so far as to pin Germany's hopes for the 1928 Summer Olympic Games on UV therapy, since American victories in previous years had been ascribed to this treatment.[145]

No one who experimented with UV understood how it affected human physiology. Fritz Lickint of Zwickau suggested three possible modes: (1) a purely psychological response; (2) a powerful general organismic effect impacting on circulation, breathing, metabolism, blood composition, and enzymes that might well boost athletic fitness; or (3) a local effect on specific muscles.[146] The experiments of Karlheinz Backmund found that aiming the rays at specific muscles had no effect, but irradiating the entire upper body including the head and arms from both front and back increased the performances (of finger muscles!) by factors ranging from 20 to 100 percent. (He knew that observations of "improved" performances after UV irradiation at competitions could not be judged scientifically.) While Backmund did not believe in the metabolic effects of UV, he rather assumed that UV exerted a combined effect on the central and vegetative nervous systems.[147] Dr. Baur of Marburg reported that UV treatments had improved the times of runners and swimmers over a distance of 100 meters.[148] Dr. Günther Lehmann of the Kaiser Wilhelm Institute for Work Physiology spoke of 40–60 percent increases in muscular efficiency and a whole series of favorable metabolic changes. He also believed that by irradiating a control subject through a pane of glass that filtered out UV rays, he had ruled out the power of suggestion as a factor in his experiment.[149]

The debate over UV became a textbook confrontation between the antidoping purists and their "modern" opponents for whom performance was the first priority. The conservatives offered the standard critique of doping: a chivalric refusal to betray one's comrades in sport combined with a warning about medical dangers.[150] For example, the Sports Medical Commission of the German Swimming Federation unanimously rejected UV both on the grounds of sportsmanship and the apparent ineffectiveness of the treatment.[151] Proponents of UV treatments, on the other hand, denied it was doping, arguing that it strengthened only "natural processes" and was actually comparable to massage—another therapy that, having started out at the sickbed, had found many healthy clients.[152] Dr. Hans Seel of Hamburg split the difference by recommending that UV treatments be banned only during the training period; the grounds for censure were the clear "physical and pharmacological" differences between these artificial light sources and natural sunlight.[153]

The UV controversy also revealed a kind of ambivalent fixation on American civilization that expressed itself in scientific and athletic competitiveness. German nationalists resented the widely held view that UV was an American invention. A look at the scientific literature, writes a Dr. Hering in 1926, makes it clear that Germans understood the effects of radiation therapy well before Americans did.[154] Eight years later, with the UV issue still alive and the Nazis in power, a more assertive scientific nationalism was in style. According to Dr. Kusserath of Berlin, it was German technology that had devised the quartz irradiation lamp, a German physician who had discovered that UV therapy cured rickets, and German doctors who had treated wounds with UV during the war. Now that Adolf Hitler had called for better German bodies, here was a medical technology that could actually help build them.[155] As for the athletic rivalry with America, UV was felt to be a necessary equalizer. UV lamps have been used in America with great success, writes a Dr. Bach, and no one there objects to them[156]—an eminently practical reason not to defame the "invisible rays" as "doping."

Few appear to have disagreed with this argument. It is surprising, in fact, that there was not more open German resistance to this "American" innovation, and that the "doping" epithet was not heard more often in the polemics about UV. The political and cultural conservatism of the German medical establishment of this period is well known,[157] and this conservatism included both an antiscientific strain and a profound distrust of America as a source of unwholesome modern trends. The prominent German surgeon and sports physician August Bier (1861–1949) was an antimodernist of this kind who described "Americanism" as "repulsive" and "fundamentally alien to the soul of the German," while decrying the illusory progress of technology and "all the triumphs of cold intellect."[158] Another German doctor raised the possibility that the scientific approach to sport might not be compatible with German values.[159] The representatives of this mindset often pursued the hard line against drugs in sport; what is more, they showed a persistent tendency to associate the more scurrilous aspects of doping with Americans. It is the Americans who are the predominant dopers, wrote the physiologist A. Loewy in 1910, and their concoctions are a notoriously well-kept secret.[160] After the first American six-day cycling races, a physician says, some of the riders went crazy, climbing in trees like apes; although people called these antics the effects of overexertion, the fact was that the riders were high on cocaine.[161] (It is quite possible this was a true story.) It was Americans who combined kola nuts and coca leaf extract, an American doctor who had fed pills from the Amazon to unsuspecting athletes, Americans (and European professionals) who injected "poisons" to boost their performances.[162] There is a suggestive comparison to be made between this besmirched image of Americans in German eyes and later ideas about East Germans athletes cultivated in the United States and elsewhere. In both cases, political xenophobia is combined with a projection of forbidden impulses—here, the urge to practice doping—onto a society that is regarded as ideologically alien and in some ways inhuman (see Chapter 6).

But the problem of doping could not be resolved by scapegoating foreigners. The German sports medical literature was full of contradictory views on the subject and quite unable to define in any unanimous fashion what doping actually was. One approach was explored by a Swiss doctor who wrote that he would prefer to draw the crucial line between nutrients ("in the broadest sense of the term") and stimulants that are not part of ordinary metabolism, but this distinction had proven to be impractical in the real world of ambiguous substances.[163] Indeed, said Otto Riesser, many people had already contributed toward blurring the distinction between doping and innocent dietary regimens for athletes in training.[164] In the meantime, those who talked in terms of nutrients and stimulants overlooked the fact that the term "stimulus" remained unclarified and almost meaningless. Doping was, in fact, virtually synonymous with stimulation. But it was easier to assume than to demonstrate the efficacy, let alone the mechanism, of any given "stimulant." The very concept of the stimulus had been one of the classic problems of physiology since the seventeenth century and was still being debated in the 1920s and 1930s. Inadequate understanding of the entire subject had not, however, prevented the spread of fashionable terms like "stimulant cells" and "cell stimulation."[165] In short, the nutrient/stimulant distinction was hopelessly blurred by the impossibility of defining these terms in a consistent and contrastive way.

A second approach was to define doping by differentiating between short-term and long-term effects on the organism. Riesser, for example, drew a distinction between quick measures taken just before competitions to boost performance and more gradual, sustained efforts to improve the entire organism for the long term.[166] The latter regimen had the obvious advantage of being less "artificial," of involving "natural life processes," of being part of "a natural way of life." Riesser called this a "dietetic" procedure.[167] In a similar vein, another scientist contrasted doping (and its risk of medical complications) with healthy "supporting substances" that have a genuine physiological basis.[168] This need to make the boosting of the organism approximate as closely as possible the normal course of physiological events expresses the conservative attitude toward the human organism we noted earlier in this chapter. It was less evident in the 1930s than it is today that this attitude is incompatible with high-performance sport.

A third (though seldom mentioned) approach to resolving the doping issue was the possibility of providing equal access to performance-enhancing substances and techniques. One fervent opponent of ultraviolet treatments for athletes argued, for example, that UV should be banned as long as it was not continually available to every athlete.[169] When the Viennese physician Alexander Hartwich proposed the distribution of (unspecified) stimulants to all takers, this was rejected by a Swiss colleague as an unthinkable contravention of the meaning of sport.[170] Yet another physician pointed to the problem of whether two athletes would necessarily react in the same way to equal doses of the same stimulant[171]—a reminder of how little was known about how these agents worked and how such effects might be measured.

The most interesting argument invoked to legitimate "doping" was that certain substances were therapeutic rather than performance-boosting in nature, a distinction of vexing subtlety that reappeared several decades later in the debate over anabolic steroids (see Chapter 7). The use of drugs that restored or repaired the athlete's body after a stressful competition made obvious sense to a doctor. It was well known, for example, that the sports physician Wilhelm Knoll had administered the analeptic stimulant Coramin to exhausted athletes completing distance events at the 1928 Winter Olympic Games in St. Moritz.[172] The fact that the drug was taken after competing appeared to rule out a case of genuine "doping." A more ambiguous situation arose when Alexander Hartwich gave Coramin to untrained athletes "to help them through the initial stages of fatigue"[173]—a procedure another physician had carried out on military recruits subject to overexertion and even physical collapse. For the military physician, Coramin represented an improvement over other analeptic compounds like caffeine, digitalis, and camphor that appeared to boost circulation and breathing.[174] The use of such drugs by German mountain climbers on the famous Himalaya expeditions seemed to Hartwich another model worthy of emulation. But even if Hartwich's argument-by-analogy—that the physiological state of the athlete is comparable to that of the soldier or alpinist—was medically correct, it overlooked the special cultural status of sport as an exercise in "pathological physiology." For the purely utilitarian approach of the military doctor could not be applied to sport without downgrading the element of risk that is inherent in the idea of sport.

Hartwich steadfastly denied that his use of Coramin was "doping." He described it rather as "medically indicated" and recommended that this stimulant be made freely available to all athletes who wanted it.[175] Since he was serving as a medical consultant to the Austrian Olympic Committee, his recommendations were all the more difficult to ignore, and the reaction was not long in coming. To Professor Rudolf Staehelin of Basel, Hartwich's advocacy of Coramin and Cardiazol, an analeptic similar to Coramin, was both medically irresponsible and damaging to the ethos of sport. For one thing, the manufacturer's promotional material for Cardiazol promised more than mere recuperation or protection against circulatory problems; it bluntly promised to boost athletic ability. Using such a drug, says Staehelin, was a case of doping that required the strongest protest from the medical community, even though Cardiazol had proved itself in the case of acute respiratory weakness following strenuous athletic competition. That restorative function did not legitimate its general use as an ergogenic aid. But the most penetrating part of Staehelin's critique is directed against the "pathological physiology" of sport itself. High-performance sport was already pushing the muscular and circulatory systems to their physiological limits, he said, and the use of analeptics to drive them even further by suppressing symptoms of fatigue and other inhibitory mechanisms was simply inexcusable, even if their use was already widespread. If sport now involved the risk of physiological collapse, then the obligation of the physician was to challenge this type of physical culture as medically unacceptable.[176] The moral of the story, as another observer pointed out, was that the prophylactic use of Cardiazol had led to its use as a performance-enhancing drug.[177]

We can now see why medical objections to doping in Germany did not command universal support among sports physicians. Some of them, of course, like their modern counterparts, were simply spellbound by the prospect of boosting athletic performance in ingenious new ways. But the more fundamental problem, then as now, was that there were simply too many ways to rationalize the use of drugs within the standard guidelines for medical practice. Thus one doctor used the so-called *Tonikum* Roche to treat "overtrained" athletes, assuming that it would not be abused ("like so many other drugs in sports circles") because it required a prescription.[178] In a similar vein, an implacable foe of UV treatments for athletes saw no reason why he should not give a nonnarcotic derivative of the baldrian root (marketed as Recvalysat) to athletes suffering from precompetition anxiety—by his account, a wholly successful remedy. He was justified in giving this "harmless" substance to his patients, he argued, because a physician is expected to provide a cure. In addition, the drug had other uses. The sexual abstinence required by training had caused many young athletes to complain of nocturnal erections and emissions, and Recvalysat had effectively dealt with these symptoms.[179] The frequent appearance of such arguments in the medical literature showed that the line between restoring the organism and boosting it was being eroded in a variety of ways. An entire spectrum of substances required what amounted to individual interpretations to which all medical men could subscribe—a project comparable to interpreting Shakespeare in a way that could please all tastes.

By the end of the interwar period, the complexities of the doping issue seemed intractable. "The record of these controversies," a clearly frustrated observer wrote in 1939, "shows the futility of discussions on 'doping' on any but a medical basis."[180] Such a Gordian Knot approach attempted to reduce a multidimensional issue to the single dimension of medical safety, but sports physicians knew better; the resistance of the doping problem to strictly logical analysis was no excuse to oversimplify it. Otto Riesser, a master of the biochemical complexities of doping who fully recognized the limits of logic on this terrain, noted with admirable lucidity that in difficult cases "common sense and conscience must be the final judges."[181] As intellectually (and ethically) unsatisfying as it is, this intuitive solution to the doping conundrum is the only practical option for the individual athlete or physician who refuses the comforts of cynical opportunism. The "mental attitude" of the athlete, as one of Riesser's contemporaries put it, is a critical aspect of the doping question,[182] and the same applied to the physician. For example, when Otto Riesser wrote about digitalis in 1930, he speculated that it might actually help the long-distance skier. "I don't know whether that sort of thing has been tried," he went on. "But all of us feel a healthy inner resistance to such experiments in artifically boosting athletic performance, and, perhaps, a not unjustified fear that any pharmacological intervention, no matter how small, may cause a disturbance in the healthy organism."[183] If men would not punish the doping athlete, Riesser implied, nature itself might take on the assignment.

Ultimately, then, doping was treated as a private issue for those involved. At a time when drug testing did not exist, athletes and physicians answered to their consciences. It would be a great mistake, however, not to see these individual decisions in the context of the sports subculture of this era—a community consisting of athletes, physicians, coaches, bureaucrats, and the pharmaceutical companies that have lurked in the background of the doping issue for almost a century.

The German sports medical literature of the interwar period makes it clear that the doping practices of this era were entangled in a network of relationships linking these interest groups to each other. Some physicians, recognizing that some athletes had an unwholesome interest in drugs, argued that information about these substances should be held back from their clients.[184] But it was evident that doctors involved in the world of sport could not expect to enjoy the same degree of authority they took for granted in the ordinary practice of medicine. At least one doctor warned that the physician should not cede his authority to coaches and officials,[185] but this was easier said than done. It was inevitable, for example, that sports clubs and federations would pressure physicians to do anything and everything to get athletes into shape or out of bed and onto the track, even if such efforts might violate medical ethics.[186] Since a strict separation between the responsibilities of physician and trainer was not always possible, and some trainers were willing to dope their athletes, conflicts between a trainer's ambitions and the physician's code of conduct could not always be avoided.[187]

Despite these admonishing voices and the general antidoping consensus they represented, the German sports medical establishment was vulnerable to pressures that encouraged doping. Differing opinions about what constituted doping were only one part of the problem. Again and again doctors warn that the overly strict sports physician will be held suspect by athletes, that doctors should somehow get closer to their athletes, that the sports physician must realize that competition and high performance are absolutely inherent in sport.[188] We also learn that pharmaceutical companies were handing out pharmaceutical drugs at sports competitions, while some well-known physicians were endorsing these products.[189] As one skeptical observer commented in 1931: "Most of the substances that are known in sports circles and are being vigorously marketed as rejuvenating agents and strength-boosters work either psychologically or not at all."[190] This portrait of an early elite sport culture will be recognizable to any informed observer of our own high-performance sports scene. As we will see in Chapter 7, the sociology of doping and the debate over its place in sport have changed little over the last half-century.

The Early History of the Anabolic Steroid

The development of the anabolic steroid belongs to the long tradition of scientific speculation and experimentation on the significance of male sexual biology. As we have seen, the essence of this development is a transition from primitive but vaguely empirical beliefs about the powers of the male sexual fluid to scientific confirmation of its power to engender physical strength in both men and women—hence its great cultural importance as the most effective performance-enhancing substance ever used by athletes.

Anabolic-androgenic steroids are synthetic versions of the male sex hormone testosterone. The term *anabolic* means that they stimulate muscle growth, *androgenic* that they promote such male secondary sex characteristics as facial hair and a deepened voice. These male traits (along with sexual and physical vigor) have been associated with the testes since the time of Aristotle, but demonstrating this connection in a scientific fashion was not possible until the nineteenth-century ideas about "internal secretions" formulated by Claude Bernard matured into the science of endocrinology during the first decades of our own century. As noted previously, Charles-Édouard Brown-Séquard (see Chapter 3) was an important, if not infallible, contributor to the theory of internal secretions and the first scientist to associate these glandular products with physical strength.

The history of the male sex hormone and its derivatives has transcended sexual chemistry per se by reinforcing judgments about the meaning of what it is to be male or female. As a performance-enhancing substance, in other words, the anabolic steroid is nothing less than an expression of male biology as power, since there is no female hormonal derivative that can match its ability to promote muscle growth and endurance. The historical background of this chemical asymmetry is, of course, the prestige of maleness that has been an important part of our cultural heritage for millennia. In this sense, testosterone and steroids have exercised a kind of gender tyranny by requiring female athletes to accept the risk of virilization—for instance, hirsutism, deepened voice, male pattern baldness—as the price of improved performance. In addition, these side-effects seem to be reversible in males but not in females.[191] From a strictly biological perspective, then, the uninhibited pursuit of athletic performance is essentially a *male* project to which females may subscribe voluntarily or even involuntarily, as in the case of East German women who were given steroids without their knowledge.

The gender asymmetry of sexual biology was anticipated during the eighteenth century by the British experimenter John Hunter (1728–93), who, using fowl, transplanted male organs into females and vice versa and observed the results.[192] This apparent gender symmetry of his work is misleading for two reasons. First, Hunter's stature as a forerunner of modern endocrinology stems primarily from his transplantations of cock testes into hens—experiments that were rediscovered only at the beginning of the twentieth century and affirmed male primacy. The second and more interesting point is that Hunter himself, prompted no doubt by cultural assumptions about gender, seems to have taken for granted the biological dominance of the male organism. He concluded from his transplantation experiments "that there is a material difference in the powers of the male and the female. The spurs of a cock were found to possess powers beyond those of a hen, while at the same time, the one animal as a whole, has more powers than the other."[193] A century later Brown-Séquard assumed, in similar fashion, that an ovarian extract could not boost the human organism like a testicular extract.[194]

In retrospect it is possible to see testicular extracts and their apparent effects, in Brown-Séquard's eyes, as both anabolic and androgenic. The traditional interpretation of the male fluid, as we have seen, was androgenic in that it was associated with virility, as were the extracts that Brown-Séquard prepared for himself and gave away free of charge to many other physicians and researchers. His important conceptual innovation, however, was to ascribe to the extracts a kind of anabolic property he associated indirectly with increased athletic capacity. In addition, by expressing the "dynamogenic" effect of his testicular extracts in quantitative terms suitable to the physiological energy of the racing cyclist, Brown-Séquard initiated the conceptual process by which the male hormone came to be associated with athletic potential as well as virile traits. Progress in endocrinology thus entailed a demystification of the male fluid and the eventual separation of its anabolic from its androgenic properties, thereby making possible the engineering of steroids that maximize the production of proteins for muscle-building and minimize their virilizing side-effects.[195]

This "athleticizing" of the testicular extracts was already underway when Brown-Séquard died in 1894. Oskar Zoth, a junior scientist at the Physiological Institute at the University of Graz (Austria) as well as a cyclist and swimmer, and his colleague Fritz Pregl, a hiker and swimmer, injected themselves with a liquid extract of bulls' testicles and then tested the strength of their fingers with a Mosso ergograph. Zoth concluded that this "orchitic" extract had boosted both muscular strength and the condition of "the neuromuscular apparatus." Autosuggestion had not played a significant role in the experiment, he claims, because both he and Pregl had expected a negative result. The final sentence of Zoth's paper can even lay claim to a certain historic significance: "The training of athletes offers an opportunity for further research in this area and for a practical assessment of our experimental results."[196] This appears to be history's first proposal to inject athletes with a hormonal substance in order to boost performance. In a separate pair of trials he carried out on two other athletic types, Pregl confirmed his original results and made the prophetic observation that it was the combination of exercise and orchitic extracts that boosted performance, endurance, and recovery[197]—a formula we know applies to anabolic steroids.[198] In 1898 Zoth reported the results of additional work and commented that previous experiments of this kind had neither been repeated by other investigators nor had they found any practical application.[199]

From the standpoint of the late twentieth century it appears odd that this work was not applied to the rudimentary high-performance athletics of the period. All of Zoth's test subjects were athletes, and he had specifically proposed the use of the extracts during training sessions. Once again, however, we must resist the temptation to impose our own perspective on the inhabitants of a different age. An attentive reading of Zoth's "historic" proposal shows that he, like Tissié, saw sport in the service of science rather than the other way around.

Nor did Zoth have to reckon with "modern" reservations about applying hormonal physiology to the assault on record performances, since there was as yet no proscription of scientific performance-enhancement on ethical grounds. The partnership between athletics and physiological experimentation had yet to lose its innocence. The development of sport into a highly competitive subculture in which physiological advantages would really matter lay years in the future.

The association of sport with testicular extracts is more explicit in a 1910 paper by the important German physiologist A. Loewy, who had done work on the chemistry of respiration, body temperature, blood composition, high-altitude physiology, and fatigue. Loewy begins by referring to the unknown nature of the chemical mechanisms of the "secret substances" used by the notorious six-day cyclists, a practice he calls "doping." Following the lead of Brown-Séquard, Zoth, and Pregl, his purpose was to see whether injections could not postpone the onset of fatigue in dogs by neutralizing the acidic metabolic products of tired muscles.

The substance in question was a crystalline compound called "spermine," first isolated from the testis in 1891 by the Russian chemist Alexandr Poehl,[200] who identified it as a crucial catalyst of oxidation present in almost all human tissues. Poehl also claimed that, in the words of a later commentator, spermine offered "an extraordinary action as a physiological tonic."[201] But the central problem posed by spermine was its relationship to the testicular extracts of Brown-

Séquard. In 1901 the British pharmacologist Walter E. Dixon sought a solution to this problem by injecting spermine into rabbits and observing its effects on blood pressure, body temperature, involuntary muscles, and the testis. But the actual "relation of spermine to the Brown-Séquard fluid" remained a mystery for this generation of investigators, and the "spermine" concept eventually dropped out of sight.[202] We may assume that Poehl, trying to identify the active principle of the testis, produced a crude extract using the best equipment available to him.[203] It is also interesting to see that, like his contemporary Brown-Séquard, Poehl found his own extract to be a "physiological tonic."

The originality (and fatal flaw) of Loewy's investigation was its fusion of the hormonal principle and the acidic theory of fatigue. He injected spermine into dogs in order to measure its effect on their consumption of oxygen while they ran on a treadmill device. These injections seemed to produce reductions of oxygen consumption of between 2 and 14 percent, persuading Loewy that he had confirmed "in a more objective and satisfactory way" the findings of Brown-Séquard, Zoth, and Pregl by demonstrating a respiratory strategy that could slow the onset of fatigue during physical exertion. The crucial factor, he believed, was a boosting of the alkaline content of the blood to buffer the acidic waste products of fatigued muscle.[204]

We now assume that steroids increase the rate of protein synthesis in muscle (and other) tissues by bonding with androgen receptors in target cells. The end results of this bonding are increased production of "messenger" RNA and muscle protein synthesis.[205] Lacking this kind of knowledge, Loewy and his contemporaries had to grope after plausible physiological mechanisms that could count for the apparent ergogenic or stimulating effects of these extracts, and the acidic theory of fatigue was a prime candidate. (Here, in fact, Loewy anticipated the widespread interest in using alkaline buffering against fatigue that would appear during the 1930s.)[206] At the same time, however, Loewy realized that his buffering theory was not compatible with the long-lasting effects of testicular extracts found by Zoth and Pregl, and he reported that he was continuing his investigations.

From the earliest days of Brown-Séquard's campaign on behalf of his *liquide testiculaire*, the scientific status of these substances was very uncertain. In 1914 a spermine enthusiast in Kharkov noted that, though widely used as a medication, the controversial compound was being dismissed or ignored by many scientists, in part because of the flamboyant way it was being marketed to the public. This author described spermine as a catalytic oxygen-carrier that promoted the physiological resiliency of the body: Wounds healed faster, the effects of poisons like strychnine and chloroform were mitigated, and young dogs and guinea pigs grew bigger and heavier than control animals. In human subjects, spermine diminished irritability, improved sleep, appetite and digestion, and lowered the respiratory and pulse rates. "The actual mechanism of the spermine effect is still not entirely clear," he wrote, but he did not doubt that spermine boosted human physiology in a significant way.[207] As late as 1934, an observer still felt the need to note that "the remarkable oxidative catalytic action of Poehl's spermine has not been substantiated."[208] Needless to say, it never would be; but the scientific errors of these investigators were actually less important than their preservation of Brown-Séquard's doctrine that male extracts were remarkable and "dynamogenic" substances.

By 1930 scientists were closing in on the exact chemical structures of the male and female sex hormones. Male hormone activity could be detected and even measured by its effects on castrated cocks. As one team of chemists reported that year, "The urine of young men contains a hormone (or hormones?) which induces comb growth in capons when a properly prepared extract of such urine is injected."[209] The isolation of the male hormone testosterone in 1935[210] was the culmination of decades of work on male extracts going back to the first preparations of the late nineteenth century. But what had happened to Brown-Séquard's theory of the "dynamogenic" extract and its implications for athletic performance?

Loewy's report of 1910 presented his experiments with spermine as a scientific response to the mysterious doping compounds of the six-day cyclists. At this point, however, two factors cause a blanket of silence to fall over the entire subject of hormonal performance-boosting in sport until the advent of anabolic steroids in the 1950s and 1960s. First, belief in the efficacy of testicular extracts fell victim to the rise of a more scientific endocrinology during the 1920s. Second, the synthesis of testosterone in 1935 and the explosion of steroid research that followed was not applied to sport until after World War II. In 1919 the prominent British anthropologist Arthur Keith had associated "an hormonic mechanism" with "the needs of athletic training," but here Keith meant nothing more than the need for a vague "co-ordinating mechanism" that could harmonize all of the organs of the body under stress[211]—a concept that prefigures recently published (1991) East German research on "hormonal regulation" in high-performance athletics.[212] In 1924 a mention of the "pharmaco-dynamic effect" of gland extracts referred to a variety of therapeutic procedures that had nothing to do with athletics.[213] The key to this lack of interest in sportive performance was the absence of a special conceptual framework—of the idea that an anabolic hormonal effect might benefit athletes.

The endocrinologists of the 1920s and 1930s were preoccupied instead with the relationship between the sex glands and reproductive biology; in short, it was the androgenic (or estrogenic) rather than the anabolic (muscle-building) effects of hormones that occupied center stage. The only "performance-enhancing" function of the male hormone at this time was the sexual "rejuvenation" of aging men[214] rather than the strengthening of younger athletes. This was also the purpose of certain popular surgical procedures that aimed to boost sexual functioning. The Russian-French surgeon Serge Voronoff, for example, earned an international reputation—and a great deal of money—by transplanting slices of monkey testicles into aging men seeking a new lease on life. Voronoff's operation was, in fact, performed on a former boxing champion and a couple of racehorses, but these cases were exceptional.[215] And while Eugen Steinach identified "increased muscular strength" as one effect of his famous vasectomy operation, its primary purpose was a general rejuvenation of the entire organism.[216] As late as the 1920s Francesco Cavazzi was injecting patients with extracts of animal testicles in the manner of Brown-Séquard, claiming that they reduced fatigue and increased the frequency and duration of erections.[217] In other words, even during this first "golden age" of sport, none of these dubious innovators (and talented self-promoters) expressed any interest in boosting the performances of athletes.

Nor do references to the recently isolated sex hormones show up in the German sports medical literature, even though the crucial papers on the male hormones were appearing in German-language scientific journals that German sports physicians may have been reading. The only hormone of interest to sports physiologists was adrenaline.[218] In 1922, for example, the American physiologist Frank A. Hartman associated adrenaline injections with the "second wind" phenomenon experienced by runners (and his experimental cats) and theorized that when an athlete "is put to the test he is able to start with a higher muscular efficiency, partly on account of the extra epinephrin already released, although of course there are other factors involved."[219] There was, however, at least once case of athletic interest in unorthodox hormone treatments that had been widely publicized. In 1939 the Danish exercise physiologist Ove Bøje wrote:

> Quite recently, the newspapers announced that the remarkable performances of the Wolverhampton Wanderers football team were due to gland extract treatment provided for the players by their manager, Major Buckley. The Portsmouth team consequently decided to follow their example. Such cases show that, nowadays, no hesitation is felt in administering even *hormone* treatment as a method of improving athletic performance. I do not know what hormones the English footballers use to score their goals, but this, presumably, is irrelevant, as we are probably dealing with a purely subjective phenomenon.[220]

It is theoretically possible, Bøje concedes, that "sex hormones" might boost athletic performance, but he has no physiological model to offer. For despite the fact that German research on steroids escalated dramatically toward the end of the 1930s, the work was too highly technical to yield an adequate conceptual framework for understanding what hormones actually are. What, for example, was the relationship between hormones and stimulants?[221] Were hormones distinguishable from vitamins? Did a stimulant have the same active principle as an organ extract? At this point the relationship between the male hormone and athletic performance was scarcely more advanced than it had been in the days of Brown-Séquard; the specific hormones were being isolated, but their anabolic effects had not been confirmed in the laboratory. Major scientific findings on the protein-anabolic, or muscle-building, potential of steroids would not actually appear until the 1950s,[222] more or less simultaneously with their introduction into the world of high-performance sport.

The psychological dimension of doping was recognized as early as the 1890s. The uncertain emotional consequences of giving gland extracts or more conventional stimulants to human subjects was evident to early investigators like Brown-Séquard and Oskar Zoth, who persuaded themselves that they had eliminated the power of suggestion as a factor in their experiments. Later investigators, however, realized that they could not predict what might or might not happen in a psychophysiological sense once a drug had been injected or ingested. This uncertainty eventually gave rise to the "double-blind" procedure that keeps both investigator and subject unaware of what the latter is receiving. But even these precautions do not suffice for drugs, like steroids, that some subjects can recognize by their immediate effects.[223] Thus the psychological factor has greatly complicated the problem of measuring the effects of drugs on athletic performance and continues to be a major topic of research on anabolic steroids.[224]

The pharmacological problem is only one facet, however, of the psychological dimension of high-performance sport, a topic often discussed around the turn of the century by physiologists investigating intense exertion. Of course, the ultimate sources of extraordinary physical performances were as mysterious then as they are to us a century later. The difference between the fin de siècle and our own period is that our high-performance sport culture has created a demand for a "sport psychology" that carries scientific cachet. Yet there is good reason to doubt, as we will see in the next chapter, whether modern sport psychology has advanced much farther than its nineteenth-century models.

5

The Last Frontier
Mental Energy and the Quest
for Human Limits

Enter Psychology: The Discovery of the
Athletic Psyche

Back in the 1980s a West German racing cyclist, accompanied by an anxious coterie of sports officials, paid a visit to a psychologist at the University of Heidelberg. The young rider's custodians explained that, while he was a spectacular hill climber and a flyer across level ground, he could not rid himself of the fear that prevented him from hurtling down mountainsides at 100 kilometers an hour. "Take the brakes out of his head, doctor," they demanded. The professor, though confident he could have managed such a feat of psychosurgery, refused to do so on ethical grounds.[1]

Several years later, an Italian rider afflicted with the same problem found a composite cure. A music therapist had him listen to Mozart at different speeds and volumes; an allergist took him off wheat and milk products and prescribed new pills; and a psychologist went to work on a timidity complex dating from the athlete's childhood. By 1990 the music therapy had cured his vertigo, and Gianni Bugno sat atop the computerized rankings of the world's top 600 professional riders.[2]

This brand of "sport psychology" and its indiscriminate eclecticism have little to do with the scientific method that formulates and

154

tests hypotheses. Rather, these scattershot, or "pragmatic," approaches to boosting performance have resulted from the experimental subject's escape from the laboratory, its measuring devices, and the physiological models of a bygone age. Today, what we call sports psychology consists of a wide variety of therapeutic episodes of this kind, while the idea that scientists would eventually understand the constituent elements of performance in a genuinely scientific fashion has faded along with the physiological laboratories (and the innocent confidence) of an earlier era. This loss of ambition was inevitable. For it was precisely the methodological limitations of the confined world of laboratory-bound experiments that forced physiologists to think about athletic performance in psychological terms. It became clear that human performance could not be explained as solely the product of biological forces. This theoretical concession to the complexity of human functioning implied a methodological concession as well. The physiological complexity of athletic performance (and the feats of soldiers and mountain climbers) had expanded beyond the laboratory investigator's ability to describe it. This meant, in turn, that athletic physiology could not be miniaturized or modeled in an artificial setting. The discovery that controlled experiments could not reproduce the conditions of uncontrolled exertion recurs throughout the scientific literature of the fin de siècle and beyond.

The static and easily monitored organism on the dissection table was now replaced by a dynamic organism experiencing physiological stresses that could not be measured. One response to this relocation of the experimental subject outdoors was to use the ingenious instruments that allowed Étienne-Jules Marey (See Chapter 3) to study human and animal motion. But these devices described only the external dimension of physical activity. Was there, in fact, any way to bring the subtler techniques of the laboratory to the athlete or to the marching soldier? The easiest solution was to extrapolate from small biological events to larger ones. For example, following their testicular extract experiments, Oskar Zoth and Fritz Pregl had not hesitated to interpret ergographic trials of finger muscles as indices of athleticism on a grander scale, but some of their contemporaries had well-founded doubts about this sort of extrapolation. The cautious Philippe Tissié noted in 1894 that many physicians knew virtually nothing about physical exercises "apart from a few laboratory experiments on muscular contraction, respiration, and circulation,"[3] while he, by contrast, had taken the trouble to monitor the cyclist Stéphane under racetrack conditions. Similarly, Gustave Le Bon was more impressed by studies of the effects of kola nuts on marching soldiers and mountain climbers than by "laboratory research."[4]

This important distinction between performance in the laboratory environment and the unrestrained physical effort possible outside it often appears in the medical literature on pharmacological aids to performance. In a frequently cited 1922 study of the effects of alcohol on sprinters, the German sports physician Herbert Herxheimer insisted that real sportive effort is not comparable to ergographic trials. While the laboratory subject exerts only a few muscle groups, the athlete in the field uses virtually all of them. In addition, the central nervous system of the athlete is more highly activated than that of his sedentary counterpart and is inseparable from muscle functioning itself—neurophysiology in action. These quantitative and qualitative differences between the laboratory and field experiences, said Herxheimer, might also account for the contradictory results of the alcohol trials indoors and out. Contrary to the prevailing gossip in athletic circles, the alcohol doses given to his subjects seemed to reduce performance rather than provide the prerace stimulus many had taken for granted. He found it understandable that alcohol might boost performance on the ergograph, but argued that actual sportive performance could not be "dosed" with this kind of precision if only because so much more coordination is required.[5] Fifteen years later, another sports physician used this distinction to deflate the widespread idea that pharmacological doping worked: "It is my judgment that the performance *in actual competition* of an organism that has been trained to perfection *in a mental and physical sense* cannot be boosted by pharmacological means, although this does not apply to performances on the bicycle ergometer."[6] The crucial distinction separated natural from artificial experience; thus doping could "boost" only what was not real to begin with.

Of course, these investigators were not the first to understand that the difference between an experimental setting and a competitive venue transcended physiological processes and was actually a mental phenomenon. A French psychologist suggested in 1899, for example, that the electrical stimulation of a muscle was not the same thing as a normal contraction provoked by the psychological force of willpower,[7] and by the 1920s the artificiality of the experimental setting (and a corresponding emphasis on psychological factors) had become commonplace. Robert Werner Schulte, the sports- and instrument-oriented psychotechnician, warned against measuring the performance of "an abstracted, artificial segment" of experience in

place of the "total organism."[8] Another German psychologist, studying the effects of altruistic motivation on performance, reported that
imagining a selfless act was not comparable to performing it in real
life.[9] Herxheimer, too, was well aware that his "controlled" experiments on alcohol and performance were vulnerable to the psychological effects of weather and competition and what we simply call
"mood."[10] In his *Fundamentals of Sports Medicine* (1933), he refers
frequently to the psychological dimension of athletic performance,
describing the much discussed "overtraining" syndrome, for example, as a mental condition. To his credit, Herxheimer was not afraid
of pointing out what science did not know, and this intellectual honesty mandated a role for psychic factors no one could explain. The
willpower of a Paavo Nurmi remained as mysterious in 1933 as that of
a six-day cyclist at the turn of the century.[11]

The early sports physiologists discovered that scientific study of
athletic performance must operate at this frontier where physiology
and psychology overlap. Only a psychophysiological approach could
begin to explain the stress phenomena—pain, trauma, anxiety, fatigue—that are an inherent part of high-performance sport. We have
already seen that the early investigators of this "pathological physiology" of athletic exertion showed little interest in using science to
boost performance, and this observation applies as well to the psychological realm. Consequently, what we find emerging at the turn of
the century is a diagnostic rather than prescriptive interest in the
mental phenomena associated with sport. The idea of manipulating
the mind to enhance human performance—a popular preoccupation
of our own era—seldom appears during this period. Alfred Binet's
1893 study of chess prodigies merely contemplates a wonder of nature; it does not offer mental strategies to improve the minds of
aspiring players. Even the occasional positive identification of a
performance-boosting psychological factor was not necessarily regarded as a practical solution for athletes. In 1905, for example, the
German physiologist Caspari argued in a long scientific paper that the
remarkable performances of vegetarians in long-distance races had
nothing to do with their diet and everything to do with their ideologically motivated fanaticism, the "struggle for their ideals."[12] He
did not believe, however, that such character traits could be im-
planted in people or turned into self-improvement techniques, and
the even more interesting point is that there appears to have been
little interest in doing so.

This "premodern" character of psychological thinking about

sport at this time is clearly evident in the writings of Pierre de Coubertin, founder of the modern Olympic movement. Coubertin published hundreds of pages on "sports psychology," but not one mentions anything about boosting performance. This lack of interest in practical techniques was not due to an ignorance of contemporary scientific developments. For example, in "The Psychology of Sport" (1900), he points out that even as much study was being devoted to "the physiological effects," the psychological dimension of sport was being neglected, and he further notes that it was impossible to separate these two disciplines. "The first thing to keep in mind," he writes, "is that physiology and psychology share common and imperfectly defined frontiers."[13] But he adds that he had "no intention whatsoever of throwing light on so delicate an area." In fact, Coubertin had a very limited interest in the scientific side of sport, and virtually none in scientific schemes to make athletes stronger and faster. The "human thoroughbred" imagined by some, he wrote, would be a monster if it ever came to pass.[14] So what, then, does he mean by a "psychology of sport"?

Coubertin the intellectual was primarily a social theorist. His distinctive contribution to this field, dated now in most respects, was a social psychology of sport that had nothing to do with improving athletic performance.[15] He offered sport to his countrymen and to the world at large as a mass therapy that was necessary to mitigate what he called the "intensive character" of a "pulsating and complicated" society: "Considering the substantial expenditure of nervous and mental force demanded of people by modern civilization, they need an equivalent dose of muscular force" by way of compensation.[16] Having absorbed a Victorian view of sport, Coubertin was primarily interested in how sport developed, not better athletes, but "the moral musculature of man," and he firmly believed that it did.

Coubertin's idea of "sportive instinct" had nothing to do with physical or mental aptitude. It was a propensity, an affinity for sport in response to modern life, that appeared in some people and not in others. It was not an extension of the child's need for physical play and appeared first during adolescence. By calling sport "neither a proof of health nor an extra measure of constitutional strength," Coubertin deëmphasized the idea that the athlete was a physical specimen (the heavily muscled "human thoroughbred") or that he served the performance principle implicit in the Olympic motto: faster, higher, stronger. Yet Coubertin himself was ambivalent toward his own nondynamic conception of sport, because it obviously did not account for the emotional excitement experienced by Olympic athletes.

The key to this ambivalence was his idea of "excess," which could refer to a phenomenon as vast as the mood of modern civilization or to the mental state of an individual. On the larger scale, "excess" had to be restrained to prevent conflict between nations or social classes. But on an individual scale, "excess" was an indispensable ingredient of the athlete's competitive spirit. For that reason, Coubertin argued that "the idea of [wholly] suppressing [the element of] excess is a utopian notion of the anti-sportive types."[17] For there exist sportsmen, he says, "of the instinctive kind, active types belonging to a certain category, whom one does not have the right to stop, and whose élan should not be compromised in the name of a principle of equality which has recklessly been pushed to the point of the absurd." Coubertin realized that Olympic sport was simply incompatible with this sort of temperance. For "we know," he wrote, "that [sport] tends inevitably toward excess, and that this is its essence, its indelible mark."[18] As early as 1900 Coubertin had called sport's tendency toward excess its "psychological characteristic par excellence."[19] What he did not foresee was that this endorsement of the drive toward "excess" and the "active type" of athlete would lead directly to the development of the "human thoroughbreds" who now compete at the Olympic Games.

Physiologists and psychologists of the turn of the century were no more interested in devising strategies to boost athletic performance that the *rénovateur* of the modern Olympic movement himself. Yet they were interested in extraordinary physical performances. Indeed, the gradual conflation of the "normal" and the "pathological" in nineteenth-century medical and biological thinking created a new interest in extreme physiological states and the extreme psychological states that accompanied them. On a less dramatic level, science could study the distribution of talent throughout a population and speculate on its origins. In both cases we find a strategy for assessing aptitude rather than for attempting to magnify it.

An example of the interest in talent is the notion of "athletic capacity" proposed in 1903 by Francis Galton's admirer and biographer, the eugenist Karl Pearson, who discusses this type of ability in a study of the inheritability of mental and physical characteristics. "We may define the athletic individual," Pearson writes, "as one not only keen on sports and games, but as capable in them. This denotes a training and a *mental control* of hand and eye, and approaches psychical efficiency."[20] Pearson's idea of "athletic capacity" thus combines interest, aptitude, and enough practice to amount to "training." His reference to "mental control" points forward to the practical techniques of modern sports psychology and back to Galton's pioneering experiments with mental imaging. By modern standards, this is a very casual approach to athletic performance. Furthermore, Pearson was studying schoolchildren rather than the accomplished athletes of his day. His choice of younger subjects had been dictated by the overriding interest in inheritance he shared with Francis Galton, whose own work on inheritance had been limited to the study of mature oarsmen. This emphasis on heredity—an analytical, as opposed to manipulative, approach to both mental and physical aptitude—is characteristic of the performance-oriented science of the fin de siècle.

Psychology and Athletic Potential in the Nineteenth Century

Exactly how did nineteenth-century scientists regard extraordinary physical feats or more routine examples of athletic ability at a time when the idea of high-performance sport was still in its infancy? Where did they think the physical strength or energy for such biological events actually came from? Their explanations relied for the most part on two ways of thinking about the human organism: theories of human "constitution" or "temperament"—terms that will be used interchangeably below—and the study of extreme stimuli, or what the modern psychologist would call "emotional arousal."[21] Of these two intellectual traditions the first had virtually expired by about 1940, while the second has evolved into speculations about "peak performances" in various realms of human endeavor. A third and less well-noted approach to finding the emotional sources of physical strength and endurance identified racial aptitudes that also can be considered premodern examples of psychological thinking about the origins of athletic performance.

Constitutional typologies of human beings are theoretical constructs designed to classify a diverse population into several basic types. They attempt to establish correspondences between physical and mental traits that serve to distinguish these human types from each other. The classical model is the fourfold system of Hippocrates and Galen that survived in only slightly altered form for many centuries. It held that health and disease in human beings were governed by the varying relationships between four bodily "humours": blood, lymph, black and yellow bile. These substances corresponded in turn to the four temperaments: The phlegmatic (lymphatic) type was obese and slow in both movement and intelligence; the plethoric (sanguine) type—large, robust, and sexually active; the bilious type—thin, energetic and healthy; and the melancholic type—thin, dark, constipated, and undersexed. The health of an individual depended on preserving a balance among these four humours.[22] For the historian of ideas, the improbable longevity of this theory has a fascinating quality comparable to that of an ancient fish like the coelecanth—a genuine fossil that has, almost miraculously, extruded itself into our own century. In fact, the idea of temperament is not yet extinct, even in academic writing, in part because finding correspondences between physique and temperament appears to satisfy a certain human need to discover visible patterns in our fellow human beings. The "instinctive" association of muscularity and aggressiveness is only one of many such correspondences that have thrived as cultural stereotypes since ancient times. Aristotle applied this principle to the problem of assessing the physical abilities of nonhuman creatures as well, stating in the *Physiognomica* that "experts on the lower animals are always able to judge of character by bodily form: It is thus that a horseman chooses his horse or a sportsman his dogs."[23]

The theory of temperaments, combining as it does both physical and psychological assessments of the human organism, would appear to be ideally suited for identifying athletic talent. As constitutional theory evolved over the centuries, it did not aim at finding promising athletic material. From the beginning, the four classifications were used in the service of medical diagnosis and treatment, and this continued to be the case during the golden age of constitutional theory that followed the publication of Ernst Kretschmer's medical bestseller *Physique and Temperament* in 1921.

Constitutional theory began to react to developments in physiology during the Enlightenment. By the time the French physician Cabanis (see Chapter 4) presented his version of the ancient theory of temperaments in the late 1700s, it had acquired two additional classifications reflecting the investigations of Albrecht von Haller (1708–77), the most important physiologist of the eighteenth century. Specifically, his work on the relationship between nerves and muscles prompted Cabanis to add fifth and sixth temperaments: the predominance of the nervous system over the muscular system and vice versa. It is of particular interest that Cabanis renamed Haller's *musculosum-torosum* the *tempérament musculaire*, thereby introducing—inadvertently—the idea of an athletic temperament into the constitutional typologies of the nineteenth century.[24] Later French theorists of the nineteenth century like Rostan and Sigaud reduced Cabanis's six basic temperaments back to four: the respiratory, the digestive, the cerebral, and the muscular. At the same time, however, we should not assume that Cabanis and his contemporaries saw the "muscular temperament" in modern terms.

"Muscular temperament" was a static rather than a dynamic term, pointing to ancient classical statuary rather than to the athletes of the future. Believing that the "modern" thinkers of the Enlightenment could improve upon the ancient classification of temperaments, Cabanis noted that the ideally equilibrated "muscular and robust subjects" (*musculosi quadradi*) pointed out by Haller constituted a naturally occurring human type the ancients had overlooked.[25] Unlike the sports-minded legions of our own century, Cabanis was unimpressed by great muscular strength except in those cases where it took the mysterious form of a sudden and unexpected manifestation of energy issuing from an apparently weak organism. A century before Philippe Tissié would make the same point, Cabanis recalled an ancient association of athleticism and pathology. "Hippocrates," he wrote, "points out that extreme athletic strength borders on illness." Hypermuscular development, Cabanis continues, impedes an individuals's ability to sense threats to his health. In addition, physical strength is only "mechanical strength" and therefore less important than "the true energy, the radical energy of the nervous system" that can surge forth from frail bodies in dramatic fashion. Cabanis also subscribed to the law of compensation that found an inverse relationship between physical and intellectual ability.[26] It is worth noting that Cabanis's views match those of Pierre de Coubertin, who not only showed no explicit interest in developing the muscles of athletes but who also believed that the "sporting instinct" had nothing to do with "constitutional strength."[27]

Changes in the meaning of the term "muscular temperament" would be determined by evolving cultural attitudes toward the human physique and its social functions. For our purposes, the crucial question is when the term became associated with athleticism rather than the capacity to perform work, since this transition marks an important stage in the emergence of a "scientific" interest in sportive exertion. Cabanis describes an "athletic regimen" based upon "bodily exercises" as having some hygienic value, but he also believed that this muscle-building "regimen" diminished longevity by diverting energy away from the nervous system and by exposing the body to new forms of stress, a special disadvantage to men who cultivated the arts and sciences.[28] In other words, for Cabanis the "muscular temperament" was precisely that—a diagnostic category, a syndrome of medical interest rather than the focus of society's fascination with athletic types.

Fifty years later, the French army doctor Michel Lévy (1809–72) had little to add to Cabanis's treatment of this topic.[29] It is interesting to note, however, that by this time Lévy had reduced Cabanis's six temperaments to three—nervous, the sanguine, and the lymphatic—and made a point of labeling the muscular temperament an "idiosyncrasy" rather than a full-fledged temperament. Lévy's definitions of these and related terms are also somewhat more precise that those of his predecessor. Constitution, which can be modified but not destroyed by a "regimen," is the foundation [fond] of a personality, whereas temperament is a personality's more or less permanent [durable] form. Before defining idiosyncrasy, Lévy complains that the term "has been employed in a very arbitrary fashion by a variety of authors; it has referred to tastes, feelings of revulsion of cerebral origin, as well as the effects of habit or morbid deviations." For him, an idiosyncrasy resulted from the effect of a "nutritive or stimulating fluid" on a specific organ and reflected the state of balance among the system bodily organs. As an example of an idiosyncrasy, he cites Rousseau's need to urinate whenever he heard a bagpipe.[30]

At first glance, it is tempting to assume that the relatively low status of muscular development throughout this period reflected the absence of a popular cultural vehicle (like modern sport) for its display. But while such a relationship between a constitutional typology and social developments is possible, it appears in this case that scientists like Haller, Cabanis, and Lévy simply regarded musculature in purely anatomical-functional terms without assigning to it any particular symbolic significance. In fact, Lévy saw muscular vigor as relatively insignificant from a biological point of view. Judging a constitution in terms of its muscular development, he says, is a mistake that derives from misunderstanding strength as muscular strength, which Lévy calls "trivial" in contrast to the more comprehensive strength [force d'ensemble] that issues from a person's overall constitutional makeup. Muscular strength did not, for example, furnish a man with his "reactive power," his biological resiliency. Indeed, says

Lévy, men of an "athletic cast" [*complexion athlétique*] are rarely examples of good health, and the "exuberance of the muscular system" tends to rule out a lively mind. The "massive constitutions" of the insensate Nordics, who are almost impervious to pain, confirm this point. The "athletic temperament" is thus not "a special kind of health," and "the exaggerated nutrition of the muscles" is merely "an epiphenomenon of the sanguine temperament."[31]

Writing in 1850, Lévy was enough of a "modern" to have heard about the idea of "training." The long-distance race-walkers in England, he reported, were capable of prodigious feats, one of them having covered the 62 miles from London to Brighton in eight hours.[32] "These men," he noted, "have submitted to a course of preparation they call training, the point of which is to reduce the weight of the body and increase respiratory force. To this end, one reduces the fat content of the body and the excess of liquid which impedes the cellular tissue with the help of purgatives, dieting, and morning fasts supported by the ingestion of tea. After this first state, which expels useless fluids from the body, one sets about developing the muscles and providing more energy to the nutritive processes through regular and gradual exercise combined with a proper diet."[33] It is instructive to hear this modern routine described as the experiment in human physiology it was a century and a half ago.

Constitutional theorists were interested in physical exertion because it was an experience shared by so many laborers of this epoch. Diagnosing the physiological efficiency of the various constitutional types was of obvious practical value. Thus, when Lévy speaks of the mind-numbing consequences of "the continuous and violent exercising of the muscular system," he notes that this unhappy condition had arisen in "many of the mechanical professions."[34] Interest in the labor capacity of each temperamental type is evident in a long French encyclopedia article on *Tempérament* that appeared in 1858. The author, a Dr. Fourcault, proclaims three basic temperaments—the nervous, the sanguine, and the cellular—along with no fewer than seven others to represent "intermediate nuances" of the fundamental triad: the lymphatic, the adipose, the sclerotic, the muscular, the gastrolimic, the melancholic, and the erotic. In every case but the last, the author addresses the capacity of the type to perform physical labor. At the same time, his portrait of the muscular temperament is more positive than that of Lévy. Fourcault's muscular types are essentially healthy people who are not condemned to the mental inferiority proclaimed by the law of compensation.[35]

The modern reader may be surprised to learn that the "nervous" temperament did not refer to fragile or fearful personalities. On the contrary, this term indicated a vibrant nervous system that poured energy into the limbs. According to Dr. Fourcault, "it confers on those men who are endowed with it an ability to perform sustained and heavy labor and all the bodily exercises. If they are not as strong as the athletes, they are more supple, more agile, and better able to withstand such labor and the fatigues of war."[36] A British contributor to *The Anthropological Review* offered a similar interpretation in 1870: "The nervous temperament is characterised by the body being small and almost feminine, with narrow sloping shoulders. The bones are small, the muscles of soft and fine, capable of sudden great effort, but soon fatigued." Despite these apparent deficiencies, nervous temperaments represented "almost all the miners in the kingdom" and made good soldiers. "It is called *nervous* because full of nerve—strong." And: "Weight for weight they are the strongest of men." By now it should be clear that, even though the primary interest in temperaments originated in concerns about labor efficiency, these assessments of the human organism were becoming protoathletic. At the same time, they were charged with value judgments that lent themselves to invidious comparisons. Did constitutional types correspond to racial or national types? And if so, were some people more athletic—both physically and temperamentally—than others? This kind of thinking, which enjoyed a small boom in Germany during the Nazi period, had already appeared in England by 1850. To take one example, the British interpreter of the nervous temperament quoted above was pleased to identify his own nationality with the (conspicuously virile) sanguine type: "This forcible temperament I believe to be handed down to us from the Danes."[37]

The theory of temperaments made it easy to invoke "scientific" support for the idea that athletic aptitude was a national character trait. While these descriptions of national temperament offered different degrees of racial chauvinism, all stressed the characterological rather than the purely physical dimension of this superiority. In his widely read book *The Races of Man* (1850), Robert Knox describes the Saxons as "a tall, powerful, athletic race of men" whose cultural savagery is matched only by their irrepressible energy:

His genius is wholly applicative, for he invents nothing. In the fine arts, and in music, taste cannot go lower. The race in general has no musical ear, and they mistake noise for music. The marrow-bones and

cleaver belong to them. Prize-fights, bull-baiting with dogs; sparring
matches; rowing, horse racing, gymnastics: the Boor is peculiar to the
Saxon race. When young they cannot sit still an instant, so powerful is
the desire for work, labour, excitement, muscular exertion. The self
esteem is so great, the self-confidence so matchless, that they cannot
possibly imagine any man or set of men to be superior to themselves.[38]

Knox's portrait of the Saxons as boors is at first somewhat surprising
since he describes himself as one of them. But he finds more than
adequate compensation for this lack of culture in the aggressiveness
and limitless male vanity—tempered by a Saxon "love of fair play"—
that he regarded as a self-evident virtue as the races struggled for
position in the "Zoological history" of man.[39] What interests us most
in Knox—the most primitive and least nuanced of these racial commentators—is the straightforward connection between sportive activities and sheer emotional energy and its celebration as a national trait.
Later, as psychological thinking about athletic performance became
more scientific, and elite sport became more international, this kind
of anthropological chauvinism virtually disappeared. It has survived
only in Western speculations about the racial and/or cultural factors
that might be of value to the athletes of black Africa (see Chapter 2).

Another example of anthropological chauvinism appears in an
1866 essay "On the Psychical Characteristics of the English People."
This author, Owen Pike, repeats much of what Knox had to say while
adding some thoughts on "national characteristics" and a vaguely
scientific foundation to his own doctrine of temperaments:

> One of the best elements in the English is its energy. It is that energy
> which is, above all other elements, the cause of the Englishman's
> various successes; it is that energy which causes his genius to appear so
> versatile, which forces into action the talents that in a phlegmatic
> people lie dormant. From that energy results the great diversity of
> forms in which the Englishman's restless desire for athletic exercise
> displays itself. And from the same kind of energy resulted that similar
> diversity of forms which athletic exercise took among the ancient
> Greeks. Energy—restless, insatiable energy—has been the leading
> characteristic of the two peoples, and it is a characteristic which we
> cannot find equally conspicuous—equally uniform—among the Ger-
> mans, the Dutch, or even the Danes.[40]

Pike's racial chauvinism knew no bounds, for he ascribed to the
English ice skater a "perfect command over all his movements" of

which the French and—*pace* Hans Brinker—even the Dutch were supposedly incapable. The scientific basis for this typologizing was provided by the Scottish philosopher Alexander Bain's theory of "muscular feelings," since "the muscular feelings and movements" were "of very great importance as an index to character and disposition."[41] (In fact, psychological investigation of the so-called "muscular sense" enjoyed a vogue in Europe toward the end of the nineteenth century.) But Pike's attempt to athleticize "muscular feelings," or what the French called the *sens musculaire,* was eccentric and in all likelihood an expression of the special British fixation on sport during the Victorian period. In contrast, Bain's extensive commentaries on muscular experience contain only the most casual references to "active sports and amusements."[42] Similarly, an international bibliography on "the muscular sense" that appeared in 1899 does not include a single item related to athletic performance.[43] As we have seen again and again in our survey of fin de siècle science, this work, too, was of potential rather than current value to sportsmen. French work on the psychology of fatigue carried out under the rubric of the *sens musculaire* is one example of how this kind of psychophysiological speculation represented a precursor to an applied psychology of sport.[44]

The theory of temperaments facilitated racial comparisons between European ethnic groups or between Europeans and Africans. Employing terms like "nervous temperament" and "mental constitution," one British observer of the Continental scene explained the one-sided outcome of the Franco-Prussian War by invoking a basic temperamental difference between the Celtic and Germanic races. Whereas the former (in this case, the French) showed a "more powerful development of the nervous system as contradistingished from the osseous and muscular," the latter were "the reserve force of the West, which always comes into play when the more nervous races have been exhausted by the morbid excitement of their corrupt civilisation. They are the osseous and muscular pole of European humanity."[45] But the characterological contrast was found to be sharpest in the case of non-Europeans and especially blacks, who were frequently criticized as indolent and cowardly. "The Negroes of Africa are eminently a home-keeping unadventurous race," wrote one British ethnologist. Their missing trait was "the spirit of adventure."[46] In the same vein, an American surgeon in charge of the General Hospital for Coloured Troops at New Orleans expressed the view that the Negro soldier was "*at present,* too animal to have moral courage or endurance." In the face of prolonged hardship in the field, another physician wrote, "the *morale* of the white man steps in and often aids him in overcoming the situation."[47] These Anglo-Saxon commentators were firmly convinced that this characterological fortitude also expressed itself on the fields of sport.

In addition to the theory of temperaments, nineteenth-century scientists developed a primitive psychophysiology of extreme states to account for the sudden bursts of energy that could push the human organism beyond its apparent limits. That these two approaches overlap is already evident in the idea of the "nervous" temperament described above, since its apparent delicacy conceals mysterious reserves of strength that can explode when triggered by factors known or unknown. Cabanis, too, saw a triangular relationship connecting temperament, physiologically extreme states, and unusual physical strength.

Great muscular strength, he says at one point, can arise from either an "inherent primitive disposition" or sudden physiological events that "depart from the normal order of nature" and constitute what for the healthy would be states of disease.[48]

These two major categories—robust temperament and the physiologically extreme state—do not appear to include certain case studies that appear in his work. One of his male types, for example, is a demasculinized creature like those who appear in one variation or another in every European characterology published during the nineteenth and twentieth centuries. Sad-faced, pale and scrawny, weak of pulse, and timid of manner, they flee the presence of other men for the comforts of solitude. And yet these sorry creatures of frail aspect are possessed of a "remarkable bodily strength," an improbably physical endurance, and a prodigious memory. Another kind of temperament, characterized by a capacity for profound feeling, is sometimes combined with "an extraordinary energy." All of the "energetic passions," says Cabanis, can cause any man to "find inside himself a strength [*vigueur*] he did not suspect" and make him "capable of executing movements the very idea of which would have frightened him in a more sober state of mind."[49]

The most dramatic cases of unexpected physical strength originated in pathological states. When certain illnesses affect the nervous system, Cabanis says, they can have a dramatic impact on its functioning or render it susceptible to similar influences from outside the body, at which point "the most feeble muscles instantly acquire a capacity to execute movements endowed with an energy and violence that are scarcely conceivable."[50] "Energetic movements," Alexander

Bain wrote in 1872, "arise under the influence of drugs and stimulants acting on the nerves and nerve centers; also from fever and other ailments. Convulsions, spasms, and unnatural excitement, are diseased forms of the spontaneous discharge of the active energy of the nerve centers."[51] Cabanis identified five pathological types who could suddenly acquire unusual strength: maniacs, hydrophiliacs (victims of rabies), melancholics, epileptics, and "vaporous," delicate women. The first three disorders, he says, can cause "weak and stunned men to burst the strongest constraints, sometimes even heavy chains that would tear apart their muscles if they were in their natural state."[52]

How could such biological events be explained? Cabanis believed that there was "a great difference between the mechanical strength of the muscle fibers and the various living forces which animate them." Almost a century later, the philosopher-psychologist Bain offered his own version of the same theory: "Distinct from mere muscular power is Spontaneity, or the active temperament; meaning the natural proneness to copious muscular activity. This must be regarded as a property, not of the muscular tissue, but of the nerve-centres on the active side of the brain." And it is the resident of the British Isles who points out the athletic dimension of this theory: "It is usually men of abounding natural activity that make adroit mechanics, good sportsmen, and able combatants"—an example of that range of performance types so often referred to in commentaries on human performance toward the end of the nineteenth century. Given a strongly developed nervous system, Bain says, there is "a natural exuberance of all the mental manifestations; and energy of mind is then compatible with much bodily feebleness, yet not with any circumstances that restrict the nourishment of the brain."[53] The critical organ, in other words, was not the musculature but the mind. As in Cabanis, it is sometimes difficult while reading Bain to separate the constitutional and the neurological factors, for he clearly meant to combine them. For it is "the Natural Vigour of the constitution" that makes possible the discharge of an accumulated store of inward energy:

> The effect is explosive, like a shot, or the bursting open of a floodgate. It would not be difficult at those moments, indeed it would be the natural thing, to perform some great feat. The boy let out from school, incontinently leaps over ditches, breaks down barriers, and displaces heavy bodies; and should these operations be required at the moment, no special or extraordinary stimulus would be needed to bring the requisite power into play.[54]

We would say in our modern idiom that this boy is "psyched up" the way an athlete should be in preparation for performing "great feats" of his own. The difference between Bain's and our view of this state of mind is that we bring to it new ambitions about human performance and thus a new set of expectations about the exploitation of mental energy. Modern sports psychologists describe these mental states with more theoretical sophistication and attempt to manipulate them, but they have not created a scientific psychology of performance that is much more advanced than that of a Victorian like Bain. He was a painstaking psychologist of "the muscular feelings," and he well knew that "muscular exertion" involved a special state of mind "signified by such phrases as 'the sense of power,' 'the feeling of energy put forth,' 'the experience of force or resistance.' "[55] But Bain was a taxonomist rather than a potential manipulator of such feelings, and that is what makes him a "premodern" thinker about the mental dynamics of performance. When he writes of "*mental* stimulants," he is classifying a natural phenomenon rather than describing potential techniques for boosting human capacities.

Cabanis's "vaporous" women are a striking addition to the theory of pathological energy. The idea that delicate women could, in his words, "in their convulsive episodes burst restraints that would be beyond the powers of several men"[56] had the appeal of a charming and scientifically interesting paradox. Could a "nervous woman" ever lose "the turbulence of her electric sensibility?" Michel Lévy asked rhetorically in 1850.[57] By the turn of the century the "muscular force" of the human female in an agitated state had been quantified by the French physiologist Vaschide, who described his thirty-year-old subject as follows:

> She was a normal subject, but in the course of her life she had experienced several unusually violent shocks, considerable worry and unexpected emotions. One evening, under the impression that burglars were entering her house, she seized in self-defense the dynamometer which lay on her table and had been used each day to test her muscular force. The investigator was astonished to find a record of 53 kgs., an amount which in her natural state the subject could never attain even with her two hands.[58]

As Vaschide had recently pointed out, the fear of death was "an emotion which has a physiognomy entirely its own from a psychological standpoint,"[59] and now the dynamometer had verified its special powers. His ideas about the sources of abnormal strength were almost indistinguishable from those of Cabanis, although presented in a more up-to-date scientific vocabulary: "A large number of dynamographic and ergographic experiments have convinced me that muscular force has a far more complex nature than is generally supposed, and that to our unusual ideas of purely muscular force must be added a conception which, for lack of a better term, I propose to call 'neuro-muscular force' or 'subconscious muscular excitability.' " Vaschide seems unaware that Cabanis, Bain, and no doubt other scientists had been convinced of this distinction long before he announced it. Like his predecessors, Vaschide noted that extraordinary strength could result from a variety of disorders: epilepsy, melancholia, hysteria, somnambulism, and delusions. But the passage of a century had produced little more than an updated vocabulary for describing these puzzling states of mind. As we will see later in this chapter, the passage of yet another century has yielded little more in the way of scientific findings that could be applied to athletic performance.

The physiological traditions articulated by Vaschide and constitutional theory have been absorbed and modernized in the writings of Philippe Tissié, the pioneering sports psychologist and sports physician of his epoch. Tissié was very interested in the relationship between psychopathological states and athletic training, but his own treatment of this connection is diametrically opposed to that of Cabanis and his successors. While Cabanis had seen the pathological state as the source of prodigal energy and performance, Tissié saw athletic training as a source of psychopathology. Intensive training, he wrote in 1896, causes the same "psychopathological phenomena" found in hysteria and hypnotic states, including hallucinations, phobias, and obsessions.[60] More than twenty years later Tissié was still warning against the consequences of exhaustion [forçage], including split personality, hallucinations, delirium, amnesia, and even heart failure.[61] An echo of the tradition that conjoined pathology and high performance can be heard in Tissié's observation that certain psychopathological states like neurasthenia, phobias, and epilepsy are actually advantageous for physical training.[62] Here is the ambivalence toward physical exertion that appears in his writings from time to time: His predominant note is a warning against forcing the organism into unnatural states, while the scientist inside him cannot resist thinking about the physiological implications of what he has found. Nevertheless, what Tissié brought to the subject of athletic exertion was primarily a physician's genuine concern. Cabanis the physician did not live long enough to observe cyclists pedaling themselves into various states of exhaustion; writing a century before Tissié, it did not occur to him to analyze the toxins in their urine as Tissié did (see Chapter 3). Given the simultaneous occurrence of pathology and great strength, Cabanis marveled at the strength and assigned the pathology to its proper place in nature. For the later physician like Tissié who both saw and predicted the consequences of high-performance sport, this kind of medical voyeurism would be ethically indefensible.

In appropriating nineteenth-century French constitutional theory, Tissié used the terms "constitution," "temperament," and even "idiosyncrasy" as late as 1919, but always in the modern context of his own physiology of exertion. Constitution, he says, determines a man's "nervous potential" and therefore his susceptibility to fatigue; "temperaments" now refer to degrees of health or illness. While thereby medicalizing the idea of temperament, Tissié did not really propose a variation of the classic fourfold model, though it is at least detectable in the three "classes" of men, based on their "physical, psychological, and psychophysical reactions," he had proposed in 1901. The *muscular* type comprised athletes with powerful muscles and undeveloped brains, the *cerebral* types were physically stunted despisers of all physical exercise known by their "impotent smile," while the *cerebro-muscular* types exhibited normal development of both physical and intellectual faculties. Tissié's reduction of the traditional classification to the single cerebro-muscular axis reminds us that Cabanis, too, had stressed the relationship between muscles and nerves.[63]

Tissié subdivided the athletic temperament into three types, an innovation that points forward to many future speculations about the relationship between personality and athletic aptitude. In other words, he functionalized the idea of "temperament" by making it nothing more than the athlete's emotional response to his coach. The "passive" type responds directly to the will of his trainer; the "affective" type requires assurances of his ability and a soft touch; the "affirmative" type is wholly unreceptive to either of these approaches, requiring the coach to doubt his ability so that the athlete can prove the contrary. According to Tissié, it is those who belong to the last category who make the superior athletes, competing to the point of exhaustion and transcending themselves, "since their will-power increases along with the obstacles they face."[64] Once a coach has categorized the athlete, Tissié suggests, he can manipulate the psyche of his protégé in order to get the most out of him.

Tissié's dramatic portrayal of the relationship between the athlete and his trainer was in striking contrast to his lack of interest in pushing the human organism to its limit. He believed, in fact, that training itself was a kind of hypnotic suggestion, that athlete and trainer were bound together in an unconscious partnership in which each sacrificed a part of his autonomy. "As a rule," he says, "the man who is trained is worth no more than his trainer, whose role is to exhaust himself on behalf of the man he is training." At the same time, the athlete had to subordinate his own personality to that of the coach. The result, says Tissié was a two-part creature whose brain was the coach and whose spinal cord was the athlete, a kind of automaton analogous to a man in a hypnotic trance.[65] This idea of a team approach to developing sportive force of will is a prescient tour de force.

The most powerful of all the "dynamogenic agents," Tissié wrote, is willpower.[66] In this formula he invoked one of the predominant psychological mysteries of the turn-of-the-century period. "We have learned but little concerning the nature of the voluntary nervous impulse," an American physiologist wrote in 1892, "and almost nothing as to its source, and the influences which determine its strength." It was clear to him, however, that willpower was a key component of human performance and that the fatigue studies of this period could not ignore its role in sustaining or subverting physical endurance. This scientist's experiments on voluntary muscular contractions had convinced him that it was not "the will power as a whole" that experienced fatigue but rather "certain of the central nervous system mechanisms" whose endurance could be increased by exercise—an optimistic finding, indeed. Why? Because in 1891, by contrast, another scientist had pointed out that, while willpower could not contract the fatigued muscle of an experimental subject, an electrical current could. Hence the will must be deficient.[67] In retrospect, we can see that these findings were relevant to the potential boosting of athletic performance, but these men were not thinking about willpower in these terms. The American physiologist does mention running and boat races as productive of fatigue, but only incidentally. The aim of his work was to explore the psychophysiological complexity of the fatigue mechanism, not to boost the performances of runners and oarsmen.[68]

At the same time, the study of human volition was, of course, recognized as having potential uses. Clearly, the link between willpower and fatigue was of practical interest if boosting or preserving the former could diminish or abolish the latter. The fatigue researcher

Angelo Mosso had pointed out that climbers who led the way up a mountain tired much faster than those who followed, perhaps because the greater degree of attention required fatigued the laboring body more quickly. This might be why the insane sometimes appeared immune to fatigue, since they were incapable of focusing attention on their own bodies.[69] From a modern perspective one is tempted to ask whether there might be artificial insanities that could boost athletic performance, and whether the sporting public would tolerate such methods. As the following suggests, I think it would not.

The concept of willpower is, after all, inherent in our traditional idea of the athlete. Willpower gives authenticity to athletic performance because this form of desire is characteristically human and suggests courage; machines can perform, but only human beings can *will* a performance. The possibility of unauthentic desire in the stadium accounts for the instinctive revulsion we feel toward the robotic athlete—doped or hypnotized into a trance—who haunts the future of sport.[70] Modern civilization's sensitivity to such altering of human identity to boost athletic performance can be traced back to concerns about "psycho-doping" that appear after the First World War.

Such ethical concerns about boosting athletic performance psychologically (or pharmacologically) do not appear, however, in the scientific literature of the fin de sièle. There is much curiosity and even wonderment at the capacities of the human organism, but anxieties about boosting it too far seem to have been confined to science fiction (see Chapter 4). The fact that this anxiety was still a rarity is, of course, a significant cultural marker of this period. In his physiological studies of vegetarian athletes, the German physiologist Caspari noted "the enormous influence of willpower on maximal physical performances" and pointed out that the discipline required to maintain a meatless regimen already suggested that the vegetarian possessed superior willpower. Caspari called this state of mind out-and-out fanaticism, but he never suggests that this is somehow an unfair advantage, and he discusses the use of alcohol by Tissié's rider Stéphane with similar equanimity.[71]

Evidently, the similarity between willpower and the socially prized faculty we call courage helps to account for this lack of concern about the ethics of psychological performance-boosting. For one thing, boosting the strength of the will against the threat of fatigue had obvious military significance and was a widespread popular preoccupation. For these reasons alone, artificial constraints on developing force of will simply made no sense. Fin de siècle France, as

Robert A. Nye has shown, saw a boom in "popular self-help books on will-therapy" and the conquering of timidity, spurred in part by the enduring national trauma of the Franco-Prussian War.[72] Anti-Semitic defamations of the Jewish male inside and outside of European military establishments often included allegations of cowardice, or an innate lack of will, and the Zionist press of this period carried articles both challenging the traditional idea of courage and in one case proposing a "psychological exercise" to develop courage in the same manner as logical thinking and moral fiber. The latter author's point was that real courage was an acquired rather than an inborn faculty and thus more reliable than reckless daring. Gymnastics, fencing, and mountain-climbing, he says, are the best sports for developing courage in young Jews.[73]

The scientific basis of these will-therapies was uncertain at best, because no one understood the conditions that gave rise to bravery, cowardice, or timidity. In his study of fear, Mosso offered a physiological explanation to account for sudden and unexpected reactions to this kind of psychological stress. "One must be a physician," he wrote, "in order to see how the most courageous men become faint-hearted at a trifling loss of blood, and timid people, in consequence of a more abundant flow of blood to the brain, perform miracles of bravery. Weakness quickens the heartbeat even when we are not moved by anything." Having separated the psychological (the emotion of fear) from the physiological (blood flow to the brain), Mosso now confronted the problem of establishing their sequence, the relation of cause to effect. In the passage above he implies that blood flow precedes the eruption of bravery into the timid psyche: A physiological cause produced a psychological effect. Yet in a later passage he suggests the reserve, that it is the man who "resolutely determines to overcome a difficulty" who actually modifies the circulation in his own brain, with the result that "we sometimes see deeds performed by the pusillanimous such as were never expected of them."[74] In the last analysis, Mosso pronounced excessive fear a "disease," but the psychophysiology of courage and cowardice remained as much a mystery to him as to others.

The battlefield was another "laboratory" for the testing of willpower. In the psychological comparisons of the solder and the athlete that appear from time to time in the constitutional and psychological literature of the nineteenth and twentieth centuries, the military man is consistently held in higher regard than his athletic counterpart. In his encyclopedia article on *Tempérament*, Dr. Fourcault had claimed that the "nervous" temperament stood up better than the athletic types to the stress of war.[75] During the First World War, according to Tissié, many star athletes had been sent from the front to the rear echelon on account of a "pathological incapacity for combat."[76] Every military doctor knows how inferior sports stars and professionals can be when confronted with the military's demand for hardness, all-round performance capacity, and mental attitude, a Swiss doctor wrote in 1937,[77] and the German Wehrmacht apparently agreed with him. A degree in sports, its military psychologists insisted, was not an adequate assessment of willpower.[78] Only the British psychologist Karl Pearson, steeped in traditional views about the playing fields of Eton, went on record claiming that "the athletic boy . . . should make a better soldier than the non-athletic."[79]

These observations suggest that medical men did not always see sport as the school of courage many others took it to be, and here was one more reason not to worry about excessively stimulating the will in the stadium. Questions about the legitimacy of psychologically boosting athletic performance arose instead in the context of the doping debate in Germany, because drugs and the psyche are related themes. As one physician in Berlin put it, doping worked psychologically or not at all; therefore, if the many drugs and concoctions being marketed as rejuvenating and fortifying formulas counted as doping, then inspirational cries of encouragement belonged in the category of "psychological doping."[80] Similarly, an outspoken critic of pharmacological doping condemned excessive encouragement directed at an athlete, since the issue for a traditionalist like him was the difference between assisted and unassisted performance.[81] On the other side of the debate was the industrial psychologist ("psychotechnician") Robert Werner Schulte, who argued that relieving an athlete's precompetition anxiety was not at all different from lifting a friend's spirits when he was depressed.[82] This position was still being argued in 1968 (at the Second International Congress of Sport Psychology held in Washington, D.C.) by a Spanish psychologist who argued that using tranquilizers "to normalize an unusual state in an athlete" should not be considered doping.[83]

German Sports Psychology Between the Wars

Psychological writing on sport flourished in Germany between the world wars, and much of this interesting work can be traced back to the extraordinary achievements of German physiology and medicine. The sheer size and ability of this scientific establishment, the recognition of the psychological factor in sport by many physicians and physiologists, and the rise of sport as a form of mass culture during the 1920s combined to produce a large and diverse body of commentary on the psychophysiological foundations of athletic performance. This scientific literature belongs to a cultural and intellectual world quite different from that of today's sports psychologist, who is neither medically trained nor interested in the history of psychological thinking about sport. Our sports psychologists are interested in techniques that produce results; the German medical men and others we are about to meet were concerned about understanding rather than enhancing the performances of athletes. Because to them the harmonious development of the individual counted for more than technical innovation, these men often opposed the cult of performance to which modern sports psychology is primarily devoted.

Psychological thinking about sport in Weimar Germany continued to use four approaches that dated from the nineteenth century: constitutional theory, pathological physiology, hypnotic techniques, and psychological testing. The dramatic revival of constitution and temperament in the medical literature resulted from the work of the psychiatrist Ernst Kretschmer, whose 1921 work *Physique and Temperament* had a profound effect on European psychiatry. His theory of constitutional types was a refurbished, if ostensibly more scientific, version of the nineteenth-century French systems built on the fourfold division into respiratory, digestive, muscular, and cerebral types. His novel achievement was to demonstrate an apparent correlation between three newly defined body types and two forms of mental illness.[84] He had observed that a disproportionate number of manic-depressive patients showed the heavy, compact, fatty body structure he called the "pyknic" type; whereas a disproportionate number of schizophrenic patients showed the body types he called "athletic" and "asthenic," the former characterized by a well-developed skeleton and musculature, and the latter by thinness and above-average height.[85] But these findings alone were not enough to make Kretschmer the controversial figure he became. His revolutionary step was to apply this classificatory system not only to abnormal personalities but also to the population at large, thereby erasing even more of the line separating the normal and the pathological that had begun to erode during the nineteenth century.

Kretschmer was not interested in sport; indeed, *Physique and*

Temperament refers to sport only as an eccentric interest of certain subjects described in the book. The athletic type [*Athletiker*] is a constitutional type rather than a sportive one, and its male and female representatives are subjected to aesthetic criticism: "The bodily constitution of the athletic woman gives us on an average more the impression of abnormality, of extreme overdevelopment, of unpleasant stolidity and massiveness than does that of the athletic male, and for this reason: these men at times come quite near our aesthetic ideal, while our ideal of female beauty is far overstepped by the athletic female."[86] This viewpoint was promulgated in a more polemical fashion by some of his contemporaries, but Kretschmer saw himself as the objective observer. His athletic type is thus intended as an empirically valid scientific construction, not as a modern version of the Germanic hero.

Kretschmer's unromantic attitude toward sport is further evident in his 1936 monograph *The Personality of the Athletic Type*, in which he defends his claim that the athletic type is not simply an intermediate form between the pyknic and asthenic types, but rather one of the fundamental human types. Franz Weidenreich had argued in 1927 that Kretschmer had erred in basing the athletic type on as superficial (malleable) a trait as muscular development. "It seems questionable," Weidenreich wrote, "that the degree to which the musculature can be developed is linked to the presence of a special constitutional factor,"[87] although he does concede that extraordinary physical performances may be connected to a special constitutional factor.[88] In his rebuttal, Kretschmer, who was not interested in looking at constitution from this point of view,[89] portrayed the "athletic" type as a unitary syndrome, associating the physical performances of "athletic" soldiers and athletes with their phlegmatic dispositions and diminished responsiveness to external stimuli.[90] In addition, he shows no interest in devising ways to improve physical performance.[91]

Nor does Kretschmer show any interest in promoting the athletic type as an ideal type. At a time when some sports physicians and scientists were invoking German athletic successes at the 1936 Berlin Olympiad as evidence of the nation's new-found greatness, Kretschmer offered his colleagues a portrait of the athletic type that is downright unflattering. According to Kretschmer, the "athletic" temperament has a bipolar structure that includes both a "viscous placidity" and an "explosive tendency." He presents these people as physically clumsy and as intellectual and emotional dullards. Relative to other human types, they lack imagination, humor, and the capacity to be critical; even their gait and speech habits have a distinctively sluggish quality.[92]

Kretschmer even makes a point of debunking the contemporary image of the athletic lifestyle:

> There is a widespread notion that the athletic individual is above all the active and energetic person, where the musculature is regarded as standing for the will pure and simple. This idea does not stand up to scrutiny, but rather contradicts the conclusions we have reached. . . . The energy of the athletic type is far more and predominantly passive, oriented toward calmness and tenacity.[93]

Following a different line of reasoning than this skeptic, German physicians and trainers were hoping that constitutional theory could develop a "doctrine of types" the could select athletic talent for specific events. Kretschmer's "athletic" type, for example, represented a version of the traditional insensate mesomorph—a human type who offered obvious advantages to the athletic trainer looking for brute strength. In 1923 Wilhelm Kohlrausch published the results of an anthropomorphic survey of athletes he had carried out at the Deutsche Kampfspiele competitions the previous year. He describes the following types according to body structure and temperament: sprinter, middle-distance runner, long-distance runner, long-distance skier, ski jumper, high jumper, multievent athlete, swimmer, throwing athlete, weight-throwing athlete, wrestler, boxer, soccer player, gymnast. But how accurately could one really predict the specific body type—let alone the character traits—of a particular type of athlete?

The answer, Kohlrausch argued, lay in correlations between athletic specialty and temperament. He claimed, for example, that sprinters and high jumpers were generally "sanguine" types, while long-distance runners and weight-throwers were predominantly "phlegmatic." Although he did not mention Kretschmer, his constitutional types corresponded to those of his fellow researcher to a striking degree. Like others at this time, he presented the multievent athlete (pentathlete, decathlete) as a physical and characterological ideal type.[94] Kohlrausch's sport typology was, then, an applied constitutional psychology that looked for the foundations of performance within the body as it was naturally constituted. It was prescriptive only in that it proposed to match constitutional types with appropriate athletic challenges, its function being to identify talent rather than develop it further. This conservative approach was by definition an "early" sports psychology as opposed to the more interventionist techniques that have become a familiar, if scientifically unproved, part of high-performance sport.

The application of constitutional theory to sport was only one example of what eventually became known in Germany as "aptitude testing," a branch of industrial psychology. A 1930 essay on this topic by the physical educationalist Carl Krümmel illustrates the limited role of body typing within the sportive aptitude testing of this period. His point of departure, like Kretschmer's, was the trained observer's total impression of a human being, for which Krümmel used the term *Habitus*. It included both the "external impression" and the "internal state" of the body, incorporating such components as age, growth pattern, biological reactivity, inherited traits, and lifestyle.[95] But Krümmel concluded that it was simply too early to apply constitutional theory to sport, because the basic research had not been done. "The value of pursuing typological questions in sport," he wrote, "depends on training the observer to spot those natural abilities which are expressed in the body structure." But he, like Kohlrausch, had to ask whether this kind of talent-spotting was even possible. In the last analysis, Krümmel's assessment of sportive aptitude had more to say about the mind than about the body. The most effective form of "doping," he said, is the carefully trained athlete's will to win. Yet he did not consider winning the real point of sport. For the goal of sports psychology, says Krümmel, is "to train a human being to transcend himself at a given moment"; the value of sport lies in this experience rather than in competitive success.[96] Here is an affirmation of quality over quantity that would retain its prestige in German sports circles well into the twentieth century, even though such cultural conservatism was, of course, incompatible with the cult of performance Germans could see proliferating all around them.

By the end of the 1920s, the body-structure approach to finding athletic aptitude was recognized as a failure. But if the key to athletic ability could not be found in physique, some speculated that it was associated with temperament. This was the approach of Dr. Walther Schulz, who attempted to correlate personality and sportive aptitude within Kretschmer's constitutional model. Schulz began by demonstrating the inadequacy of the body-typing approach to sportive talent. He had no trouble showing that body types varied widely within groups of elite sprinters and other performers, and he bolstered his argument by pointing to the case of the great Finnish running star Paavo Nurmi, whose multiple world-records and Olympic championships, he says, had astonished medical science. According to a Finnish sports expert, Nurmi had once been "a heavy-limbed youth with a barrel chest" who had transformed his body through training. His high-performance body could not, therefore, be identified with a specific constitutional type.[97]

In this vein, Schulz emphasized environmental factors over genetic ones. The formative influences, he said, are ethnological and climatic. The hard winter of Northern Europe promotes the toughness and endurance of the long-distance skier, the lively and impulsive Rhinelander differs from the more taciturn and self-willed Westphalian type, and so forth. But Schulz adheres to the constitutional model by claiming that these "essential inner differences" are manifested in such outer (physical) traits as language, gesture, and movement. These differences become evident, say, in the contrasting physical styles of "mechanical, almost machine-like" distance runners like Nurmi and the "more temperamental, more elastic, more rhythmic" sprinters.[98]

The theoretical basis of Schulz's system was the "structural psychology" of Professor Erich Jaensch, whom Schulz describes as "one of the most distinguished minds in the world of German scholarship." (Jaensch eventually became a pillar of Nazi psychology.)[99] Jaensch's bipolar model contrasts the "disintegrated type" (D-type) with the "integrated" type (J-type). Whereas the D-type is characterized by his willpower and insensitivity toward those around him, the J-type allows feeling a greater role in his life and forms emotional ties to other people. Similarly, in the world of sport, there are "two completely different [personality] structures." The first is characterized by an iron will to win, the second by self-consciousness and sensitivity to external stimuli that is absent in the former type.[100] It is not surprising that the physician Walther Jaensch, brother of the more famous Erich, took the latter's typology even farther than Schulz by equating the D-type and J-type with masculine and feminine types, respectively. This dualism enabled him to contrast the characterological style of the "sportive man of willpower" with that of artists, women, and children—the unvirile multitude.[101] Such developments within constitutional theory show how easily it could be adapted to the ideological program of the German cultural conservatives.

Racialistic thinking was basic to this conservative agenda, and constitutional theory easily lent itself to racial interpretation. Given their fixation on the appearance of the human body, it is hardly surprising that theories of "constitution" and "temperament" had been haunted by racial ideas since the growth of "scientific" racism during the latter part of the nineteenth century.[102] It was inevitable that the struggle for and against the racializing of Kretschmer's constitutional types would begin shortly after he proposed them,[103] and that the search for sportive "types" would lead to the usual thinking about racial types as well. Were certain races better suited to some sports than were others? Did some races possess athletic aptitudes that other peoples did not? Both Krümmel and the sports physician Ferdinand Hueppe took up this nineteenth-century anthropological question (see Chapter 2) in some detail but reached few conclusions about racial abilities in sport.[104] (These observers regarded the prodigious high-jumping ability of the Watusi and Finnish achievements in throwing events and distance running as the conspicuous exceptions to this rule.)[105] Krümmel, in particular, was quite ambivalent about this kind of speculation. On the one hand, he did believe that some race-specific physical and characterological traits signified difference rather than superiority or inferiority; he also noted that universal demands for physical performance had produced a full range of body types within each racial group, and that such differences *within* races were always greater than differences *between* races.[106] Once again, the body had proved to be an inadequate criterion of difference between human types.

The more subtle alternative to body typing was character typing, and in 1929 the fine German-Jewish sprinter Ernst Jokl[107] applied "the epochmaking work" of Kretschmer to the problem of identifying athletic temperaments. Jokl's innovation was to contrast an "imperturbable" Type I, exemplified by the indefatigable and preternaturally calm Paavo Nurmi, with a "sensitive" Type II, represented by the neurologically high-strung Jewish boxer, sprinter, or soccer player.[108] It is hardly necessary to point out that Jokl's emotionally inert endurance athlete and hyperactive speedster were variations on the muscular and nervous types of the nineteenth century. They were also athleticized stereotypes of Germans and Jews that had established themselves in German racial folklore over many decades prior to their exploitation by Jewish self-reformers and anti-Semites alike during and after the fin de siècle.[109] The inherent athletic inferiority of the Jews was generally taken for granted, and Jokl was only one of many authors to address this "problem."[110] That a self-respecting Jew like Jokl could publish this typology in a Zionist newspaper in Berlin as late as 1929 tells us a great deal about the respectability of racialistic thinking before its definitive disgrace by the Nazis.

Although the constitutional theories we have just reviewed represented a new wave in medical psychiatry during the 1920s, this was clearly an outmoded type of scientific thinking, largely intuitional and based, of course, on an ancient model. Its bid for scientific status rested on the "modern constitutional pathology" that defined constitution in terms of biological reactivity, function rather than form. The claim that it was an "idealistic" medicine of German origin, disdaining specialization in favor of treating "the whole person," only confirmed its attachment to the past.[111] Merely dressing up nineteenth-century ideas about the mind-body relationship could not produce a biological psychiatry of lasting value.

The second nineteenth-century theory that appeared in Germany during the 1920s was the idea that extraordinary physical performances were rooted in extreme psychophysiological states. In the writings of Cabanis, as we have seen, "extreme" physiology meant some sort of disorder or acute sensitivity. In the wake of the Darwinian revolution, abnormal physiology in this sense came to include the physiology of the "primitive," as well. Thus in his essay on "Wild Men and Beast-Children" (1863), the prominent British anthropologist E.B. Tylor wrote of the extraordinary climbing and leaping ability of "Peter the Wild Boy" and others who had grown up as exiles from civilization, including "the two boys seen to leap from crag to crag, like goats, in the Pyrenees, in 1719."[112] This association of physical ability with atavistic human types is implicit in the racial analyses of Hueppe and Krümmel, who believed that savage peoples [*Naturvölker*] possessed special physical aptitudes. But the relationship between sport and primitive man did not end here. Krümmel saw modern sport itself as a reversion to a primitive stage of human development.[113] Was there, then, a link between physical performance and the most primitive level of human personality?

August Bier thought so. This prominent surgeon and former high-jumper argued that the amazing physical feats of epileptics and the mentally disturbed offered clues to the psychophysiological origins of high-performance achievements in sport. Bier believed that the human being could never exert all of his muscular strength in a normal state of mind. "This kind of exertion is a very rare event made possible by powerful mental stimuli and the simultaneous elimination of inhibitions." He himself watched a mentally disturbed man execute a fantastic jump in the waiting room of another doctor's office, a performance Bier reckoned as equivalent to what the current world champion might have done. He theorized that the human organism possessed "reserves of strength" that even experienced scientists had ignored; more specifically, he speculated that individual groups of muscle fibers almost never experience simultaneous maximal stimulation, which accounts for the limited range of "normal" performances. To support this view, he cited the observation of the psychiatrist Richard Krafft-Ebing that there are mentally ill people who are virtually immune to feelings of fear, exhaustion, and pain.[114]

In a second theory about exceptional physical performances, Bier applied his observations about mentally disturbed subjects to the problem of fatigue. He cited findings that involuntary ("automatically performed") effort had been found to be less fatiguing than ordinary effort. While accepting the traditional theory that fatigue substances caused muscles to tire, Bier also believed that mental states could suppress the effects of those substances in certain situations—mind conquering matter—and that this source of extraordinary energy within the human organism did not have to be of pathological origin. The exhausted hunter who is suddenly energized by the prospect of an imminent kill is "not crazy, but rather completely healthy." The "passion of the hunt" originated, not in insanity, but in "an inherited, idealized version of the predatory instinct."[115] In this sense the primitive part of man was a unique source of energy for a variety of performances.

Bier's meditations on the uninvestigated sources of high performance accentuated the importance of sheer emotion. The fear of death or stirrings of maternal love, for example, could summon up the "reserve strength" that remained quiescent until an emergency called it to life. Science, he noted, had hitherto ignored the fact that "joy, interest, passion that becomes fanaticism and even madness—it is a gradual transition from one to the other—boost performance to an extraordinary degree." Having learned that epileptics, like apes and primitive peoples, climbed with their feet, Bier concluded that "in these people the thin veneer of civilization so-called has been stripped away, and that primeval drives and capacities concealed in their genomes are brought back to life again."[116] But he did not so much as hint that there might be ways to reach the atavistic core of human nature and release its concealed energies. As in the case of constitutional theory, this was diagnostic rather than prescriptive thinking about sport. Yet even a man with a method, as our next case study shows, was not necessarily interested in boosting performance.

While the German psychiatrist Johannes Heinrich Schultz (1884–1970) is remembered by modern sports psychologists as the inventor of "autogenic training," a self-hypnosis technique used to promote relaxation, his scientific descendants seem to know nothing of the cultural context in which he worked and wrote. [117] Schultz is an interesting example of how an otherwise conscientious professional adapted his career to the political climate of Nazi Germany. The historian Geoffrey Cocks has provided a memorable portrait of Schultz as "the prototype of the in-house pragmatist who regularly snapped 'Heil Hitler' over the telephone but who, in actuality, had no real party or government affiliation." [118] His acquiescence to the Nazi regime was rooted both in nationalistic feelings and in the cultural conservatism of the interwar period. This antimodern attitude shaped his view of sport in ways that would undoubtedly surprise those who have tried to turn his techniques to the task of boosting athletic performance.

Schultz's interest in the practical application of hypnotic techniques was stimulated by the work in the 1890s of the psychologist Oscar Vogt, whose research journal was filled with contributions from other scientists describing the application of hypnotism to drug addiction, bedwetting, constipation, hysteria, paralysis, and the pregnant woman in labor. [119] The foundation of Schultz's own method, he wrote in 1932, was "rational-physiological exercises" that made possible the "performances" achieved by the suggestive mental states of traditional hypnosis. Far from being the sort of cookbook self-therapy with which we are so familiar, this "autogenic" training was to be practiced only under medical supervision. In this area, Schultz says, it is obviously impossible "to provide recipes." What he did claim was that this "focused inner gymnastics" enabled the patient to control otherwise autonomic functions, calm himself down, eliminate pain, and improve his memory to an extent that traditional gymnastics exercises could not. [120]

Schultz's interest in relaxation mandated an interest in the body and the physical experiences that could affect it. He believed that feelings and bodily states were intimately bound together, "that every feeling experience is a total experience, so that our feelings respond above all to the totality of the body's movements," and he recognized an "analogy" between his own autogenic training and the various schools of therapeutic gymnastics. But this also meant accepting the cultural conservative view of sport as "one-sided" exercise that trained men like racehorses, a critique that in Germany dates from the 1880s.[121] For the cultural conservatives, sport's fixation on performance made it an antitherapeutic experience that turned the living organism into "a dead mechanism that moves." Schultz subscribed to this view and even described traditional German gymnastics (*Turnen*) in the same terms, criticizing its "one-sided" cultivation of strength and tension.[122]

Schultz's view of sport was not, however, entirely negative. Pursued with moderation, he thought, sport could offer some of the benefits of his autogenic training. But he consistently opposed the high-performance ideal, preferring to see in sport a means of cultivating self-esteem that was more important than the performance itself. A sport like riding could develop willpower by exposing the athlete to moments of danger, yet, Schultz insisted, the psychological goal of this exercise was just the opposite of conventional approaches to pumping the athlete full of "energy" and "courage." The contemporary fixation on setting records was exactly what he regarded as a deformation of physical culture. Perhaps the crucial observation here is that Schultz went out of his way to dissociate sport from the military model of training: It was not a school of "hardness" or of "steeling" the recruit.[123] This refusal to accommodate the performance principle makes Schultz an anomalous predecessor of the achievement-obsessed psychologists who today market their services to athletes and many others who want to "perform" in the modern world.

Sports Psychology as Psychic Engineering

Our contemporary "sports psychologists" have, in fact, completely shifted the emphasis from assessing the human organism to boosting whatever capacities it has. The only remnant of constitutional theory left today is the elusive search for personality traits that may promote athletic achievement.[124] Wonderment at the physical feats of epileptics and frightened women has been replaced by attempts to produce unusual mental states. Only the autogenic training of J.H. Schultz survives as the prototype of relaxation therapies that might benefit the anxious athlete. While the scientific value of the modern procedures remains uncertain, the global search for competitive advantages in high-performance sport has created a market for practitioners whose theories and credentials deserve examination. The quest for scientific credibility has also lead to the transformation of sports psychology into a form of popular culture analogous to the "human potential" movement of the 1960s. Its romantic theories of untapped energy and mind-body unity recall the naive psychophysiology of the fin de siècle and its speculations about human limits, the power of "nerve-force," and the conquering of fatigue. What is new is the idea that the mind can be manipulated to improve athletic performance, and that these manipulations can be understood in a scientific manner. We will find, however, that both of these claims are difficult to confirm, and that sports psychology is most interesting as a receptacle for the fantasies of its practitioners, their clients, and others who find their wishes fulfilled by this late twentieth-century attempt to re-create, if unwittingly, the optimism of late nineteenth-century psychophysiology and its promise of unlimited human performance.

The idea that the athlete can be liberated from performance-inhibiting restraints, that he or she can transcend the normal state, is the romantic core of modern sports psychology, as confirmed by many anecdotal accounts of this kind. The British psychologist John E. Kane once described the case of a runner who underwent hypnoanalysis to find out why he was unable to repeat a peak performance. After the first phase of the procedure had been completed, the athlete was asked whether he wanted to continue with this "insight training." He chose not to, apparently because his record race had been a very painful experience. "Of course," Dr. Kane commented, "it would have been quite simple to reconstruct 'cognitive strategies' during hypnosis with an aim toward dissociation of pain during running competition in the waking state. However, since the athlete did not wish to pursue such avenues, 'the case was closed.' "[125] Here, as in the case of the inhibited cyclist that opened this chapter, the blithe technical confidence of the psychological practitioner suggests that psychological engineering is a routine, and routinely effective, part of elite sport. A similar but less orthodox method used on swimmers was once described by the German psychologist Henner Ertel: "Through a receiver in one ear we send a continuous barrage of nonsense questions to the part of the brain which handles conscious perception, until it has virtually ceased to function. Simultaneously, through a second receiver in the other ear, we send simple messages to the unconscious which penetrate directly because the conscious mind is blocked off."[126] Once again, the efficacy of the procedure is taken for granted, not least because many of us have an irrational tendency to assume that invasive or "surgical" procedures are effective ones.

The much less dramatic truth is that "sports psychology" is an eclectic group of theories and therapies in search of scientific respectability, as its more sophisticated academic theorists openly acknowledge.[127] Its methods include behavior modification techniques; somatic procedures like biofeedback, progressive relaxation, and anti-anxiety drugs; cognitive-behavioral procedures such as rational-emotive therapy, cognitive restructuring, and hypnosis; stress management; goal setting; positive thinking; and the "covert rehearsal" strategies better known as "visualization" or "mental practice."[128] In one case, a psychologist using family therapy methods counseled the trainer of a West German handball team over the telephone—a group dynamic as opposed to the more common individual approach.[129] Our focus, however, is less the techniques themselves, which are explained in many popular manuals, than their origins and reception by elite athletes and the wider public to whom they are marketed. For judging from the evidence to date, these techniques and the promotional campaigns that sell them are more significant as cultural trends than as demonstrably effective factors in high-performance sport.

The most popular and scientifically credible of these methods are the so-called covert rehearsal strategies, which have been defined as "imagined, symbolic rehearsal of an activity"[130] for the purpose of improving actual performance. The popularity of these methods has resulted in some terminological confusion, since the same basic procedure employing mental imagery has been called "symbolic rehearsal, imaginary practice, implicit practice, mental rehearsal, conceptualizing practice, and mental preparation."[131] One example of this technique that has been used with elite athletes is visuo-motor behavior rehearsal (VMBR), developed by the American psychologist Richard Suinn, whose ultimate goal was to effect a fusion of mind and body that produces perfect physical movements. This attempt to triumph over classic mind-body dualism is the holy grail of elite sports psychology, and Suinn's version of mind and body dissolving into each other is fairly typical: "In my work with relaxation and stress management, I have been extremely impressed by the quality of imagery that is possible after deep muscle relaxation. This imagery is more than visual. It is also tactile, auditory, emotional and muscular." Suinn's "muscular imagery" is a modern version of the "muscular feeling" Alexander Bain had described a century earlier. The difference is that feelings are now called images that are somehow "more than visual"; in addition, these "images" can be put to use in improving athletic performance. In another passage, Suinn once again resorts to metaphor to convey the theme of mind-body unity: "The imagery of visuo-motor behavior rehearsal is more than sheer imagination. It is a well-controlled copy of experience, a sort of body-thinking similar to the powerful illusion of certain dreams at night."[132] The happily paradoxical notion of "body-thinking" expresses the sports psychologist's idea of optimal human functioning.

Similar interest in the relationship between mental imagery and human performance appears as early as Francis Galton's *Inquiries into Human Faculty and its Development* (1883). Like modern proponents of mental practice routines, Galton believed that the ability to create mental images could to some extent be developed. He cites the examples of blindfolded chess players who visualize the separate boards on which they play and musicians who visualize the scores they are playing. There are others, he says, who have "a complete mastery over their mental images," including the ability to visualize a human figure "by mounting it on a bicycle or compelling it to perform gymnastic feats on a trapeze."[133] The crucial difference between Galton's visualizer and his modern counterpart is that the former does not imagine himself as the man in motion. It was a decade later, however, that Étienne-Jules Marey (see Chapter 3) proposed the visualizing exercise that today's entrepreneurs are selling as the latest development in "neuromuscular programming." Marey was the world's premiere photographer of the body in motion, and he believed that an attentive observer could internalize images of athletic movements to good effect by contemplating his photographs:

> In order to render chronophotographs of movements more instructive, these images should be taken from very strong and competent athletes; for example, from the prize-winners at athletic sports. These champions will thus betray the secret of their success, perhaps unconsciously acquired, and which they would doubtless be incapable of defining themselves.
>
> The same method could equally well be applied to the teaching of movements necessary for the execution of various skilled industries. It would show how the stroke of a skilful blacksmith differed from that of a novice. It would be the same in all manual performances, and in all kinds of sport.[134]

Today, Marey's most successful entrepreneurial imitators[135] have adopted his idea of skill emulation and added a purportedly scientific theory of "neuromuscular programming" to attract a modern audience. The self-improvement programs of SyberVision Systems,[136] for example, advertise a "neuropsychology of achievement" that employs "images of achievement" to boost a wide range of human performances. There is "The Neuropsychology of Successful Marriage," The Neuropsychology of Staying Young," a "Creative IQ Booster Kit," "The Neuropsychology of Self-Discipline," "The Neuropsychology of Memory Power," "How to Be a No-Limit Person," and many, many more. An instruction manual for golfers offers the following explanation of the program's effects: "The more you see and hear pure movement, the deeper it becomes imprinted in your nervous system . . . and the more likely you are to perform it as a conditioned reflex," and "The decomposition of what is seen and sensorily experienced into an electromagnetic wave form is accomplished by a complex mathematical operation (Fourier Transform) by the brain." And there is a program titled "Your Holographic Brain: The Power of Three-Dimensional Visualization."[137] Suffice it to say that a team of expert evaluators sponsored by the National Research Council found little merit in this theoretical apparatus. Its members concluded that, while "it is conceivable that programs like Syber-Vision could improve performance," there is no scientific evidence that they do so.[138]

The SyberVision model is little more than the naive psychophysiology of the fin de siècle presented in the cybernetic language of "programming" as well as in the behaviorist language of the "conditioned reflex." "While you watch," says an advertising brochure, "you actually feel a slight rhythmic movement in your own muscles as they imitate and memorize the movements on the screen." This is 1914-vintage speculation about the muscle-brain link once promoted by the American behaviorist John B. Watson.[139] In fact, from an historical standpoint, the supreme irony of the SyberVision program is that its ultracapitalist developers have appropriated behaviorist jargon about the thinking body that was once associated with the Bolshevist conception of human nature (see Chapter 6). In addition, they have reintegrated sport into the broad range of performance types from which it began to emerge a century ago (see Chapter 3). In this case, at least, marketing acumen has re-created an historical event of genuine, if ironic, interest to the cultural historian of sport.

While mental practice exercises are commonly used by athletes, hypnosis has been more significant as an object of fantasy than as a technique. It is striking that early references to hypnosis in relation to sport do not include a hypnotist. Philippe Tissié, as we saw earlier, believed that the athlete in training was in a kind of hypnotic state. But he does not make the athlete's trainer into a hypnotic therapist.

The mental state to which he alludes is presented as an emotional pact between the trainer and his protégé or as a condition accompanying exhaustion; it is not the result of a conscious effort to induce a hypnotic state.[140] The American psychologist Norman Triplett, a contemporary of Tissié's, reported another theory of athletic hypnosis in his study of the psychological effect of competition on cycling performance: "A curious theory, lately advanced, suggests the possibility that the strained attention given to the revolving wheel of the pacing machine in front produces a sort of hypnotism and that the accompanying muscular exaltation is the secret of the endurance shown by some long distance riders in paced races."[141] The fact that neither of these authors proposes a hypnotic procedure to boost performance is additional evidence that manipulative strategies aimed at developing athletes were not characteristic of the 1890s.

Today, hypnosis is seldom mentioned by sports psychologists. An exception is a German psychologist who has argued that hypnosis could replace doping as a performance-enhancing technique, on the grounds that the elite athlete's intuition, emotions, and power of imagination remain underdeveloped with conventional training and could be thus enhanced to provide a competitive advantage.[142] But an American psychologist has argued the reverse, that hypnotic suggestions tend to be effective, not with elite athletes, but with untrained ones.[143] An oft-cited 1961 study of hypnosis and strength associates athletic performance with a "psychologic limit" that can be breached by removing inhibitions, but one of the experiments carried out by these investigators already called this theory into question.[144] And while there may be "controlled cases of phenomenal endurance breakthroughs by well-conditioned athletes after post-hypnotic suggestions,"[145] none that we know of are inscribed in the annals of sport.

In fact, hypnotherapy in sport is less a method than a stimulant to fantasy. It is also a screen onto which our culture projects certain unfulfilled wishes about expanding human potential. It is not surprising that many anecdotal accounts of hypnosis-driven performance breakthroughs circulate among athletes, or that for many people hypnotizing an athlete is considered equivalent to drugging him[146] or unleashing his aggressions.[147] What is more, the imagined power of hypnosis can be applied to more than one field of human achievement. Is it really true that Rachmaninov composed his Second Piano Concerto while hypnotized,[148] we wonder. But what actually took place is less important than our fantasies about what happened if he did. If we assume that a hypnotic trance must have assisted rather than impaired his natural ability—and we do—it is because we take for granted the effectiveness of technical procedures. This unreflective attachment to *techniques* is the real secret of sports psychology.

This infatuation with technique makes the athlete seem to be a one-dimensional being whose mind has dissolved into his or her body. For despite its scientific appearance, the aim of elite sports psychology is to abolish thought itself. As one practitioner has put it, "at times, the goal in sports is to remove psychology, not change it."[149] This is the anthropological dimension of sports psychology, its ideal model of the human organism, and it possesses an unmistakable charisma in a technologized world. In the world of fantasy, the hypnotized athlete is a robot possessed of an inhuman force of will. But in the real world, the athlete who is manipulated with drugs or mental techniques may well be a volunteer. "I could not care less whether I am manipulated or not," a West German champion said in 1972. "The only thing that is important to me is whether I am on the victory stand."[150] Such cynical surrender to manipulation further complicates the ethics involved in trying to boost performance through hypnosis. If these techniques do work, then the athlete who "benefits" has forfeited a psychological vulnerability that is inherent in being an athlete. For the humanity of one's competitor is expressed in that willingness to test his or her emotional resources in the heat of competition.

Even if we agree with these statements of principle, we must also recognize that there is a contrary trend within sports psychology to dehumanize the elite athlete by eliminating emotional vulnerability. Until recently, Westerners have dealt with the temptation to robotize their own athletes by projecting their desire onto the sports scientists of the now-crumbling Communist world and by imagining that Soviet and East German athletes were somehow different from our own. In this episode of mass projection, sports psychologists who romanticized mental techniques from behind the Iron Curtain played an important role in creating the myth of Communist sports science. In other words, some of our legends of Soviet and East German tampering with human nature were projections of our own wishes to perform experiments we dared not attempt ourselves. Other tales and rumors served to inflate the achievements of Communist sports science and obscure the similarities between Western and Eastern European sport. For this reason our next chapter examines, not only the history and ambitions of Communist sport, but Western fantasies about the ideological alien and what they reveal about ambitions of our own.

6

The Myth of Communist Sports Science

The Soviet Origins of the Myth

The phenomenal successes of Soviet and East German athletes over the past four decades raise interesting questions about the relationship between high-performance sport and the nature of communism as both an ideology and a way of life. Why have societies founded and ruled by Marxist-Leninists produced so many world-class athletes? Why have the proponents of this ideology showcased the elite athlete as an ideal human type? Has Communist ideology played a role in inspiring these people to extraordinary athletic achievements? Have Communist bureaucracies exploited the human material at their disposal with a uniquely cold-blooded efficiency? Has the secrecy that has always shrouded Communist societies made possible a secret science of sport? Are Communist athletes the products of scientific breakthroughs based on a willingness to carry out human experiments the West would consider immoral?

These questions cannot be answered in simple yes-or-no terms, but rather call for comparisons between Soviet and East German practices and comparable activities in the West. In this respect we are fortunate that the collapse of world communism has produced an avalanche of information about the high-performance sports cultures of the East, so that we are now in a position to measure East-West differences and similarities with more precision than ever before. It

193

appears that these differences, while real and important, have been
exaggerated, and that an honest encounter with the Communist
sports "machine" can teach us a great deal about ourselves. This
learning process requires in turn an examination of how Westerners
have perceived (or imagined) the Communist athlete, of how this
ideological alien has been at one and the same time demonized and
romanticized. We must also acknowledge that the resulting images
are not simply figments of the Western imagination, and that they
have a real historical foundation. Let us proceed, then, to explore the
historical foundations of Communist sport and see how they played an
important role in generating our mythological images of the sportsmen and sportswomen from beyond the ideological divide.

Soviet and East German triumphs at the Olympic Games and
other world championship events have made the Communist athlete
a familiar figure in Cold War mythology. Images of these exotics
began to appear shortly after the 1952 Helsinki Olympic Games, the
first Olympiad ever attended by the Soviet Union after decades of the
Stalinist regime's self-imposed exile. American impressions during
this period emphasize the ideological fervor and utilitarian sobriety of
Soviet sport. "Russia is building the greatest mass army of athletes
the world has ever known," wrote Avery Brundage, president of the
International Olympic Committee, in 1955. The ambivalent Brundage saw the Soviet athlete as not just fiercely tenacious but also
curiously demoralized and devoid of élan. "By American standards,"
he continued, the Soviet sports program seemed "harsh and severe.
It is both Spartan and puritanical. Most of the spirit of fun seems to
have been bled from it, and it thrives on regimentation and fierce
national pride."[1] "Their athletes are deadly serious," another American observer wrote. "When Mikhail Krivonosov smashed the world
hammer-throw record, he merely sat down on a bench and pulled a
cap over his eyes. He had been given a job to do and he did it—that
was all."[2]

Here are early examples of the myth of the Communist athlete—the despiritualized automaton, the sportive alien. Yet we would
do well to keep in mind the profound ambivalence of the self-
proclaimed conservative Brundage—his simultaneous reactions of fascination and disapproval. There is a great deal of evidence that the
fundamental Western response to the great Communist sports cultures has always combined fascination with disgust, envy with puritanical rejection. As the American psychologist Jerome Bruner
pointed out in that fateful Olympic year of 1952, Westerners would

understand Soviet society better if they learned "to respond to Russia as something more than a screen upon which we project our fears and aspirations."[3] But if our fears concerning the scientifically manipulated athlete are easy enough to acknowledge, our aspirations to create such a creature are not. It is easier, in other words, to project the temptation to play Dr. Frankenstein onto the ideological alien while proclaiming one's own immunity to temptation. The historical record shows, however, that the elite sports cultures of the West have not resisted the appeal of illicit performance-enhancing techniques.

Over the past forty years Western ideas about the Communist sports program and its scientific basis have evolved along with Cold War trends. From the beginning, images of the dehumanized Communist athlete have served the psychological needs of populations who doubted the full humanity of all Communists. At the same time, Stalinist dehumanization throughout the Eastern bloc provided a realistic basis for such images even as they were embellished by fantasies about the effects of communism on human nature. When the gender testing of female athletes during the 1950s revealed a number of male or quasi-male imposters from Eastern Europe, Western suspicions about the essential strangeness of the inhabitants of Stalin's closed realm were confirmed. In recent years the idea that Communist man is somehow essentially different from his Western counterpart has been connected to the doping issue, even if East-West similarities in this regard have now become increasingly evident to informed observers of international sport. As of today, however, our perceptions of East-West differences bearing on high-performance sport have changed in two important ways. The image of the robotlike automaton is dead, and fantasies about the performance-boosting manipulations of Soviet scientists and psychologists have acquired a positive aura among a large Western audience fixated on achieving its own "peak performances."

One example of the wish to believe in "scientific miracles" behind the Iron Curtain appeared in the respected Danish newspaper *Politiken* in 1983. Based on a series of "remarkably candid interviews," it is an enthusiastic account of two Soviet experiments in what might be called anthropological engineering. The first story concerns the development of "a new breed of superhumans" taking place in the then-closed central Asian city of Alma Ata, the site of many secret projects. Under the supervision of the gynecologist Igor Tyarkovsky, a forty-seven-year-old naval officer who had been given official permission to proceed with this project at the end of the 1960s, children were being born underwater and spending their first 96 hours of life in a tank. Playing almost exclusively in the water, these children were embarking on a "strict program to allow them to reach the outer limits of human ability, both mentally and physically." Now that a small number of these "superchildren" were entering their teenage years, Dr. Tyarkovsky could confirm their all-round superiority; they were taller, stronger, more intelligent, and "very athletically built." In the second experiment, Professor Georgi Dshabinava of the Georgian city of Tbilisi was reported to be directing red laser beams at "the more vital acupuncture sites" of fetuses, thereby producing children who were both unusually robust and free of disease. "We are firmly convinced," Professor Dshabinava stated, "that these children will become the first in a series of supermen and -women—precisely the kind of people needed by our colleagues in the space program."

Such apocryphal reports of dramatic scientific breakthroughs are, of course, among the standard legends of the technological age. The short-lived legends of Dr. Tyarkovsky and Professor Dshabinava—I have seen them referred to nowhere else—belong to a sub-genre that has to do with the idea that anthropological transformation might make performance breakthroughs possible. But why have most of these stories come out of the Soviet Union? Is it coincidence that in 1938 the Nobel Prize-winning geneticist Herman J. Muller confided to a colleague that "there had been talk in the Soviet Union of crossbreeding human beings and apes, and stories of Russian women prepared to volunteer for artificial insemination with ape sperm"?[4] An indispensable element of legendary science is the secret laboratory in which unorthodox or forbidden procedures can be carried out beyond the prying eyes of regulatory commissions or hostile foreign observers. This isolation from the everyday world of "normal" limits and controls does not always require a Communist setting. The fetal-cell injections administered to wealthy clients in Swiss clinics, for example, partake of the same romantic aura as the Soviet experiments described above.[5] But if Switzerland is known for the secrecy it can provide to wealthy people, their bodies, and their money, the Soviet Union was "a society that until recently was purportedly proscientific, rational and even 'scientifically' designed."[6] It is Communist secrecy, not its decadent capitalist equivalent, that fascinates Westerners who yearn for the transformation of the human organism and new horizons of performance. This yearning has created new myths and a new market for Soviet "secrets" that is likely to shrink as Cold War mythology is replaced by more sober assessments of the Soviet scientific "threat." Today, as Soviet society is literally falling apart at the seams, it is pathetic to see a former Soviet sports psychologist selling "the theories and techniques of Soviet sports psychology that are used by Russian athletes, chess players, politicians [!] to give them the competitive edge that has earned them an enviable reputation as superachievers."[7] Given the magnitude of the Soviet debacle, Western consumers may be skeptical about secret techniques that did not enable these "superachievers" to prevent the collapse of the Soviet system.

The myth of Soviet science and its secrets originated during the 1920s, at a time when the slogan "science is the religion of the Soviet Union" was often cited to capture the temper of the times.[8] Of particular interest to us is the widespread conviction of this era that Soviet scientists would soon solve the riddles of human nature and make possible the creation of a "rational" society. "Spectacular advances in the scientific understanding of behavior aroused the belief that human conduct would soon be completely explained in terms of reflexes and reactions and that all other schools of psychology would become useless and disappear," Alex Kozulin has written. "Scientific popularizers were eager to foretell the decisive victory of physiological methods and the emergence of a unified theory of human and animal behavior."[9] This "unified theory" of human functioning included the infatuation with the idea of extending human limits that has become an integral part of the modern experience. Half a century before the "human potential" movement began to attract large American (and Soviet) audiences, early Bolshevist visionaries believed that the science of the future would vastly extend man's mental and physical capacities. This was an intoxicating idea at the time, and its continuing hold on the modern imagination is demonstrated by the enormous popularity of record-breaking athletes today and by our many fixations on performance and productivity. To understand these ambitions to boost the human organism to new levels of performance, we have to examine how two important figures of this period viewed the human organism and imagined what might be done with it.

The physiologist Ivan Pavlov (1849–1936), regarded as the greatest Russian scientist of his age, became world famous for his theory of conditioned and unconditioned reflexes.[10] But Pavlov's significance for us has less to do with the substance of his scientific work than with its enduring image in the mind of the West. The famous experiments on salivating dogs and his skeptical attitude toward the field of human psychology created a powerful (if erroneous) impression that he saw

human beings as little more than animals. As a noted historian of
Soviet science has pointed out, "Pavlov cannot be described fairly as
a person who believed that human behavior can be reduced to the
simple stimulus-response action of the noted experiments with dogs."
Yet even this observer concedes that "Pavlov tended to see psychic
phenomena . . . in somewhat mechanistic and elementary terms."[11]
The important point is that a great scientist was seen to be simplifying
the human organism, reducing it to an object of purely physiological
interest, under the auspices of the Soviet regime. The irony is that
Pavlov was never a Marxist and that it was his students who attempted to apply his doctrines to so many areas of human behavior,
including education.[12] Nevertheless, he always enjoyed the favor of
the Soviet regime, and by the early 1950s he had become a virtual
cult figure of the Soviet scientific establishment. Despite his lack of
interest in the official ideology of dialectical materialism, Soviet ideologists valued his work for its tendency to subordinate psychology to
physiology and its emphasis on the environmental conditioning of the
human organism. We must now explain why these Pavlovian ideas
were compatible with Communist ideology and how they played a
role in Soviet thinking about the importance of the elite athlete.

In his "Reply of a Physiologist to Psychologists" (1932), Pavlov
wrote that "identifying the physiological with the psychological, the
subjective with the objective . . . is the most important scientific task
of our time." His interest in fusing mental and physical processes was
inspired by his teacher Ivan Sechenov (1829–1905), who held that "all
conscious activities, including those regarded as spontaneous, were
nothing other than reflexes." For Pavlov the goal was to establish the
scientific truth about the functioning of the human organism, but his
political sponsors had something more at stake. Proof of a reflex theory of human nature would deny the autonomy of mental life and
open the door to "conditioning" the citizen in politically desirable
ways. One observer noted "how Pavlov's teaching seems to open up
opportunities for 'psychagogic moulding-processes', i.e., for an unlimited power of shaping men and guiding their thought and behavior
by appropriate manipulation of their two 'signaling systems.' "[13] The
fundamental issues for us can be phrased as three questions. Is this
Orwellian project latent in Pavlov's theory of human functioning?
Does Pavlovian man represent a crudely simplified image of man that
can be presented in the charismatic figure of the high-performance
athlete? And are Communist regimes more likely than other political
systems to develop and glorify athletic achievement?

The Orwellian implications of Pavlov's pronouncements on human nature were followed up, not by the scientist himself, but by those Stalinists who used him as a monument to the Soviet state. Yet the very fact of his exploitation by the regime suggests that some aspects of Pavlov's thinking were all too compatible with the brutally simplified human image cultivated by the Stalinists. Indeed, one historian of Soviet psychology, Alex Kozulin, has argued persuasively that Pavlov's reductionist approach to human nature was not only real but rooted in his own personality. "I myself am psychasthenic," Pavlov wrote. "There is nothing artistic in me at all." The typically psychasthenic personality is pedantic, monotonously repetitive, has little imagination and is firmly attached to what is "real," operating within the limited confines of his own mental world. "It is thus clear," Kozulin writes, "that Pavlov's psychasthenia was the specific reason for his 'scientific' typology. The perceptual stimuli prepared in the laboratory and artistic creativity appear to have been one and the same in his mind. Pavlov linked artistic creativity with primary signals [e.g., a bell] and the animal aspect of human nature because true artistic talent was simply unknown to him. His mind recognized only commonplace compositions of everyday objects."[14] Pavlov's sensibility foreshadows the official Soviet doctrine of art known as Socialist Realism, a politically militant aesthetic that turned art and literature into forms of state propaganda featuring the mindless optimism of selfless tractor drivers and other proletarian heroes.[15] In a similar vein, the high-performance athlete became a conveniently mute and self-disciplined hero, always subordinated to the state, as his body expressed exactly what the state wanted to hear.[16]

The early Soviet doctrines of human functioning—Pavlovian reflex theory, the reactology of K.N. Kornilov, and the reflexology of V.M. Bekhterev—were united in denying an independent status to psychology as an approach to understanding human nature. They are all forms of behaviorism, a doctrine that insists on confining the study of human beings to objectively observable phenomena and emphasizes the role of environmental factors in determining behavior. It would be inaccurate, however, to simply equate behaviorism and Soviet doctrine and suggest that a behavioristic outlook accounts for the Soviet cult of the elite athlete. First, the materialist tradition in Russian physiology long antedates the Revolution of 1917;[17] second, behaviorism appeared independently in the United States around 1914. It is clear, then, that behaviorism as a philosophy or mindset transcends the familiar ideological divide separating communists and capitalists. Even so, there is a special affinity between behaviorism and Marxist-Leninist doctrine that does not occur in the West, and there are two ways to account for this difference. First, Stalinist ideologues appropriated the field of psychology as a political instrument to enforce their own conception of the ideal Soviet citizen; the history of Soviet psychology is filled with the unseemly maneuverings and denunciations of psychological theorists trying to keep up with the party line. In the United States and Europe political philosophy and psychology did not combine into a single entity, while "in Russia they fused, and under the Soviets psychology took the form of a philosophical ideologization of behavioral research."[18] The second factor is an important but overlooked aspect of this intellectual authoritarianism, namely the Soviet behaviorists' persistent effort to fuse the mental and the physical dimensions of man at the expense of individual intellectual autonomy. While the effects of this strategy to decomplexify human nature have been largely overlooked, this corporealizing of the human organism has played a role both in generating the image of the Communist-as-soulless-automaton and in promoting the official glorification of the elite athlete as the apex of human development.

The idea that the mental and the physical are one, that thought is a substance comparable to blood or saliva, developed during the nineteenth century as a form of "naive" materialism. "We conclude," wrote the French physician Cabanis, "that the brain after a fashion digests impressions; that it organically performs the secretion of thought [fait organiquement la sécrétion de la pensée]." In 1805 the French philosopher Destutt de Tracy followed suit by calling the brain "a special organ of digestion, or the organ that secretes thought [digesteur spécial, ou l'organe sécréteur de la pensée]." This notion scandalized contemporary thinkers who insisted on the dualism of mind and body. In addition, it is easy to see how any believer in the concept of the soul would have regarded such an idea as virtual heresy. This indignation is a historical precursor to the Western indignation once directed against the robotlike athletes of the Communist bloc. When the nineteenth-century German materialist C. Vogt wrote that "thought bears the same relationship to the brain as bile does to the liver or urine or to the kidneys," he achieved a notoriety among historians that persists to this day, because biological materialism of this kind guarantees scandal in the Western world.[19]

And there is another interesting historical parallel. One historian has argued that Cabanis's attachment to this kind of "vulgar materialism" (a Soviet term) has been greatly overestimated, as was Pavlov's, and that "even careful scholars have designated Cabanis an atheist or a bold mechanical materialist who crassly compared the formation of thought in the brain to the digestion of food in the stomach."[20] As this historian correctly notes, an attentive reading of Cabanis's *Reports on the Physical and Moral Aspects of Man* contradicts the idea that he regarded human beings as physiological automata. This tendency to read reductionist views of human nature into major scientific authors is interesting in its own right. The most important point, however, is that Judeo-Christian civilization regarded the physiologizing of human nature as a scandal in the last century and that it continues to do so today. The mere impression that an alien culture is treating the human body in this manner is simultaneously offensive and exciting, a syndrome that helps to explain why Western observers have consistently exaggerated Soviet manipulations in the area of sports medicine: Only materialists like the Soviets would be capable of such medical indecencies.

Outside the Soviet Union behaviorism scandalized many psychologists but never posed a moral threat to society at large. Within the world of academic psychology, as in the United States, behaviorists competed successfully in the marketplace of ideas for decades, but the American political system did not provide the political organization that might have enabled one school of psychology to establish an intellectual dictatorship over the entire field. The historical irony is that the fusion of mind and body—and the use of sports images to express this absorption of mind by muscle—appears most eloquently in the work of Anglo-Saxon psychologists who recognized the "Bolshevist" flavor of behaviorist thinking. In the 1930 edition of his classic textbook *Behaviorism*, John B. Watson points out that he and his fellow behaviorists had been called "bolshevists" for challenging "that comfortable introspective psychology" which had reigned for decades in American and European universities. Indeed, all one would have to do to make *Behaviorism* a model Bolshevist text—and, in some respects, a blueprint for Orwell's *1984*—would be to remove Watson's single anti-Soviet outburst and expand its handful of references to Pavlov into a more reverent encomium.[21]

The success of American behaviorism showed that the "Bolshevist" dream of transforming human nature was not (and is not) peculiar to Communist visionaries. It was Watson, not Lenin, who claimed that "we can change personality as easily as we can change the shape of the nose." It was Watson, not the early Soviet mechanist Aleksei

Gastev (discussed later in this chapter), who said, "Let us try to think of man as an assembled organic machine ready to run." It was Watson, not Trotsky, who said: "We no longer believe in faculties nor in any stereotyped patterns of behavior which go under the name of 'talent' and inherited 'capacities.' " It was Watson, not Pavlov, who conditioned fear into an 11-month-old infant and looked forward to "hospitals devoted to helping us change our personality." And it was Watson, not the materialist V.P. Rozhin, who called thinking "a kinaesthetic or 'muscular' habit."[22] But it is the Soviets who represent all of these ideas in the modern imagination.

Descriptions of behaviorism seldom refer to its notion of the thinking body, a pseudoscientific conceit that piques the scientific imagination without satisfying it. Elevating the status of muscular functioning came naturally to the behaviorist, whose evidence consisted of the movements ("behavior") of his laboratory animals or human subjects. Suppressing the intangible, and therefore irritatingly inadequate, evidence of introspective psychology required a kind of rehabilitation of the muscles that made "behavior" real to the scientific observer. Just as nineteenth-century physiology was shaped by the limits of the instruments available to measure and record certain variables,[23] so twentieth-century behaviorists shaped the human image by considering only what was physically observable to be valid evidence of human functioning. Watson saw athletic performances as useful evidence of this kind because they could be accurately measured and were straightforward examples of "complex conditioned responses" and the development of "habit systems." "One can describe in well chosen words," he wrote, "every act of two boxers, two fencers, and can criticize each individual detail of their responses, because there are verbal manuals of procedure and practice in the performance of these skillful acts." The next step, as in the Soviet Union after 1954, was to elevate the athlete's "skillful acts" to the level of thought: "The behaviorist advances a natural science theory about thinking which makes it just as simple, and just as much a part of the biological processes, as tennis playing." Small wonder that Watson, like postwar Soviet ideologists, admired a man who had excelled at one sport or another.[24]

The most eloquent assimilationist of mind and muscle, the British psychologist T.H. Pear, was neither a Bolshevist nor a behaviorist, confirming that the appeal of the thinking-body model is not limited to doctrinaire temperaments. Pear's lecture on "The Intellectual Respectability of Muscular Skill," read before the British Psychological Society in 1921, articulates the implications of the behaviorist view of the body with a nonpartisan clarity neither Pavlov nor Watson could match. Pear's argument was that "muscular skill has a higher intellectual value than is usually assigned to it," and that intellectuals held "kinaesthetic knowledge" in unfair contempt. He distinguishes between two "different types of mentality" who he called *visiles*, or people who think in terms of images, and *motiles*, meaning those who "think" in terms of "kinaesthetic processes"—the silent and invisible "language" of the body. Pear also addressed the political implications of his argument. He claimed that "the powerful mechanisms of class tradition and class distinction" had maintained the power and prestige of the visual types at the expense of the motile segment of the population, including athletes. And he noted that it was "the left wing of behaviourism" that had taken up the banner of the disparaged motiles of the modern world.[25] In short, it did not take a behaviorist or a Bolshevist to see a connection between affirmation of the prestige of the body and the revolutionary culture that was attempting to transform Russia.

The significance of the athlete in Bolshevist Russia during the 1920s transcended competitive sport. For the visionary social planners of this period the efficient movements of the sportsman were a model for streamlining the labor process; the extremists of this approach to boosting productivity were the so-called mechanists. The most important was Aleksei Gastev, head of the Central Institute of Work in Moscow, a man who dreamed of turning men into machines who would build a new industrialized civilization. Like Pavlov, Gastev was not a Marxist; his fascination with the popular "time-and-motion" studies of this period has been inspired by the American management expert Frederick W. Taylor—an interesting example of cross-cultural fanaticism focused on a common goal. As early as 1882 Taylor had begun to use a stopwatch to analyze workers' movements in search of perfectly efficient motion. During the 1920s the scientific management system known as "Taylorism" swept across the United States, Germany, and the Soviet Union as the wave of the future in industrial management. In the ideological hothouse of the new Russia this innovative industrial psychology took on a sometimes surreal quality that included the mind-body fusion we have encountered above. Despite the fact that Taylorism was of American origin, its association with the robotizing of the labor force has survived in our images of despiritualized workers and athletes of the Soviet Union.

Gastev was described by a Western eyewitness in 1926 as one of "the modern ecstatics of rationalism," people who "labour to become like the machine and finally to be asborbed into bliss in a structure of driving-belts, pistons, valves, and fly-wheels. People began eagerly to investigate the mechanical elements in man himself, the technical foundations of the bodily organism, which must in the future be encouraged and religiously developed."[26] Gastev saw athletic skill as a precursor to this new anthropological type. "He especially admired the skill of sportsmen and circus artists and greatly enjoyed watching performances of jugglers, acrobats, and magicians. He regarded their dexterity as a result of practice, proof that muscles and reflexes could be trained to perform phenomenal feats of precision and agility." Gastev dreamed of "training" children starting at the age of two: "The new age demands a generation with tempered nerves, strong physiques and unreflective agility. To do this we must develop a system of precise exercises"—as perfect a prescription for scientifically developing the high-performance athlete as anyone could imagine.[27] And Gastav understood that this sort of "training" meant altering the status of mental life: "The principle of mechanization of biological automatization must go very far, all the way to man's so-called mental activity. . . . *We recognize no difference* between so-called physical work and so-called mental work."[28] Here, in short, is the myth of the Soviet robot when it was an ideal rather than an epithet.

In retrospect it is easy to see how the utopian anthropology of the early Soviet period prepared the way for the scientific development of athletic ability and how it fed the imaginations of foreign observers. By the time Soviet athletes began to win Olympic medals in 1952, the Western public had accumulated a repertory of images that facilitated fantasies about the mentality of the Communist athlete and the scientific manipulations that might have produced him. Gastev had called the factories of the 1920s "laboratories" in which a new human type was being developed;[29] by the postwar period it was easy to imagine that the Soviet Union had now become a "laboratory" for the development of elite athletes. Many themes associated with Soviet civilization could be extrapolated into the ingredients of alien sports science: Pavlov's reflex theory of human nature and the indelible image of his canine subjects; the nightmarish mind-control schemes of the Stalinist regime; the confident claims about the plasticity of the human organism and the power of environmental factors; the inspirational value of fanatical loyalty to the state; the Soviet cult of technology and the man-machine interface that promised limitless productivity. All of these themes appear in the two most important anti-Soviet Western novels of the Stalinist period—Arthur Koestler's *Darkness at Noon* (1941) and George Orwell's *1984* (1949)—both of which had an incalculable effect on foreign perceptions of the world behind the Iron Curtain. The Soviet dystopia portrayed in Orwell's book is, in fact, nothing other than a gigantic laboratory for the shaping and truncating of human nature. It was not long before it became natural for Westerners to talk in a special idiom about "the breeding of super sports stars" in the Soviet Union.[30]

Yet for all the talk about the New Soviet Man and the transformation of human nature, there is no indication of any extraordinary plan for the scientific development of athletes. In the case of Gastev, for example, athletic movement was viewed as a natural fact, not as the product of scientific methodology; it was a model for productive effort, not the object of scientific research. Gastev's "psychotechnical" research was oriented to the needs of the workplace. His visions of "muscles like iron rails" and "iron arms and shoulders" pertained, not to athletes, but to laborers who had somehow fused with their machines.[31] In a word, Gastev's scientific imagination was fixated on the factory, not the stadium. The imaginative literature of this period also provides insights into Soviet ideas about human performance. One novel published in 1934 depicts an engineer whose physiology undergoes a sudden transformation while working on the great White Sea–Baltic Canal project. "The authors relate how, after Magnitov began to labor on the canal, he developed a quicker pulse and faster thought processes and nervous reactions: 'He begins to take on the new tempo, to adjust his reason to it, his will and his breathing.' "[32] For all its imaginative appeal, this example does not depict the scientific boosting of human performance; on the contrary, it is the labor process that somehow creates the new physiology. Similarly, the cult of the record-breaking Stakhanovite superworker that swept the Soviet Union in 1935–36 had no scientific subplot. While the Stakhanovism movement supposedly represented "a *qualitative* leap forward in human anthropology," this transformation was never depicted as a result of laboratory experimentation. We are told that the Stakhanovite laborer possessed the sheer "daring to discount established empirical norms and 'scientifically' determined limits of technology,"[33] but this confidence was not the product of science but rather a blind willpower inspired by Stalin and the state. What is more, it was teamwork that made these super performances possible in the first place; "sportsman-like records of individual workers" were simply incompatible with maximizing industrial production. The inspirational slogan "Higher, farther, and faster"—modeled after the Olympic motto—referred not to sports champions but to production quotas.[34] As late as the 1930s the idea of "breeding" superathletes was not much more prevalent than it had been at the turn of the century, whether inside or outside the Soviet Union. Even the authors of *Psychic Discoveries Behind the Iron Curtain*, a true believer's account of parapsychology and other wonders of the Communist realm, found Communist scientists working "to improve intellectual, artistic, inventive ability."[35] But there is not a word about boosting athletic performance.

Western ideas about the manipulative plans and practices of Soviet sports scientists belong to a larger distorted image of Soviet science as a whole. It is true, of course, that the history of Soviet science includes some nightmarish chapters: the groveling for political favor by psychologists from the 1930s up to Stalin's death in 1953, the Lysenko affair[36] and its disastrous impact on Soviet genetics and molecular biology, and the infamous psychiatric hospitals for "treating" political dissidents. These all-too-real scandals have horrified Western observers, and rightly so. But these travesties of genuine science and medical practice—and, in recent years, the tales of some enterprising Soviet emigrés who claim to be experts on Soviet sports science—have also led outsiders to overestimate Soviet interest in tampering with the human organism. For all of the Pavlovians' talk about conditioning people, Soviet publications have shown little interest in applying these methods to the citizenry.[37] Despite Stalin's support of the fraudulent geneticist Trofim Lysenko, "application of Lysenkoism to human genetics was not supported in the Soviet Union."[38] In fact, research on human genetics was banned in the Soviet Union starting in the early 1930s, and opposition to human genetic engineering and cloning has persisted.[39] Unaware or incredulous of such self-restraint on the part of Communists, foreign observers have been primed to expect aggressive research programs aimed at achieving world domination in various fields of endeavor. The idea that the Soviet Union was a scientifically dynamic civilization was also conveyed in certain Soviet films: "One appreciates how the cinematographic work of [Dziga] Vertov, for example, could pulverize Western audiences while leaving them miserably uncertain whether they themselves could ever sustain life at such white heat. It took less than three hours to create an audience of fellow-travellers mesmerized by pulsating energy symbols."[40]

Western unwillingness to imagine Soviet self-restraint in the

realm of applied science has encouraged many sensationalistic fantasies about what has been going on in Soviet sports laboratories over
the years. One technique is to offer up a naive and indiscriminate
collection of rumors and "reports" about exotic initiatives taken to
boost performance. A British text of this kind talks of laboratory experiments that test the athlete's capacity to endure pain, of research
into willpower, of behavioral psychologists who manage athletic training, and of the "Russian whose drug regimen had caused his testicles
to burst." There is also the unfounded claim that "the Russians were
probably the first actually to use their leading athletes as subjects for
experimentation."[41] In all of these claims but the last there is a small
and prosaic kernel of truth that has taken on an aura of science fiction
when presented in a certain way.

The romanticizing of Soviet science has alternated between (or
even combined) this kind of infatuation and suspicion of the ideological alien. Conversely, the Soviets have not been immune to suspicions about the aims of Western scientific research. At the
International Psychotechnical Conference held in Moscow in September 1931, for example, a Soviet delegate denounced the "bour-
geois" psychotechnics of the West as a "top secret" method for the
unscrupulous manipulation of workers under capitalism.[42] This early
distrust of the relatively innocuous procedures of industrial psychology prefigured the war of accusations about doping in sport that has
finally lost its Cold War dynamic. We have seen that this dynamic
resulted in part from distortions of the Soviet past. In the next section
we will examine how our image of East German sports science has
been shaped by another historical misconception—the idea that the
most successful high-performance sports culture in history and its
scientific methods had no past at all.

The German Vision of the Myth

Western fantasies about Communist sports laboratories repeat a well-
established literary formula that conjoins remoteness and the idea of
radical transformations of a scientific or magical character. As the
author of the medieval *Polychronicon* put it: "Note that at the farthest
reaches of the world often occur new marvels and wonders, as though
Nature plays with greater freedom secretly at the edges of the world
than she does openly and nearer us in the middle of it."[43] During the
Cold War, as we have seen, ideology replaced geography as the

measure of remoteness, and the Communist world—which had once
proudly proclaimed itself the social laboratory of mankind—became a
different sort of laboratory in the eyes of many Westerners. We know
now that these fantasies were "accurate" in the sense that many East
German scientists and physicians did perform unethical experiments
on young athletes. Many adolescent women, for example, were unaware that physicians were disrupting their hormonal systems with
anabolic steroids. But why, given how little was actually known about
East German sports medicine, did the Western public assume the
likelihood of such abuses? This was certainly due in part to reports
that East German athletes were being doped.[44] In addition, the muscular appearance of some female swimmers at the 1972 Munich Olympic Games provoked much journalistic comment. Yet these episodic
reports alone cannot account for the mythic quality associated with
East German sport. In all likelihood, such medical indecencies were
actually expected of these medical personnel because they were Germans.

   After 1945 the idea of medical experimentation in Germany became synonymous with the cruel experiments carried out by German
physicians in the Nazi death camps. In reality and in the public mind,
Auschwitz was and is a mythical site known for "its openness to
virtually any form of human manipulation."[45] Given the enormous
potency of the Nazi image in the postwar world, its demonstrated
power to engage and fascinate millions of people, we may assume that
fantasies about East German experiments represent new versions of
some standard ideas about Nazi unscrupulousness in the field of science. The myth of the "Nazi steroid," as we will see, is one expression
of this impulse to put both types of "bad" German into a single
category. This perceptual link between Nazi physicians and East German Communists became painfully evident in 1991 during public
hearings on the alleged crimes of physicians who once staffed the
secret police–dominated Charité Hospital in East Berlin. Reports of
illicit organ transplants and steroid experiments on young female
athletes took on a ghoulish quality against the historical backdrop of
Nazi medical practices.[46] When a Berlin senator referred to the "criminal energy and imagination" evident in these alleged medical per-
versions, no one could miss the connection between the accused and
other German physicians who once stood in the dock at Nuremberg.
Indeed, the similarities between the concentration camp doctors and
their East German counterparts are real enough—secret experimenters using men and women as "guinea pigs," medical indifference to

the fate of experimental subjects, and uninhibited eagerness to make use of unique experimental opportunities were common to both regimes.[47] Yet despite these similarities, Germany's Fascist and Communist regimes did not adopt similar approaches to the investigation of human athletic potential. We will examine this important discontinuity after looking at older stereotypes that have affected our perceptions of East German athletes and the scientists who "service" them.

The portrait of the ancient Germanic warrior type in Tacitus's *Germania*—"huge frames that excel only in violent effort"—provided the original stereotype of the robust and aggressive German male.[48] Later variations on this type introduce the idea of a superbred or supertrained man who is capable of extraordinary feats on the battlefield. Russian epic literature, for example, features many examples of gigantism.[49] In a paper read before the Russian Endocrinological Association in 1925, a Soviet scientist described this legendary figure as follows: "Giants were considered 'supermen'; they were clothed with special qualities, with enormous physical strength; the best national characteristics were incorporated in them; every act of theirs became magnified in the songs of the common people." In later times such "patients" were often exploited for their tremendous physical strength. The German examples of this human type, he points out, were the giants Frederick the Great recruited into his army—or, as Darwin put it, "the well-known case of the Prussian grenadiers, for it is asserted that many tall men were reared in the villages inhabited by the grenadiers with their tall wives." Darwin called this "the law of methodical selection" in action.[50] This example of "military eugenics" is interesting precisely because reports of such schemes are very rare. Why the idea of artificial breeding became associated with Nazi Germany will be discussed below.

A far more common stereotype of the German soldier derives from Bismarck's one-sided victory in the Franco-Prussian War of 1870–71. Contemporary images of the super-efficient Prussian fighting man were evident, for example, at a meeting of the London Anthropological Institute in 1871 that discussed the French and Germans as distinct anthropological types. Whereas the French showed a "more powerful development of the nervous system," one speaker said, the German constitution was dominated by "bone and muscle": "They are the reserve force of the West, which always comes into play when the more nervous races have been exhausted by the morbid excitement of their corrupt civilisation. They are the osseous and muscular pole of European humanity." Another speaker offered a more up-to-date image of the Prussian soldier: "iron discipline," he says, had transformed "the disciplined warriors of Germany" into "animated machines," and this image persisted for many years.[51] The ramrod-stiff (*gestrafft*) Prussian body, its aura of muscular tension, and the self-disciplined personality it represented became the ideal human type for German army psychologists during the Nazi period.[52] It is also a symbolic precursor of both the conscienceless SS monsters developed by the Nazis and the Communist robot-athletes of the Soviet Union and East Germany.

The temptation to equate Nazis and East German Communists in vague but suggestive ways is both seductive and misleading; any comparison of the Nazi state and East Germany should avoid drawing false parallels. A willingness to experiment on human beings, for example, does not necessarily mean that these experiments are designed to boost the physical or mental powers of the human guinea pigs. Thus the parallels between Nazi and East German medical crimes, while interesting, are of limited value, owing to the different ideologies and practical goals of these two German dictatorships. Their respective attitudes toward the development of elite athletes, for example, were very different. Virtually from the day of its founding on October 7, 1949, the East German state (the German Democratic Republic, GDR) aimed at creating an exemplary high-performance sports culture that could serve as a model for other sectors of East German society.[53] This determination to produce champion athletes did not flow from Marxist-Leninist doctrine, but was rather the personal decision of Walter Ulbricht, leader of the East German Communist Party (SED) from 1945 until his retirement in 1971. Eventually, East German social scientists proclaimed the sports establishment "the most highly developed subculture"[54] of a Communist society whose leaders went to great lengths to disassociate themselves from the Nazis. In the case of sport, the key difference concerns the idea of achievement or performance (*Leistung*).

National Socialism proclaimed the "performance principle" (*Leistungsprinzip*) one of its basic tenets.[55] Thus the Nazi author of *Race and Soul* (1933) refers to "the man of achievement [*Leistungsmensch*] and "the Nordic life of achievement [*Leistungsleben*]."[56] A 1937 pamphlet celebrating the young participants in a "Labor Olympiad" idealizes "the will to on-the-job performance."[57] Like its East German successor the Nazi regime also declared that its athletes were representatives of the state who could demonstrate its superiority in competitions with the other "peoples of the earth,"[58] and for many Germans the 1936 Berlin Olympiad confirmed the correctness of this view.[59] Nevertheless, the official Nazi attitude toward high-performance sport was profoundly ambivalent. For despite his or her propaganda value, the spectacular individual performer was a living contradiction of the collectivistic principle that demanded absolute obedience to the Nazi state. This conflict between the performance principle and the conformity principle was never resolved by the Nazi theorists who wrote about sport. One of them, Bruno Malitz, condemned the pursuit of the record-breaking performance in the same terms used by conservative German gymnasts a half-century earlier—high performance sport meant "one-sided" and "hypertrophic" development of the body; the point was to strengthen the Fatherland, not "to breed the greatest possible number of star athletes." In a similar vein, the more prominent racial theorist Alfred Rosenberg wrote in 1939 that Nazi physical culture was not interested in pursuing world records or in developing a "bunch of sick and artificially bred outsiders (*einige krankhaft gezüchteten Aussenseiter*]."[60] The crux of the high-performance problem was that extraordinary achievements had to embody social values (*hochwertige Leistungen*) and not be the product of apolitical egocentrism. In short, the Nazi authorities regarded the performance as less important than the politically correct attitude of the performer.[61]

High-performance athletes were not the primary "action figures" of Nazi Germany. They were of no direct value to military mobilization or in wartime, and this confirmed their inferiority to real soldiers, a view accorded quasi-official status by the Wehrmacht. When a psychologist proposed in 1940 to test the willpower of potential soldiers by means of "tough" sports tests, the Wehrmacht rejected such trials as unrealistic assessments of a man's strength of will. The transfer of courage developed in sport or acrobatics to the harrowing conditions on the battlefield was regarded as problematic at best.[62] Similarly, the athlete was of little importance to economic productivity. In *Human Performance as the Foundation of the Total State* (1936), the Nazi physician Hans Hoske treats sport as only one of many ways to create a more productive population. The "social value" of a person, Hoske says, is his "will to achieve." Yet even in the year of the Berlin Olympiad, there is no mention of the elite athlete as a role model. A man's highest worth is his readiness to go to war for Germany, a type of "human high-performance that transcends purely physical ability." Only the militarily fit are worthy of being called "healthy" and "normal."[63] A similar emphasis on the social utility of performances is evident in a paper by the labor physiologist Gunther Lehmann published during the war (1942). Lehmann's attitude toward the high-performance idea is related to the fact that his model of productivity is based on the combination of man, machine, and organization. To strive for higher performance does not mean to exhaust the worker's potential energy, but rather to make more efficient use of him. Lehmann does discuss the high-performance athlete when he addresses the problem of squeezing the last energy reserves out of a human being, but even here, however, Lehmann sees the athlete's experience as somewhat artificial. Only great and real danger can activate "the will to extraordinary achievements" to the fullest extent. The athlete can approach, but never reach, the absolute point of human exhaustion.[64] Another scientific paper that also appeared in 1942 discusses protein needs in relation to boosting physical performance, but here, too, the primary focus is on the war effort. Although this author singles out the Olympic athlete as a peak performer, the "enormous practical significance" of this physiological problem concerns, not German Olympians, but the "tremendous physical performances" demanded of German troops by the "Blitzkrieg."[65]

The relatively low status of the high-performance athlete did not wholly eliminate scientific speculation about how to boost athletic performance. For example, a paper on artificial alkalosis—a "very promising" strategy aimed at reversing the build-up of lactic acid in tired muscles—appeared in 1937.[66] Nor did an emphasis on the "noble contest" and the "chivalric attitude" of German sports teams necessarily exclude an interest in scientific approaches to high-performance athletics, provided that such analyses aimed at illuminating the "totality" of the human being as a physical performer.[67] In general, however, German physiologists and sports physicians were not interested in developing performance-boosting techniques beyond the limits of conventional training. Dr. Hanns Baur's lecture on "Applied Sports Medicine," presented before an international group of sports physicians at the 1936 Winter Olympic Games in Garmisch-Partenkirchen, conceives of "performance-boosting" (*Leistungssteigerung*) in terms of diet alone and categorically criticizes doping.[68] Similarly, the labor physiologist Lehmann rejected pharmacological performance-boosting in his wartime paper on the grounds that it just did not work.[69]

Nazi lack of interest in creating superathletes contradicts our deeply rooted assumption that these unscrupulous people stopped at nothing to ensure their success in every field of endeavor. It seems improbable that the enormous achievements of German science over the past two centuries did not culminate in scientific experiments aimed at producing the super-race of which the Nazis boasted, including superhuman athletes. Our eagerness to believe that the Nazis did carry out such a project suggests that the world outside Germany has projected its own experimental impulses onto this ultimate gangster regime and assumed that on morally alien territory these forbidden wishes would be fulfilled. One such fantasy has long focused on the *Lebensborn* ("Fount of Life") nurseries administered by the SS. "Fantastic rumors" surrounded these establishments, Hans Peter Bleuel has noted, "not only during the Third Reich but even more so after its downfall. SS brothel or stud-farm, or a cross between the two—such were the sensational constructions placed upon it by each according to his particular flight of fancy."[70] Popular lore transformed these strictly run nursing homes and orphanages into breeding farms of the super-race. This fantasy was further reinforced by a fundamental misunderstanding of the Nazi eugenics program. This project, carried out in the 1930s and 1940s by the German medical establishment at the behest of the Nazis, resulted in the murders of thousands of people deemed not fit to live.[71] Popular thinking apparently assumes that such an extermination of the "worst" must be matched by a comparable effort to produce the "best." A similar assumption has probably shaped our response to the medical "experiments" performed in concentration camps. The sheer sadism of such procedures, and the aura of absolute power that attaches to them, suggests to the imagination that any transformation or manipulation of human "material" would have been possible in these circumstances.

Such powerful wish-fulfillment fantasies tend to persist and adapt to new developments rather than disappear entirely. Inside the drug-ridden worlds of high-performance sport and bodybuilding, therefore, the basic fantasy of Nazi-inspired scientific ingenuity has lived on as the myth of the "Nazi steroid"—a perfect commingling of stormtrooper "masculinity" and the secret science of the East German sports laboratories combined into a single idea. (East German scientists did, in fact, investigate the potential use of steroids to produce aggressiveness in soldiers.)[72] Combining Nazis and male hormones fulfills a longstanding stereotype about German national character. Germany "is the country where the claims of Masculinism are most loudly asserted," Havelock Ellis wrote in 1917, and the

Nazis promulgated the most extreme "masculinism" of all, glorifying the German male as both warrior and racial paragon.[73] Small wonder, then, that various stories about Nazis and hormones have been circulating for years, including the widespread rumor that Hitler himself had been given secret drugs. He was, in fact, given many doses of Testoviron (testosterone proprionate) by his physician Morell in 1944, but this was hardly a secret substance at the time.[74]

Published rumors about Nazis and steroids focus on the military significance of the drugs rather than their use by athletes.[75] These reports, including those which have appeared in reputable journals, never offer documentary evidence. "The first use of male steroids to improve performance is said to have been in World War II, when German troops took them before battle to enhance aggressiveness," *Science* told its readers in 1972. In 1988 this prestigious journal elaborated on the tale: "The German government under Hitler developed and used [anabolic steroids], allegedly in an attempt to create an army of supermen."[76] That same year two American physicians cited reports that the German steroids had been given to Hitler's especially vicious SS troops.[77] (In 1990 Switzerland's finest newspaper reported that steroids were given to U.S. Marines during World War II.)[78] In the United States, the outbreak of World War II diverted resources away from important work on adrenal steroids when "research teams were sidetracked into the search for the mythical steroid supposedly helping Nazi pilots to fly higher than our own."[79] Rumors about hormones even reached anti-Nazi German exiles in California. In his journal entry of May 7, 1942, the playwright Bertolt Brecht notes that the novelist Lion Feuchtwanger had told him that "they now have hormone injections in the [German] army that remove all traces of homosexuality (though they have to have boosters every few months)."[80] In short, the male hormone acquired a uniquely legendary status. In contrast, the actual use of amphetamines by German (and Allied) troops to counteract fatigue during night marches and night flights did not become the focus of rumor and fascination during or after the war.[81] Similarly, the use of steroids during the war to restore the health of starvation victims has excited little interest.[82] The emotional appeal of the male hormone is based primarily on its alleged power to "masculinize" whoever takes it.

Conspicuous by its absence is the claim that German athletes used testosterone or steroids to prepare for the 1936 Berlin Olympiad. In fact, I have found only one (indirect) indication that this might have occurred. The source of this ambiguous evidence is

Friedrich Percyval Reck-Malleczewen, a Prussian aristocrat and anti-Nazi who was arrested by the Gestapo in October 1944 and executed in Dachau several months later. His *Diary of a Man in Despair* (1947), which has received much critical acclaim, contains a fascinating but inconclusive reference to what East German sports scientists would later call "hormonal manipulation." Reck's book offers a caustic philosophical critique of twentieth-century life, including the observation that "the complete somaticizing of life"—or scientific treatment of the body—has disturbed the harmony between body and soul. Having recourse to "technical, chemical, hormonal, or any other sort of magic tricks," he says, is a chimera. And at this point he remarks, with unconcealed sarcasm, that "sports physicians with whom I have discussed the recent [1936] Olympiad of blessed memory told me that menstrual disturbances among the young women and sexual insufficiency among men who appeared to be bursting with strength" were common.[83] What he does not say, of course, is that these sexual disorders were the result of hormone treatments.

Were such treatments—of athletes *or* SS killers—technically feasible at this time? Testosterone was first synthesized in Germany in 1935; a year later the Ciba corporation was manufacturing commercial quantities (in its proprionate ester form).[84] But there is no hard evidence in or out of the scientific literature that this material was being used outside research laboratories except as a therapy for testosterone-deficient men. As late as 1942, a general discussion of testosterone that appeared in a German scientific journal made no mention of athletic or military applications.[85] In addition, testosterone was only one "hormone" among many others, including therapeutically important substances such as insulin and adrenalin. During the 1920s and 1930s a wide variety of "hormonal" remedies were on the German market. Hormokutin, used to combat rickets, combined three separate gland extracts.[86] Hormo-Vesculan, administered by tablet and intramuscular injection, combined a fat-burning compound with "metabolic hormones of both sexes."[87] Prolan was marketed as a "sexually unspecific sexual hormone" that promoted sexual organ development in both sexes.[88] A Hungarian firm was marketing a "skin hormone" containing a testicular extract for both men and women. Hormonal treatments of gynecological problems were especially popular: Perlatan and Progynon for ovarial insufficiency, Owowop for menopausal disorders, Prolutan for uterine bleeding.[89] In short, there was extensive coverage in the pharmaceutical literature of the commercial exploitation of hormonal remedies. It is therefore reasonable to assume that these observers would have noticed the diversion of testosterone or early versions of anabolic steroids into the world of sports. Rudolf Ismayr, a German weightlifter who won a silver medal at the 1936 Berlin Olympic Games, wrote to me in 1991 that he never heard about testosterone or any other drug use at this time, and that he would certainly have caught wind of such practices had they been in use. Similarly, even the sports and medical journals that circulated reports of sports doping during the 1930s do not mention testosterone. On the other hand, the Nazis would presumably have wanted to conceal the diversion of testosterone for military use.

The myth of the Nazi steroid is part of the historical background of East German sports science. It illuminates our recent stereotypes of what it means to be German, including what we expect German scientists to do behind the closed doors of their laboratories. As Brigitte Berendonk notes, the world expected an unusual degree of efficiency from the East German sports leadership: "Teutonic rigor combined with German industriousness and Prussian discipline."[90] These anticipations of "German" behavior are also related to the widespread and erroneous impression that East German sports medicine sprang into existence with the founding of the German College of Physical Culture (DHfK) in 1950. In fact, German doctors developed the world's first and most advanced sports medical establishment during the 1920s and 1930s.[91] The substantial (and sometimes ethically dubious) postwar accomplishments of both West and East German sports physicians therefore represent separate continuations of a common tradition. Indeed, our examination of the pre- and postwar sports medical establishments will show that the much-vaunted sports scientists and physicians of the German Democratic Republic introduced few new ideas between 1950 and the crumbling of the East German state in 1989. Their major contribution to modern sports medicine was the development of a new anabolic steroid (Oral-Turinabol) and the vast experimental program, using hundreds of athletes, that perfected its use for high-performance athletes in many disciplines.[92] For the most part, however, postwar German sports physicians on both sides of the Iron Curtain pursued a scientific agenda that had already generated an enormous amount of published research prior to the Second World War.

But the antecedents of the massive East German sports project are not all found in the field of sports medicine. Perhaps the most remarkable feature of the East German high-performance sport establishment was the Communist-style *mobilization* of thousands of people for the purpose of producing elite athletes, and the lengths to which the state would go to mobilize the human organism itself both chemically and psychologically in order to make it athletically and therefore politically productive. This mass effort made the GDR by far the most successful sports nation in history on a per capita basis; only the USSR has made a comparable effort. But scientific investigations into *mobilizing* the human organism on behalf of productivity and the state did not first appear in Germany in 1949. For example, in his 1921 monograph titled "Boosting Performance By Means of Inspirational Stimuli," the psychologist Rudolf Schulze states that his research into this topic had been inspired by the courageous behavior of the German people during the recent world war. The terrible psychological stresses created by the war were counterbalanced, he says, by "altruistic drives" amounting to a "mass psychosis" that enabled people to do things they could not have done before. He believed this impressive store of energy pointed to "undreamed of forces" in every human being that could boost both mental and physical achievements. The question, he said, was to what extent a person suddenly extricated from an emotionally transported crowd could exploit these feelings to boost his own performances. The goal was to transform "mass suggestion" into "autosuggestion."[93]

Schulze's procedure was to direct three kinds of stimuli at his experimental subjects (all veterans of the recent war) and then measure the strength of the index finger by means of an ergometer. The emotional stimuli included a competitive situation, military songs, and exhortations to imagine wartime situations in which the subject either had to save himself or rescue soldier-comrades from impending death (the latter two stimuli could also be combined). Needless to say, this was neither exact nor dispassionately objective research. Schulze acknowledged that no "feelings meter" existed and that the imagined act in the laboratory was not the true equivalent of actual experience, although this scientifically cautious maxim was actually challenged by the combat veterans. "The soldiers who had been at the front assured me over and over again that they had 'put out everything' in the experiments just as if they had been in the field." In short, one gets the impression that this "experiment" amounted to a deeply emotional veterans' reunion under the auspices of German science, and one is not surprised to hear that all of these inspirational techniques caused either significant or genuinely staggering improvements in performance.[94]

East German sports personnel often worked at creating a similar group mentality. Prior to the 1988 Calgary Winter Olympic Games, for example, the East Berlin Secretariat for Physical Culture and Sport issued a statement on "the consolidation and promulgation of basic images of the enemy" and the likelihood that Olympic rules would be bent and broken "in an ingeniously fomented anti-Communist atmosphere" to benefit capitalist athletes forced by economic pressures to take drugs and otherwise risk their health.[95] This combination of German nationalism and Marxist-Leninst militancy did, in fact, succeed in motivating some East German athletes. Schulze's nationalism, on the other hand, which was still fixated on the German war disaster, did not use sport as a self-expressive vehicle. Two crucial developments—the sports boom of the 1920s and Hitler's conversion of Olympic glory into political prestige—still lay in the future. At the same time, however, Schultze's approach to performance already contains the basic elements of the East German sports science of the future. That he compares the performances he is aiming for with sportive efforts is not surprising. Far more interesting is his rhetoric of psychophysiological ambition. Inspirational stimuli, he claims, can be intensified by means of practice. The overall aim of cultivating these feelings is to break through the inhibitions rooted in the organism's instinct for self-preservation so as to unleash the muscle's full potential. If properly handled, this process can lead to an "almost limitless" boosting of performances. What is more, the younger the organism the more susceptible it is to this kind of influence.[96]

Schultze even wrestled with the temptation of doping. Almost two decades after the German immunologist Wolfgang Weichardt first claimed to have found an antidote to fatigue ("antikenotoxin"— see Chapter 3), Schulze reveals himself to be a true believer in this miraculous substance. At the same time, he demonstrates both prescience and self-restraint as he contemplates the possibilities that seem to be opening up before him:

> At this point, we are presented with a seductive look into the future of work physiology. Should it not be possible to counteract the formation of [the fatigue substance] kenotoxin by innoculating the worker with antikenotoxin, thereby eliminating all fatigue and raising human performance capacity to undreamed of levels? In fact, experiments of this kind have already been carried out; and it has been reported that they have produced very promising results. We have also heard fantastic prognoses regarding the possibility of applying kenotoxin immunity to the boosting of human potential.[97]

But despite this intoxicating prospect, Schultze refused to endorse a procedure employing "poison and antidote" to boost human performance. It is hardly necessary to point out, he says, that, as Weichardt himself had maintained, such a powerful substance (*Gewaltmittel*) should be strictly reserved for emergencies, especially since his psychological techniques produced analogous results.[98] This instinctive refusal to use drugs would appear many times during the German doping debate of the 1920s (see Chapter 4). But we should also take note of what Schulze *was* willing to do in order to boost human performance, and where this sort of ambition could lead later on in the minds of Marxist-Leninists. His crucial idea in this respect—that there are no apparent limits to what "inspirational stimuli" can do to boost performance[99]—was a fundamental tenet of Communist psychology from Stalin to Mao. The Stakhanovite superworker who paid fealty to Stalin is a case in point. "The secret of his success lay in his *daring* to discount established empirical norms and 'scientifically' determined limits of technology. Any man who had the courage to go beyond that threshold, it was claimed, could outdo production norms by 'ten to one hundred times.' "[100] Even prior to the launching of the Stakhanovism movement in 1935, the Soviet psychotechnician I. N. Spielrein had emphasized that human "psychological norms" (such as the fatigue threshold) were dependent, not on the physical condition of the organism, but on "stimulation from a politically charged environment ("social motivation").[101] Nevertheless, as Schulze's work makes clear, this challenge to the limits of human performance is not a specifically Communist theme. Rather, it is rooted in the performance-oriented psychophysiology that developed in Europe and the United States in the late nineteenth and early twentieth centuries (see Chapter 3).

East German sports medicine was largely built on the achievements of the world's first organized sports medical establishment. The world's first sports college, which included a sports medical curriculum, was founded in Berlin in 1920. The world's first sports medical journal was founded in 1924 by the German Association of Physicians for the Promotion of Physical Culture (DÄFL). Some of the German physicians who did so much to develop modern sports medicine during the 1920s and 1930s continued to work in the GDR after 1945. Former DÄFL members began organizing in the eastern zone of Germany in 1947 even before the founding of the East German state.[102] Let us now compare the German sports medicine of the interwar period with the sports science developed in East Germany from the 1950s to the present day.

The German sports medicine of the interwar period comprises several distinct branches. Muscle physiology investigated the biochemistry and thermodynamics of muscular contractions, measured muscular strength with the ergograph, studied the effects of alcohol and other drugs on muscle functioning, and looked at the effects of muscular exertion on blood pressure, glycogen consumption, and other physiological variables.

Respiratory physiology studied the relationship between metabolism and the oxygen content of exhaled air, the effects of drugs such as alcohol and morphine derivatives on breathing, the effects of rapid air-pressure changes on organisms, and the physiological effects of breathing at high altitudes, including the critical red blood cell count. The development by Nathan and Leo Zuntz of an apparatus for collecting and analyzing exhaled gases greatly facilitated the study of extreme physical exertion, including that of athletes.[103]

The neuromotor physiology of this time looked at such issues as the anatomical structure of the nervous system, the relationships between nerves, muscle tissues, and organs such as the glands, lung, and heart, the effects of drugs and other chemical compounds on nervous functioning, the effects of electrical stimulation, and the speed of nerve impulses. The preoccupation with fatigue during this period raised the intriguing question of whether nerves, like muscles, experience exhaustion.

The cardiac physiology of this era probed the neural regulation of cardiac functioning, rhythmic and arhythmic heartbeats, the effects of drugs and toxic substances, including the boosting of cardiac functioning with aspirin, artificial stimulation (chemical, electrical, mechanical) of the heart, the heart-lung relationship, reviving the heart after cardiac arrest, and the detection of audible heart anomalies. Contemporary sports physicians were particularly concerned about the effects of athletic exertion on the size of the heart.[104]

This scientific agenda was continued by East German researchers who eventually adapted it to the political requirements of a Communist party bent on producing high-performance athletes at any cost. State intervention into the management of East German sports medicine began as early as the first Sports Sciences Conference held in March 1952 and throughout the 1950s caused a growing rift between many sports physicians, including prominent members of the DÄFL, and state institutions such as the German College of Physical Culture in Leipzig (1950–), the Scientific Council for Physical Culture and Sport (1951–), and the State Committee for Physical Culture and Sport (1952–). These organizations became, in effect, the state lobby for the development of world-class athletes at the expense of sport for the masses. During the 1950s it became clear that these institutions were risking the health of child-athletes at the state-sponsored Youth Sports Schools (KJS), thus provoking bitter (and unsuccessful) resistance from many sports physicians who were now effectively excluded (or had withdrawn) from the increasingly closed world of high-performance sports medicine. When a group of physicians at the University of Leipzig protested this new state-sponsored approach to sports medicine, the chairman of the State Committee, Hans Schuster,[105] stated that trainers and athletes should not take such objections seriously and should overcome any "obstacles" that might stand in the way of their developing a "correct assessment of the political importance of high-performance sport."[106]

In 1960 the party ordered the State Committee to improve the scientific basis of high-performance sports medicine. The resulting research included work on the effects of training on the heart, the performance capacity of children's circulatory systems, the physiology of nutrition for elite athletes, and the effects of physical training on growth.[107] By the 1980s East German sports scientists had developed more specialized research strategies, including the increasing of training loads (for children as well as adults), investigating untapped energy "reserves," and developing an oxygen-starvation (hypoxia) training method for endurance athletes. The world's best-coordinated high-performance sports medicine also included many effective (and occasionally original) investigative and training techniques such as the use of muscle biopsies to identify "fast-" and "slow-twitch" muscle types or to assess the biochemical effects of procedures such as hypoxia-assisted training, biochemical techniques to distinguish sprinters from endurance athletes in terms of genetic endowment, computer-assisted film analyses and "force platforms" that analyze jumping movements, and moving-water chambers in which swimmers' strokes were photographed as they swam against a current. Electromyostimulation (EMS) to strengthen muscle fibers remains an unproven technique.[108] Wrestling robots, controlled by electric sensors and driven by compressed air, were used as programmable training partners.[109] The most sensational revelation of this kind concerned the underground chamber in which athletes trained while breathing artificially thin air—in effect, simulated altitude training in a country with no mountains. The first Olympic champion to train in this device was the long-distance walker Peter Frenkel, who at the

1972 Munich Games broke the Olympic record in the 20-kilometer walk by an astonishing three minutes.[110]

The achievements of East German elite athletes were made possible by the willingness of a small state to spend enormous sums to carry out the following program: scientific methods for identifying athletic talent, systematic selection and development of athletically gifted children, high-quality training for coaches, scientifically optimized training routines, and excellent coordination of the various members of the interdisciplinary group responsible for developing talent.[111] But following the dissolution of the East German state a flood of new information confirmed what had long been suspected— that the unmatched successes of East German athletes in international competitions were also built on the systematic doping of athletes with anabolic steroids, in particular the domestically produced synthetic hormone Oral-Turinabol.[112] The first documented use of this compound occurred in 1966 and 1967, just prior to dramatic increases in performance among East German female shotputters and javelin throwers. Intensive use of steroids was prompted by several factors. First, steroid use in conjunction with weight-training increases muscle size; second, the athlete can train harder with shorter recovery periods; third, the athlete experiences a feeling of unusual well-being that can also take the form of an extreme aggressiveness or sexual arousal;[113] fourth, steroid use can increase endurance capacity, especially among female athletes; finally, steroid use can virilize (and therefore strengthen) the female athelete, including young teenagers. The doping of both male and female minors, often without their knowledge, has been thoroughly documented.[114]

The doping of East German athletes was a secret and centrally administered program unlike that of any other society on earth.[115] Among the institutions that played important roles in this project were the German College of Physical Culture (DHfK), the Research Institute for Physical Culture and Sport (FKS), the Central Institute for Microbiology and Experimental Therapy (ZIMET), the pharmaceutical company VEB Jenapharm, the Central Institute for Sports Medical Services, the Central Doping-Control Laboratory in Kreischa, the Institute for Aviation Medicine, and the Health Ministry in East Berlin.[116] A Sports Medical Commission passed doping instructions down the line to sports physicians and trainers who would distribute the drugs and often extract a vow of silence from the athletes. Some athletes actually complained that teammates were getting more potent drugs than they were and, hence, an unfair competitive advantage.[117]

The pharmacological ambitions of East German sports scientists extended beyond the familiar world of steroids to more exotic compounds. Dr. Winfried Schäker, a zoologist at the FKS, experimented on athletes with combinations of steroids and the neuropeptide hormones oxytocin and vasopressin, which are credited by some scientists with improving the ability to learn, remember, and concentrate on a specific task.[118] Other researchers gave athletes doses of the mysterious "substance P"—a protein consisting of 11 amino acids—to test its reputed ability to suppress anxiety and rejoiced over the fact that it could not be detected by doping controls.[119] However, several months before the collapse of the East German state at the end of 1989, the temptation to flaunt purported secrets overcame Ekkart Arbeit, the head trainer of the East German track and field establishment. Responding to accusations of the recently defected ski-jumper Hans-Georg Aschenbach, Arbeit claimed that Aschenbach's stories about steroids were leading "our adversaries" to jump to false conclusions. "For if everyone believes that we are constantly developing new doping substances and procedures, then we can quietly work on very different ways to boost performance. For example, we have been working for some time now on altering metabolic processes, the nervous system, and—as we put it—the person's head." Arbeit refused to explain further on the grounds that "a country as small as the GDR needs secrets to maintain its lead in the area of sport."[120]

The justification of doping as a replacement therapy that restores the body to is natural state has long been a basic element of this illegitimate medical subculture in the GDR. On the other hand, the idea that doping is essentially a therapeutic procedure is not peculiar to East Germany. On the contrary, this notion has many defenders around the world, and in Germany (East and West) it is known as "substitution." In 1990 Prof. Hermann Buhl, chief of medical research at the FKS, went so far as to accuse his West German counterparts of having invented this term to justify their own use of steroids: "Then it occurred to somebody to call it a therapeutic procedure." In the same interview, however, Buhl stated that East German physicians used steroids "out of concern for the condition of the athlete" who had been run down by the excessive demand of high-intensity training.[121] (A day later Dr. Lothar Pickenhain, a founder of the FKS, dismissed this explanation as a "fraud.")[122] Such apologias could also take on a more personal note. Rüdiger Häcker, another doping scientist at the FKS, declared in December 1990, "We haven't given the athletes anything we would have regarded as hazardous for ourselves or our families."[123] Finally, as an argument of last resort, the doping doctors could present themselves as the unwilling instruments of medal-hungry sports officials.[124] By this point, of course, the elite sports establishment of the GDR was in a state of dissolution. Let us now take a look at how this secretive and tightly controlled network of institutions, along with its Soviet counterpart, eventually came apart as Communist rule came to an end behind the Iron Curtain.

The End of Communist Sport

The disintegration of the two great Marxist-Leninist sports cultures proceeded along separate paths and followed different chronologies. In the Soviet Union the reforms of Mikhail Gorbachev, who assumed power in 1985, catalyzed change within the sports establishment by weakening the authoritarian climate that had prevailed for decades within this Stalinist subculture. One factor in this development was the new Soviet sports journalism, which now reported with unprecedented freedom on fixed soccer games, elite athletes' resistance to the authoritarian methods of certain trainers, and the administration of dangerous drugs to child-athletes.[125] In 1990 the editor of *Sovietski Sport* claimed that the press had become a force unto itself that was intervening in the political process and even making policy.[126] At the same time, we should recognize that the loosening of constraints within Soviet sport transcended Soviet politics, that it was more than a symptom of the crisis of political authority in the Soviet Union. For on another level, these changes were a response to severe discipline and dehumanizing limitations endured by athletes wherever high-performance sport is practiced. In 1987 the three-time Olympic champion figure-skater Irina Rodnina complained publicly, "Success and records are all that count in the USSR."[127] But the enforcement of this iron rule and the impoverished experience it has inflicted on many athletes was not confined to the Soviet Union, even if the nature of Soviet rule made many elite athletes captives of a particularly harsh system and vulnerable to state-sponsored doping as in the GDR.

The gradual dissolution of the Soviet sports establishment after 1985 seemed to offer a new beginning for elite sport in the USSR. Fundamental criticisms of the old order became commonplace. Revelations by the *Medical Gazette* that children as young as twelve had been given steroids suggested that a reform of doping practices was

within the realm of possibility.[128] The press told the Soviet public
that the use of performance-enhancing drugs had for years been a
routine part of the sports medical preparation of athletes for international competitions, and in November 1987 there was a concerted
antidoping campaign in the Soviet media. *Sovietski Sport* reported a
scandal from Novisibirsk involving the doping of an entire swimming
team and described the plight of a female athlete made sterile by
steroid abuse and a male who had become "totally impotent." Professor Vitaly Semyonov of the Moscow Testing Institute warned that
many athletes and "certain sports physicians" continued to ignore the
medical dangers of doping.[129] By 1987 foreign observers noted a
marked falling-off in the performances of Soviet women in the middle-
distance running events, indicating a reduction in or perhaps even
the elimination of doping in this area. As a West German trainer put
it in 1989: "Once again performances on a human scale."[130] And the
new president of the Soviet National Olympic Committee, Vitaly
Smirnov, stated in 1990 that the old equation between Olympic champions and political superiority was now a thing of the past.[131] However, this trend did not continue indefinitely. For example, during
1991 Soviet female runners ran four of the world's ten fastest 800-
meter-races, and three of the world's six fastest 1,500-meter races,
with a Soviet woman at the top of each list.[132] It is reasonable to
assume that anabolic steroids played a role in at least some of these
performances.

A conspicuous beneficiary of *glasnost* in sport was Yuri Vlasov,
the legendary 1960 Olympic weightlifting champion who for many
years was a writer and often-resented critic of the Soviet sports establishment. When Vlasov's athletic career came to an end during the
late 1960s, he turned into a critic of the system, and the bureaucrats
he was now offending turned him into a kind of invisible man. For
eighteen years he was denied both recognition at home and the right
to travel abroad. The ascendancy of Mikael Gorbachev in 1985
brought Vlasov out of the shadows. He was elevated to the presidency
of the Weightlifters' Federation and made a member (if still an outsider) of the powerful Sports Committee of the USSR. He denounced
Soviet measures against doping as limited and therefore counterpro-
ductive, in that antidoping strategies had done nothing more than
show athletes and their handlers how to beat the tests. He called the
well-established Soviet tradition of high-performance sports training
for children "a crime," and declared that "from now on nothing should
be beyond criticism."[133]

This "Prague Spring" of Soviet sports has come and gone. In 1990 the deputy sports minister, Vassily Gromyko, linked an apparent increase in doping to food shortages, raising the alarming possibility that steroid hormones were replacing protein and vitamins in the diets of elite Soviet athletes, including children.[134] In 1991 the head trainer of the Soviet weight lifters, the former Olympic champion (1972, 1976) Vassily Alexeyev, called doping "only a minor problem," and of the 240 elite Soviet athletes polled in one survey, 44 percent called doping "necessary or simply unavoidable" to give them a chance in international competitions.[135] These unhappy developments make it clear that Soviet sport could not achieve real and lasting reforms without virtually seceding from global sport and its uncompromising demands for performance. In addition, the international market for athletic talent has enabled track and field stars from many countries, such as the Soviet pole-vaulter Sergi Bubka, to become entrepreneurs who can offer themselves to meet promoters around the world. Communist incentives have been replaced by market incentives that promote doping almost as effectively as state apparatchiks once did. Finally, one must reckon with the mysterious power of sportive nationalism. "How can it be," *Komosomolskaya Pravda* demanded to know in 1986, "that the most important scientific discoveries and developments that promote improved performances in sport are being achieved outside our country?"[136] This sort of ambition will survive *perestroika* on the territory of the former Soviet Union, and it will survive antidoping reforms in other countries well into the foreseeble future. Indeed, as we will see in the next chapter, the non-Communist world is only too eager to receive doping assistance from the Communist-sponsored scientists who perfected it.

The collapse of the politically powerful East German sports establishment was both late and abrupt compared with events in the Soviet Union. The tearing down of the Berlin Wall began on November 9, 1989, but the party's resistance to *glasnost*-inspired liberalization continued to the bitter end, even if the elite sports culture of the GDR had been undergoing significant if unheralded changes for several years prior to the Communist party's precipitous fall from power. One example of the erosion of authoritarian norms was the diminished authority of the state to shape the lives of child-athletes against the wishes of their parents. This, in fact, was only one part of the recruitment problem faced by sports officials responsible for replenishing the ranks of elite international athletes. Parents typically refused to send their children to the special sports schools on the grounds that they would be better off learning an ordinary profession.[137] A modest degree of material prosperity, more opportunities for travel to the West, and an awareness of the medical risks involved made elite sports careers less attractive to many parents and children than had once been the case.[138] One result was that sports officials undertook a campaign in 1989 to allay the fears of parents about the medical hazards of boxing.[139] There is, in fact, much evidence that the vaunted East German sports "machine" had been in decline for years when the Communists fell from power.

The sports establishment's abrupt loss of authority revealed a lot of suppressed public resentment directed against the privileged cast of elite athletes. The reform group New Forum called for a redressing of the balance between elite and mass sport.[140] Even before the end of 1989 the Olympic champion (1968, 1972) swimmer Roland Matthes had moved to West Germany because of threats and harassment from ordinary citizens and what he called a "mass hysteria directed against the elite sport of the GDR." Looking back on his career, Matthes called elite athletes the "billboards of this Stalinist system."[141] But more recent beneficiaries of the elite-sport system offered no apologies and even sounded a defiant note. The multi-gold-medal winning swimmer Kristin Otto rejected the insults of the crowd and stated proudly that the GDR's best athletes had incarnated the performance principle better than any other group that served the state. "I think that many of our country's artists have more reason to stick their heads in their shells," she added, invoking a Marxist-Leninist dogma that made athletes the equals of writers and painters.[142] In an open letter to the party newspaper *Neues Deutschland*, the two-time Olympic champion javelin thrower Ruth Fuchs said that sports stars like her "have nothing to be ashamed of so far as our performances or behavior is concerned," and she called for an ever greater commitment to the performance principle.[143] In a similar vein, her fellow javelin thrower Petra Felke noted haughtily that those accused of doping should answer their critics with better and better performances.[144]

This defiant attitude was shared by the scientists, sports physicians, and state officials who had conducted the most extensive and cold-blooded doping program in the history of drug-enhanced sport. "There was no Dressel case in our country, because we didn't leave the field open to medical charlatans," said Dr. Manfred Höppner, director of Sports Medical Services (SMD) in Berlin.[145] Manfred Ewald, who had directed the sports establishment for three decades before retiring in the mid-1980s, issued blatantly contradictory statements. "There has never been any doping in GDR-sport," he lied at one point. Yet only a few days earlier his arrogance had gotten the better of his discretion. "In the capitalist countries they are doping more incompetently than ever," he said, "and for that reason sports medicine must make a contribution here, as well. We will make use of every medical advance."[146] As we will see in Chapter 7, this determination to exploit everything medical science has to offer has become a defining characteristic of international sport. It would therefore be inaccurate to say that East German sports science has disappeared along with the bureaucracy that sponsored it. It has, in fact, been migrating to hospitable research and sports programs around the world.

7

A Conspiracy So Vast
The Politics of Doping

The Ordeal of Sandra Gasser

On September 12, 1987, Sandra Gasser and five other Swiss track-and-field athletes flew home from Brussels to the town of Kloten on a private jet made available by a wealthy admirer. A middle-distance runner of international caliber, Gasser at age twenty-five was at the top of her career. The day before she had won the women's mile run at the Brussels Grand Prix meet in a time of 4 minutes 23.84 seconds, a new national record and the fastest time in the world that year. For this victory and her third-place ranking in the overall Grand Prix standings she would collect $20,000. A week earlier, on September 5, she had won an unexpected bronze medal in the 1,500-meter run at the quadrennial World Championships in Rome, finishing in the excellent time of 3:59.06, a mere half-second behind the Soviet champion.[1] In only a year she had lowered her best time for the distance by an astonishing ten seconds, a fact that would not go unnoticed in the storm of controversy that was about to break over her head.[2]

Upon landing in Switzerland, Gasser was urgently summoned by the director of the Swiss Athletics Association (SLV). On September 11, the International Amateur Athletics Federation (IAAF), the ruling body of world track and field, informed the SLV that the urine sample Sandra Gasser had provided to IAAF drug testers after her race on September 5 contained methyltestosterone, an anabolic steroid banned by both the IAAF and the International Olympic Committee.[3] The analysis of the first (or "A") sample of Gasser's urine was performed in Dr. Felice Rosati's IAAF-sanctioned doping laboratory in Rome. The mandatory second (or "B") sample was tested there on September 23, with the president of the SLV, Georges Kennel, in attendance. Although the chemical profile of the second sample differed wildly from that of the first, the presence of methyltestosterone was confirmed and the result was reported to the IAAF. Of the 192 athletes subjected to drug testing in Rome, only Gasser had tested positive for a banned substance. Meeting in Moscow on September 29 the IAAF Medical Committee, by a vote of 2 to 1, stripped the Swiss runner of her bronze medal, nullified her victory in Brussels, cancelled her $20,000 in prize money, and banned her from officially sanctioned competition for a two-year period to end on September 5, 1989.

The stage was now set for the kind of protracted legal battle and scientific controversy that exemplify the tangled politics of doping in international sport. Typically, the accused athlete, who may well consider performance-enhancing drugs a perfectly acceptable procedure within the subculture of high-performance sport, confronts a powerful international organization and its scientific team of drug testers. The national federation for which the athlete competes is caught between its obligation to guarantee the rights of the athlete and its countervailing obligation to adhere to the procedures and rulings of the international body to which it belongs. The state of which the athlete is a citizen may bear responsibility for having funded a doping conspiracy with taxpayers' money; in addition, as would happen in the Gasser case, the foreign ministry of this state may be asked to intercede on the athlete's behalf against the ruling of an international federation, since international law is the only forum in which the athlete can seek redress against an imposed penalty. Typically, the athlete's sports physician, who may also be employed by the national sports federation, will support the athlete's innocence, though perhaps on highly technical grounds that indicate that some sort of questionable drug therapy did in fact take place. The public, faced with the conflicting claims of a national hero(ine) and an international regulatory body, will either side with the athlete or remain indifferent to doping episodes, despite credible press reports about a doping "crisis" in sport. Indeed, the sheer complexity of some doping cases, including Sandra Gasser's, will tend to dull whatever public outrage there might be to begin with. Unsupported personal testimonials, abstruse laboratory procedures, legal technicalities, and the opaque functioning of remote committees combine to make these affairs appear quite intractable to any sort of satisfactory resolution. The apparent stalemate is exploited by sports officials in many countries to delay or subvert the development of effective doping controls. Their resistance is at the core of the doping system, as I will explain later in this chapter.

The central figure in any major doping scandal is the accused athlete, who has few resources other than legal counsel to rebut the charges. Sandra Gasser's response to the accusation that she doped herself was actually unprecedented in its vehemence and sheer tenacity. Since the IAAF banned anabolic steroids in 1974, the organization had investigated 89 alleged doping violations, yet Gasser was the first to mount an aggressive defense against this reputation- and career-shattering kind of accusation.[4] "Honestly," she stated, "I took nothing that is prohibited; I was never doped. I was always against that and I have said so publicly many times. Doping is a disgrace that damages sport."[5] She emphatically separated herself from the kind of cheater who had doped, been caught, confessed, and finally been readmitted to the track-and-field "family." "Whenever I see [the Finnish runner] Martti Vainio, a real doper, I think, what does he think he's doing among us. He doesn't belong here anymore." But it was not long before Gasser herself felt the invisible curtain of disgrace falling silently around her. "Superstars: Sandra is clean," proclaimed one Swiss tabloid, but the shunning of this new doping pariah had already begun.[6] Her friendship with Switzerland's only other world-class female runner, thirty-four-year-old Cornelia Bürki, dissolved in the course of bitter accusations and countercharges. Bürki, who had finished two places behind Gasser in Rome, found the IAAF verdict "too severe" but refused to affirm her former roommate's innocence. "It's all over between us," said Bürki, "a friendship that probably never was one in the first place." For one thing, Gasser's claim that Bürki might have sabotaged her by slipping the drug into a drink was, she said, "absolute impudence." A four-hour interrogation by Swiss investigators seeking the true "perpetrator" of this alleged underhanded deed left Bürki stunned by the sheer hostility of their questions.[7] Two years later, as her exile ended and she began an eventually successful comeback, Gasser wondered about how she would be received back into the sport. Would her former comrades assume she was guilty and give her the cold shoulder? "I couldn't blame them if they did," she confessed, "because two years ago I thought that way myself."[8]

How firmly established was Gasser's guilt in the first place? Doping control depends upon the reliable behavior and accurate analytical work of two groups of people. First, there is the team of physicians and others who collect urine samples at athletic competitions, label them in coded fashion to preserve anonymity, and convey them to an officially sanctioned laboratory for testing. Second, there are the scientists and laboratory technicians who perform sophisticated biochemical assays on the samples in the hope of detecting any of the many hundreds of banned substances that can lead to an athlete's disqualification. Perhaps the most controversial participants in Sandra Gasser's protracted ordeal were the people who operated these instruments at the laboratory in Rome, since the treatment of both her "A" and "B" samples appears to have been irregular from start to finish.

Gasser had provided a urine sample in the doping-control room inside the Olympic Stadium about an hour after her bronze-medal run. The rules that were supposed to govern this procedure were violated in several ways, or so she declared shortly after her appeal to the IAAF was rejected on January 18, 1988. She complained that there were too many people in the control room, that she had not been permitted to choose the beaker that would hold her sample, and that she had had to urinate in the presence of another athlete. The IAAF arbitration panel replied that she had consented to the procedure by signing the required form.[9] Gasser and the Swiss team physician, Dr. Bernhard Segesser, had joked when the IAAF official responsible for dividing her sample into "A" and "B" portions had spilled some of the urine on his hand. But even this minor mishap had its significance for what followed, since it turned out that the total sample sent to the Rome laboratory was only half of the 70 milliliters required by IAAF regulations. Even so, the Bulgarian physician who supervised the procedure accepted the sample as satisfactory.[10]

These irregularities were followed by more serious ones in the laboratory itself. Analysis of the "A" sample revealed clearly the presence of methyltestosterone. Later, however, an investigative report by two chemists from Basel pointed to the absence of any written record confirming that Dr. Rosati had actually performed the required repeat analysis of the "A" sample, as he claimed. Even at this early stage, they maintained, an error might have been committed.[11] But it was the analysis of the "B" sample that caused an uproar and gave some hope to Gasser and the SLV that the IAAF might overturn its original finding, for everyone agreed that the results of the "A" and

"B" analyses were improbably and inexplicably different. Whereas the "A" sample had only a small amount of the steroid, the "B" portion appeared to contain an enormous dose. According to Dr. Manfred Donike, the famed doping expert at the German College of Sport in Cologne, the second test had been carried out with an ether compound containing peroxide, thereby inadvertently eliminating an important chemical reaction necessary for detecting the metabolites of methytestosterone. Consequently, these compounds did not show up in the computer profile of the "B" sample, rendering it at best inconclusive. In fact, Donike suggested, the two samples might even have come from different people.[12] Reasoning along the same lines, the two Basel chemists went so far as to propose that "sample 'B' could be virtually anything, perhaps even dog urine."[13] For his part, Donike backed up his strong words with action. As a member of the IAAF medical subcommittee adjudicating the Gasser case in Moscow on September 29, he cast the one dissenting vote. In a fitting coda to the whole affair, Dr. Rosati's laboratory lost its license to perform doping tests while Sandra Gasser was still waiting for her ban to expire.[14]

As a world-class runner representing a small country, Gasser was a national figure whose predicament became front-page news at home. Caught in the middle of the conflict between this pugnacious athlete and the IAAF—now denounced as a "monopolistic international federation" by the Swiss press—was the SLV, whose president, Georges Kennel, was the runner's most vocal defender. After the IAAF announced Gasser's ban on September 29, the SLV demanded "a scientifically based explanation of this discrepancy" between the two test results.[15] But the power of the IAAF meant that the national body could not support Gasser without reservation even if it wanted to. Indeed, when she obtained a restraining order in late December from a judge in Berne—the first athlete in history to take a doping ban to court—she was pursuing actions against both the SLV and the IAAF, since the national organization had to enforce the international ban or risk the disqualification of any Swiss athletes who ran against her in their officially sanctioned national competitions.[16] Because even Gasser did not expect this kind of sacrifice from the SLV or other Swiss athletes with Olympic ambitions, she withdrew from the traditional *Silvesterlauf* run scheduled for December 27. Her career as an elite runner, pronounced dead by some observers, would not resume until almost two years later, when she became the first Swiss athlete to ask for random drug testing during her training periods.[17]

A less conspicuous participant in this complicated drama was the SLV's Dr. Segesser, who came to Gasser's defense. "Taking testosterone before a race is completely senseless," he said, a claim that was quickly challenged by a Swiss magazine.[18] In fact, Segesser's relationship to the doping issue—like that of many sports physicians—was both complex and ambiguous. In 1976 he had warned against giving steroid doses he "wouldn't even give to an elephant."[19] But ministering to high-performance athletes eventually brought him into that "twilight zone" of sports medicine where the lines between licit and illicit treatments seem to disappear before the eyes of the practitioner. At the Seoul Olympiad in 1988 Segesser administered "therapeutic doses" of steroids to the Swiss shot-putter Werner Günthör, who went on to win a bronze medal.[20] As Günthör's personal physician, Segesser had to be aware of the far more extensive steroid regimen Günthör was following, one that would be described later in a once-secret master's thesis (1989) by the West German sports scientist Norbert Wolf. In 1990 Segesser finally admitted—after furious denials by Günthör and the SLV—that the shot-putter had been using the anabolic steroid Stromba since 1985.[21]

Segesser's unhappy predicament grew out of his membership in a national sports establishment bent on producing elite athletes who would compete with the world's best, and this meant using steroids whether by hook or by crook. The Swiss Sports School (ESSM) at Magglingen had secretly sponsored the use of steroids until 1975, or a year after the IAAF and IOC had banned them.[22] Now, in the age of Werner Günthör and Sandra Gasser, the conspiracy of silence was operating in full force. In 1988 the head of the research institute at Magglingen, the prominent sports physician Hans Howald, told an interviewer that sports physicians were, in fact, the most entrenched opponents of doping control. According to a member of the Swiss Federal Parliament, Dr. Lukas Fierz, Howald's subsequent "voluntary" resignation was the work of the SLV and the Swiss National Olympic Committee.[23] Similar attempts by established and supposedly reputable national organizations to suppress the truth about steroid use are part of a worldwide pattern of activities that has proven resistant to international regulation. We must not assume, however, that *international* supervision is immune to the temptations that have corrupted the national groups a world body ought to control.

In fact, the most interesting aspect of the Gasser case may well be this international dimension. World-class sport is a global, multinational enterprise, and the Olympic movement is only the most prestigious of many organizations that govern sport on an international basis. As the Gasser case demonstrates, the problematic nature of drug testing has further complicated the administration of these far-flung empires by making their headquarters into virtual courts of international law dependent on fallible technical testimony. Indeed, the Gasser case turned into a contest between conflicting expert witnesses. The IAAF rejected the appeals of its Swiss counterpart and ignored the decision of the cantonal court in Berne, the headquarters of the SLV, as a matter of bureaucratic self-preservation. As the IAAF general secretary John Holt said two weeks before its arbitration panel met on January 18: "The decision of the court in Berne was absolutely extraordinary. We can't have the national courts of 181 member nations telling us what to do."[24]

Yet the logic of this argument conflicts with the realities of how international organizations actually function—a long-neglected topic that will be addressed later in this chapter. Suffice it to say that the basic premise of any international body like the IAAF is that its leadership has relinquished the pursuit of national interests in favor of supranational goals, and one of these goals is the impartial investigation and arbitration of disputes. A real-life flaw in this ideal model is that the major international sports bodies have not produced a caste of cosmopolitan bureaucrats who can be counted on to manage a global system of justice, and the arbitration panel that met in London and rejected Gasser's appeal is a case in point. All three members—the chairman, Lauri Tarasti (Finland), Robert J. Ellicott (Australia), and Evelyn Herberg (East Germany)—had undeclared interests in the outcome of this proceeding. Tarasti had seen his compatriot, the disgraced Finnish runner Martti Vainio, banned without mercy despite the Finnish team physician's desperate attempt to take the blame himself—a ploy that, if accepted, would eviscerate the ability of the IAAF or the IOC to prosecute doping cases.[25] Ellicott had seen Australian athletes banned for doping only months before. And Herberg, as a critic of the "professional" athletes of the decadent West, was not inclined to pursue the weaknesses of the scientific case against Gasser.[26] Indeed, the assignment of an East German functionary to judge a doping case already made a mockery of the proceedings—only one example of the East German fifth column that has infiltrated the IOC and IAAF medical commissions over many years.[27] In short, this panel incarnated the fraudulent internationalism of global sport, which amounts to competing national interests pursued under the inspiring banner of shared cosmopolitan values.[28] The ethical vacuum within this cosmopolitan bonhomie was symbolized by a meeting in November 1991 between Juan Antonio Samaranch, the president of the IOC, and Manfred Ewald, an ideological hardliner who served as the virtual czar of East German sport from the mid-1950s through the mid-1980s. ("From the athletes," Ewald said privately in 1987, "I expect creativity and a willingness to take risks"—i.e., steroids.)[29] Samaranch's willingness to receive the wholly unrepentant prime architect of the East German doping program suggests that the IOC leadership does not take the doping issue as seriously as it claims.[30] In this setting the "control" of doping by international bodies is pursued as a hit-or-miss ritual designed to reassure a global public that might lose its taste for world-class track and field if cynicism about top performances becomes too widespread.

Ideally, the power of international bodies like the IAAF should be adequate to preserve the coherence of policy while also ensuring the rights of individuals to be heard and judged fairly. But after the arbitration panel rejected her appeal, Gasser complained that, so far as the IAAF was concerned, she scarcely existed. She had expected a hearing that would address her concerns, a hearing "about me as a person, about Sandra Gasser, about someone who has something to say." But in the course of a proceeding that lasted eight hours, she was allowed to speak exactly once, and only in response to a question.[31] In fact, this humiliating experience was emblematic of the larger power imbalance not just between accuser and accused but also between administrators and athletes. During the world championships, while IAAF officials were being escorted through the streets of Rome with police sirens howling, athletes labored inside the stadium to fill the bank accounts of a conspicuously profitable international organization (the IAAF) whose president, Primo Nebiolo, was soon implicated in a notorious cheating incident that had benefitted an Italian athlete at the world championships in Rome.[32] (In January 1989 Nebiolo was driven from his position as president of the Italian Track and Field Federation (Fidal) but remained president of the IAAF—an instructive example of how international organizations can serve as refuges for certain energetic but dubious personalities.) In short, Gasser had no way of challenging an international body on equal terms. Her one court victory was in Berne, the seat of the SLV; a high court in London, site of the IAAF headquarters, refused to lift her ban, even though her appeal had been sent to the court by the Swiss foreign ministry.[33] One Swiss newspaper called this "an anachronistic gentlemen's justice" dating from a period when sportsmen had regulated their own disputes.[34] This telling observation points to the implausibility of comparable self-regulation when enormous sums of money are at stake and the specter of doping threatens to undermine the entire enterprise. The promotion of commercialized track and field by the IAAF and the IOC requires in turn a complex and fragile system of drug testing that has failed to establish either scientific or political credibility. Let us now examine the inner workings of this troubled international community of athletes, doctors, scientists, national federations, international bodies, and the dominating personalities among them who have conspired to suppress the truth about doping practices in sport today.

The Politics of Doping in Germany

Our anatomy of this doping subculture focuses on Germany for two reasons. First, Olympic sport is taken very seriously there and is financed by the federal government; therefore, the German parliament (Bundestag) has a legal and moral responsibility for any doping that is supported by German taxpayers, and its sports committee has held periodic hearings on the doping issue. Second, the West German press has thoroughly documented the various dimensions and factions of the doping scene in Germany. Nowhere else in the world can the strategems, deceits, alliances, and conflicts of this previously hidden world be followed as closely as in the new Germany, whose sport establishment now combines the wealth and ambition of the West with the scientific expertise of the East.

Because the nation's elite sports program is a public policy issue that is debated in the Bundestag, the German government has had to confront directly the human and scientific complexities posed by doping. In the United States, by contrast, the attitude of the state toward doping is harder to ascertain, since doping issues are handled by nongovernmental bodies like the United States Olympic Committee (USOC), The Athletics Congress (TAC), and comparable organizations. Elite sport is thus a highly "public" issue that is essentially under "private" control. This privatization of high-performance sport has had the effect of suppressing real public debate about performance-enhancing drugs in the United States. For example, a lengthy and impressive public hearing held before a Senate subcommittee in 1973 had little impact and was quickly forgotten.[35] (Indeed, the lack of public interest in such hearings suggests strongly that

American society has become habituated to drug use of all kinds.) In Germany, too, the doping issue has risen and fallen in the press, typically, in reaction to specific scandals. The furor over Birgit Dressel's death in 1987 and the East German revelations of 1990–91 resulted in sustained media coverage of the doping that gradually subsided until it was revealed in October 1991 that the Federal Interior Ministry itself had sponsored research that involved injecting testosterone into high-performance athletes.

In general, however, the German press has covered this issue year in and year out over the past decade with a thoroughness that is extraordinary by international standards, largely because of the political status of sport in the society that produced the concept of "high-performance" a century ago.[36] In Germany at least some politicians must, however reluctantly, announce their positions on doping. Public hearings in the Bundestag are only one part of a public debate among worried politicians, defensive sports officials, nervous sports physicians, and athletes who feel betrayed by a system that cannot control the use of drugs in sport. German politicians, sport bureaucrats, and business sponsors alike assume that doping scandals are bad public relations, but public reaction to doping is very hard to gauge, as it is everywhere, since it is both deeply ambivalent and hard to define even as it plays an important role in the minds of sports officials and the corporations that help to fund sporting operations. What is clear is that the political will to eradicate doping is lacking, and that this reluctance to eliminate doping from sport is a global phenomenon. Athletes and officials everywhere recognize that, especially in strength events such as weightlifting, shot-putting, and discus throwing, steroids are required to achieve international norms. But in Germany, thanks to government involvement, prominent sports physicians, and a vigilant press, the hypocrisy of the campaign against doping is most transparent, since the contending parties sometimes say what they actually think in addition to offering pious denunciations of doping.

Of these interest groups—athletes, officials, trainers, sponsors, politicians, physicians—none has the power, and some lack the will, to eradicate doping from sport. To date the sum total of their interactions has amounted to a massive holding action against reform. It is tempting to see in this failure a unified and orchestrated fraud, but no single interest group is actually powerful enough to coordinate such a plot. The orchestrating principles of this vast process originate from modern societies who view performance-enhancing drugs as an inevitable part of technological progress, an attitude that encourages sports bureaucrats to believe that the campaign against doping is hopeless in practical terms. The spokesman for Germany's track-and-field athletes, for example, claimed in 1991 that highly placed officials had simply given up in the face of apparently insurmountable obstacles.[37] A month later, the former president of the German Swimming Federation, Harm Beyer, called for the limited use of steroids on the grounds that German sports officials had shown themselves to be both unwilling and unable to eradicate doping. Beyer proposed the formation of a "circus troup" of elite athletes "subject to different rules and laws" who would be eligible to receive steroids and other performance-enhancing drugs.[38]

The German debate about doping represents nothing less than a referendum on the importance of high-performance sport to the nation, and high German officials have virtually stated that success in international sport is a kind of national security issue. For example, Professor Klaus Heinemann, chairman of the Scientific Council of the German Sports Association (DSB), stated in 1988 that "we must invest in sport because it facilitates the citizen's identification with the state."[39] Similarly, the German interior minister, Wolfgang Schäuble, has bluntly rejected the view that the end of the East-West conflict should lead to a withdrawal of state support for elite sport.[40] This political resolve has had consequences, since the failure of the antidoping campaign is a direct result of Germany's determination to field competitive teams of elite athletes. Publicly acknowledging this direct contradiction (the pursuit of national prestige through sport versus the control of doping) violates an important taboo, and those who broach unmentionable subjects are treated as renegades who must be discredited. In 1989, for example, the (retired) West German record-holder in the shot-put, Ralf Reichenbach, denounced the hypocrisy of two prominent sports officials for giving "Sunday-school sermons" against doping while continuing to enforce Olympic qualifying norms so difficult they require the use of steroids. Reichenbach compounded his offense by calling for the controlled distribution of steroids as a healthier alternative to the potentially fatal doses being taken by athletes in steroid-dependent throwing events such as the shot, discus, and javelin.[41] Having retired from competition, Reichenbach was relatively immune to retaliation from the sports bureaucrats. He was, however, criticized by the chairman of the Federal Committee on Elite Sport (BAL) and the prominent sports physician Wildor Hollmann.[42] Reichenbach is only one of many prominent West German athletes who have criticized official policies pertaining to qualifying norms and antidoping measures.[43]

The political conflict between representatives of the German sports establishment and their critics took on new life during the 1980s as members of the "Green" Party were elected to the Bundestag and other public positions. By 1984 they had begun to revive the critique of high-performance sport developed by West German neo-Marxists during the late 1960s and early 1970s.[44] The Green mayor of Leverkusen, Klaus Wolf, outlined a party platform that did not reject elite sport outright but recommended that state funds also provide for mass sport, sports for the handicapped, and appropriate sporting activities for children.[45] In 1985 Winfried Herrmann, the Green spokesman on sport matters in the provincial parliament of Baden-Württemberg, sharpened the critique by demanding that no public funds be spent on the "war of bodies" taking place at international sports competitions. This Green critique attacked medically hazardous training regimens, the biochemical manipulation of athletes, the "Darwinistic" selection of national teams, the athletic exploitation of children, and the "ruthless exploitation of the inherent limits of human nature."[46] In 1988 the Greens' attack on the exploitation of children was renewed in the Bundestag. On this occasion the party spokesman on sport, Jochen Brauer, called for the exclusion of athletes under the age of 18 from high-performance sport,[47] thereby reiterating demands made two months earlier by the German Children's Protection Society.[48]

These criticisms of high-performance sport were part of a more comprehensive campaign against technological interventions into human biology such as genetic engineering and the "misogynistic" high-tech procedures behind in vitro fertilization.[49] As technophobes, the Greens resemble the British antivivisectionists of the nineteenth century, who rejected "a social order that allowed scientists to appropriate animals for experimentation with the unthinking confidence that they were serving the ends of progress. [They] abjured a set of values that prized progress above all else, preferring a more spiritual code."[50] The Green critique of high-performance sport should also be seen in its international context, for it was virtually identical to the reaction against athletic exploitation that appeared at the same time in the Soviet Union as a result of glasnost (see Chapter 6). The political irony is that this attack on high-stress sport and the doping it requires was more effectively suppressed in democratic Germany than in the tottering dictatorship to the east. For by this time the

West Germans had worked out a political equilibrium, both in the Bundestag and in the major sports federations funded by the parliamentarians, that would preserve an effective prodoping consensus camouflaged by antidoping rhetoric.

At this point the real question was whether or not any political challenge to this consensus could succeed. With the political establishment supporting the status quo, such challenges would ordinarily have to come from political outsiders like the Greens. The one apparent exception to this rule was the president of the Federal Republic, Richard von Weizsäcker. Addressing the West German National Olympic Committee in Munich on November 16, 1985, he offered these notables an impressive philosophical argument against exploitation of the human organism for sportive purposes, citing the multiple threats to the integrity of sport posed by doping, genetic manipulation, violence, the abuse of child-athletes, the hunger for political prestige, and commercialization. He called upon "sport" to preserve its "humanizing influence" upon mankind by reëxamining its "moral-intellectual foundations" and the "existential issue" posed by its relentless assault on human limits.[51]

But von Weizsäcker's speech was not an act of radical protest comparable to the initiatives of the Greens, appearances notwithstanding. For the president of the Federal Republic, elected by a committee of the Bundestag and Bundesrat, is primarily a symbolic figure who is expected to take the moral high ground on controversial issues; in this respect he is comparable to royal figures in constitutional monarchies or even to the pope. Invested with the moral authority of the politically neutral, he is in no position to offer serious challenges to specific measures unless he discerns a genuine national emergency (such as the rise of a Hitler). He can refuse to sign legislation, but such action will only delay the implementation of these measures for a short period of time. In fact, von Weizsäcker underlined this political neutrality in his speech by expressly refusing to make specific recommendations and by treating high-performance "sport" as an abstraction rather than as the tangle of interest groups it really is. In addition, by invoking the humanistic tradition and earnestly talking about "existential" situations, he was making the familiar associations between sport and high culture that have traditionally, and frequently, been invoked by Olympic enthusiasts. (And, perhaps, by Germans in particular. Five years later, West German athletes heard the same sort of lofty discourse from Willi Daume, president of the National Olympic Committee and the grand old man of West German sport, as we will see later in this chapter. As the athletes' spokesman put it after a Daume speech in December 1990, the old man had invoked Aristotle and Horace, Plato and Goethe, but had "not addressed a single word to the real problems" facing German sport.)[52] At a ceremony honoring elite athletes in January 1988, von Weizsäcker renewed his diplomatically phrased assault on the distorting effects of modern sport. The idea of measuring the value of a society by the number of Olympic medals it produces is false, he declared, and he decried the inordinate pressure on West German athletes to win medals at the upcoming Olympic Games in Calgary and Seoul. Yet he diluted the effect of his criticism by hailing "the Olympic idea" that, despite threats of boycotts and counterboycotts, "is living and blossoming with great vitality."[53] Once again the president had transformed the distasteful realities of international sport into a soothing abstraction ("the Olympic idea") from which conflict, doping, subterfuge, and ambition had been banished by the magic of rhetoric. On both occasions, then, von Weizsäcker lapsed into a rhetorical style that declared, perhaps unintentionally, its establishment affinities.

The enormous success of East German athletes at the 1976 Montreal Olympic Games produced a traumatic effect on the West German sports establishment that ended only with the collapse of the Communist state. The widespread assumption that anabolic steroids had played a role in this harvest of Olympic medals convinced many West German sports physicians that the time had come for controlled distribution of these drugs. At the Congress of German Sports Physicians held in Freiburg in October 1976, prominent figures like Armin Klümper, Alois Mader (a recent defector from GDR), Wildor Hollmann, Herbert Reindell, and Wilfried Kindermann minimized the medical hazards presented by steroids and recommended they be used under medical supervision.[54] This initiative provoked the shot-putter and antidoping activist Brigitte Berendonk to publish a critique of doping the following February that was followed by a wave of television programs, conferences, newspaper articles, and discussions among the general public.[55] The Bundestag took up the doping problem, and the federally financed Federal Institute of Sports Science (BISP) launched studies on the "Possibilities and Limits of Humane Performance-Enhancement."[56]

On September 28, 1977, the Sports Committee of the Bundestag held a hearing on doping policy, yet, according to Brigitte Berendonk, the invitations to testify before the committee went exclusively to advocates of steroid use.[57] Several months earlier, on June 11, the National Olympic Committee and the German Sports Federation (DSB) had issued a "Declaration of Principle" against "every form of medical-pharmacological performance-enhancement," popularly known as the "Anti-Doping Charter." But at the Bundestag hearing, the spirit of this document was not much in evidence. One of the conservative parliamentary deputies, Wolfgang Schäuble, wondered out loud whether the recently concluded charter would not better be replaced by a very different policy position: "We advocate only the most limited use of these drugs and only under the complete control of the sports physicians . . . because it is clear that there are [sports] disciplines in which the use of these drugs is necessary to remain competitive at the international level."[58]

With this candid statement Schäuble articulated what would be West Germany's unofficial doping policy for years to come. At the time, of course, he could not foresee his future role in the doping debate. Speaking in December 1988 as Chancellor Helmut Kohl's chief of staff, he gave a tough anti-doping speech, calling the use of these drugs a scandal and a crime against the health of the athlete. The national appetite for Olympic medals was no excuse for doping, he warned, even if West Germany had to walk the path of abstinence alone and suffer the inevitable consequences in international competitions.[59] A year later, as Kohl's interior minister with responsibility for federal sports policy, Schäuble sounded a different note. Now he warned against a "doping hysteria" that was threatening to make every successful athlete a doping suspect. At the same time, he was careful to invoke the humanistic doctrine of sport; like Richard von Weizsäcker before him, he declared that human limits must be respected. But Schäuble's principal agenda was clear in his call for "a new definition of the doping concept," a maneuver that appeared aimed at opening the door to the "controlled" and "therapeutic" use of steroids. Many West German sports physicians in the prosteroid lobby had waited years to hear such a proposal from a federal official, but for the time being this opening remained merely a tantalizing prospect. In December 1990, following a tidal wave of revelations about East (and some West) German doping, interior minister Schäuble, the National Olympic Committee, and the DSB announced an "Independent Doping Commission" headed by a prominent judge named Heinrich Reiter. For five months Reiter's investigators were stonewalled and lied to by doctors, officials, and athletes, but they were finally able to submit a report to the federal government the following June. The commission concluded that many West German sports officials had known about doping since 1976 and done nothing. But it saw no reason for the state to intervene in the doping problem, since the ability of sport "to clean itself up" would suffice to eliminate drugs in the long run. It called in addition for a general doping amnesty, thereby skirting the potentially explosive (and virtually tabooed) idea of revising the world-record lists in sports where steroids had clearly inflated performances. (In November 1990 many East German records were ratified as all-German records.)[60] Finally, echoing Schäuble's prophetic words of 1977, the commission emphasized that high-performance sport was a significant part of Germany's national identity (*nationale Selbstfindung*).[61]

Meanwhile, the doping debate in the Bundestag has clearly revealed the ideological split between the Greens and a few Social Democrats (SPD) on one side and the conservative parties on the other. The Greens have been the driving force behind the Bundestag's episodic and unenthusiastic engagement with the doping problem.[62] Insisting that high-performance sport and doping are inextricably tied together, they have argued that German society's relationship to sport must change fundamentally if a genuinely "clean" sport culture is to be achieved. They have also consistently stated, perhaps disingenuously, that they have nothing against elite sport per se, but their initiative titled "An Inquiry into Measures Against Doping in Sport" (June 1987) suggested otherwise and went unanswered by the other parties. The basic ideological divide between these numerically unequal fractions was evident in a debate in the Bundestag in March 1988. The (conservative) Christian Democrat Roland Sauer criticized the Green program for an ideological rigidity that simply made elite sport into a whipping boy. Doping, he said, was indeed a problem but not a problem for sport in particular, since drugs were ubiquitous in modern society. Yet Sauer reserved his sharpest criticism for the IOC's unfettered commercialization of the games and the West German National Olympic Committee as well. Gerhard Baum of the centrist Free Democrats (FDP) emphasized the positive, declaring the need for a middle way between alarmism and indifference. The great majority of athletes are honorable types, he said, and he too attacked the IOC and the sports-promoting media. The Social Democrat Wilhelm Schmidt, a former vice-president of the German Swimming Federation, took a sharper line by stating that the SPD saw little difference between doping in elite sport and the tawdry drug scene associated with body-building studios. In addition, he warned of the "genetic manipulation of future world-record holders."[63]

This debate demonstrated that the strategy of the conservative majority in the Bundestag was to focus on extraterritorial adversaries such as the IOC and the media, thereby directing public attention away from the specific interest groups within Germany that actually practiced doping. The unspoken premise of this strategy had been enunciated by Wolfgang Schäuble in 1977 and would be reiterated by the Reiter Commission: It was imperative that Germany remain competitive in world-class sport. "We have no interest in letting the elite sports system of the GDR collapse," Schäuble stated in April 1990,[64] and it was his interior ministry that presided over the large-scale importation of East German doping experts into West German sports federations and universities during the period 1990–91.

Not surprisingly, it was a Social Democrat, Peter Büchner, who challenged the royal treatment accorded such compromised figures as Dr. Claus Clausnitzer, former head of the doping laboratory at Kreischa, and Dr. Harald Tünnemann, former director of the now notorious FKS research institute in Leipzig.[65] (In October 1990, at a meeting of the German Sports Medical Association, a member of Schäuble's staff stressed that Article 39 of the Reunification Treaty specifically mandated the preservation of both institutions.)[66] In 1987, following the death of Birgit Dressel, Büchner had listened incredulously as leading West German sports physicians such as Heinz Liesen and Joseph Keul told the Bundestag that the doping problem was being exaggerated, that doping did not occur in most sports, that steroids were both safe and effective.[67] Small wonder that the "reunification" of East and West German sports physicians proceeded so smoothly several years later.

The ideological division between soft- and hardline antidoping factions in the Bundestag has persisted. While conservative spokesmen have roundly condemned doping on some occasions, they have also been more likely to support the sports federations that have lost the confidence of many athletes.[68] The Social Democrats, on the other hand, have continued to resist the idea that elite sport is a self-evident national priority and have criticized the proposed general amnesty for athletes who practiced doping before January 1, 1991. "Even if the 1992 Olympics turn out to be a debacle for us," the party spokesman Wilhelm Schmidt said in 1991, "we can only engage in elite sport if it is clean."[69]

This political dividing line appeared again in late 1991 in response to revelations about the testosterone experiments sponsored by the Federal Institute of Sports Sciences and its supervising agency, the Federal Interior Ministry, during the 1980s. West German medical researchers, led by the prominent sports physician Joseph Keul—for two decades chief physician to the West German Olympic team—administered doses of testosterone to fourteen experimental subjects chosen from the "B" division of the national skiing team. (Other skiers who refused the injections served as a control group.) The stated purpose of this project, titled "Regeneration in High-Performance Sport," was to counteract rumors among West German athletes that testosterone and anabolic steroids permitted faster recovery after training and higher stress loads during training. In their published paper (1988), the research team claims to have demonstrated that testosterone is without value for endurance training—a politically correct result that may also be scientifically valid. Their claim that this work was motivated by antidoping intentions met with a mixed reception (along party lines) in the Bundestag.[70]

In fact, the first reports of this project stimulated protests from parliamentarians across the political spectrum. Eventually, however, the member of the sports committee representing the Christian Democrat party of Chancellor Helmut Kohl and his interior minister, Wolfgang Schäuble, defended the project on the grounds that it had been publicized and that it had been acceptable research during the 1980s. The most visible doping critics in the Bundestag, members of the opposition SPD, strongly criticized this research as "an official research project carried out with an officially prohibited substance."[71]

West German athletes have watched this political drama as mere spectators, although many of them have had conflicts with the sports bureaucrats (such as those of the DLV) whose decisions have profoundly affected their athletic careers. Like other groups of elite athletes around the world, the West Germans present a fairly heterogeneous mix of attitudes toward doping, even if it seems clear that most of them would accept antidoping measures that ensured fair competition. For example, according to Dr. Manfred Donike, the Cologne doping expert, 95 percent of elite West German athletes would accept drug tests during training periods; the resistance to effective doping control, he said in 1989, "comes only from physicians, trainers, and federation officials."[72] In fact, when West German decathletes announced plans in late 1990 to have themselves tested with Donike's assistance,[73] their initiative was actually rejected by officials of the DLV on the grounds that it would make athletes in other disciplines look guilty by comparison.[74]

Many elite athletes, however, have developed profoundly ambivalent or uncritical attitudes toward doping. For some of them, drug treatments are only one part of a round-the-clock medical regimen they have come to rely on. The professional cyclist, for example, who has good reason to think of his body as his indispensable capital, is likely to regard official attempts to prevent chemical manipulation by himself or a physician as restraint of trade.[75] One West German athlete threatened in 1990 to end his career unless given access to East German doping secrets.[76] The same year, a high official of the DLV confirmed that some athletes were training abroad—in the United States or on resort islands off the Moroccan coast—in order to evade drug tests.[77] The following year German swimmers threatened to boycott the upcoming European Championships to show their solidarity with former East German trainers accused of doping their athletes.[78] All of these behaviors are actually part of a larger syndrome, since the point of steroid use is to enable the athlete to train with the greatest possible intensity. Many athletes dope themselves only because they are driven by the fear that they will be at a serious disadvantage if they do not.[79] The Viennese doping expert Dr. Ludwig Prokop has predicted that "when the athletes know they can't dope themselves any more without being disqualified, they will just train harder than before."[80]

The doping crisis has greatly exacerbated the traditionally difficult relationship between athletes and the bureaucrats of the German sports federations. Many West German athletes watched in disbelief as federation officials hired large numbers of former East German trainers and physicians who were implicated in the doping programs of the now-defunct Communist state. The antidoping campaigner Harald Schmid, a widely respected former intermediate-hurdles champion who was appointed in December 1990 to head the Doping Commission of the DLV, could only wonder at the values of his bureaucratic superiors who had made these appointments. "A federation with principles, morality, and a sense of honor would reject these people," he commented.[81] Previously, the director of the Federal Committee on Elite Sport had conceded that absorbing the former East Germans would be a ticklish matter. Involvement in secret police activity, he said, might disqualify some of these people, but a witch-hunt should be avoided.[82] In fact, nothing resembling a witch-hunt ever developed. Before West German sports scientists and scholars fully realized what was happening, the chance to resist these developments was past. The chairman of the German Association for Sports Science (DVS) pointed out that no procedure for checking on the secret activities of the East Germans had been instituted, and subsequent hirings indicated that such vetting would not have been taken seriously anyway.[83] As early as February 1990 the head trainer of the West German swimming team, Manfred Thiesmann, had invited Dr. Jochen Neubauer, physician to the Potsdam swimming club and a man who had given steroids to thirteen- and fourteen-year-old East German children, to apply for a job.[84] Indeed, there were many opportunities in the West for the enterprising and well-informed. Shortly after the fall of the Honecker regime, Dr. Michael Oettel, director of the Central Institute for Microbiology and Experimental Therapy (ZIMET) and a direct participant in the massive East German doping project, was already in contact with West German pharmaceutical companies and the office of the federal minister for research.[85] Volker Kluge, the former press spokesman for the East German Olympic Committee who in 1989 had openly lied in denying the doping allegations of the defector Hans-Georg Aschenbach, joined the newly united German National Olympic committee (NOK) at the invitation of its president, Willi Daume.[86] Dr. Joachim Weiskopf, another member of the East German NOK, had presided over the canoeing establishment and its doping program; but on November 17, 1990, he too joined the new NOK with Daume's blessing.[87] "My task as vice-president of the German National Olympic Committee," Weiskopf stated, "is to prevent and control every form of doping." It would be a terrible thing, he added, if allegations of doping in East Germany proved to be true, but rumors and mere reports were not enough to go on. "Everything must be proved beyond a doubt."[88] In November 1991 he was forced to resign because of his previous involvement in doping in the GDR.

The smooth and scandalous "reunification" of the East and West German sports establishments was based on shared values, ambitions and—not least—a common if tacit understanding of how to play the public relations game practiced by both sides since the 1970s. Doping would be deplored in public but continued in private. But the frequent announcements by high officials of the NOK or DLV about ambitious drug-testing plans could not disguise their own role in promoting the use of performance-enhancing drugs. When, for example, the DLV announced its harsh Olympic qualifying standards in November 1989, there was a groundswell of protest from the athletes.

Sabine Everts, who had won a bronze medal in the heptathlon at the 1984 Los Angeles Olympic Games, called the new standards "an invitation to doping." The discus thrower Alwin Wagner was even more blunt: "These gentlemen are well aware that a mere mortal cannot achieve such results without aids to performance [steroids]." The long-jump trainer Hans-Jörg Holzammer criticized the DLV for proposing qualifying norms "that in Year One after Ben Johnson are no longer relevant to international standards."[89] Nor was this the first public protest directed against the minimum-performance system of choosing Olympic athletes.[90] In January 1989 the shot-putter Ralf Reichenbach had set the entire qualifying norms issue in its larger context: "First, people like IOC-president Samaranch set the Olympic qualifying standards so high that they can only be achieved with banned substances, and then they throw out the athletes they catch doping."[91] The new chairman of the Federal Committee on Elite Sport, Uli Feldhoff, announced: "We will never distribute anabolic steroids [to the athletes]. We would rather lower the qualifying norms or simply give up being competitive in one or two sports."[92] Several months later Dr. Wildor Hollmann, president of the International Federation of Sports Medicine (FIMS), announced an initiative of the German Association of Sports Physicians (DSÄB) calling for the abolition of qualifying norms.[93] But these arguments made little impression on the highly placed sports officials who make policy. In 1990 Dr. Manfred Steinbach of the DLV responded to the norms challenge with a subtle circumlocution: "I am reluctant to trace the problems our athletes are having to doping," he commented.[94] Later that year an angry Willi Daume replied more directly: "I refuse to negotiate about this."[95] But shortly thereafter the DLV capitulated in the face of mounting criticism and eliminated its system of performance norms, conceding in an official statement the legitimacy of athletes' and trainers' concerns that "certain performances are only possible by means of doping."[96]

The qualifying norm issue is directly tied to another aspect of the doping problem that may be termed the "steroid deficit." This widely presumed difference between what an athlete can do with and without the benefit of anabolic steroids has not been scientifically demonstrated. As Wildor Hollmann put it in 1989: "We still do not have real scientific data about measurable increases in distances and heights achieved that are directly attributable to anabolics." But the absence of such data is easily explained. First, medical ethics have not permitted Western scientists to carry out the experiments required to

confirm it, for as Hollmann has observed: "Anyone who takes anabolics over a long period of time is putting his longevity at risk."[97] A
second reason is that experiments aimed at assessing the influence of
drugs on human athletic performance are notoriously difficult, since
many factors that affect performance—including the athlete's emotional state—must be taken into account (see Chapter 5).

East German scientists, on the other hand, after years of secret
research, can speak to this issue with more confidence than their
Western colleagues. East German trainers told an 800-meter runner
that steroids could make her three seconds faster over that distance.[98]
Professor Hermann Buhl, formerly of the FKS, claims that steroids
can give a 100-meter sprinter a half-second advantage and extend a
shot-putter's throws by an extra meter.[99] Alois Mader, who served as
a sports physician in East Germany from 1965 until his defection to
the Federal Republic in 1974, has called all shot-put throws over 19
meters (62 feet 3 inches) "anabolic performances,"[100] suggesting in
some cases an enormous "steroid deficit" as large as four meters. A
once-secret (1989) study of several elite shot-putters (including
Werner Günthör) by the West German scientist Norbert Wolf esti-
mates a "deficit" of 2 to 3 meters in the shot and 7 to 10 meters in the
discus and hammer-throw.[101] Similarly, when the (West) German
Federation for the Modern Pentathlon forbade its athletes to boost
their shooting scores with pulse-lowering beta-blocker drugs, they
fell hopelessly behind their Communist rivals. "The foreigners are
laughing at us," their trainer commented gloomily.[102] Such testimo-
nies make it clear that there is a perceived doping deficit in high-
performance sport even though its existence has not been established
in a scientific fashion. The widespread assumption that such deficits
are real drives many elite athletes to use banned drugs even if they
would rather not do so.

The doping phenomenon has an important economic dimension.
Corporate sponsors of elite German athletes, for example, have
watched the doping crisis with concern. Like many German sports
officials, they assume—even in the absence of hard evidence— that
drug scandals make for bad public relations, and their spokesmen
have demanded that their money support only drug-free athletes. As
one case in point, the DLV's contract with the Daimler-Benz company specifies that "improvements in performance must result from
fair practices" and notes that "doping is unfair and harmful." Small
wonder that a DLV vice-president promised sponsors an "absolutely
clean sport" in 1990,[103] but that very year the widespread lack of

confidence in the DLV felt by some decathletes and women high-jumpers prompted these athletes to declare themselves drug-free and to search for sponsors willing to support genuinely "clean" sports events outside of the DLV. This strategy was endorsed by Harald Schmid, the DLV's newly appointed (and morally isolated) antidoping czar, but it evoked an evasive response from a Daimler-Benz spokesman, who stressed the company's ties to such official representatives of German sport as the DLV and the German Sports Federation.[104] In the face of this solidarity between corporations and the sports federations, a plausible first step out of the doping morass was not taken.

For many years the most important manager of this coalition, and the reigning grand old man of German sport, has been Willi Daume, an industrialist who claims to have participated in the 1936 Berlin Olympiad as a basketball player.[105] He has occupied many leadership positions within the world of West German sport. In 1956 he became a member of the IOC as well, serving as a vice-president of that organization during the period 1972–76, and he remains an influential member of the inner circle. Since 1961 he has been president of the West German (now simply German) National Olympic Committee, giving him great influence over policy-making in the area of elite sport.[106] Daume's power within the Olympic movement has been strengthened by his ability to play the charming cosmopolite, a role well suited to the upper echelons of the movement. "Generous gifts for officials' wives and after-dinner speeches full of profound quotations for a shallow public have given Daume the reputation of a gentleman and a connoisseur," Brigitte Berendonk wrote in her polemical portrait of Germany's First Olympian.[107] This patina of culture, rooted in the sentimental neo-Hellenism that has attracted Germans to the Olympic movement since the turn of the century, has contributed mightily to Daume's image and to the prestige of the Olympic movement as a whole. After all, devotion to ancient Hellas or to the cosmopolitan Goethe are surely incompatible with corruption or narrow partisanship, let alone the use of illicit drugs.

On November 16, 1985, Daume sternly announced that any West German athlete involved in a doping case would be banned from Olympic participation, a threat he reiterated in late 1991.[108] In the years that followed he would call doping "the evil of all evils" and "the moral sin of elite sport."[109] His public reaction to revelations about systematic doping in East Germany was a model of sober concern: "The situation is grave," he said, "and we should act with dispatch." Like Joachim Weiskopf, he stressed the need for definitive proof before making judgments, then called for an "international investigation" and announced that he had already contacted the IOC Medical Commission.[110] These public statements were in all likelihood a charade. It is difficult to believe that the best-connected man in West German sport, this popular confessor figure and all-purpose fixer, could have been unaware of doping in his own sports establishment. If anyone was in a position to expose and reform the West German doping scene, it was Willi Daume, and he chose not to act. Why, for example, was he a consistent and bitter opponent of doping critics like Berendonk as far back as 1977? Why did he not act then on information from a DLV doping investigator? Why, as late as 1984, did he ignore an athlete's report about drug-test cheating? Why did he refuse to "negotiate" Olympic qualifying norms with his own athletes in 1990? And why has he expressed confidence in two sports physicians, Joseph Keul and Armin Klümper, who are known to be steroid advocates?[111]

The German Sports Medical Establishment

It was Willi Daume who, as president of the German NOK, presided over the merger of the East and West German sports medical establishments during 1990 and 1991. This elaborate mating ritual completed a process begun in 1974 when Dr. Alois Mader left Halle in East Germany for the German Sports College in Cologne in West Germany, bringing with him both a knowledge of how anabolic steroids could improve performances of elite athletes and a willingness to use them. (On one occasion in 1976, Mader had to be cautioned by West German officials not to give "performance-boosting injections" to young female swimmers.)[112] The next sports physician to arrive from the East was Dr. Harmut Riedel, a doping expert of vast experience who defected in May 1987 at a track meet in Austria. Shortly afterward Riedel was introduced to the West German public in a sympathetic magazine article that never mentioned doping. He claimed to have fled from East German officials dissatisfied with the performances of track-and-field athletes under his supervision. In fact, Riedel had already recorded his unparalleled knowledge of steroid doping in the now-famous "Dissertation B" (1986). Once in West Germany, he became "a sought-after conversational partner" among such West German colleagues as the eminent Dr. Wildor Hollmann of Cologne.[113] Unlike his new colleagues, Riedel had been able to carry out steroid experiments on hundreds of elite athletes in order to fine-tune their doping schedules and dose levels. Brigitte Berendonk has described his activities, including the doping of minors, as "criminal sports medicine." Riedel's doping experiments did not, however, prevent his finding a prestigious position at the University of Bayreuth, thanks in part to supporting letters from Joseph Keul and Wildor Hollmann, the president if FIMS. (Hollmann later said he had refrained from asking Riedel about doping since this topic was irrelevant to his possible employment at Hollmann's institute in Cologne.)[114] On the contrary, Riedel's "substantial knowledge of anabolic and catabolic hormones" made him an especially desirable colleague.[115]

The reunification of German sports medicine was best symbolized, however, by a conference at the FKS in Leipzig in May 1990 that brought together many of the leading East German steroid researchers with such distinguished West Germans as Manfred Donike and Horst de Marées, the new director of the Federal Institute of Sports Sciences. The proceedings of this meeting (published in Cologne in 1991) reveal the nature of the East Germans' seductive overture to their new colleagues in the West. While these sanitized scientific papers disguise the real nature of the East German steroid experiments, in particular their inhumane and involuntary aspects, they also present the case for the "controlled" administration of steroids to elite athletes. Come join us, these scientists seem to say, in the brave new world of medically safe "hormonal regulation" of high-performance athletes.[116] (Their specific proposals are discussed in the final chapter of this book.)

This reunified world of German sports medicine is unique among the sporting nations because it is the product of two separate and opposed medical traditions that have deep roots in the culture of nineteenth-century Germany. The first is the great tradition of clinical medicine built by men like Rudolf Virchow, Robert Koch, and Paul Ehrlich on the basis of laboratory science. The German sports medical establishment of the 1920s—the first of its kind in the world (see Chapter 6)—derived from this scientific enterprise and the professionalization of medicine that accompanied it. On the other hand, a "natural healing" tradition (*Naturheilkunde*) arose in opposition to this scientizing trend within nineteenth-century medicine. By the 1920s this conflict developed into a major cultural schism, which was frequently referred to by German doctors as the "crisis" of modern medicine. The crucial factor was the apparent dominance of scientific procedures that encouraged a "mechanistic" approach to the human organism. "Natural methods of healing (*Naturheilkunde*)," Robert Proctor points out, "had as a result been replaced by exclusively physicochemical models and techniques; time-tested methods such as homeopathy had been supplanted by modern pharmacology and mass-produced chemical products."[117] This antagonism between old and new medical models was only one part of a larger contest between tradition and modernity that lasted well into the Nazi period.[118] Its reappearance in the context of postwar German sports medicine, and indeed the widespread popularity of "alternative" therapies throughout the country today, testifies to a deeply rooted German ambivalence toward modern medical science.

The cultural conservatism of the medical establishment (and its small band of "sports physicians") was exemplified during the first decades of the twentieth century by the prominent surgeon and sports physician August Bier, who served as first rector of the German College for Physical Education in Berlin. Like many Germans of the Weimar period, Bier was profoundly disturbed by the ineffectiveness of parliamentary government and by the "political poisoning" of the body politic.[119] He looked back nostalgically to the Prussian state of Frederick the Great and Bismarck's *Reich* and called for the "towering statesman" who might redeem modern Germany.[120] Such attitudes made Bier a typical German conservative of his era, inside or outside of the medical profession. His antimodernism is primarily concerned with what one might call the nature of modern experience. He describes "Americanism," for example, as "repulsive" and "fundamentally alien to the soul of the German" because of the "specialized" and "mechanized" nature of modern work, the illusory progress of technology, and "all the triumphs of cold intellect."[121]

Bier was, however, a selective antimodernist whose primary interest was not to promote blind reaction, but rather to assert the healing authority of a classical past over a confused and superficial modern age. As a physician, he could not reject modern science out of hand, since to do so would have meant joining "the army of fakes and quacks" who had attempted to exploit his prestige for their own ends."[122] Instead, Bier's conservatism paid homage to a venerated medical canon rooted in a philosophy of "healing" (*Heilkunde*) and based on "teleological concepts" that had been forgotten by modern physicians in favor of mere "medicine."[123] Heraclitus, the creator of a doctrine of the world's ultimate "harmony," had anticipated the basic principle of homeopathy—the curative power of minute doses of poisons—to which Bier subscribed.[124] Hippocrates, "the greatest physician who ever lived," had made "observations and discoveries that are still valid and superior to what the most refined technical instruments have taught us."[125] Bier makes much of the fact that Hippocrates had called the physician both a philosopher and an artist and emphasizes the invidious comparison between the pretechnological, "godlike" physician and a modern medical establishment, imprisoned within a "mechanical" materialism, that is content to believe that it can live and prosper without a grounding in philosophy.

Bier's cultural conservatism thus had several dimensions: the need to romanticize and spiritualize science that resulted in his sympathy for homeopathy,[126] the cult of the ancient Greeks that merged effortlessly with an analogous reverence for Germanic heroes like Paracelsus and Goethe, the hostility toward specialization and "materialism," the homophobia that anticipated the "masculine self-image of Nazi medical science,"[127] and the nationalism that yearned for a *Führer* to heal Germany.

Yet Bier was also a modern physician who embraced genuine scientific developments. His belief in the "autonomy and uniqueness of living things," for example, had its limits. "For the physician who thinks biologically," he wrote, "it goes without saying that he may not disregard the physiochemical dimension of life."[128] Nor did he endorse the racial biology that many of his right-wing peers espoused in the 1920s. He objected vigorously to the "one-sided" genetic doctrine promulgated by the racial hygienists and eugenicists of the time, who included the prominent sports physician Ferdinand Hueppe.[129] Bier denied that the biological "constitution" of the human being was subject to an "iron and immutable" law of heredity.[130]

Finally, Bier favored scientifically based training in sport, while noting that "for the [sports] physicians everything remains to be done."[131] Yet it is important to recognize that Bier's endorsement did not refer to scientific performance-boosting in the modern sense. His primary point was that physical culture should serve medicine, not the other way around.

As remote as it may seem from our own day and age, August Bier's philosophy of medicine helps us understand some of the most publicized figures and doping controversies that have arisen within the German sports medical community in recent years. For example, the traditional conservative critique of "scientific" medicine deplored the transformation of the physician into a mere technician, a development that supposedly diminished the humanity of both doctor and patient. Bier's contemporary, the renowned surgeon Ferdinand Sauerbruch, was only one of many voices calling for a "return to the primacy of 'the personal character of the physician' over mere medical technique."[132] But this emphasis on the *character* of the physician could also become a longing for the *charisma* of the physician, hence Bier's image of the "godlike" physician of yore. In that age as well as in our own, the charisma of the practitioner belonged, not to the scientifically trained doctor, but to the nature-healer whose exotic techniques benefitted from his aura. Thus the (nonmedical) Dr. Heinrich Pudor (b. 1865)—vegetarian, immunization-resister, sexual revolutionary, anti-Semite—was only one of many bizarre personalities who promoted the German nudist movement as a means of spiritual, medical, and a kind of political healing.[133] From the 1920s to the 1950s the role of the European *Wunderheiler* ("miracle-healer") was occupied by a series of (non-German) physicians who specialized in exotic treatments to bring about sexual rejuvenation. The Russian-French surgeon Serge Voronoff made a fortune during the 1920s transplanting slices of monkey testicles into aging men. At the same time, in postwar Vienna, the Austrian surgeon Eugen Steinach performed many "Steinach operations"—vasectomies of one or both testicles—on the grounds that this procedure would conserve sperm; the treatment for his infertile female patients was to irradiate their ovaries. The Swiss Paul Niehans began his career as a transplanter of glands but switched to injecting animal tissue into human patients when gland-grafting was discredited during the 1930s. He became a very wealthy man and achieved the pinnacle of his fame in 1953 when he injected Pope Pius XII with cells taken from unborn sheep.[134]

The celebrity of these practitioners was inseparable from the primitive character of their treatments—scientifically unfounded techniques based on the ancient belief that animal organs could heal their counterparts within the human body. As one German scientist noted in a 1937 article on "hormone preparations," animal organs had been used by alchemists and *Wunderdoktoren* during the Middle Ages.[135] Nevertheless, the profound appeal of these primitive therapies kept them alive well into our own era. Modern endocrinology has put an end to gland grafting, but injections of *Frischzellen* (animal cell tissues) are still common in Germany today. At least five thousand West German doctors are adherents of the Niehans method, and as late as 1990 the Belgian cyclist Eddy Planckaert received cellular therapy at a *Spezialklinik* in Switzerland and proceeded to perform very well. [136] A few German sports physicians, too, inject fresh animal cells into athletes, and it is no coincidence that practitioners of "cellular therapy" such as Armin Klümper, Heinz Liesen, and Hans-Wilhelm Müller-Wohlfahrt belong to an elite group of five or six sports physicians in Germany who have been publicized like movie stars and famous athletes.

The celebrity sports physicians are modern versions of the traditional *Wunderdoktor*. But these charismatic healers, ministering to the "best" German bodies, are more than clinical wizards, for while they are not themselves racists, they have unwittingly acted out German racial preoccupations that have been difficult to acknowledge during the post-Holocaust era. We should recognize that their "premodern" predecessors shared the political conservatism of the German medical establishment as a whole and sometimes expressed racial obsessions in their scientific publications. Ferdinand Hueppe's fin de sièckle interest in physical culture was wholly compatible with his assertion that the Jews were a degenerate race. [137] In his 1913 article on "Sport and Stimulants," Hueppe invoked "the Germanic storm-god Wodan" (as a despiser of alcohol) and propounded a *Weltpolitik* that called for Germanic racial hegemony over the entire world. [138] His *Hygiene of Physical Exercise* (1922) promotes physical culture as a salvational strategy of the German race and European culture as a whole. [139] Arthur Mallwitz, in his address to the Sports Medical Congress accompanying the 1936 Winter Olympic Games at Garmisch-Partenkirchen, hailed sport and the performance principle in the spirit of the new racially fit Germany. [140] In 1939 the director of the Biological Institute of the National Academy for Physical Culture, Dr. Bruno K. Schultz, published an essay on "Sport and Race" that linked race and performance and commented acerbically on the willingness of Americans to count the victories of Negro athletes as part of their medal harvest. [141] The postwar writings of Wilhelm Knoll, a prominent Swiss sports physician professionally active in Hamburg, seethe with the fierce homophobia and sheer contempt for inferior human specimens that made him an eager Nazi sympathizer during the Third Reich. [142] Racial themes, in short, were an integral part of German sports medicine for many years prior to and during the Nazi era. Given the persistence of racial consciousness in postwar Germany, we may assume that the apparent absence of racial ideas in its sports medicine is in some sense illusory, and that the medical man who ministers to Germany's athletic stars is a symbolic custodian of racial health. "Medicine," the great pathologist Rudolf Virchow once said, "is politics writ large,"[143] and in this sense elite sports medicine is a symbolically charged instrument of the *Volk*. This emotional link between sports medical ambition and the national community helps to account for the reluctance of German politicians to separate themselves from prominent *Wunderdoktoren* who practice or countenance doping.

The high-profile sports physician also symbolizes a return to the empathy and personal presence of the traditional doctor who treated the "whole person." But this public display of sports medical skills being applied to popular athletes has also provoked resentment among more retiring colleagues. The "telegenic appearances of doctors in stadiums" have annoyed the Swiss sports physician Bernhard Segesser, among others. "Anyone who can do an instant prognosis may be a hero," he said, "but he is not a responsible sports physician."[144] This alleged conflict between public visibility and medical responsibility, a familiar part of the West German scene, has been dramatically exemplified by the enormous popularity of Dr. Armin Klümper, who founded a "Sport Traumatology Clinic" in Freiburg and has cared for hundreds of elite West German (and foreign) athletes. In fact, Klümper's stormy career over two decades of federally funded activity illustrates both the vulnerability and the power of the charismatic outsider.[145] Following the death of his patient Birgit Dressel in 1987, he was disowned by both Willi Daume and the DLV. Yet within months of his ouster from the ranks of the officially approved, Klümper was welcomed back into the fold by Daume and later by the new leadership of the DLV.[146] For despite Klümper's controversial reputation, the sports establishment had concluded that the tremendous demand for his services by West Germany's Olympic athletes outweighed his liabilities, including a reputation for unorthodox treatments described below.

The celebrity sports physician is himself a curious example of "reactionary modernism," that is to say, the resurgence of antimodern instincts in modern garb. Dr. Hans-Wilhelm Müller-Wohlfahrt, who regards Armin Klümper as his mentor and has treated many stars, exemplifies this paradoxical combination of traditional medical virtues and allegedly advanced techniques. In a 1991 interview in *Der Spiegel*, Müller-Wohlfahrt spoke of his empathy with his patients, his need to listen to their personal stories, the superiority of sensitive hands to technological diagnosis, and the "courage" required of the doctor to "really engage" with his patient. But the charismatic sports physician also challenges the modern world by contesting the validity of its science and claiming he can do better. Thus the appeal of this "old-fashioned" medical style is rooted, not in nostalgia, but in the promise of medical wonders. Claiming that half of all muscle injuries are misdiagnosed, Müller-Wohlfahrt offers elite athletes a dream come true—overnight repair of muscle tears and resumption of training the next day. When he was reminded that orthodox physicians attribute his cures to the power of suggestion, Müller-Wohlfahrt boldly replied that 40 to 50 percent of all medical therapies are "of a questionable nature" yet are not merely the result of suggestive placebo effects.[147]

Such challenges to scientific orthodoxy make this sports medical *Naturheilkunde* a kind of medical populism that is explicitly intended to circumvent academic medicine or *Schulmedizin*, and this conflict is itself a contemporary version of the great medical schism of the nineteenth century. "We are both frontline people," Armin Klümper once said of himself and Heinz Liesen, "who really take care of athletes instead of sitting in the ivory tower of science."[148] The strategic advantage of this alternative sports medicine—or, in Klümper's phrase, "creative medicine"[149]—among high-performance athletes is precisely the suggestive power of strong personalities. The loyalty of Klümper's clients is legendary, while Heinz Liesen has been described by one journalist as "a man who exerts an inexplicable power of attraction over elite athletes, a psychosomatic magician."[150] In other words, these men benefit from the psychological factor in sport discovered by German physiologists almost a century ago (see Chapter 5), while the protests of respectable clinicians are simply irrelevant to elite athletes who are desperate for confidence rather than the support of scientific theories. Referring to the supposedly regenerative injection known as the "Klümper-cocktail," the sports physician Joseph Keul once commented: "There is no scientific work in which the effect of his mixtures is described."[151] Similarly, the honorary president of the German Association of Sports Physicians (DSÄB), Dr. Herbert Reindell, stated in 1987 that "anyone who, like Mr. Liesen, gives injections according to unproven hypotheses violates medical ethics."[152] And even stronger terms have been used. When he sees someone like Heinz Liesen "rushing all over the place giving immunity-boosting injections," Manfred Donike said in 1988, "the first word that occurs to me is 'charlatan.' "[153]

The mystique of the injection exemplifies the charismatic appeal of "radical" therapy. Surrounding the needle is an ambiguous aura that combines the miraculous with the sadistic, the power to heal and the power to violate. In German sports medicine today the injection is also associated with unorthodox substances, including both traditional herbal remedies (*Hausmittel*) and unorthodox substances that are in all likelihood as chemically innocuous as they are exotic. The famous "Klümper-cocktail"—though the exact recipe is secret—contains, in addition to a potentially dangerous drug like cortisone, various antibiotics, denucleated animal cells, extremely diluted plant extracts (following the homeopathic principle), and amino sugars.[154] When Heinz Liesen was attending the West German national soccer team at the 1986 World Cup in Mexico City, he was reported to have administered 3,000 injections containing plant extracts to boost the immune system, megadoses of vitamins C and B-12, bee honey extract for the circulatory system, and calf-blood extract to ward off the effects of the high altitude.[155] In 1987 Hans-Wilhelm Müller-Wohlfahrt earned headlines and the outspoken criticism of Manfred Donike when he injected cells and calf blood into West German soccer players at the European Cup final.[156] In short, the conspicuous use of the needle on elite athletes generates publicity by merging tabloid science and the aura of the *Wunderheiler*. But the high-profile charismatic physician is not limited to the dubious therapies described above.

The charismatic sports physician's intense identification with the ambitions and requirements of his patients can encourage a kind of medical megalomania that disdains limits on performance-boosting treatments as a matter of principle and disparages the competence and devotion of all but a tiny handful of elite practitioners. Armin Klümper said in 1984 that of the 6,000 sports physicians in West Germany perhaps two dozen were worth anything at all. In 1989 Heinz Liesen declared that there were not more than ten physicians in the country who were "really concerned about taking care of high-performance athletes."[157] Ten years ago Klümper called for East German-style care of elite athletes, and Liesen has since called West Germany's sports medical capacity "wholly insufficient" to meet the needs of high-performance athletes.[158] This sort of wholesale criticism can take the form of an impatience with rules and regulations about prohibited substances and techniques, and the definitional problems that result have important consequences for the concept of doping. Thus Liesen maintains that injections that fortify or stabilize the body "really have nothing to do with doping," because the concept of "substitution" holds that the sports physician can legitimately replace what the body loses. But while Liesen usually administers vitamins, minerals, and trace elements, he has also given steroid hormones to marathon runners to "regenerate" their bodies. "Doping," he said in 1987, "is a legal concept that includes whatever is on the doping list. Everything else is up to the personal judgment of the physician." Klümper has effectively concurred: "Everything that helps is permitted."[159]

But the legalistic interpretation of doping exploited by Liesen has failed to satisfy many scientists and physicians for many years. In 1933 the pharmacologist Otto Riesser (see Chapter 4) maintained that in borderline cases it was "common sense and coincidence"—not legalistic reasoning—that guided the physician in determining whether a specific treatment was or was not doping. Four years later the Swiss sports physician G. Schönholzer argued that, far from being a dry technical matter, the idea of doping also addressed the whole issue of what one intended, or one's "mental attitude" (geistige Einstellung). In 1930 Dr. Otto Blau had even wondered whether the search for performance-enhancing techniques was compatible with German values at all—a cultural-ideological approach to the issue.[160] Despite the passage of time and many pharmacological innovations, the idea that doping must be defined according to intuitively determined limits is still very much alive. In fact, two prominent German sports physicians have recently criticized certain of Heinz Liesen's practices in precisely these terms. Herbert Reindell[161] has called this "doping with permitted substances," while Manfred Steinbach termed it, not doping, but rather a "doping mentality."[162] The intuitive definition of doping is important, because the only alternative to a consensus built on self-restraint and a respect for human limits is endless technical and legalistic wrangling over what "doping" actually is.

The high-profile physicians have meanwhile gone their own way. Determined to boost their clients' performances by almost any means, most have favored the supervised use of anabolic steroids since the mid-1970s. As of 1976 some of the most prominent—Armin Klümper, Herbert Reindell, Joseph Keul, Wilfried Kindermann, and Wildor Hollmann—either favored or were relatively unconcerned about giving steroids to athletes,[163] although Reindell and Hollmann eventually took positions against doping.[164] Today steroid proponents within the medical establishment regard the officially sponsored (and politically mandated) antidoping campaigns as hypermoralistic and/or ignorant interference in their relationships with their clients. The attention paid to steroids, Heinz Liesen said in 1985, is the fault of the press, and the sporting press in particular. They should concern themselves with the bodybuilders, who are constantly abusing [these substances]. The world-famous hormone researcher Adlerkreutz from Finland says at every conference that giving testosterone to a man is much less dangerous than giving birth control pills to a woman. Why do we make such a drama out of this? If a body cannot regenerate itself by producing a sufficient amount of hormone, then it is certainly appropriate to help it out, just as one would give vitamin C, B-1 or B-2 or stimulate its immune system, so that it can recuperate rather than remain sick.[165]

Not surprisingly, this kind of uninhibited talk is more the exception than the rule among German sports physicians. Even the steroid proponents have learned to hold their tongues or speak in code so as not to offend public opinion. Dr. Erich Spannbauer, who caused a scandal in 1986 by giving testosterone to the (allegedly unwitting) biathlon champion Peter Angerer, is another one of the few who have spoken their minds in public. Testosterone is "harmless," he stated, and its status as a banned substance because of its cardiac, reproductive, and psychological hazards is simply "an edict of the doping committees, who do nothing but boil urine." The permanent banning of Spannbauer by the German Skiing Association and the International Biathlon Federation was an unusual—and perhaps a hypocritical—event that illustrated the vulnerability of the lesser-known physician who can be sacrificed to save the career of a champion athlete.[166]
Over the past decade the German sports physician who best combined prominence and respectability was Wildor Hollmann, president of the DSÄB and the World Federation of Sports Medicine (FIMS). In 1990 he retired from his position as head of the Institute for Circulatory Research and Sports Medicine at the German Sports College in Cologne, where over many years he conducted research on measuring and boosting physical performance, including a 1966 paper on the potential benefits of certain drugs (caffeine, alcohol, digitalis, nicotine, and other nonhormonal substances) to athletes.[167] During the 1980s Hollmann became a distinctive voice within the West German sports establishment, issuing Cassandra-like warnings about the future of doping and ostensibly cynical predictions about the future of sport. "Never again, not even in the distant future, will we see a type of high-performance sport without doping," he said in 1984.[168] A year later he warned of the coming "waxworks museum of specially bred athletes."[169] But Hollmann's position as a public

spokesman on doping has always been ambiguous. For more than a decade Heinz Liesen served as an assistant to Hollmann, conducting doping-related research while his boss issued dire statements to the national press.[170]

Hollmann has stated repeatedly that doping will last as long as sport, and that new substances will continually appear to frustrate the efforts of those who seek to control the practice. He opposes the medically supervised use of steroids both on account of their unpredictable effects on human metabolism and because he sees the elite athlete as a role model whose behavior will be imitated by children.[171] He has proposed an "honest solution" for high-performance sport that attempts to sever the inevitably doped athletes of the present and future from sport in its traditional sense. "The chemically prepared athlete has been a reality for a long time," Hollmann said in 1989. "We must introduce a fifth category into sport, the sports show (*Sportshow*), that is no longer associated with our traditional definitions of sport. I said eleven years ago," he continued, "that the time would come when we would have to say good-bye to sport and its traditional values. In some sports that time has come."[172] Inevitably, this candid assessment of Olympic-level sport brought Hollmann into conflict with the IOC. In 1985 he criticized its president Juan Antonio Samaranch for promoting "a totally commercialized professional sport circus," since professionalization of the games has been a major cause of doping. Two years later he met with Samaranch and the president of the IOC's Medical Commission, Prince Alexandre de Merode, and pronounced himself satisfied with their exchange of views. The tangible result of this meeting was a joint IOC-FIMS commission that would, according to Hollmann, allow the doctors to exert some influence on events. "The setting-up of the commission," he said with satisfaction, "is a first step in the direction of humanizing high-performance sport."[173] Suffice it to say that the achievements of this commission have not been conspicuous over the past five years.

Hollmann's basic point is that the demands of high-performance sport have driven the human organism to its physical limits. "We have reached the maximum," he said in 1984, "the athletes have entered the biological border zone."[174] Three years later he offered examples of specific physiological limits that had been reached and could not be surpassed. By the early 1960s, he wrote, physiologists had determined the maximal oxygen-uptake of elite athletes. A quarter-century later these values had not been exceeded. On the contrary, readings achieved by professional cyclists in 1964 and 1976

(the famous Eddy Merckx) were still unmatched by their counterparts of the 1980s. Nor had the size of the "athletic heart" increased
among high-performance athletes. In addition, Hollmann argued, lactic acid production in elite 400-meter runners had pushed pH-values
down to the point where lower numbers would trigger the self-
destruction of muscle cells.[175]

Hollmann's ambivalence toward high-performance sport makes
him a particularly interesting contributor to the doping debate. While
he sees doping and other abuses of the human body as intrinsic to
elite competition, he has refused to quit the scene because it is, in
human terms, much more than the sum of its corruptions. "The drive
toward performance," he says, "is inherent in man,"[176] and it is this
elemental need for achievement that makes the abuses of the sports
world more of a tragedy than a crime, as primal ambitions collide with
fated limits. So what is the far-sighted physician to do? "Sports medicine," he said in 1985, "takes the pulse of high-performance sport.
Our task is to look at the professional issues in the widest context and
call questionable developments by their proper names." At the same
time, he went on, the conscientious physician is more than an observer, and the refusal to abandon ship will confront him with some
challenging dilemmas. He could, for example, separate himself from
this corrupt subculture: "The question arises as to whether we physicians can keep on being a part of this." But Hollmann has refused
the option of becoming a conscientious objector to sports medicine:
"That is wholly incompatible with our professional code. As physicians, we are obligated to give help to anyone who requests it."[177]
The problem, of course, is that "help" in this context is an ambiguous
concept. For the central ambiguity of high-performance sports medicine may be posed as a question: Is this medical practice "humane"
or is it "functional"? Is the physician there to serve the patient as a
human being who is separate from his athletic self, or is the physician
there simply to maximize performance? Hollmann himself once
pointed out that ethical objections to steroid use "do not change the
fact that it is clearly possible to improve recovery in specific situations
that occur only at the limits of human ability."[178] But what does
"recovery" mean in this context? Is one recovering to live or to perform? Or are these categories separate at all for the elite athlete?

Hollmann eventually found that in the age of commercialized
Olympic sport the physician "accommodates to pressures that have
very little to do with health, ethics, and morality in the classical
sense."[179] "Every day," he said in 1987, "I am confronted by athletes

asking whether doping is appropriate. But I can't say anything, because if I do I run the risk of losing my license to practice medicine."[180] This is an intriguing formulation from Germany's most prestigious antidoping crusader. What, one wonders, would the doctor say if the law were not looking over his shoulder? But it is important to understand that, here as elsewhere, moral rigorism has its limits, and that even an adversary of doping can feel a profound ambivalence toward drug use. Conversely, the medical colleague who defies antidoping regulations can be something other (and better) than a pariah. For example, both Hollmann and Brigitte Berendonk have praised Armin Klümper's almost superhuman devotion to his athlete-clients, a style that virtually dissolves the traditional distance between doctor and patient.[181] What is more, Klümper's stature among elite athletes translates into political power. It was the loyalty inspired by his devotion to West Germany's best athletes that eventually persuaded Willi Daume to express his "complete confidence" in the doping-doctor. And a year later the only sports official to vote against Klümper's nomination to be an Olympic physician lost the presidency of the DLV. "If conditions like this become the norm," Eberhard Munzert declared before his forced resignation, "then this is no longer my sport."[182] Back in the 1920s this kind of moral clarity was the order of the day among German sports physicians (see Chapter 4). Today the national alliance among sports physicians, officials, and politicians discourages statements of principle while perpetuating the bureaucratic arrangements that guarantee the future of doping. Our final question is whether or not international governance might break this monopoly of power.[183]

The Prospects for International Doping Control

To outside observers the victory of the IAAF in the Gasser case might have suggested that athletes who doped themselves would be caught and dealt with severely by the international body. We must remember, however, that of the 192 athletes tested for banned substances in Rome Sandra Gasser alone was reported to have tested positive. This improbable result drew the following comment from Dr. Robert O. Voy, chief medical officer of the United States Olympic Committee: "I don't know whether the athletes were tested or whether the samples were thrown down the sink. In my mind, one positive for the

track and field championships is unbelievable."[184] Originally, the
IAAF had appointed Dr. Manfred Donike of West Germany and Dr.
Arnold Beckett of Britain, the world's foremost experts on gas chro-
matography/mass spectrometry drug testing, to supervise the drug
testing at Rome. But a few weeks prior to the competitions, for unspecified reasons, they were replaced by a Bulgarian and a Swede of
lesser stature, and Dr. Voy does not rule out the possibility of an
organized cover-up by top officials.[185] It is now known that, in addition to Ben Johnson, at least five gold-medal winners in Rome were
using anabolic steroids for long periods during the 1980s. Four of
these athletes were East Germans—Thomas Schönlebe (400 meters),
Jürgen Schult (discus), Torsten Voss (decathlon), and Silke Gladisch
(100 meters)—while the fifth was the Swiss shot-putter Werner
Günthör.[186] Here is empirical proof that the drug testing performed
in conjunction with a world championship competition as late as 1987
was little more than a farce.

The anabolic steroid epidemic began in the 1950s and is usually
traced back to the actions of one man—Dr. John Ziegler, the team
physician attached to the American team at the World Weightlifting
Championships held in Vienna in 1954. Carefully observing the Soviet team, he concluded that they were boosting their performances
with testosterone, a suspicion later confirmed by one of the Russian
doctors. Upon returning to the United States, Ziegler tested testosterone on himself and others. The first American anabolic-
androgenic steroid, Dianabol, was introduced by the Ciba company
in 1958. Reports about steroids spread among athletes and an epidemic was born.[187]

After three decades of doping it is clear that international controls cannot put an end to doping. Incredibly, the IOC Medical Commission, which introduced the first testing program in 1968, now tests
for no fewer than 3,700 banned substances.[188] At the 1988 Seoul
Olympic Games, its testing procedure produced a mere dozen positives. In light of what we now know about East German doping
during the 1980s and the various techniques used to "beat" the tests,
these athletes certainly represented a small fraction of the participants who doped. Given the similar results of the IAAF's drug-testing
operation in Rome in 1987, its announcement in 1989 of a plan for
worldwide random out-of-competition testing for anabolic steroids
and the drugs that mask them should be taken with a grain of salt.[189]

Drug testing is difficult for both bureaucratic and scientific reasons. As the Gasser case makes clear, the collection, custody, and

accurate scientific analysis of an athlete's urine sample require the personal integrity and competence of all parties concerned if the system is to work and inspire the confidence that is vital to upholding the moral reputation of elite sport. In addition, scientific knowledge is easily abused: It is common practice to discontinue steroid use long enough in advance of testing to escape detection.[190] Indeed, the East German scientists developed this method to near perfection.

More important than these technical difficulties, however, is the bureaucratic nature of sportive internationalism and the inherent problems it shares with other international organizations. First, it is not easy to exercise centralized "international" authority over many national organizations, as the International Atomic Energy Agency among others has discovered. (To make matters even more complicated, the IOC must rely both on national Olympic committees and on international federations like the IAAF.) Second, the leaders of international organizations are often unwilling to assume important responsibilities. Juan Antonio Samaranch, for example, his rhetoric notwithstanding, has rejected the idea that the IOC should lead the campaign against doping. Both he and IAAF-president Nebiolo have called the German doping crisis "a German problem," and Samaranch has said he is not interested in pursuing retroactive sanctions against athletes who have doped themselves.[191] In addition, national sports federations will often appeal positive doping tests on behalf of accused athletes. Take, for example, the case of Harry ("Butch") Reynolds, the American world-record holder in the 400-meter dash. Following a track meet in Monte Carlo on August 12, 1990, Reynolds tested positive for the anabolic steroid Nandrolone and was suspended from further competition in accordance with the rules of the IAAF and The Athletics Congress (TAC). On October 22 of that year TAC stayed the suspension. In June 1991 Reynolds successfully petitioned the USOC to lift the suspension so he could take part in the TAC outdoor championships. On October 4, 1991, the TAC Doping Control Board exonerated Reynolds on the grounds that many irregularities had occurred in the handling and analysis of his urine sample. It is significant that, while the Reynolds case resembles the Gasser case in both its complexity and specifics, exoneration came from his own national federation.[192] Whereas the TAC Review Board's case against the IAAF presentation appears to have been quite substantial, other cases exhibit blatant national bias. For example, when the Norwegian shot-putter Georg Andersen tested positive for an anabolic steroid in 1991—four years after five other Norwegian shot-putters were caught

doping—the Norwegian Track and Field Federation proclaimed his
innocence on no grounds whatsoever. Andersen's retinue surpassed
in inventiveness all previous alibis for positive drug tests by claiming
that he had ingested hormones from the chicken he had eaten at a
banquet in Portugal, a claim that did not stand up to even a brief
scientific examination.[193]

Nor is it easy to keep track of individuals who possess the expertise to flout international rules and regulations. Indeed, the mi-
gration of East German doping experts to various parts of the world
may be followed by a similar exodus of Soviet nuclear scientists who
are prepared to sell their services to the highest bidder.[194] But the
crucial question is whether an international organization is truly *internationalist* in theory and practice, or whether it is primarily an
arrangement for facilitating the expression of nationalist impulses
whose purpose is continually disguised by internationalist rhetoric.
Because the Olympic movement belongs to the second category, the
Swiss sports physician Hans Howald concluded in 1984 that neither
the IOC nor the international federations with which it must collab-
orate are interested in publicizing positive drug tests.[195] But this
managerial indifference to rules violations is not limited to the Olympic movement and its affiliates. In the Nobel address he delivered in
1970, Alexander Solzhenitsyn referred sarcastically to the United Nations as "a United Governments Organization" having nothing to do
with internationalist idealism.[196] Until this fundamental structural
defect is remedied, the Olympic movement will continue to sponsor
doping even as it spends millions to "control" it. Or, perhaps, the
steroid will prevail and the definition of doping will be revised to
make it compatible with current practices. The final chapter of this
book explores the implications of such a scheme for the future of
sport.

8

Horses and Humans
Equine Performance and the Future of Sport

The doping of racehorses throughout the twentieth century[1] is only one of many parallel developments that link the human and equine athlete. Yet the physiological conceptions of and training techniques applied to the athletes of these two species have not always evolved in synchrony with each other. The use of breeding to improve equine performance appeared centuries before speculations about the genetic manipulation of human beings. And at the turn of the century, investigations into the physical capacities of horses were considerably more advanced than those pertaining to the physiology of human athletic performance. As the prominent fatigue-researcher Angelo Mosso pointed out in the 1890s, the physiological laws associated with training and work performed by horses were much better understood than those pertaining to human beings.[2]

Breeding and Drugging the Equine Athlete

On January 6, 1912, *The Pharmaceutical Journal and Pharmacist* of London published a short but direct reply to an anonymous correspondent under the rubric of "Doping Racehorses." The inquirer had apparently solicited advice that the better sort of person simply did not pursue. "We have no special information on the subject," the editors wrote, "and as the use of drugs for the purpose would be illegal you would be well advised to have nothing to do with the matter."[3] In fact, the relationship between drugs and large animals had been addressed in the same journal five years earlier, but in a rather different spirit. In an essay titled "Subduing Restless Horses," a pseudonymous "Centaur" described the stealthy machinations of a farmhand in pursuit of the "ingredients of a mysterious compound" that would tranquilize unruly colts, including restless animals that "would not submit to the machine" that castrated (or "clipped") them. "Through the columns of the agricultural papers," the author continued, "the carter, the cowman, and the shepherd are getting to know a good deal about drugs and their action upon animals. Query columns are open to them, and are very freely used." And woe to the misinformed "pharmaceutical brother" who recommended opium rather than chloral to the anxious farmer, since the former drug would only exacerbate a horse's restlessness.[4]

Less than a year after its laconic reply to the nameless information-seeker, the *Journal and Pharmacist* printed another report of pharmaceutical monkey business involving horses. Shortly after the Olympic Horse Show, the West London Police Court dealt with two men "charged with administering ginger and capsicum to horses to give them the appearance of being young and full of life"—a shady practice that anticipated the use of anabolic steroids to improve the appearance of young horses a century later.[5] The next report to appear in the *Journal and Pharmacist* concerned a waggoner named Carter who was charged with administering doses of aqua fortis and butter of antimony to three horses owned by the farmer who employed him. "A fine of 40s. and 12s. costs was imposed, and the offence was spoken of as being very prevalent among horsemen,"[6] presumably to envigorate the animals. A year later the stewards of the Jockey Club of London announced that it was "their intention from time to time to order the examination of racehorses with a view to satisfying themselves that drugs or stimulants have not been administered for the purpose of affecting the horses' speeds." Following the Swaffham Welter Handicap at Newmarket on July 15, 1914, a Dr. Lander of the Royal Veterinary College examined a sample of the winning horse's saliva and found "no evidence of drugging."[7] The detection method he used had been developed in Austria in 1910 following a series of unexpected victories by second-rate horses.[8] In 1913 the French Minister of Agriculture ordered that a series of experiments on the testing of racehorses' saliva be undertaken. The results showed that drugs like cocaine, heroin, strychnine, and kola were easily detectable, and that "the only question was really how long the traces of the intoxicant or stimulant lasted."[9] In other words, laboratory methods for testing the saliva of horses were developed a half-century before analogous tests were performed on the urine of human athletes.

The relatively advanced status of equine performance physiology was the result of two traditions: the animal experimentation of the nineteenth century and, more importantly, the decades of organized horse-racing that generated accurate data about equine performance. While most of the resulting literature deals with thoroughbreds, the American trotting horse was the subject of several studies that appeared between 1880 and 1900. "It is as an implement of gambling and sport," an American author noted in 1883, "that the trotter has his chief value to the biological student. Sporting events are published or recorded as the mere everyday use of animals is not, and the records of races give numerical data by which to measure the rate of progress. Similar data do not exist for the study of the evolution of any other breed." In addition, science advanced along with the human impulse to make bets. During the early years of the nineteenth century the three-minute mile was for the trotting-horse what the four-minute mile would be to the human athlete a century later. In 1818 the report that a horse had trotted a mile in three minutes prompted a bet of a thousand dollars that it could not be done—a bet that was lost.[10] Shortly after the publication of the American study, Francis Galton (see Chapter 3) used its data on trotting-horses to calculate that "the rate per mile of the hundred fastest American trotting-horses has become 2 seconds faster in each successive period of 3 years, beginning with 1871, and ending with 1880," and he expected this improvement to continue indefinitely.[11] Similarly, by 1894 the free-running "fast horse" was only a second-and-a-half away from breaking the two-minute barrier for the mile.[12] In short, voluminous data provided a basis for calculations that simply could not be made for humans. (For example, the "pedestrianism" of the nineteenth century, as exemplified by long-distance walking feats, did not involve standardized performances that could be followed and compared over a number of years.)[13]

Yet even the apparent wealth of horse racing data did not satisfy Galton. "It is strange," he wrote in 1898, "that the huge sums spent on the breeding of pedigree stock, whether of horses, cattle, or other animals, should not give rise to systematic publications of authentic records in a form suitable for scientific inquiry into the laws of heredity."[14] For the father of eugenics, of course, the purpose of any such data was to improve the breed.

But how could the equine athlete be improved at all, assuming this were possible? Such speculations had focused on breeding, training, and the energy sources of the "animal engine," in that order of frequency. At the turn of the century a number of scientists considered how these sources of performance capacity were related to each other. The French physiologist E.-J. Marey, a pioneering student of both human and animal motion (see Chapter 3), appears to have believed that the effects of training could be inherited, in Lamarckian fashion, as an acquired characteristic: "Thus in the course of the last two centuries the breed of race horses has diverged markedly from its primitive form. The excitation to more rapid and more energetic muscular action is the cause of the modifications revealed by comparative anatomy, which are in great part hereditarily transmitted."[15] The American author of an 1894 article "The Horse as a High Speed Engine" saw the racehorse as the supreme example of the "vital machine"—then a common term for the mammalian organism—corresponding to the steam engine. In his view, the artificial evolutionary process managed by breeders had made this creature increasingly fit for the racecourse:

> The gain by breeding and change of form of the high speed horse takes effect by improving the relation of weight of muscles, and of form of body and limb, to the new conditions of vigor and power, and of speed of the animal, by giving the creature more of the deer shape and proportion of limb, and increased power in the development and the application of energy in this specific direction.[16]

But how long could this improvement go on? In 1873 the Committee of the House of Lords on horsebreeding had recognized the genetic progress made over many equine generations, but in 1901 one British author speaks of "our exhausted stock."[17] (This pessimism was about a decade premature: winning times for the three classic English races improved from the 1840s to about 1910, but have shown little improvement since.[18] The apparent stagnation in performance prompted this connoisseur of the racing scene to raise some interesting questions about the sources of and prospects for boosting equine performance. For one thing, he frankly doubted the efficacy of the traditional breeding techniques, and he seems to take a cultural conservative's pleasure in holding up the limits nature had imposed on human ambitions to improve the breed:

> Nothing is more baffling than breeding, and I can easily believe that if men had begun to breed a racer on preconceived theories we should never have had the "material" to produce such a magnificent creature as Stockwell, or Persimmon, or a dozen more, at all.
>
> Many and complicated have been the theories by which breeders have endeavoured to avoid these losses and produce a "certainty." But year after year the animals under their charge have refused to be treated as so many four-legged multiplication tables, and the foals thrown have shown much the same proportion of "rank bad 'uns." Nature deals out the cards by processes known only to herself.[19]

But if breeding meant playing in nature's lottery, was training a more rational and effective procedure? Here, too, this observer was concerned about the wisdom of modern methods and their potential for causing harm to the breed as a whole:

> Those modern trainers, who deliberately train a young brute into the cramped and unnatural habits necessitated by a hurried bucket off [start] the instant the flag falls, are not likely to encourage the long, low, sweeping action and powerful stride which are associated with stamina over a long course. In other and even more important details too, many modern trainers and breeders seem to me to affect artificial methods of education and training which cannot benefit the breed. In the early eighteenth century a horse was at least naturally treated as a natural animal, and I believe he was the better for it.[20]

This conflict between the traditional and the modern, between the "natural upbringing" of the thoroughbreds of yesteryear and the "artificial methods" of modern horse trainers, was the fundamental problem in human as well as equine athletics. In his 1908 dissertation on the physiology of Olympic athletes, the German sports physician Arthur Mallwitz compared the oversized hearts of professional athletes to those of racehorses and warned that the animal as well as the human athletes were likely to die of heart disease.[21] In other words, the new training methods were literally life-threatening.

In contrast with the medical pessimist, others took a more strictly mathematical approach to the sportive feats of man and beast. In his 1906 essay "An Approximate Law of Fatigue in the Speeds of Racing Animals," the American scientist A.E. Kennelly studied the kind of trotting-horse data used by Galton and predicted "final limits" for the one-mile times of both trotters (98 seconds) and thoroughbreds (91.5 seconds).[22] But men, too, were racing animals, and Kennelly surveyed the human performance data for running, walking, rowing, swimming, bicycling, and skating. Although he did not predict final record times in these events, he did produce a formula relating the increases in distance covered by these various performers to the increases in the time required to cover them.[23] Most remarkably, he found that plotting the time-versus-distance relationships for trotting, running, and pacing horses along with those for running, walking, rowing, swimming, and skating men, *all* followed parallel lines when plotted on logarithm paper.[24] This was perhaps the most impressive evidence produced by fin de siècle science justifying the frequent comparisons of this era between the animal organism and the internal combustion engine, since quantifiable data appeared to predict performance.

By the turn of the century, then, racehorses as well as human athletes were experimental subjects for the exercise physiologists of the era. "If there is any thing in the world of nature that seems clear, morally," an Englishman wrote in 1874, "it is that man has an authentic right to require reasonable service from the horse."[25] As physiology became an increasingly interesting science toward the end of the century, this right included equine service in the laboratory. The German physiologist Nathan Zuntz was testing horses on treadmills as early as 1889 and debating the merits of his equine respiratory mask—a baglike device that measured and analyzed exhaled air—in the scientific literature.[26] A few years later, a British military veterinarian calculated the maximum muscular power of the horse.[27]

During the twentieth century the science of equine performance has advanced on several fronts, but this has not meant consistent improvements in performance. While times for the longer British races remain essentially static, winning times continue to improve in shorter races such as the Kentucky Derby.[28] As one observer summed it up in 1986: "The speeds of galloping racehorses have not improved much this century, unlike speeds in human athletics, or even equine trotting races."[29] These mixed results have prompted increased scientific interest in determining how breeding and training contribute to equine performance. For example, could it be that the thoroughbred stock has become genetically exhausted? Apparently not, since recent calculations have suggested that "the failure of winning times to improve is not due to insufficient genetic variance in the thoroughbred population as a whole."[30] If this is in fact the case, then we may assume that training methods have failed to exploit real genetic opportunities to boost equine performance. If, on the other hand, these calculations are in error and exploitable genetic variance really has disappeared from the stock, then it is important to learn why this has occurred.[31] In short, while selection has been improving *average* racing performance,[32] there is no longer an efficient "science" of breeding that can boost top performances, even if there are those who would claim otherwise. (Shortly before the animal-cruelty scandal bearing his name toppled Paul Schockemöhle from his position as Germany's leading horse-trainer, he announced that he would in the near future be producing "an almost perfect racehorse" by computer.)[33]

But the physiology of training is better understood than it was at the turn of the century. One investigator estimated in 1991 that about 35 percent of equine racing performance results from heritable factors, while the remaining 65 percent is traceable to such factors as training and nutrition.[34] Horse trainers have debated, for example, whether or not "interval training" is of value to equine athletes, as it is to humans. Interval work consists of a series of short, intense efforts separated by rest periods in order to build endurance, as opposed to long steady training exercises. Some trainers have claimed that interval training has improved the speed of trotters, though research by scientists at Ohio State University "found no differences in standard measurements of physiology, such as changes in heart rate, or in the biochemistry of the blood, between animals trained by interval methods and those trained by more continuous methods."

Today, in the search for new training techniques, horses are still being put onto treadmills and made to breathe into respiration bags while skin electrodes monitor their heart rate and catheters inserted into blood vessels in the neck divert blood for biochemical analyses that illuminate the secrets of equine muscular physiology.[35] In fact, horses are remarkably powerful athletes that enjoy several physiological advantages over humans. First, they possess more glycogen, or respiratory fuel, in their muscles. Second, they can actually increase their red blood cell count during exercise, thereby facilitating the transport of oxygen to muscle tissues. (Human athletes take the drug erythropoetin [EPO] or practice blood doping to achieve the same effect.) In addition, the horse is able to increase its heart rate during exercise to a much greater extent than a human athlete.[36] But it is still unclear whether or not this awesome mammalian physiology can be trained to even greater achievements.[37]

For one thing, this scientific knowledge is, like most comparable work on human exercise physiology, diagnostic rather than of immediate value for boosting performance. Similarly, our knowledge of physiological limits to equine (or human) performance remains speculative. Such limits would not necessarily, however, mean an immediate end to improved performances:

> Even if one assumes that such a physiological ceiling exists, further progress should be possible. In human athletics, training regimens are now often targeted specifically on shifting the lactic acid clearance rate. Such methods could well have an application in the training of horses. Furthermore, it might well be possible to select deliberately for more efficient lactic acid metabolism. In horses, that project would be very long run, although it might be feasible to test its applicability in a selection experiment in mice.[38]

That human and equine athletes might share futuristic training techniques is only one example of how similar they are as physiological subjects. In the field of equine neonatology, for example, horses and humans have converged in a medical context. "We've reversed the common course for medical research," an American veterinarian said in 1989. "Ordinarily, treatments are used on animals before they are tried in human patients. In this case, the human baby is our experimental model."[39] Such developments raise the possibility that these two athletic species will converge to an even greater extent in the future. Nowhere is this convergence more evident than in the area of doping.

Two weeks before the Ben Johnson scandal engulfed the Seoul Olympic Games, the turf writer of the *New York Times* described the drug predicament of another famous athlete: "Alysheba," Steven Crist wrote, "must prove he can win a race in New York without Lasix to remove the clouds hanging over his reputation."[40] Three years later Johnson, in virtually the same position as the horse, could not remove the clouds hanging over *his* athletic reputation, because he was unable to run world-class sprint times without his steroid regimen. The fact that man and horse shared this predicament points to their shared status as performers and experimental subjects.

In fact, horse racing in Europe and the United States is haunted by what Crist calls "the one issue that won't go away: the widespread use of both legal and illegal medication, and the resulting public perception that this is an unsavory game run by chemists and crooked gamblers."[41] This drug scene is eerily similar to its human counter-part. Here, too, drug fashions change, new drugs appear to frustrate testers, drug use is discontinued just before competitions, and the very stimulants, depressants, and other drugs originally intended for human use are given to horses. According to one American veteri-narian, applejack and brandy were the favored drugs at the turn of the century while heroin was the drug of choice of the 1920s. In recent years painkillers, stimulants, tranquilizers, camphor, theobromine (the active ingredient in tea), caffeine, heptaminol (for the heart and circulatory system), anabolic steroids—all of these drugs have been fed to or injected into racehorses to boost performance. As one Amer-ican jockey put it: "You often have drug-addicted jockeys mounted on sick horses."[42]

The most controversial racehorse drug in the United States is Lasix (furosemide Hoechst), a diuretic that has been used to mask the presence of anabolic steroids or other drugs in the bodies of both human and equine athletes. Lasix advocates maintain that it prevents exercise-induced bleeding in horses' lungs. But as with so many drugs that allegedly enhance performance, the physiological effects of Lasix on the racing animal are poorly understood. "Folk wisdom," accord-ing to Steven Crist, "holds that Lasix, by draining fluid from a horse, keeps him from bleeding again." Another physiological mechanism has been proposed by the American veterinarian Robert W. Copelan, who believes that Lasix "lowers pulmonary arterial pressure, which decreases pressure in the damaged vessels responsible for the hem-orrhage."[43] But exactly how Lasix works is less important than how people think it works and why they are motivated to draw certain conclusions. "Some horsemen, preferring anecdotal to scientific evi-dence, genuinely believe that Lasix is a humane and helpful bleeding treatment"[44] despite the lack of credible data. But these trainers also know there is scientific evidence[45] suggesting that Lasix makes horses run faster by a crucial half-second per mile, a factor that can only encourage belief in its "humane" role. Similarly, in the world of human sports medicine, physicians who see anabolic steroids as ther-apeutic drugs are conspicuously unconcerned about whether or not they may also enhance performance. Indeed, some would call this a false distinction to begin with, claiming that steroids just restore the body to its normal state—an argument that has appeared during the Lasix debate. Dr. Copelan, for example, claims that the drug's effi-cacy as an antibleeding agent "allow[s] horses to perform at a level commensurate with natural ability" and that "no evidence of enhancement of racing performance beyond natural ability has been demonstrated to my satisfaction."[46] In short, uncertainty about the efficacy of "performance-enhancing" drugs has the same impact on the sporting worlds of both man and beast.

As we saw in the previous chapter, doping involves specific interest groups whose motives deserve scrutiny. So, too, do the motives of those who oppose the use of drugs, and in the world of horse racing this faction has an economic stake that is (so far) unique to equine sport. The chairman of the New York State Racing and Wagering Board, for example, has argued for a ban on Lasix because it "has a pharmacological effect on horses that enhances their performance in a race" and therefore threatens the "integrity" of the sport.[47] New York is the only state to ban the drug (and only within 48 hours of post time). But both the horse racing industry and some sports journalists have pressured the New York Board to liberalize this rule. Their rationale is that racing fans deserve to see first-rate horses that depend on Lasix to perform at their best—an argument that could just as well be applied to human athletes in the foreseeable future. For its part, the board that regulates horse racing uses antidrug rhetoric about "integrity and fair play" to veil its own interest in preserving a healthy betting environment—$3.5 billion a year in New York alone. Performance-boosting drugs introduce yet another uncertainty into handicapping racehorses, and that is bad for business. "Fans routinely talk about which horses 'have the juice,' and wonder how much a 'first-time juice horse' might improve today. How can they be anything but cynical?"[48] In fact, the economics of horse doping are particularly vicious from the standpoint of anyone concerned about animal cruelty. Racing officials want horses to run "clean," even if that means foregoing a drug that might conceivably alleviate their suffering, while revenue-hungry state legislatures and other economic interests promote doping by forcing horses to run as often as possible, sometimes to the point of exhaustion or death—a misfortune that is considered no more than the price of doing business.[49] (The new biannual world championships schedule of the IAAF (International Amateur Athletics Federation) for track and field athletes will have essentially the same effect, encouraging elite athletes to rely on doping rather than permitting them enough time to rest and recover naturally from injuries.)[50]

But the potential disadvantages of Lasix do not spring solely from economic considerations, for the drug may achieve in horses what some sports scientists dream of doing to human beings—tapping the "last reserves" that the organism normally protects for its own survival. "Race horses are bred to run their hearts out in a race," says one Lasix opponent. "They do not have the benefit of a higher intellect to avoid doing damage to themselves in competition."[51] What is more, boosting the performance of genetically inferior horses with drugs could mislead breeders and thereby endanger the future of the thoroughbred line.[52] One might add that both of these situations—namely, drugging athletes into a state of recklessness and committing drug-induced breeding "errors"—may eventually appear in the context of human sport.

In addition to Lasix, anabolic steroids have became a serious problem in the American horse racing industry, even if hormonal manipulation of horses has generally been much less common than among humans. It has also been much less controversial, since hormonal interventions into horses do not pose problems for human sexual identity. Indeed, the English Jockey Club actually permits small amounts of testosterone in racehorses.[53] One interesting account of hormonal experimentation was published in 1942 by the American physician Walter M. Kearns. He had noted the "startling effects" of giving sex hormones to human patients, and he was well aware that castrated animals were used to test the potency of various hormone preparations. His own experiments with human subjects had confirmed that testosterone increased muscular endurance, and it was "these remarkable results on endurance in human castrates which suggested experimentation with castrated male horses."[54] The fact that geldings did not perform as well as stallions in both trotting and running races suggested that castration weakened the muscular system of the horse. The question now was whether testosterone, administered to geldings as a replacement therapy, could make up for this physiological deficit. Kearns found, in fact, that testosterone implanations improved racing performance to a remarkable degree, and one gelding even established a trotting record at the age of nineteen.

But the most interesting part of this report is the author's spirited argument that administering testosterone to these horses was absolutely proper. Indeed, Kearn's logic is indistinguishable from that of many sports physicians who want to prescribe steroids for human athletes:

> There is apparently no reasonable objection to the use of testosterone in racing geldings. Certainly no legal complications could arise from its administration because *in no sense is testosterone a drug or stimulant.*

The illegal and unsportsmanlike use of drugs like heroin, caffeine, or alcohol excites the animal to an abnormal and possibly harmful exertion, followed by late ill effects. On the other hand the administration of testosterone replaces in the animal *a normal constituent of his body which nature intended for him* and supplied through the normally functioning testicles before man removed them. In geldings who exhibit signs pointing to a need of this hormone, it supplies a long term effect in his reconditioning. Along with the administration of vitamins, iron, and other minerals *it belongs in the category of sound therapeutics* [emphasis added].[55]

This guileless apologia for testosterone appeared decades before the hormonal manipulation of human athletes emerged as an ethical problem. It is obvious that Kearns knew about the doping issue and was aware that certain kinds of "stimulation" might be seen as unfair. But he saw testosterone as nothing more than a "substitution" therapy that restores the body to its "natural" state, and to a castrated horse this must have seemed like elementary logic, indeed.

Doping and the Future of Sport

What can the current status of the equine athlete tell us about the future of the human athlete? How likely is a further convergence of these two sportive types? Predicting such developments has less to do with the biochemistry of performance-enhancing drugs than with the behavior of individuals and bureaucracies (see Chapter 7). In short, although new drugs will certainly appear, the future of doping is more a problem for the sociologist or the medical ethicist than for the biologist. It is possible, for example, that the role of the sports physician will become even more like that of the veterinarian. As one American vet has put it: "In the veterinarian's world the client and the patient are not the same. Our first loyalty is to the patient. But you can't force an owner to treat. You are under obligations to follow their requests."[56] This veterinary model describes quite accurately the late East German system, and it is by no means impossible that similar systems will be sponsored by non-Communist states, perhaps employing former East German emigrés. Such arrangements tend to destroy the autonomy of the doctor or vet. As a Swiss observer noted: "There are already schizophrenic situations where veterinarians must evaluate horses they themselves are treating."[57] This type of "schizophrenia" inheres in the whole concept of the "sports physician," and it may become an even more institutionalized feature of sports medicine than it already is. Such a development would occur in conjunction with a redefinition of the doping concept and thus a new frankness about drug use by famous athletes. The model for routinizing doping in this fashion was initiated in the equine world in 1990 when the *Daily Racing Form* began adding drug information to its charts and past-performance lines. Now a horse running on Lasix was designated with an "L," while a horse treated with the analgesic Butazolidin (phenylbutazone) had a "B" next to its name.[58] The purpose of this scheme, of course, was to repair a gap in the handicapping process and attract business to the betting windows.

An alternative possibility is that current measures to control the doping of horses could be applied to humans. The personal freedoms of Olympic athletes are still taken more seriously than a horse's right to privacy, but official frustration over the failure of doping controls could prompt the IOC and its national affiliates to take desperate steps to guarantee "clean" competitions for their global public. The American Horse Show Association (AHSA), for example, has ruled that any horse that "acts abnormally" or is entered and then withdrawn from competition can be selected for drug testing. In what may be a sign of things to come, an official publication of the United States Olympic Committee has described the AHSA horse testing program as a model for Olympic sport.[59] At the World Equitation Games in Stockholm in 1990, security measures included stewards provided by the International Equitation Federation (FEI) to watch all 700 stalls, 49 supervisory veterinarians (not counting team vets), video cameras, and identification numbers that horses wore around the clock.[60] Video surveillance of horses will be standard at the 1992 Barcelona Olympic Games.[61] A French Olympic riding champion, Pierre Durand, proposed in 1989 that, in addition to installing video cameras, authorities should require all those with access to horses to wear numbers on their backs, and that investigators should check under leg-covers and bandages to prevent the pain-inducing (and performance-boosting) techniques known as "mechanical doping" (see below).[62] The European championships held in Rotterdam the same year featured barbed wire and patrol dogs in the campaign against both doping and animal cruelty.[63] In 1990 the FEI announced that so-called Security-Level 1 measures would be adopted at events offering more than $60,000 in prize money: two-meter-high steel fences surrounding the area, guarded exercise grounds, and tightly controlled access to stalls.

The most difficult security challenge of all, however, is to protect horses from their own riders and trainers, as was clear in the animal cruelty scandal that erupted in Germany in the summer of 1990 and shook the world of Olympic equitation to its foundations.[64] Paul Schockemöhle, Germany's leading horse-trainer, was videotaped hitting the most sensitive parts of horses' legs to make them jump higher during training exercises. (This practice is prohibited by Article 243 of the FEI's bylaws.) The "Schockemöhle Affair" provoked a public debate among the luminaries of the sport as to where legitimate training ended and animal abuse began. Schockemöhle had previously declared that he was not the sort of trainer who beat a horse on its legs. But after the scandal broke and the notorious tape was broadcast, he changed his tune. Hitting a horse, he said now, was simply a "training method" that did not fall into the category of animal cruelty when carried out by a professional. The former Olympic riding champion Josef Neckermann sharply disagreed, since it was well known that this practice caused great pain to the horse.[65]

Even worse is "mechanical doping," a crude form of behavioristic conditioning that involves the use of chemicals, sharp objects, or electroshocks to inflict pain on a horse's legs during training or competition. The purpose of this pain is to provoke greater muscular exertion to which the horse will become habituated. Mechanical doping is used because no known drug can make a horse jump higher. The training is achieved, in effect, by means of torture. In Switzerland trainers have bound sharpened bottle-caps to the legs of horses during competition or smeared their legs with turpentine.[66] Other European trainers have used thumbtacks, formic acid, or created skin abrasions for the same purpose.[67]

Behavioristic therapies that offer human subjects positive or negative reinforcements to eradicate or reinforce certain behaviors have been used for decades, but I have seen no evidence that they have been used to boost athletic performance. Nevertheless, pain-oriented techniques resembling mechanical doping could play a future role in human sport as athletes encounter the limits of doping and training methods. The Viennese doping expert Ludwig Prokop, for example, has predicted that athletes will pursue training into new areas of stress: "When the athletes know that they can no longer dope themselves without being disqualified, they will simply train harder than before."[68] Harder training will mean more pain, and the athlete will require a trainer of some kind to help him or her inflict and endure this suffering. One extreme development (not mentioned by Dr.

Prokop) would be "torture contracts" between athletes and their handlers that would attempt to establish the trainer/torturer's legal immunity from prosecution. In this scenario the athletes of the future, like the horses of today, would literally require protection from their "trainers." One resolution to the potentially deadly conflict between trainer and protégé would be a horrific vision imagined by Dr. Prokop: a dehumanized, robotlike athlete operating in a state of hypnosis, a creature either immune to pain or unable to stop it.

Such developments might even lead to a Society for the Prevention of Cruelty to Athletes. Performance-boosting cruelty to horses, after all, has become an animal rights issue in Sweden, where laws protect the young, the weak, and the powerless to a greater extent than in other societies. A year before the 1990 world riding championships were to be held in Stockholm, Swedish animal rights activists threatened to blockade the entrance if the painkiller Butazolidin were not banned. At the same time, the Swedish riding federation warned the FEI that a new animal-protection law prohibiting the doping of animals would apply to the event. The FEI quickly ruled that a horse with more than a thousandth of a gram of "bute" would be disqualified as doped. The sad backdrop to this reform was the fact that many of the top horses simply could not perform without Butazolidin in their bodies.[69] The humane treatment of animals has deep roots in Germany, as well, and since 1987 horse doping has fallen under the nation's animal protection laws.[70]

Would modern societies react with similar outrage to the bondage and tormenting of athletes who had formally agreed to such an arrangement? The East German example suggests that state-sponsored abuse of athletes is more vulnerable to public criticism than similar but private arrangements. For one thing, the Western critique of East German sport was always one aspect of a larger political hostility directed at a Communist state. In general, however, any government-sponsored doping or athletic servitude will generate the sinister overtones that do not attach themselves to more informal schemes. (One irony of the Ben Johnson case is that a state inflated the sinister qualities of private parties to safeguard its own image.) Primed by the political science fictions of Aldous Huxley and George Orwell, our imaginations are naturally inclined to suspect the worst if it appears that a government has sponsored manipulations of people or events.

But the bondage issue would not be decided by any state alone. How would the general public, for example, react to reports of such practices? It is in fact no secret that athletes suffer, and it may be that the public expects them to suffer for their fame and their fortunes. In addition, there is no persuasive evidence that "the public" of any modern society really condemns athletes who practice doping and win. For example, the drug-tainted victory of the Spanish cyclist Pedro Delgado in the 1988 Tour de France produced euphoria in his home country. The scandal that erupted when he tested positive for the steroid-masking drug Probenecid seems to have made no different there at all.[71] Similarly, the blood-doping scandal that involved American cyclists at the 1984 Los Angeles Olympic Games caused no public protest. *Sports Illustrated*'s devastating account of the athletes' and trainers' cheating mentality and the medical malfeasance sponsored by the USOC did not animate the American public to demand reforms. Seldom, in fact, has such a genuine scandal left such shallow marks upon the institution responsible for it.[72] These two incidents suggest that one could inflict unprecedented physical, pharmacological, or psychological abuse on athletes without repercussions if it were presented as part of the inevitable stress of high-performance training. Such arrangements could, of course, degenerate into lurid scandals in the event of serious injury, death, or a falling out between trainer and protégé.

We must not assume, however, that such abuses would guarantee improvements in performance, even if the natural tendency to exaggerate the effectiveness of sadistic methods might suggest otherwise. For looking at high-performance sport from a strictly physiological standpoint, it is clear that even our customary expectations about applied science have tended to exaggerate the practical value of sports physiology (excluding doping) to the high-performance athlete. By the 1950s it was possible to correlate performance capacity with quantitative data about the heart, lungs, circulatory and metabolic systems, and by the early 1970s physiologists could scientifically assess individual fitness. But it was not until about 1980 that physiologists could help plan the training regimen of an elite athlete,[73] and even this modest level of assistance remains somewhat problematic. The limitations of laboratory-based science in this area ("physiologic testing") were spelled out in some detail in 1989 by the American sports physiologist Carl Foster. "There is a continual quest for the correct way to train," he noted. "Unfortunately we know so little about the quantitative aspects of adaptation to training that it's hard even to ask the right questions." According to Foster, there are several reasons why "the results of laboratory studies of athletes have rarely led to changes in preparation schedules or competitive strategies." For one thing, the widely used lactic acid profile becomes less reliable as the time of competition approaches, and unexpected test results can be "psychologically devastating" to the athlete who has become emotionally dependent on seeing encouraging "right shifts" in his profile after continuous training and testing. In addition, physiologic tests are still not useful for advising an athlete as to whether he or she should change events or sports, while work on standard procedures for physiologic testing has lagged. Scientists have been unable to define the so-called anaerobic threshold, a level of stress some athletes regard as ideal for endurance training. The measurable effects of various training regimens on athletic performance remain poorly understood. Finally, the extraordinary physiology of the elite athlete defeats the standard research protocol. "Does physiologic testing help?" Foster asks. "One can never be sure with elite athletes at this level; the control that is necessary in research studies is impossible."[74]

One escape from these constraints is to manipulate the athlete's hormone levels. In 1987 the German sports physician Heinz Liesen (see Chapter 7) described the following futuristic possibility: "Every adaptation to training occurs in the brain, in the nervous system. It is there, through the hormonal regulation of the body, that we must do our regulating" to boost athletic performance.[75] Hormonal regulation was also the topic of the conference held in Leipzig in 1990 that brought together the most prominent East German doping doctors and eminent West German colleagues like Manfred Donike and Horst de Marées. This colloquium, and the proceedings published a year later, constituted a scientific overture on the part of the former East Germans to their new sports medical colleagues in the Federal Republic of Germany. Their argument was that "hormonal regulation"— the scientific use of anabolic steroids as perfected in East Germany—is the key to boosting athletic performance. Prior to their own efforts, they argued, scientists had not understood how to manage the hormonal regulation of energy metabolism with anabolic steroids. The international scientific literature had, in fact, dealt with the hormonal regulation of energy metabolism in relation to psychophysical stress, but had not addressed managing the stress and intensity of training. Ethically responsible research on steroids, they said, must be based on adaptational processes in general and hormonal regulation in particular. By intervening in these informational processes, anabolic steroids affect adaptation to the stresses of training and competition. The East Germans claimed to have thoroughly investigated the effects of steroids on the various physiological systems linked to training. "The results," they claimed, "suggest that high-performance training offers medical opportunities that are scientifically well founded and can specify doses without side-effects." In short, the holy grail of high-performance sports medicine had been found: The physician could prescribe effective doses of a steroid secure in the knowledge that he was doing no medical harm. The crowning diplomatic touch of this presentation was the assurance that the integrity of the human genome was secure. "The probing and extension of human capacities in sport," these doctors declared, "is neither unphysiological in a fundamental sense nor objectionable so long as it is achieved in the context of the human genetic endowment."[76] Even as hormonal manipulation advanced, human identity would remain intact.

This East German initiative was by no means the first proposal to bring the concept of doping into line with modern realities, but it was the most scientifically advanced and that was its appeal. The West German cyclist Dietrich Thurau (among others) had called for a new doping concept in 1987, but this had been the self-interested cry of an athlete demanding relief from the inhuman stress of the professional circuit.[77] Today the question is whether the sweat-stained athletes and the men in the white coats will be able to persuade publics and parliaments that the future of sport requires a new medical realism. The German sports medical establishment will remember Wolfgang Schäuble's call for a "new definition of the doping concept."[78] But the crucial deliberative body will remain the IOC Medical Commission. If these gentlemen accede to the importunings of the prosteroid lobby, then a new age of hormonal manipulation will have dawned.

It is genetic engineering, however, that promises to bring about the most profound biological transformations of the human being, and it is likely that this technology will be used to develop athletes before it is applied to the creation of other kinds of human performers. As the Canadian physiologist Claude Bouchard has pointed out, high-tech societies that put a premium on competition and success will want to apply genetic engineering to an entire range of performers, including writers, musicians, and scientists. Athletes will serve as the most promising experimental subjects because it will be easier to identify correlations between the actions of particular genes and performance-related traits if the test performances are physical and quantifiable in a way that musical and scientific talent are not.[79]

The genetic engineering of athletes in the laboratory does not exist at this time, and its future as a biotechnology is necessarily a matter of speculation.[80] The feasibility of developing such a biotechnology is closely tied to the international Human Genome Project, a scientific enterprise now underway that will supposedly identify in sequence all three billion base pairs of the DNA that constitutes the human genome by about the year 2005. Having defined a "standard" genome, scientists would be able, at least theoretically, to compare the DNA sequences, and thus the genes, of outstanding performers to those of less gifted people. Such comparisons would presumably lead to the identification of performance-linked genes and even, perhaps, their synthesis and in utero insertion into the genome of a gestating fetus. An even more futuristic scenario would be the "cloning" of genetically identical individuals from the genome of a great athlete or some other kind of overachiever.

Genetic engineering, like doping and any other important innovation in the life sciences, has both scientific and sociological dimensions. As a scientific problem, the search for the genetic basis of strength or trainability in the athlete—like research on "performance-enhancing" substances—is bedeviled by the sheer complexity of the human organism. "It is the almost infinite number of variables involved in athletic prowess that make it difficult to measure the genetic contribution to it." This kind of research is also complicated by the fact that one is looking for the genetic bases of extreme physiological traits rather than "normal" ones: "Selection is likely to have acted upon the occasional peaks of exertion rather than on the resting state; second, such peaks may be attained by calling into play reserve physiological mechanisms, and it is these that must be considered in any study of the genetic basis of genetic ability."[81] These extraordinary traits typically express themselves in the course of athletic competitions.

The sociological impact of genetic engineering on elite sport is more predictable than what will happen in the laboratory as the Human Genome Project unfolds in the years ahead. As Bouchard has pointed out, it is inevitable that trainers, parents, and sports officials will pressure scientists to make available genetic tests that identify athletic ability in children or even in utero, and it is likely that certain political leaders would make their own, more forceful demands upon their scientific communities. Nor is this mere speculation: Ambitious parents in the United States have already asked pediatricians to give anabolic steroid treatments to their athletically promising children; and the former East German state created and sustained a scientifically

administered doping community for many years (see Chapter 6). However, the genetic engineering of athletes would be complicated by two
factors. First, as the East German model showed, secret government-
sponsored installations for genetic research would require political dictatorships to protect them from public scrutiny and criticism. Indeed,
recent developments in Europe have shown that the social restraints
on producing genetic "improvements" in humans are quite real. In
January 1992 a British committee on the ethics of gene therapy recommended a ban on the enhancing of human characteristics (intelligence and personality traits) through genetic engineering. In addition,
molecular biologists in Germany who want to do recombinant DNA
research now face an intimidating set of regulations prescribed by a
new "gene technology law."[82] Second, confirming the efficacy of an in
utero procedure would take a minimum of one human generation to
enable scientists and trainers to test the performance capabilities of the
manipulated offspring. What is more, the sudden appearance of an entire cohort of phenomenally endowed athletes would probably create
a demand for DNA tests to detect genetic engineering—assuming, of
course, that these techniques had been outlawed in the first place. This
hypothetical chromosomal test already has a kind of precedent in the
case of Olympic sex tests, which employ gene amplification technology
to confirm that female competitors are genetically female. Significantly, the inherent problems involved in defining gender on genetic
grounds prompted one prominent Spanish geneticist to refuse to participate in the sex testing of women prior to the 1992 Barcelona Olympic Games. Yet abandoning this procedure may well result in a
questionable liberation for female athletes, since its failings could res-
urrect a more primitive approach to gender identification. Before
1966, female athletes were sometimes required to parade naked before
sex-determination committees, and as of this writing (February 1992)
a medical committee of the IAAF has suggested that physicians simply
examine an athlete's genitals to determine gender.[83]

The development of athletes by means of the manipulation of
genetic material would occupy its own place within the eugenic tradition. Modern scientific thinking about improving the human race
through heredity begins with Francis Galton, who invented the term
"eugenics" in 1883 and also attempted to study the heritability of
athletic ability in rowers (see Chapter 3). Since then eugenic theory
and practice have assumed two forms.[84] The "negative eugenics"
movement that was active during the early decades of this century in
Great Britain, the United States, and Germany aimed at reducing the

reproductive capacity of the lower classes. "Positive eugenics," on the other hand, encouraged those deemed socially and intellectually superior to have more children for the good of society. From the beginning eugenicists gave priority to intellectual ability and rarely mentioned physical aptitudes. The Eugenics Record Office founded by the American Charles Davenport in 1911 collected information on the athletic abilities of its large human sample, but this was only one among many traits. Similarly, the Fitter Families competitions, conducted in the "human stock" sections at some American state fairs, did not aim at finding athletically talented offspring in particular. However, the potential relationship between positive eugenics and human athletic performance was never far from the surface. According to Davenport, "the most progressive revolution in history" could be realized if only "human matings could be placed upon the same high plane as that of horse breeding."[85]

Genetic engineering will be the great bioethical issue of the next century because it concerns nothing less than human identity itself. It will be far more controversial than doping because it involves reproductive biology—including the rights and responsibilities of parents and their offspring—in profound ways that doping does not. Indeed, the struggle over this biotechnology will constitute one of the great conflicts of human history, an ideological battle royal, pitting a "proscientific" faction against its "antiscientific" adversaries. And as the Human Genome Project gets underway, the contest for public opinion has already begun.

The principal conflict in this case is between scientific ambition (including its genuinely therapeutic intentions) and the "instinctive" or "ethical" restraints we feel about modifying the human organism in a permanent way. As an editorialist put it in *Nature* last year, "Questions that seem cut and dried to professional people may be deeply worrying for the more general public. . . . It would be a shame," this writer continued, "if biology's megaproject, with all its promise, encountered the incoherent opposition that has blocked the path of great endeavours in other fields."[86]

It is in the nature of this "proscientific" mentality to see an "incoherent opposition" where others might see intellectually qualified partners in dialogue who want to think through the mind-boggling implications of refashioning the human species in the laboratory. "The politically correct position," the *Nature* editorialist goes on, "often defined without prompting by molecular geneticists, is that the human genome must not as such be interfered with, and *should* not be inter-

fered with directly, even if that could be done safely (or without substantial risk of introducing genetic mutations)."[87] The fallacy of this
argument is that it conflates "negative" and "positive" eugenic efforts
into a single category. For there is a qualitative difference between
preventing or correcting genetically based disease and reshaping the
human organism. The first procedure removes or reduces suffering
within the context of an otherwise stable human nature, while the second procedure introduces a fundamental instability into the definition
of what a human being actually is.

The dilemma inherent in genetic engineering is summed up in
the figure of the remarkable British scientist J.B.S. Haldane (1892–
1964)—a physiologist, geneticist, evolutionary theorist, statistician,
and all-round virtuoso intellect. Haldane was an early and ingenious
eugenic dreamer whose book *Daedalus* (1924) foresaw the age of in
vitro fertilization ("ectogenesis") with impressive accuracy. As a living
embodiment of scientific daring, he was also a kind of physiological
athlete who conducted many dangerous experiments on himself. "You
cannot be a good physiologist," he once said, "unless you regard your
own body, and that of your colleagues, with the same sort of respect
with which you regard the starry sky and yet as something to be used
and, if need be, used up."[88] Haldane was also more than a bit of a
bully, and his heroic service as an officer in the Great War taught him
the discomfitting lesson that he liked to kill.[89]

Haldane anticipated the genetic engineering of athletes in his
meditation on "the divorce between muscular skill and symbolic expression. Once a craftsman can explain in words or other symbols how
he uses his hands, a singer how she uses her larynx, a new era in
physiology will begin."[90] The physiological self-control of the yogi, he
said, corresponded to the physical self-control of the athlete. The
identification of such exceptional capacities would make possible the
genetic engineering of superendowed individuals capable of amazing
athletic or surgical feats. Haldane also dreamed of gene-grafting techniques that would permit the crossing of men and beasts, of legless
astronauts, and other specially adapted creatures—a vision perfectly
suited to the development of athletes who would be monsters as well.
The supreme biological question confronting mankind today is
whether Haldane's vision of the pursuit of organismic efficiency will
prevail over the human image that appeared in the Old Testament
thousands of years ago.

Notes

1. In the Penal Colony

1. This account is based on "Rutschbahn in den legalen Drogensumpf," *Der Spiegel*, (September 7, 1987): 228, 229, 232, 235, 238, 241, 245, 248, 249, 250, 251. The official report on the case of Birgit Dressel, upon which this article is based, has not been published.

2. It is even possible that Dressel's "toxic-alergic reaction" resulted from pain-killing injections she received in the hospital, although this is not the predominant view. See Michael Sehling, Reinhold Pollert, Dieter Hackfort, *Doping im Sport: Medizinische, socialwissenschaftliche und juristische Aspekte* (Munich: BLV, 1989): 114.

3. For a description of Armin Klümper's career as a sports physician, see Chapter 7.

4. The Viennese doping expert Dr. Ludwig Prokop has put the figure at 70 known doping deaths and speculated that the actual figure is substantially higher. See "Unheilbarer Drang," *Der Spiegel* (April 8, 1985): 179. In 1977 the German weekly *Der Spiegel* claimed (without documentation) that a thousand professional cyclists had died of drug overdoses. See "Bisschen Damenbart," *Der Spiegel* (April 4, 1977): 193. The Czech physician L. Schmid of the Prague Institute for Sports Medicine performed autopsies on 780 dead athletes and found 218 malignant tumors he regarded as related to drug use. See "Viel Profit," *Der Spiegel* (July 1, 1985): 129.

5. "Schlamm in den Adern," *Der Spiegel* (June 10, 1991): 191–98.

6. Vera Rich, "Mortality of Soviet athletes," *Nature* 311 (October 4, 1984): 402–3.

7. "Viel Profit," *Der Spiegel* (July 1, 1985): 126.

8. Klaus Blume, "Im Osten ein Paradies der Giftmischer," *Die Weltwoche*, (June 23, 1989).

9. "DDR-Institut Kreischa will Olympiastützpunkt werden," *Frankfurter Allgemeine Zeitung* (February 14, 1990).

10. "Doping aus Fürsorge," *Süddeutsche Zeitung* (February 15, 1990): 51.

11. "Zu schlank, um zu siegen," *Süddeutsche Zeitung* (March 15, 1990).

12. "Athleten als Sklaven," *Die Zeit* (January 26, 1979).

13. See "Da reißen Mädels Bäume aus," *Der Spiegel* (September 12, 1988): 215–23. Professor Manfred Donike has discounted these reports, noting that none of the female urine samples collected at the 1988 Calgary Winter Olympic Games tested positive for a specific hormone associated with pregnancy. This evidence alone, however, does not prove his case. See "Fraglich und fragwürdig: Doping—geht es nicht mehr ohne?," *Das Parlament* (September 2/9, 1988): 4. For a popular treatment of the "pregnancy effect" that does not raise the issue of

pregnancy doping, see Shannon Brownlee, "Moms in the Fast Lane," *Sports Illustrated* (May 30, 1988): 57.

14. W[ildor] Hollmann, "Risikofaktoren in der Entwicklung des Hochleistungssports," in H. Rieckert, ed., *Sportmedizin-Kursbestimmung* [Deutscher Sportärztekongreß, Kiel, 16–19. Oktober 1986] (Berlin: Springer Verlag, 1987): 15.

15. Hans Langenfeld has pointed out that the need for a "physiological" understanding of gymnastic movements was perceived by the German pedagogue J.C.F. GuthsMuths as early as 1793. See "Auf dem Wege zer Sportwissenschaft: Mediziner und Leibesübungen im 19. Jahrhundert," *Stadion* 14 (1988): 130.

16. E[mil] du Bois-Reymond, "L'exercise" ["Über die Übung," 1881], *Revue Scientifique* (1882): 108.

17. Arnd Krüger, *Sport und Politik: Von Turnvater Jahn zum Staatsamateur* (Hannover: Fackelträger-Verlag, 1975): 34.

18. See Henning Eichberg, *Leistung Spannung Geschwindigkeit* (Stuttgart: Klett-Kotta, 1978): 41–42.

19. For a useful schematic chart of these developments, see Jacques Guillerme, "Le sens de la mésure: Notes sur la protohistoire de l'évaluation athlétique," in Christian Pociello, ed., *Sports et société: Approche socio-culturelle des pratiques* (Paris: Editions Vigot, 1987): 64–65.

20. On the early history of European sports medicine, see Hans Langenfeld, "Auf dem Wege zur Sportwissenschaft: Mediziner und Leibesübungen im 19. Jahrhundert," *Stadion* 14 (1988): 125–48; John M. Hoberman, "The Early Development of Sports Medicine in Germany," in Jack W. Berryman and Roberta J. Park, eds., *Sport and Exercise Science: Essays in the History of Sports Medicine* (Champaign: University of Illinois Press, 1992).

21. Du Bois-Reymond, "L'exercice," 102.

22. Alfred Binet, "Mnemonic Virtuosity: A Study of Chess Players" [1893], *Genetic Psychology Monographs* 74 (August 1966): 132–33.

23. W. Caspari, "Nathan Zuntz zu seinem 70. Geburtstage," *Die Naturwissenschaften* (1917): 619–20.

24. Leo Zuntz, "Ueber den Gaswechsel und Energieumsatz des Radfahrers," *Pflüger's Arkiv* (1898): 346–48. On Nathan and Leo Zuntz, see Langenfeld, "Auf dem Wege zur Sportwissenschaft," 135.

25. See Robert A. Nye, *Crime, Madness & Politics in France: The Medical Concept of National Decline* (Princeton: Princeton University Press, 1984): 327–28.

26. Bentley B. Gilbert, "Health and Politics: The British Physical Deterioration Report of 1904," *Bulletin of the History of Medicine* 39 (1965): 143, 144.

27. Anonymous review of Archibald Maclaren, *Training in Theory and Practice* (1874) in *Nature* (March 26, 1874): 401.

28. Archibald Mclaren, "University Oars," *Nature* (March 27, 1873): 398.

29. Philippe Tissié, "L'entraînement physique," *Revue Scientifique* (April 25, 1896): 518.

30. Philippe Tissié, *L'Éducation physique et la Race* (Paris: Flammarion, 1919): 157, 159, 155.

31. A comparable remark not dealt with in Chapter 5 is Félix Regnault, "Les types et les vocations musculaires," *Revue Scientifique* (1912): 460.

32. Alexander Brandt, "Ueber den Bart der Mannweiber [Viragines]," *Biologisches Centralblatt* (1897): 227.

33. Norman Triplett, "The Dynamogenic Factors in Pacemaking and Competition," *American Journal of Psychology* 9 (1897–98): 507.

34. Triplett notes that he had borrowed this term from (Charles) Féré, who had used it as a psychological concept. It was also used by another prominent French physiologist, Charles-Edouard Brown-Séquard (see Chapter 3), but as a physiological term. See also J.M.D. Olmsted, *Charles-Edouard Brown-Séquard: A Nineteenth Century Neurologist and Endocrinologist* (Baltimore: The Johns Hopkins Press, 1946): 165.

35. Triplett, "The Dynamogenic Factors in Peacemaking and Competition," 508.

36. This preference for cyclists as subjects is evident in the case of an experiment reported in 1910 by two American biochemists: "No special effort was made to study the metabolism of athletes in particular, save in the observations with a professional bicycle rider." These authors note that even athletically active men "were not in that degree of training which might be expected of a professional prize fighter or a 6 day bicycle rider." See F.G. Benedict and H.M. Smith, "The Metabolism of Athletes as Compared With Normal Individuals of Similar Height and Weight," *Journal of Biological Chemistry* 20 (1915): 224, 245. These authors refer to the earlier (1910) report in a footnote.

37. André Lebois, *Alfred Jarry L'Irremplaçable* (Paris: Le Cercle du Livre, 1950): 150, 147.

38. For discussion of Darwin and the idea of performance at this time, see Chapter 2.

39. James McGurn, *On Your Bicycle: An Illustrated History of Cycling* (New York and Oxford: Facts on File Publications, 1987): 122.

40. T.S. Clouston, M.D., "Female Education from a Medical Point of View," *Popular Science Monthly* (December 1883): 215.

41. See, for example, Cynthia Eagle Russett, *Sexual Science: The Victorian Construction of Womanhood* (Cambridge, Mass.: Harvard University Press, 1989): 22, 126–27, 162.

42. Oskar Zoth, "Ueber die Formen der Pedalarbeit beim Radfahren," *Pflüger's Arkiv* 76 (1899): 319–55. Zoth's 1896 paper on his self-administered testicular exact injections is one of the few scientific papers of this period that expresses an interest in boosting athletic performance (see Chapter 4).

43. See, for example, "Cycle Novelties in England," *Scientific American* (March 24, 1900): 20, 266–67. An exception to the rule is "Cycling and Vitality," *Scientific American Supplement* (September 24, 1892): 13,957–58.

44. H. Lichtenfelt, "Ueber den Nährstoffbedarf beim Training," *Pflüger's Arkiv* (1901): 177–84.

45. Thomas Andrew Storey, "The Immediate Influence of Exercise Upon the Irritability of Human Voluntary Muscle," *American Journal of Physiology* 9 (1903): 52–55.

46. "Cycling and Vitality," *Scientific American Supplement* (September 24, 1892): 13,597–98. See also Sir Benjamin Ward Richardson, M.D., "Health and Athletics," *Scientific American Supplement* (March 23, 1895): 16,032.

47. See, for example, R.H. Thurston, "The Horse as a High Speed Engine," *Scientific American Supplement* (December 1, 1894): 15,778–79.
48. See, for example, "A Phenomenal Jumper," *Scientific American Supplement* (May 12, 1894): 15,318; "An Athletic Feat," *Scientific American Supplement* (February 26, 1898): 18,477.
49. Archibald V. Hill, "The mechanism of muscular contraction" [Nobel Lecture, December 12, 1923], in *Physiology or Medicine: 1922–1941* (Amsterdam, London, New York: Elsevier Publishing Company, 1965): 19.
50. A.V. Hill, "Are Athletes Machines?" *Scientific American* (August 1927): 126.
51. A.V. Hill, "The Scientific Study of Athletics," *Scientific American* (April 1926): 224.
52. Hill, "Are Athletes Machines?" 124–25.
53. Ibid., 125.
54. Regnault, "Les types et les vocations musculaires," 461.
55. "The Gas 'Dope' " [probably 1908] appears in the Beaurepaire Collection Scrapbook (1909–13) and may have appeared in the English periodical *The Athletic Journal* (p. 2). I am indebted to Ian Jobling (University of Queensland) for providing me with a copy of this document.
56. "A Bicycle Tournament," *Scientific American Supplement* (January 13, 1894): 15,038.
57. See James Turner, *Reckoning with the Beast: Animals, Pain, and Humanity in the Victorian Mind* (Baltimore and London: The Johns Hopkins University Press, 1980).
58. [C.-E.] Brown-Séquard, "Sur le siège de la sensibilité et sur la valeur des cris, comme preuve de perception de douleur," *Comptes rendus de l'Académie des Sciences* (1849): 672–74.
59. A. Imbert, "Influence exercée par la douleur sur la forme des tracés ergographiques de la fatigue," *Comptes rendus de l'Académie des Sciences* (1910): 767.
60. [C.-E.] Brown-Séquard, "Recherches sur le rétablissement de l'irritabilité musculaire chez un supplicié," *Comptes rendus de l'Académie des Sciences* 32 (1851): 897–902.
61. R. Regnard et P. Loye, "Sur quelques expériences exécutées sur un supplicié, à Troyes (Aube)," *Comptes rendus de l'Académie des Sciences* 101 (1885): 270.
62. Paul Loye, "Recherches expérimentales sur des chiens décapités (circulation et respiration)," *Comptes rendus de l'Académie des Sciences* (1887): 82.
63. Ch. Richet, "D'un mode particulier d'asphyxie dans l'empoissonement par la strychnine," *Comptes rendus de l'Académie des Sciences* (1880): 443.
64. George Ansiaux, "La mort par le refroidissement," *Archives de Biologie* (1890): 186.
65. Simon Fredericq, "Étude expérimentale sur l'asphyxie aiguë," *Archives de Biologie (1887): 227.*
66. Bonnal, "Du mécanisme de la mort sous l'influence de la chaleur," *Comptes rendus de l'Académie des Sciences* (1887): 83.
67. Philippe Tissié, "Concernant un record velocipédique," *Archives de physiologie normale et pathologique* (1894): 834.
68. N. Vaschide and Cl. Vurpas, "Contribution expérimentale à la physiologie de la mort," *Comptes rendus de l'Académie des Sciences* (1903): 933, 934.

69. Ibid., 933.

70. N. Vaschide, "Neuro-Muscular Force: A Psychical Element in Muscular Force," *British Journal of Psychology* (1905): 317.

71. "Schlamm in den Adern," *Der Spiegel* (June 10, 1991): 198. The drug specified by Dr. Georg Huber is Prednison.

72. H.G. Wells, *The Island of Dr. Moreau* [1896] (Harmondsworth: Penguin, 1967): 112, 73, 103, 108, 108.

73. The physiology of traumatic wounds and death on the battlefields of the American Civil War is discussed in George L. Kilmer, "First Actions of Wounded Soldiers," *Popular Science Monthly* (June 1892): 155–70.

74. Gilbert Horrax, "Contributions of the War to the Physiology of the Nervous System," *Physiological Reviews* 1 (1921): 269.

75. Ibid., 269–94.

76. "Rutschbahn in den legalen Drogensumpf," 241.

77. See, for example, "DDR-Synode befaßt sich mit 'Militarisierung des Denkens,' " *Süddeutsche Zeitung* [Munich] (April 5/6, 1986). The former East German swimming coach Michael Regner wrote in 1990 that he had finally come to realize that high-performance sport in the GDR was "exactly as organized as the army." See "Gib das mal den Mädels," *Der Spiegel* (March 12, 1990): 234.

78. Paul J. Perry et al., "Illicit anabolic steroid use in athletes: A case series analysis," *American Journal of Sports Medicine* 18 (1990): 422.

79. "Ein ganz besonderer Stoff," *Süddeutsche Zeitung* (May 5, 1989).

80. Hollmann, "Risikofaktoren in der Entwicklung des Hochleistungssports," 15–16.

81. "Typen wie aus dem Panoptikum," *Der Spiegel* (July 23, 1984): 71.

82. Hollmann, "Risikofaktoren in der Entwicklung des Hochleistungssports," 16–17. This view of the physiological limits of athletic achievement is not universally accepted. "Our investigations of footracing have led us to the conclusion that the barrier to be overcome by the runner who wants to be a champion is psychological: the last record set and the willingness of athletes to try to break it are the determining factors for the next record. See Henry W. Ryder, Harry Jay Carr and Paul Herget, "Future Performance in Footracing," *Scientific American* 234 (June 1976): 109–19.

83. "Sportmediziner uneins," *Süddeutsche Zeitung* (February 2, 1988).

84. Quoted in Sehling, Pollert, and Hackfort, *Doping im Sport*, 99. Mader's warnings about the dangers of high-performance sport are somewhat ironic given his own record as a doping doctor in the former East Germany. See Brigitte Berendonk, *Doping-Dokumente: Von der Forschung zum Betrug* (Berlin: Springer-Verlag, 1991): 20.

85. "Das Zeug hat mich wild gemacht," *Der Spiegel* (March 19, 1990): 248.

86. "Bußmann nicht nach Seoul," *Süddeutsche Zeitung* (July 9/10, 1988).

87. I have adopted much of this paragraph from Gunter Gebauer, "Das Spiel mit den Sündenbock," *SZ am Wochenende* [Munich] (February 11/12, 1990).

88. Monsignor Michael Sharkey, "When sport oversteps the moral mark," *The Times* (London) (July 1, 1989): 54.

89. Mary Shelley, Preface to *Frankenstein* [1818] (New York: Bantam Books, 1981): xxvii.

90. The enormous furor created by the Ben Johnson affair was the product of more

than one "cause" or "factor"; nor was it the "same" scandal everywhere it "played." In Canada, for example, it was a major political event that set into motion a large-scale inquiry and well-attended public hearings. For an interpretation of its political motives and modus operandi see John J. MacAloon, "Steroids and the State: Dubin, Melodrama and the Accomplishment of Innocence," *Public Culture* 2 (Spring 1990): 41–64.

91. Shelley, *Frankenstein,* 39.

92. The journalist Ernst Peter Fischer has argued that "the negative image of gene technology" in Central Europe is due to a pair of socio-historical factors. He claims that, first, Central Europeans—unlike the English-speaking world in which genetic recombination techniques originated—do not understand the theory of evolution and its principle of natural selection, and that they associate gene technology with eugenics. Second, "the intellectuals" resent the medical promise of new genetic recombinant technology because it threatens a consensus on the end of technological "progress" that resulted from the environmentalism of the seventies. In other words, Fischer treats resistance to genetic techniques as a problem in the sociology of knowledge. This is an interesting argument because it challenges my own theory that certain manipulations of the human organism cause deeply-rooted anxieties in many people, in large measure because we continue to hold on to the Old Testament doctrine of divine creation. In fact, Fischer makes a point of saying that we cannot make rational judgments about gene technology until we liberate ourselves from the influence of biblical concepts. My response to Fischer is that the biblical account of creation retains its value as a restraint on potentially irresponsible experimentation. See Ernst Peter Fischer, "Nur die Genetiker reden eigentlich nie vom Paradies," *Die Weltwoche* [Zürich] (August 8, 1991): 20–21.

93. George Levine, "The Ambiguous Heritage of *Frankenstein,*" in George Levine and U.S. Knoepflmacher, eds., *The Endurance of* Frankenstein (Berkeley: University of California Press, 1982): 9.

94. Shelley, *Frankenstein,* 83.

95. Richard von Weizsäcker, "Der Sport befindet sich in einer Grenzsituation," *Süddeutsche Zeitung* (November 18, 1985). In January 1988 von Weizsäcker critized public pressure on West Germany's athletes to win Olympic medals. See "Die Athleten nicht vorab unter Druck setzen," *Süddeutsche Zeitung,* (January 21, 1988).

96. W.M. Brown, for example, has argued that "any efforts to delimit the use of drugs and other aids to athletic prowess cannot be based on our conceptions of what is 'natural' to human experience. The concepts of fairness, danger, health, and normality are inextricably bound up with our moral and social commitments." See "Ethics, Drugs, and Sport," *Journal of the Philosophy of Sport* 7 (1980): 21.

97. The day before setting a new world long-jump record of 29 feet 4½ inches (8.95 meters) on August 30, 1991, the American jumper Mike Powell received "a 90-minute electromassage from physiologist Jack Scott." See Kenny Moore, "Great Leap Forward," *Sports Illustrated* (September 9, 1991): 17.

98. Norman Fost, "Let 'Em Take Steroids," *The New York Times* (September 9, 1983). By September 1988, Dr. Fost, a pediatrician and medical ethicist, appeared to have modified his position: "I do not advocate steroids or any other

performance enhancing drugs. But I object to the moralistic tone of the prohibition." See "Ben Johnson, World's Fastest Scapegoat," *The New York Times*, (October 20, 1988).

99. "Styrkeexpert vill legalisera anabola steroider," *Svenska Dagbladet* [Stockholm], (September 12, 1984).

100. See, for example, Brown, "Ethics, Drugs, and Sport," 15–23; Fost, "Let 'Em Take Steroids"; "Ben Johnson, World's Fastest Scapegoat."

101. See, for example, Tom Donohoe and Neil Johnson, *Foul Play: Drug Abuse in Sports* (Oxford: Basil Blackwell, 1986): 36; Michael Sehling, Reinhold Pollert, Dieter Hackfort, *Doping im Sport*, 20.

102. Donohoe and Johnson, *Foul Play*, 71.

103. See, for example, "Das Zeug hat mich wild gemacht," *Der Spiegel* (March 19, 1990): 244.

104. Brown, "Ethics, Drugs, and Sport," 22.

105. The classic study of this theme is George Canguilhem, *The Normal and the Pathological* [1943] (New York: Zone Books, 1989).

106. "Athletic Exercises as a Cause of Diseases of the Heart and Arteries," *The British Medical Journal*, December 3, 1892, 1,235–36.

107. Arthur Mallwitz, "Körperliche Höchstleistungen mit besonderer Berücksichtigung des olympischen Sportes" (Berlin: Aus dem hygien. Institut der Kgl. Universität, 1908): 49, 38, 39, 37.

108. A. Albu, "Beiträge zur pathologischen Physiologie des Sports," *Zeitschrift für klinische Medizin*, 78 (1913): 170, 171.

109. Ibid., 163, 169.

110. Philippe Tissié, *L'Éducation physique et la Race* (Paris: Flammarion, 1919): 155, 156–57.

111. "Rätselhaftes Wechselspiel," *Der Spiegel* (October 30, 1989): 248, 252, 254.

112. Joseph Fletcher, *The Ethics of Genetic Control: Ending Reproductive Roulette* (Garden City, New York: Anchor Books, 1974): 20, 3, 16, 6.

113. Ibid., xiv.

114. Charles L. Dana, "Giants and Giantism," *Nature* (February 14, 1895): 381.

2. Darwin's Athletes

1. "Als Wegbereiter einer neuen sowjetischen Lockerheit: 'Computer-Sprinter' Waleri Borsow verspricht mehr Lächeln," *Frankfurter Allgemeine Zeitung* (February 13, 1990): 31.

2. "Det sitter i hälen, inte starten," *Svenska Dagbladet* [Stockholm] (October 12, 1988): 27.

3. Die Springflut der schwarzen Sprinter," *Süddeutsche Zeitung* [Munich] (September 16, 1988): 56.

4. "Das ist erst der Anfang gewesen," *Süddeutsche Zeitung* (June 25, 1990): 35.

5. "Die Springflut der schwarzen Sieger," 56. In 1991 the German magazine *Der Spiegel* published an analysis of the African running phenomenon ascribing its enormous international success, not to biological factors, but to economic motives and a hunger for prestige and social advancement. See "Auf der Intensivstation," *Der Spiegel* (September 2, 1991): 236–39.

6. "Das ist erst der Anfang gewesen," 35.

7. As one (anonymous) British anthropologist wrote in 1866: "Does not the success of our colonisation depend on the correct application of the deductions of our science?" See "Introduction," *The Popular Magazine of Anthropology* (1866): 3.

8. "A Manual of Ethnological Inquiry," *Journal of the Ethnological Society* 3 (1854): 193–208.

9. See, for example, Kenny Moore, "Sons of the Wind," *Sports Illustrated* (February 26, 1990): 74–84. The Kenyan running stars Richard Chelimo, Moses Tanui, and Douglas Wakiihuri have moved to England, Italy, and Japan, respectively, to live and train. See "Auf der Intensivstation," *Der Spiegel* (September 2, 1991): 236, 237.

10. John Beddoe, "On the Bulgarians," *The Journal of the Anthropological Institute* [London] (1879): 235, 236.

11. Sanford B. Hunt, "The Negro as Soldier," *The Anthropological Review* [London] 7 (1869): 53.

12. See Antonio Ciocco, "The Historical Background of the Modern Study of Constitution," *Bulletin of the History of Medicine* 4 (1936): 23–38; W.H. Sheldon, *The Varieties of Human Physique: An Introduction to Constitutional Psychology* (New York: Harper & Brothers Publishers, 1940): 10–28.

13. Michel Lévy, *Traité d'hygiène publique et privée* (Paris: J.-B. Baillière, 1850): 71.

14. John C. Murray, "On the Nervous, Bilious, Lymphatic, and Sanguine Temperaments: Their Connection with Races in England, and Their Relative Longevity," *The Anthropological Review* 28 (1870): 19. The theory of temperaments could also be applied to non-Europeans. Thus the German anthropologist Theodor Waitz states: "The choleric and phlegmatic temperatments only are said to prevail among Negroes." See Theodor Waitz, *Introduction to Anthropology* [*Anthropologie der Naturvölker*, vol. I] (London, 1863): 98.

15. On April 25, 1989, NBC News broadcast a television documentary titled "Black Athletes—Fact and Fiction." The stated purpose of this program was to investigate, with an appropriate degree of racial sensitivity, an apparently widespread belief that African-American athletes in certain sports benefit from anatomical or physiological advantages of racial (genetic) origin. For an analysis of this program see John M. Hoberman, " 'Black Athletes—Fact and Fiction': A Racist Documentary?" Invited lecture presented at the Ninety-Eighth Annual Convention of the American Psychological Association, Boston, Mass., August 14, 1990.

16. George Harley, "Comparison between the Recuperative Bodily Power of Man in a Rude and in a Highly Civilised State; Illustrative of the Probable Recuperative Capacity of Men of the Stone-Age in Europe," *The Journal of the Anthropological Institute* [London] (1888): 112.

17. Waitz, *Introduction to Anthropology*, 114–15.

18. The frequent equating of lower-class Europeans with "savages" appears in this context as well as others. Thus the physician George Harley refers to the "maternity feat" of a "female tramp" who returned to hop picking a day after she had delivered her child with no apparent difficulty. See Harley, "Comparison between the Recuperative Bodily Power of Man in a Rude and in a Highly Civilised State," 122.

19. Joseph-Marie Degérando, *The Observation of Savage Peoples* [1800] (Berkeley and Los Angeles: University of California Press, 1969): 78.
20. Waitz, *Introduction to Anthropology*, 118.
21. E.E. Evans-Pritchard, "Preface" to *The Observation of Savage Peoples:* 38.
22. Waitz, *Introduction to Anthropology*, 117.
23. R.S. Woodworth, "Racial Differences in Mental Traits" [1909], *Science*, n.s., 31 (1910): 174.
24. A.S. Thomson, "Observations on the Stature, Bodily Weight, Magnitude of Chest, and Physical Strength of the New Zealand Race of Men," *Journal of the Ethnological Society* 3 (1854): 131.
25. "Sproat's Studies of Savage Life," *The Anthropological Review* 6 (1868): 369.
26. Dr. Rae, "On the Esquimaux," *Transactions of the Ethnological Society of London*, n.s. 4 (1866): 139.
27. Dr. Beddoe, "On the Aborigines of Central Queensland," *The Journal of the Anthropological Institute* [London] 7 (1878): 147.
28. J. Simms, "The Red Men of North America," *Anthropologia* [The Preceedings of the London Anthropological Society] 1 (1873–75): 212.
29. Harley, "Comparison between the Recuperative Bodily Power of Man in a Rude and in a Highly Civilised State," 108.
30. "The Indians' physical beauty, their fine bodies and noble features, were found to be the logical accompaniment to a noble nature." See Henri Baudet, *Paradise on Earth: Some Thoughts on European Images of Non-European Man* (Middletown, Conn.: Wesleyan University Press, 1988): 27. This aesthetic appreciation of the noble savage's body was distinct from a more fundamental theory of human unity based on shared biological traits such as the average life-expectancy, period of puberty, duration of pregnancy, fertility of hybrid races, and blood composition. See Robert Dunn, "On the Physiological and Psychological Evidence in Support of the Unity of the Human Species," *Transactions of the Ethnological Society of London*, n.s., 1 (1861): 189–92.
31. Quoted in J.A. Mangan, *The Games Ethic and Imperialism: Aspects of the Diffusion of an Ideal* (New York: Viking, 1986): 113, 114.
32. Harriet Ritvo, *The Animal Estate: The English and Other Creatures in the Victorian Age* (Cambridge, Mass.: Harvard University Press, 1987): 15.
33. Bruce Haley, *The Healthy Body and Victorian Culture* (Cambridge, Mass.: Harvard University Press, 1978): 64–65.
34. George Harley, "Comparison between the Recuperative Bodily Power of Man in a Rude and in a Highly Civilised State," 109.
35. Charles Darwin, *The Descent of Man, and Selection in Relation to Sex* [1871] (Princeton: Princeton University Press, 1981): 157, 171.
36. Waitz, *Introduction to Anthropology*, 121.
37. Darwin, *The Descent of Man*, 138.
38. Haley, *The Healthy Body and Victorian Culture*, 126.
39. Darwin, *The Descent of Man*, 138.
40. Agnes Crane, "The Mexican Atlatl or Spear-Thrower," *Nature* (December 3, 1891): 103.
41. Darwin, *The Descent of Man*, 117, 119.
42. See, for example, the review of [N.] Zuntz, [A.] Löwy, Frz. Müller, [W.] Caspari, *Höhenklima und Bergwanderungen in ihrer Wirkung auf den Men-*

schen (Berlin, 1905), in *Berliner Klinische Wochenschrift* (December 1, 1905): 1,572.

43. See the review of H. von Schrötter, *Hygiene der Aeronautik und Aviatik* (Vienna and Leipzig, 1912), in *Berliner Klinische Wochenschrift* (November 1, 1912): 2,187.

44. Darwin, *The Descent of Man*, 168–69.

45. Ibid., 112.

46. *American Journal of Physical Anthropology* 1 (1918): 107.

47. Darwin, *The Descent of Man*, 112, 172.

48. As George Stocking, Jr., has pointed out: "Darwin was not in general oriented toward future, but rather toward past evolution, and while he made some suggestions for the eugenic improvement of mankind, these were unrelated to race formation." See *American Social Scientists and Race Theory: 1890–1915* (Ann Arbor: University Microfilms, 1960): 250.

49. Darwin, *The Descent of Man*, 156–57.

50. The personality Galton projects in his writings resembles that of Oswald Mosley, founder of the British Union of Fascists. See, for example, Mosley's *My Life* (1968). On Mosley's sportive temperament, see John M. Hoberman, *Sport and Political Ideology* (Austin: University of Texas Press, 1984): 56–57.

51. Francis Galton, *Hereditary Genius* [1892] (New York: Horizon Press, 1952): 321.

52. Quoted in Mangan, *The Games Ethic and Imperialisam*, 28.

53. John Crawfurd, "On the Physical and Mental Characteristics of the European and Asian Races of Man," *Transactions of the Ethnological Society of London* 5 (1867): 59.

54. John Astley Cooper, quoted in Mangan, *The Games Ethic and Imperialism*, 56.

55. Alice Lee, Marie A. Lewenz, and Karl Pearson, "On the Correlation of the Mental and Physical Characters in Man," *Man. A Monthly Record of Anthropological Science* [London] 3 (1903): 12.

56. This view of superior European vitality contrasts, for example, with Waitz's version of the same idea: "The greatest energy of physical life is generally found, as indeed may be expected, among peoples in a primitive state; but the longer duration of life, a more extended power of acclimatization, a lesser destruction of life by diseases, and greater muscular strength, is found among civilized nations, owing to their protecting themselves from injurious influences of all kinds, in combination with superior nutrition and regular exercise." In a word, Galton's biologism is opposed by Waitz's environmentalism. See Waitz, *Introduction to Anthropology*, 108–09.

57. Michael Adas, *Machines as the Measure of Men* (Ithaca and London: Cornell University Press, 1989): 38.

58. Quoted in Richard King, "On the Physical Characters of the Esquimaux," *Journal of the London Ethnological Society* 1 (1848): 50.

59. Darwin, *The Descent of Man*, 95–96.

60. Hunt, "The Negro as Soldier," 43.

61. E.H. Man, "On the Aboriginal Inhabitants of the Andaman Islands," *Journal of the Anthropological Institute* [London] 12 (1883): 92.

62. See Maurice R. Davie, "The Negro Question in Wartime," in *Negroes in American Society* (New York: McGraw-Hill, 1949): 314–37. But military aptitude was not always equated with leadership potential. In a letter of March 14, 1779,

Alexander Hamilton, a young officer on George Washington's staff at army headquarters, wrote the following to the President of the Continental Congress, John Jay, expressing the view that "negroes will make very excellent soldiers, with proper management: It is a maxim with some great military judges, that with sensible officers soldiers can hardly be too stupid; and on this principle it is thought that the Russians would make the best troops in the world, if they were under officers other than their own. . . . I frequently hear it objected to the scheme of embodying negroes that they are too stupid to make soldiers. This is so far from appearing to me a valid objection that I think their want of cultivation (for their natural faculties are probably as good as ours) joined to that habit of subordination which they acquire from a life of servitude, will make them sooner became [sic] soldiers than our White inhabitants. Let officers be men of sense and sentiment, and the nearer the soldiers approach to machines perhaps the better." From Leslie H. Fishel, Jr., and Benjamin Quarles, eds., *The Negro American: A Documentary History* (Glenview, Ill.: Scott, Foresman and Company, 1967): 52–53.

63. Baudet, *Paradise on Earth*, 45.
64. J. Bernard Davis, "Oceanic Races, Their Hair, etc., and the Value of Skulls in the Classification of Man," *The Anthropological Review* 29 (1870): 185.
65. Edgar Rice Burroughs, *Tarzan of the Apes* [1914] (New York: New American Library, 1990): 122.
66. Man, "On the Aboriginal Inhabitants of the Andaman Islands," 115.
67. Fredrich Hueppe, *Hygiene der Körperübungen* (Liepzig: Verlag von S. Hirzel, 1922): 35.
68. Burroughs, *Tarzan of the Apes*, 187, 109, 71, 90.
69. Ibid., 147, 195, 238.
70. Harley, "Comparison between the Recuperative Bodily Power of Man in a Rude and in a Highly Civilised State," 116.
71. "Die Springflut der schwarzen Sprinter," 56.
72. *Münchener medizinische Wochenschrift*, (June 7, 1892): 413.
73. On the history of "fatigue" and strategies used to combat it, see Anson Rabinbach, *The Human Motor: Energy, Fatigue, and the Origins of Modernity* (New York: Basic Books, 1990).
74. "Rapport de M le barron Larrey," *Comptes rendus de l'Académie des Sciences* (1893): 947.
75. Francis Galton, *Inquiries into Human Faculty and its Development* [1883] (London: J. P. Dent & Sons Ltd., 1907): 16.
76. Emil du Bois-Reymond, "L'exercise" ["Über die Übung," 1881], *Revue Scientifique* (1882): 98, 101, 108.
77. Arthur Keith, "The Differentiation of Mankind into Racial Types," *Nature* (November 13, 1919): 302.
78. [Summary of] Charles L. Dana, "Giants and Giantism," *Nature* (February 15, 1895): 381.
79. Keith, "The Differentiation of Mankind into Racial Types," 302.
80. Cesare Lombroso, *The Man of Genius* (London: Walter Scott Ltd., 1898): 6.
81. Arthur Keith, "The Differentiation of Mankind into Racial Types," 302.
82. Edward Fawcett, "Patrick Cotter—The Bristol Giant," *Journal of the Royal Anthropological Institute* (1909): 196–208.

83. Paul Diepgen, *Geschichte der Medizin* (Berlin: Walter de Gruyter & Co., 1955): 148.
84. Darwin, *The Descent of Man*, 216.
85. W.L. Distant, "Eastern Coolie Labour," *Journal of the Anthropological Institute* (1874): 139–40.
86. R.E. Latcham, "Notes on the Physical Characteristics of the Araucanos," *Journal of the Anthrological Institute* (1904): 172.
87. See, for example, Cynthiua Eagle Russett, *Sexual Science: The Victorian Construction of Womanhood* (Cambridge, Mass.: Harvard University Press, 1989): 56.
88. Degérando, *The Observation of Savage Peoples*, 80.
89. Donald J. Mrozek has pointed out a similar relationship in the context of the American frontier: "Some officers, such as General George Crook, came to be regarded as 'friends of the Indians,' who saw the natives as sharing in the basic virtues which distinguished the manly civilised Victorian." See "The habit of victory: The American military and the cult of manliness," in J.A. Mangan and James Walvin, eds., *Manliness and morality: Middle-class masculinity in Britain and America 1800–1940* (New York: St. Martin's Press, 1987): 227.
90. Russett, *Sexual Science*, 51.
91. Gina Lombroso-Ferrero, *Criminal Man According to the Classification of Cesare Lombroso* (Montclair, N.J.: Patterson Smith, 1972): 25; Cesare Lombroso, *The Man of Genius*, 338, 26, 250, 100.
92. Russett, *Sexual Science*, 56.
93. Lombroso, *The Man of Genius*, 32.
94. Carl Vogt, *Lectures on Man* (London: Longman, Green, Longman, and Roberts, 1864): 183.
95. M. Larrey, "Remarques sur la constitution physique des Arabes," *Comptes rendus de l'Académie des Sciences* 6 (1838): 774, 775.
96. Charles S. Johnson and Horace M. Bond, "The Investigation of Racial Differences Prior to 1910," *Journal of Negro Education* 3 (1934): 334.
97. Burroughs, *Tarzan of the Apes*, 90, 88.
98. Earnest Albert Hooton, *Why Men Behave like Apes and Vice Versa* (Princeton: Princeton University Press, 1941): 108.
99. Vogt, *Lectures on Man*, 173.
100. Winthrop D. Jordan, *White Over Black: American Attitudes Toward the Negro, 1550–1812* (Chapel Hill: University of North Carolina Press, 1968): 233.
101. George M. Fredrickson, *The Black Image in the White Mind: The Debate on Afro-American Character and Destiny, 1817–1914* (Middletown, Conn.: Wesleyan University Press, 1971): 57.
102. Waitz, *Introduction to Anthropology*, 122.
103. Wilhelm Knoll, *Leistung und Beanspruchung* (St. Gallen: Verlag Zollikofer & Co., 1948): 53.
104. See W[ilhelm] Knoll, "Sportärztliche Arbeit," in A. Mallwitz, ed. *Sportmedizin und Olympische Spiele 1936: Festschrift der Sportärzteschaft* (Leipzig: Verlag Georg Thieme, 1936): 10.
105. Stocking, *American Social Scientists and Race Theory: 1880–1915*, 461.
106. R. Meade Bache, "Reaction Time with Reference to Race," *The Psychological Review* 2 (1895): 479–80.

107. Ibid., 481.

108. Waitz, *Introduction to Anthropology*, 126, 109, 114, 115, 120.

109. Ibid., 117–18.

110. As late as 1910, the American psychologist R.S. Woodworth took to the pages of *Science* to examine "whether the statements of many travelers, ascribing to the 'savage' extraordinary powers of vision, hearing and smell, can be substantiated by exact tests. The common opinion, based on such reports, is, or has been, that savages are gifted with sensory powers quite beyond anything of which the European is capable." See R.S. Woodworth, "Racial Differences in Mental Traits," *Science* 31 (February 4, 1910): 174.

111. Kenny Moore, "Sons of the Wind," *Sports Illustrated* (February 26, 1990): 79.

112. J.W. Jackson, "The Race Question in Ireland," *The Anthropological Review* (1869): 58.

113. Darwin, *The Descent of Man*, 174.

114. James Turner, *Reckoning with the Beast: Animals, Pain, and Humanity in the Victorian Mind* (Baltimore and London: The Johns Hopkins University Press, 1980): 63.

115. Stephen Jay Gould, *The Mismeasure of Man* (New York: W.W. Norton & Company, 1981): 134.

116. Quoted in a review of Paul Topinard, *Eléments d'anthropologie générale* (1885), in *La Revue Scientifique* (1885): 598.

117. Lombroso-Ferrero, *Criminal Man*, 27, 58–59, 87.

118. A. Marie and Léon Mac-Auliffe, "Morphologie des assassins, homicides volontaires et meurtriers français," *Comptes rendus de l'Académie des Sciences* 154 (1912): 296; "Sur les caractères morphologiques de 61 meurtriers ou homicides volontaires français," *Comptes rendus de l'Académie des Sciences* 154 (1912): 128.

119. For a history of reaction time measurements, with special reference to sport, see Arnd Krüger, "Die Reaktionszeit des Sportlers: Ein Überblick über ausgewählte Forschungsergebnisse," *Leistungssport* 31 (1982): 4–33.

120. Louis Lapicque, "Sur le temps de réaction suivant les races ou les conditions sociales," *Comptes rendus de l'Académie des Sciences* 132 (1901): 1511.

121. Michel Lévy, *Traité d'hygiène publique et privée* (Paris: J.-B. Baillière, 1850): 71–72.

122. Quoted in Haley, *The Healthy Body and Victorian Culture*, 225.

123. Quoted in ibid., 175.

124. Quoted in Stocking, *American Social Scientists and Race Theory: 1890–1915*, 342.

125. Adapted from Hoberman, *Sport and Political Ideology*, 87.

126. Lombroso-Ferrero, *Criminal Man*, 214.

127. A. Albu, "Beiträge zur pathologischen Physiologie des Sports," *Zeitschrift für klinische Medizin* 78 (1913): 172–73.

128. See, for example, the many articles on this subject which appeared in the *Jüdische Turnzeitung* (Berlin) and *Die Welt* (Vienna) after 1900.

129. Adolf Basler, *Einführung in die Rassen- und Gesellschafts-Physiologie* (Stuttgart: Frankh'sche Verlagschandlung, 1924): 132.

130. Ibid.

131. Christopher Hibbert, *Africa Explored: Europeans in the Dark Continent 1769–1889* (Harmondsworth: Penguin Books, 1982): 204.

3. Prophets of Performance

1. People who race cars or motorcycles are the conspicuous exceptions to this rule.
2. On the lack of scientific interest in boosting athletic performance at the turn of the century, see John M. Hoberman, "The Early Development of Sports Medicine in Germany," in Jack W. Berryman and Roberta J. Park, eds., *Sport and Exercise Science: Essays in the History of Sports Medicine* (Champaign: University of Illinois Press, 1992).
3. R.H. Thurston, "The Animal as Prime Mover" [1895], *Smithsonian Report* (Washington, D.C.: Government Printing Office, 1898): 303, 316.
4. É[mil] du Bois-Reymond, "L'exercise," ["Über die Übung," 1881], *Revue Scientifique* (1882): 101, 101, 102.
5. Ibid., 102, 103, 108.
6. Justus Gaule, "Die Blutbildung im Luftballon," *Pflüger's Arkiv* 89 (1902): 127.
7. MM. Meurisse and H. Mathieu, "Polygraphe pouvant être appliqué sur les animaux," *Archives des physisologie normale et pathologique* (1875): 257–59.
8. Carney Landis, "Emotion: II. The Expressions of Emotion," in Carl Murchison, ed., *The Foundations of Experimental Psychology* (Worcester, Mass.: Clark University Press, 1929): 503, 504.
9. Robert S. Woodworth, *Experimental Psychology* (New York: Henry Holt and Company, 1938): 273–75, 264–66, 363–64.
10. A. Mouneyrat, "Influence des rapides déplacements d'air que provoque l'automobile sur la nutrition générale," *Comptes rendus de l'Académie des Sciences* 144 (1907): 1,242.
11. See, for example, "Feld der Ehre," *Der Spiegel* (April 15, 1991): 270–74.
12. Quoted in Gina Lombroso-Ferrero, *Criminal Man According to the Classification of Cesare Lombroso* (Montclair, N.J.: Patterson Smith, 1972): 207.
13. Anatole Piltan, "Étude sur la physiologie de la respiration des chanteurs," *Comptes rendus de l'Académie des Sciences* (1886): 949–51.
14. A. Loewy and H. Schroetter, "Über den Energieaufwand bei musikalischer Betätigung," *Die Naturwissenschaften* (1926): 188–92.
15. Hans Langenfeld, "Auf dem Wege zur Sportwissenschaft: Mediziner und Leibesübungen im 19. Jahrhundert," *Stadion*, 14, no. 1 (1988): 141.
16. Tissié, "La science du geste," *Revue Scientifique* (1901): 292.
17. August Bier, "Höchstleistungen durch seelische Einflüsse und durch Daseinsnotwendigkeiten," *Die Leibesübungen* (1926): 38.
18. J.-M. Lahy, "Sur la psycho-physiologie du soldat mitrailleur," *Comptes rendus de l'Académie des Sciences* (1916): 33–35.
19. J.M. Lahy, "La sélection psycho-physiologique des machinistes de la Société des Transports en commun de la région parisienne," *L'Année Psychologique* (1925): 110ff.
20. Mark A. May, "The Adult in the Community," in Carl Murchison, ed., *The Foundations of Experimental Psychology* (Worcester, Mass.: Clark University Press, 1929): 758.
21. For an historical survey of reaction time research relating to sport, see Arnd Krüger, "Die Reaktionszeit des Sportlers: Ein Überblick über ausgewählte Forschungsergebnisse," *Leistungssport* (1982): 4–33.

22. Günther Just, "Die erbbiologischen Grundlagen der Leistung," *Die Naturwissenschaften* (1939): 155.

23. The doctrine that the different forms of energy (electrical, thermal, mechanical, chemical) can be converted into each other without loss of energy. Formulated around 1850 by several German physiologists, this was a revolutionary development in biology. "Arduous experimental researches were begun in the 1850s to prove that organisms do indeed act in full accord with the dictates of energy conservation; proof was delivered by century's end. The organism in its overall measurable relations with the external world—that world serving as source and sink for the organism's energy supply—was an energy-conversion device, a machine no less than those scrutinized by mechanics and thermodynamics." See William Coleman, *Biology in the Nineteenth Century: Problems of Form, Function, and Transformation* (New York: Cambridge University Press, 1977): 123.

24. A. Pütter, "Die Leistungen der Vögel im Fluge. I.," *Die Naturwissenschaften* (1914): 702.

25. A. Pütter, "Die Leistungen der Vögel im Fluge. II.," *Die Naturwissenschaften* (1914): 727, 725.

26. N. Vaschide and P. Rousseau, "Experimental Studies on the Mental Life of Animals" [1903], *Smithsonian Report* (1904): 546.

27. See, for example, Ed. Claparède, "Encore les chevaux d'Elberfeld," *Archives de Psychologie* 13 (1913): 244–84.

28. See, for example, Philippe Tissié, "L'entraînement physique," *Revue Scientifique* (1896): 514, 515, 518; "Athletic Exercises as a Cause of Diseases of the Heart and Arteries," *The British Medical Journal* (December 3, 1892): 1,235–36; Arthur Mallwitz, "Körperliche Höchstleistungen mit besonderer Berücksichtigung des olympischen Sportes" (Berlin: Aus dem hygien. Institut der Kgl. Universität, 1908): 37, 38, 39; A. Albu, "Beiträge zur pathologischen Physiologie des Sports," *Zeitschrift für klinische Medizin* 78 (1913): 151–80.

29. The essential text on this theme is Georges Canguilhem, *The Normal and the Pathological* [1943] (New York: Zone Books, 1989).

30. Ibid., 98.

31. Ibid., 271.

32. E.J. Marey, "The Work of the Physiological Station at Paris," *Smithsonian Report* (1896): 398.

33. [Étienne-Jules] Marey, "Mesures à prendre pour l'uniformisation des méthodes et le contrôle des instruments employés en Physiologie," *Comptes rendus de l'Académie des Sciences* (1898): 375.

34. M. Berthelot, "The Life and Works of Brown-Séquard," *Smithsonian Report* (1899): 678, 682.

35. See, for example, Emile Picard, "L'histoire des Sciences et les prétentions allemandes," *Revue Scientifique* (1915): 44–45. "Today," Picard writes, "what characterizes German science in particular is its facility for making use of ideas which have originated elsewhere."

36. V. Legros, Préface to A[ngelo] Mosso, *L'Éducation physique de la jeunesse* (Paris: Félix Alcan, 1895): xlii, vii–viii.

37. Physiology at this time was an adjunct of military medicine or *hygiène militaire*. See, for example, A. Laveran, "L'hygiène militaire et les conditions d'aptitude au service militaire," *Revue Scientifique* (1892): 804.

38. W. Braune and O. Fischer, "Ueber den Schwerpunkt des menschlichen Kör-
    pers mit Rücksicht auf die Ausrüstung des deutschen Infanteristen," *Biologis-
    ches Centralblatt* (1890): 698–701.
39. See, for example, Michael Rosenthal, *The Character Factory* (New York: Pan-
    theon, 1986): 58–59.
40. Francis Galton, *Inquiries into Human Faculty and its Development* [1883]
    (London: J. M. Dent & Sons, Ltd., 1907): 70.
41. Marey, "Mesures à prendre pour l'uniformisation des méthodes et le contrôle
    des instruments employés en Physiologie," 376, 379, 381.
42. Francis Galton, "The Possible Improvement of the Human Breed Under the
    Existing Conditions of Law and Sentiment," *Nature* (October 31, 1901): 127.
43. Ch. Eloy, *La méthode de Brown-Séquard* (Paris: Librairie J.-B. Baillière et fils,
    1893): 27.
44. [Charles-Edouard] Brown-Séquard, "Expérience démontrant la puissance dy-
    namogénique chez l'homme d'un liquide extrait de testicules d'animaux," *Ar-
    chives de physiologie normale et pathologique* (1889): 653, 657, 656, 657, 651,
    656.
45. Berthelot, "The Life and Works of Brown-Séquard," 685.
46. J.M.D. Olmsted, *Charles-Édouard Brown-Séquard: A Nineteenth-Century
    Neurologist and Endocrinologist* (Baltimore: The Johns Hopkins Press, 1946):
    187, 195, 234.
47. [Charles-Edouard] Brown-Séquard, "Recherches sur la rétablissement de l'ir-
    ritabilité chez un supplicié," *Comptes rendus de l'Académie des Sciences*
    (1851):898–900, 902; see also "Recherches expérimentales sur la faculté que
    possèdent certains éléments du sang de régénérer les propriétés vitales,"
    Comptes rendus de l'Académie des Sciences (1855): 631
48. *Dictionary of Scientific Biography* (New York: Charles Scribner's Sons, 1970):
    525; Olmsted, *Charles-Édouard Brown-Séquard.* 43.
49. Cynthia Eagle Russet, *Sexual Science: The Victorian Construction of Woman-
    hood* (Cambridge, Mass.: Harvard University Press, 1989): 102.
50. Merriley Borell, "Organotherapy and the Emergence of Reproductive Endo-
    crinology," *Journal of the History of Biology* (1985): 6.
51. Brown-Séquard, "Expérience démontrant la puissance dynamogénique chez
    l'homme d'un liquide extrait de testicules d'animaux," 653.
52. Robert A. Nye, "Honor, Impotence, and Male Sexuality in Nineteenth-Century
    French Medicine," *French Historical Studies* (1989): 56–57.
53. [Charles-Édouard] Brown-Séquard, "Nouveaux faits relatifs à l'injection sous-
    cutanée, chez l'homme, d'un liquide extrait de testicules de mammifères,"
    Archives de physiologie normale et pathologique (1890): 206.
54. "Brennendes Problem," *Der Spiegel* (February 19, 1990): 201, 204.
55. [Charles-Édouard] Brown-Séquard, "Sur l'emploi du liquide testiculaire pour
    augmenter la vigueur du fœtus dans le sein maternel, d'après un fait du Dr
    Kahn," *Comptes rendus de la Société de Biologie* (1892): 797–98.
56. [Charles-Édouard] Brown-Séquard, "Remarques sur les effets produits sur la
    femme par des injections sous-cutanées d'un liquide retiré d'ovaires d'animaux,"
    Archives de physiologie normale et pathologique (1890): 457.
57. [Charles-Édouard] Brown-Séquard, "Remarques sur le traitement de l'ataxie

locomotrice par le liquide testiculaire, à propos du cas de M. Depoux," *Comptes rendus de la Société de Biologie* (1892): 796.

58. Dr. Dubois, *Les psychonévroses* (Paris: Masson et Cie, Éditeurs, 1904): 141.

59. [Charles-Édouard] Brown-Séquard, "Du rôle physiologique et thérapeutique d'un suc extrait de testicules d'animaux d'après nombre de faits observés chez l'homme," *Archives de physiologie normale et pathologique* (1889): 742, 746.

60. Marey is generally assigned cameo roles by historians of culture and technology. See, for example, Lewis Mumford, *Technics and Civilization* (New York: Harcourt, Brace and Company, 1934): 250; Stephen Kern, *The Culture of Time and Space 1880–1918* (Cambridge, Mass.: Harvard University Press, 1983): 21, 117, 120.

61. Siegfried Giedion, *Mechanization Takes Command* [1948] (New York: W.W. Norton & Company, 1969): 21n.

62. E.J. Marey, "The Work of the Physiological Station at Paris," *Smithsonian Report* (1896): 406. This essay originally appeared in the *Revue Scientifique*. December 29, 1894, and January 8, 1895.

63. Ibid.

64. E.-J. Marey, "Étude de la locomotion animale par la chrono-photographie," *Revue Scientifique* (1886): 673.

65. Giedion, *Mechanization Takes Command*, 18.

66. E.J. Marey, *Movement* [*Le Mouvement*, 1894] (New York: Arno Press & The New York Times, 1972): 2. On the inadequacy of language in this regard, see also "La photochronographie et ses applications à l'analyse des phenomènes physiologiques," *Archives de physiologie normale et pathologique* (1889): 508.

67. Ibid., 8–12.

68. Ibid., 139.

69. [E.-J.] Marey, "De la mesure des forces dans les différents actes de la locomotion," *Comptes rendus de l'Académie des Sciences* (1883): 822–23.

70. Marey, *Movement*, 148–50; see also, Marey, "De la mesure des forces dans les différents actes de la locomotion," 823–24.

71. [E.-J.] Marey, "Natural History of Organized Bodies" [1867], *Smithsonian Report* (1872): 302.

72. Marey, "De la mesure des forces dans les différents actes de la locomotion," 823.

73. Ibid., 395, 397.

74. Marey, "The Work of the Physiological Station at Paris," 410–11.

75. *Comptes rendus de l'Académie des Sciences* 133 (1901): 721.

76. Bruce Haley has pointed out a similar comment: "With all his training, the oarsman *looked* the athlete; one could not mistake him. This was even more true of that new species of sportsman, and track-and-field athlete, who became, with the aid of journalism, the Victorian embodiment of the hero as Strong Man. Here is a contemporary [1864] account of a hammer throw in the first Athletic Sports between Oxford and Cambridge: 'He held the bottom of the handle with the grip of a vice in both hands, extending them above his head. The firm set muscles, at the top of each arm, were visible beneath his shirt.' " See *The Healthy Body and Victorian Culture* (Cambridge, Mass.: Harvard University Press, 1978): 129.

77. Ph. Tissié, "L'éducation physique," *Revue Scientifique* (1894): 338.

78. J. Thibault, *Sports et éducation physique* (Paris: Librairie Philosophique J. Vrin, 1987): 126, 179.
79. See, for example, John MacAloon, *This Great Symbol: Pierre de Coubertin and the Origins of the Modern Olympic Games* (Chicago: University of Chicago Press, 1981): 104–5, 108–9.
80. On Coubertin's internationalism, see ibid., esp. 262–68.
81. Tissié, "L'éducation physique au Japon," *Revue Scientifique* (1907): 522, 527.
82. Philippe Tissié, "La science du geste," 292.
83. Ibid., 289, 293; Ph. Tissié, "La fatigue chez les débiles nerveux et 'fatigués,' " *Revue Scientifique* (1896): 742–44. "We believe we have demonstrated," Tissié writes, "that 'fatigue' is the initial cause of all oneiric phenomena and, what is more, that a dream can reinforce this fatigue either by generalizing it or by localizing it in specific muscles, thereby provoking or revealing psychoses."
84. Tissié, "La science du geste," 293.
85. As we have seen, a relative indifference to boosting athletic performance is a general feature of the scientific literature of this period.
86. Pierre de Coubertin, "La limite du record," in *Essais de psychologie sportive* (Lausanne et Paris: Librairie Payot & Cie, 1913): 123–28.
87. Georges Rouhet and A. Desbonnet, *L'art de créer le pur-sang humain* (Paris: Berger-Levrault, 1908).
88. Pierre de Coubertin, *Pédagogie sportive* (Lausanne: Bureau International de Pédagogie Sportive, 1922): 23, 55, 56.
89. On Coubertin and the record performance see John Hoberman, *The Olympic Crisis: Sport, Politics, and the Moral Order* (New Rochelle, N.Y.: Aristide D. Caratzas, Publisher, 1986): 85–86.
90. Coubertin, "La limite du record," 133.
91. MacAloon, *This Great Symbol*, 108.
92. Ph. Tissié, "L'entraînement physique," *Revue Scientifique* (1896): 518.
93. Philippe Tissié, "Observations physiologiques concernant un record velocipédique," *Archives de physiologie normale et pathologique* (1894): 823.
94. Francis Galton, "Hereditary Stature," *Nature*, (January 28, 1886), 297.
95. Pearson, *Francis Galton*, 85.
96. Pearson cites a third-party letter to document Nietzsche's awareness of Galton and even argues that "Nietzsche took his doctrine of scorn and contempt for the feeble—with the cynicism (I should like to write the 'sardony') of a social invert—from Galton." See *Francis Galton*, 109, 119n.
97. Francis Galton, "The Origin of Varieties," *Nature* (August 26, 1886): 395–96; "The Possible Improvement of the Human Breed Under the Existing Conditions of Law and Sentiment," *Nature*, (October 31, 1901): 660, 661.
98. Francis Galton, "Terms of Imprisonment," *Nature* (June 20, 1895): 176.
99. Francis Galton, "Psychology of Mental Arithmeticians and Blindfold Chess-Players," *Nature*, (November 22, 1894): 74.
100. Daniel Druckman and John A. Swets, eds., *Enhancing Human Performance: Issues, Theories, and Techniques* (Washington, D.C.: National Academy Press, 1988): 43–46, 100–101, 169–208.
101. Bruce Haley, *The Healthy Body and Victorian Culture*, 227–51.
102. Francis Galton, *Inquiries into Human Faculty and its Development* (London: J.M. Dent and Sons, Ltd., 1907): 14–15.

103. Francis Galton, "On the Anthropometric Laboratory at the late International Health Exhibition," *Journal of the Anthropological Institute of Great Britain and Ireland* 14 (1885): 211.

104. Ibid., 15.

105. Herbert Spencer, "Physical Education," in *Education: Intellectual, Moral, and Physical* [1860] (New York: D. Appleton and Company, 1897): 227, 228, 238, 258.

106. Ibid., 256, 257.

107. Ibid., 222, 223.

108. Haley, *The Healthy Body and Victorian Culture*, 136.

109. Henning Eichberg, *Leistung Spannung Geschwindigkeit: Sport und Tanz im gesellschaftlichen Wandel des 18./19. Jahrhunderts* (Stuttgart: Klett-Cotta, 1978): 41–42.

110. Pearson, *Francis Galton*, 398–99.

111. Francis Galton, "The American Trotting-Horse," *Nature* (May 10, 1883): 29.

112. Francis Galton, "An Experimentation into the Registered Speeds of American Trotting Horses, with Remarks on their Value as Hereditary Data," *Nature* (February 3, 1898): 333.

113. Francis Galton, *Hereditary Genius* (New York: D.Appleton & Co., 1870): 305, 308.

114. Quoted in Pearson, *Francis Galton*, 91.

115. Francis Galton, "Human Variety," *Nature* (January 24, 1889): 299.

116. Quoted in Pearson, *Francis Galton*, 382. See also a report on Galton's paper presented to the British Association in *Nature* (October 24, 1889): 631–32; and especially, Pearson, *Francis Galton*, 386–96.

117. Pearson, *Francis Galton*, 358.

118. *Degeners Wer ist's?* (Berlin: Verlag Herrmann Degener, 1935): 1697.

119. Frederic S. Lee and B. Aronovitch, "On Weichardt's Supposed 'Fatigue Toxin,'" *American Journal of Physiology* 69 (1924): 92.

120. Wolfgang Weichardt, *Ermüdungsstoffe* (Stuttgart: Verlag von Ferdinand Enke, 1912): 11, 21, 44; "Zur Geschichte der unspezifischen Therapie," *Klinische Wochenschrift* (July 23, 1932): 1,270.

121. For a discussion of Weichardt in the context of the fatigue issue, see Anson Rabinbach, *The Human Motor: Energy, Fatigue, and the Origins of Modernity* (New York: Basic Books, 1990): 142–45.

122. Weichardt, *Ermüdungsstoffe*, 11.

123. Lee and Aronovitch, "On Weichardt's Supposed 'Fatigue Toxin,'" 92–100.

124. R. Schmidt, "Erwiderrung," *Klinische Wochenschrift* (July 23, 1932): 1,271.

125. Wolfgang Weichardt, "Ueber das Ermüdungstoxin und -antitoxin," *Münchener medizinische Wochenschrift* (November 29, 1904): 2,126. An earlier but much briefer account is "Ueber Ermüdungstoxin und deren Antitoxine," *Münchener medizinische Wochenschrift* (January 5, 1904): 12–13. It should be pointed out here that Weichardt's American critics accuse him of having failed to perform any meaningful control experiments: "The desirability of performing a series of control experiments, in which nonfatigued muscles were used as a source of the juice, seems too obvious to mention, but a careful search of Weichardt's papers fails to reveal that he performed adequate controls. Rare mention is, however, made of the fact that the juice of fresh muscles proved to be non-toxic or

non-fatiguing. We have endeavored to fill this gap, and the significant feature of our work here is that *results similar to those reported above were obtained when the muscle-juice from non-fatigued control animals was injected.*" See Lee and Aronovitch, "On Weichardt's Suposed 'Fatigue Toxin,'" 95–96.

126. Weichardt, *Ermüdungsstoffe*, 37.

127. Wolfgang Weichardt, "Ueber das Ermüdungs toxin und -antitoxin," 2,125. On one other occasion, in 1923, Weichardt refers to "metabolic products" associated with "muscular performances" which are of significance to "training" (*Training*), an apparent—and rare—reference to sport in his writings. See "Über im Körper unter verschiedenen Bedingungen entstehende aktivierende Spaltprodukte," *Klinische Wochenschrift* (December 17, 1923): 2,305.

128. It should be noted that psychological and psychophysiological studies of schoolchildren were common during this period. See, for example, the many articles that appeared in the *Pädagogisch-Psychologische Arbeiten* (Liepzig, 1910–) edited by Max Brahn. French and British researchers were also concerned about mental fatigue at this time.

129. Wolfgang Weichardt, "Ueber neue Methoden der Immunitätsforschung," *Berliner klinische Wochenschrift* (1908): 955.

130. Wolfgang Weichardt, "Ueber Proteinkörpertherapie," *Münchener medizinische Wochenschrift* (May 28, 1918): 582; "Fortschritte auf dem Gebiete der unspezifischen Therapie," *Münchener medizinische Wochenschrift* (March 25, 1927): 490.

131. Weichardt, "Ueber Proteinkörpertherapie," 582.

132. Wolfgang Weichardt, "Ueber unspezifische Leistungssteigerung (Protoplasmaaktivierung)," *Münchener medizinischeWochenschrift* (January 23, 1920): 91.

133. Lee and Aronovitch, "On Weichardt's Supposed 'Fatigue Toxin,'" 99.

134. Marey, "The Work of the Physiological Station at Paris," 412.

135. I became aware of Weichardt only because he is mentioned—as *Wilhelm Weichardt!*—in Anson Rabinbach's fine essay "The Body without Fatigue: A Nineteenth Century Utopia," in Seymour Drescher et al., eds., *Political Symbolism in Modern Europe: Essays in Honor of George L. Mosse* (New Brunswick, N.J. and London: Transaction Books, 1982): 42–62.

136. Tissié, "La science du geste," 294.

137. Tissié, "Observations physiologiques concernant un record velocipédique," 826.

138. Tissié, "L'éducation physique," 341.

139. Alfred Binet, review of [Philippe] Tissié, *La Fatigue et l'entraînement physique* [1897], *L'Année Psychologique* (1898): 594–96.

140. Tissié, "L'entertainment physique," 518.

141. Tissié, "La science du geste," 294.

142. Tissié, "L'entertainment physique," 519.

143. Marey, "Natural History of Organised Bodies," 302.

144. Marey, "The Work of the Physiological Station at Paris," 411.

145. Pearson, *Francis Galton*, 182.

146. Anatole Piltan, "Étude sur la physiologie de la respiration des chanteurs," 951.

147. W. Caspari, "Physiologische Studien über Vegetarismus," *Pflüger's Arkiv* (1905): 574.

148. Wolfgang Weichardt, *Ermüdungsstoffe*, 5.

149. Francis Galton, "A Rapid-View Instrument for Momentary Attitudes," *Nature* (July 13, 1882): 246.

150. Pearson, *Francis Galton*, 270.

151. Thibault, *Sports et éducation physique*, 116.

152. James Turner, *Reckoning with the Beast: Animals, Pain, and Humanity in the Victorian Mind*. (Baltimore and London: the Johns Hopkins University Press, 1980): 27.

153. *A Decade of Progress in Eugenics* (Scientific Papers of the Third International Congress of Genetics, American Museum of Natural History, New York, August 21–23, 1932).

154. See, for example, "Animal Drug Testing Made More Accurate," *Insight* (May 1, 1989): 53; 'Better Drug Testing Sought," *New York Times* (August 14, 1989); "Helfendes Plätschern," *Der Spiegel* (March 65, 1989): 216, 218; "Doping-Fall beschäftigt Dressur-Equipe," *Süddeutsche Zeitung* [Munich] August 8, 1988); "Ny rapport visar travtränares slarv med hästmedicin," *Svenska Dagbladet* [Stockholm] (September 7, 1988).

155. Galton, "The American Trotting-Horse," 29.

156. Harriet Ritvo, *The Animal Estate: The English and Other Creatures in the Victorian Age* (Cambridge, Mass.: Harvard University Press, 1987): 56, 72.

157. Charles Darwin, *The Descent of Man, and Selection in Relation to Sex* [1871] (Princeton: Princeton University Pess, 1981): 172.

158. Wm. H. Brewer, "The Evolution of the American Trotting-Horse," *Nature* (April 26, 1883): 609.

159. See, for example. H.G. Wells, *The Island of Dr. Moreau* (1896) and *The Food of the Gods* (1904).

160. Marie-Thérèse Eyquem, *Pierre de Coubertin: L'Epopée Olympique* (Paris: Calmann-Levy, 1966): 79; Marey, "The Work of the Physiological Station at Paris," 397.

161. "M. Marey présente à l'Académie deux Rapports qu'il a faits pour l'Exposition internationale de 1900," *Comptes rendus de l'Académie des Sciences* 133 (1901): 721.

4. Faster, Higher, Stronger

1. "Starke Männer mit weichen Knien," *Süddeutsche Zeitung* (November 19, 1990); "Die Gewichtheber-Krise," *Süddeutsche Zeitungs* (November 20/21, 1990).

2. Ludwig Prokop, "Zur Geschichte des Dopings," in Helmut Acker, ed., *Rekorde aus der Retorte: Leistungssteigerung im modernen Hochleistungssport* (Stuttgart: Deutsche Verlags-Anstalt, 1972): 22.

3. See, for example, W. M. Brown, "Ethics, Drugs, and Sport," *Journal of the Philosophy of Sport* 7 (1980): 17–18.

4. Sir Arthur Porritt, "Doping," *The Journal of Sports Medicine and Physical Fitness* 5 (1965): 166; quoted in *Commission of Inquiry into the Use of Drugs and Banned Practices Intended to Increase Athletic Performance* (Ottawa: Canadian Government Publishing Centre, 1990): 77–78.

5. André Noret, *Le dopage* (Paris: Editions Vigot, 1981): 22–28.

6. Ove Bøje, "Doping: A Study of the Means employed to raise the Level of Performance in Sport," *Bulletin of the Health Organization of the League of Nations* 8 (1939): 449; Peter V. Karpovich, "Ergogenic Aids in Work and Sports," *The Research Quarterly* 12 (1941): 443.

7. David Hamilton, *The Monkey Gland Affair* (London: Chatto & Windus, 1986): 30.

8. Dr. Willner, "Sport und Doping," in A. Mallwitz, ed., *Die Sportärztetagung Berlin 1924* (Munich: J.F. Lehmanns Verlag, 1925): 147.

9. This was a hot topic at the International Gynecological Conference held in Strasbourg, France, in October 1988.

10. Béla Issekutz, *Die Geschichte der Arzneimittelforschung* (Budapest: Akadémiai Kiadó, 1971): 11.

11. See, for example, *Le dopage*, 18: Tom Donohoe and Neil Johnson, *Foul Play: Drug Abuse in Sports* (Oxford: Basil Blackwell, 1986): 2; Michael B. Poliakoff, *Combat Sports in the Ancient World: Competition, Violence, and Culture* (New Haven: Yale University Press, 1987): 93; *Commission of Inquiry*: 69–70.

12. *Combat Sports in the Ancient World*: 93.

13. A.W. Buckland, "Ethnological Hints afforded by the Stimulants in use among Savages and among the Ancients," *Journal of the Anthropological Institute* [London] (1879): 240; Walther Straub, "Über Genussgifte," *Die Naturwissenschaften* (1926): 1098, 1099.

14. Walter Umminger, "Die übernatürliche Kraft," in Helmut Acker, ed., *Rekorde aus der Retorte*: 16, 18.

15. Prokop, "Zur Geschichte des Dopings," 23.

16. See the statement of Dr. Robert Dugal in *Commission of Inquiry*: 124.

17. Noret, *Le dopage*, 105.

18. Ove Bøje, "Doping," 442.

19. G. Schönholzer, "Die Frage des Doping," *Sportärztlichen Zentralkurs 1937 in Bern* (Bern: Büchler & Co., 1938): 191.

20. W. Poppelreuter, "Ist die Einnahme von primärem Natriumphosphat ein Dopingmittel?" *Die Leibesübungen* (1930): 534. I am indebted to Henry D. Hoberman, M.D., for pointing out the scientific flaw in Poppelreuter's argument.

21. Bøje, "Doping," 457.

22. See, for example, Robert O. Voy, M.D., "Education as a Means Against Doping," *The Olympian* (December 1987): 44. "Many cases of suppression of [positive test] results can be mentioned, but to be specific would do the [U.S. Olympic] program no good. . . . Nonetheless, it is now time to admit that suppression of results by officials occurs." At the time, Dr. Voy was director of Sports Medicine and Sports Science of the United States Olympic Committee.

23. "Anabolic steroids, including testosterone, are used clinically in cases of testicular insufficiency and to promote growth after severely debilitating injuries." See Tom Donohoe and Neil Johnson, *Foul Play: Drug Abuse in Sports*, 41.

24. Poppelreuter, "Ist die Einnahme von primärem Natriumphosphat ein Dopingmittel?" 536.

25. K.A. Worringen, "Über Arzneimittelanwendung in der sportärztlichen Praxis," *Die Leibesübungen* (1930): 409.

26. Alexander Hartwich, "Calcio-Coramin in der sportärztlichen Praxis," *Schweizerische Medizinische Wochenschrift* (1937): 99.

27. Bøje, "Doping," 465; Karpovich, "Ergogenic Aids in Work and Sports," 441.

28. Noret, *Le dopage*, 25.

29. Mary L. Wolfe, "Correlates of Adaptive and Maladaptive Musical Performance Anxiety," *Medical Problems of Performing Artists* (March 1989): 49–56.

30. *Commission of Inquiry*, 116. I heard an Olympic athlete make precisely this point at the International Symposium "Sport . . . The Third Millennium," sponsored by the International Olympic Committee and Laval University, Quebec City, Canada, May 22, 1990.

31. Gunter Gebauer, "Das Spiel mit dem Sündenbock," *SZ am Wochenende* [Munich] (September 11/12, 1989).

32. Balzac's drug habit has been pointed out by at least one commentator on doping in sport. See Helmut Acker, "Im Sog der Chemie," in *Rekorde aus der Retorte*, 10.

33. Honoré de Balzac, "Traité des excitants modernes" [1838], in *Études Analytiques* (Paris: Les Bibliophiles de l'Originale, 1968): 263. See also Maurice Bardèche, *Balzac* (Paris: Juillard, 1980): 266–67.

34. Pierre-Jean-Georges Cabanis, "Sur les habitudes morales," *Rapports du physique et du moral de l'homme*, vol. 4 of *Œuvres Complètes* (Paris: Bossange Frères, Firmin Didot, 1824): 91.

35. For a survey of this research, see Dorothy M. Needham, *Machina Carnis: The Biochemistry of Muscular Contraction and its Historical Development* (Cambridge: The University Press, 1971): 27–41.

36. R.J. Lee, *Exercise and Training* (London: Smith, Elder & Co., 1873): 36–37, 50.

37. Balzac, "Traité des excitants modernes," 252–55, 265.

38. Ibid., 255, 260, 263.

39. Ibid., 255–56.

40. Issekutz, *Die Geschichte der Arzneimittelforschung*, 100, 103.

41. See Martin Staum, *Cabanis: Enlightenment and Medical Philosophy in the French Revolution* (Princeton: Princeton University Press, 1980): 207–43.

42. Quoted in ibid., 228.

43. Cabanis, *Rapports du physique et du moral de l'homme*, vol. 4 of *Œuvres Complètes de Cabanis*, 5–6, 99; *Rapports*, vol. 3 of *Œuvres Complètes*, 422.

44. Staum, *Cabanis*, 231.

45. Cabanis, *Rapports*, vol. 3 of *Œuvres Complètes*, 420.

46. Poliakoff, *Combat Sports in the Ancient World*, 93.

47. Cabanis, *Rapports*, vol. 3 of *Œuvres Complètes*, 421; *Rapports*, vol. 4 of *Œuvres Complètes*, 99, 101.

48. See, for example, W. Caspari, "Physiologische Studien über Vegetarismus," *Pflüger's Arkiv* (1905): 473–594.

49. Cabanis, *Rapports*, vol. 4 of *Œuvres Complètes*, 64, 67, 67–68.

50. Ibid., 70, 91, 66, 41, 84.

51. Ernst R. Habermann, "Rudolf Buchheim and the Beginning of Pharmacology as a Science," *Annual Review of Pharmacology* 14 (1974): 5. The date of this "incredibly bold statement" is 1872.

52. Robert A. Nye, "Honor, Impotence, and Male Sexuality in Nineteenth-Century French Medicine," *French Historical Studies* 16 (Spring 1989): 56.

53. Cabanis, *Rapports*, vol. 3 of *Œuvres Complètes*, *Rapports*, vol. 4 of *Œuvres Complètes*, 309; 70.

54. Cabanis, *Rapports*, vol. 4 of *Œuvres Complètes*, 32, 63.
55. Buckland, "Ethnological Hints," 251, 240.
56. Ibid., 239–40.
57. Ibid., 240–251.
58. E.H. Man, "On the use of Narcotics by the Nicobar Islanders, and certain Deformations connected therewith," *Journal of the Anthropological Institute* (1894): 233.
59. George W. Stocking, Jr., *Victorian Anthropology* (New York: The Free Press, 1987): 82.
60. Gustave Le Bon, "Les recherches récentes sur la noix de Kola," *Revue Scientifique* 52 (1893): 528.
61. A.E. Crawley, "Sexual Taboo: A Study in the Relations of the Sexes," *Journal of the Anthropological Institute* (1895): 441.
62. C. E. Brown-Séquard, "On a New Therapeutic Method Consisting in the Use of Organic Liquids Extracted from Glands and other Organs," *British Medical Journal* (June 3, 1893): 1,145–47; (June 10, 1893): 1,212–14; "Animal Extracts as Therapeutic Agents," *British Medical Journal* (June 17, 1893): 1,279.
63. Crawley, "Sexual Taboo," 441, 442.
64. Review of Théophile Chudzinski, *"Observations sur les Variations Musculaires dans les Races Humaines"*, *Nature* 59 (1899): 244.
65. John S. Haller, Jr., "The Negro and the Southern Physician: A Study of Medical and Racial Attitudes 1800–1860," *Medical History* (1972): 246. This theme is repeated in Jerome Dowd, *The Negro in American Life* (New York and London: The Century Co., 1926): 398.
66. A. Bordier, "De l'anthropologie pathologique," *Revue Scientifique* (1881): 181–82.
67. Ferdinand Hueppe, "Sport und Reizmittel," *Berliner Klinische Wochenschrift* (March 24, 1913): 551; Max Grünewald, "Einfluß der Koffeinwirkung auf Arbeitserfolg und sportliche Leistung," *Die Leibesübungen* (1928): 359.
68. Walther Straub, "Über Genussgifte," *Die Naturwissenschaften* (1926): 1097.
69. Issekutz, *Die Geschichte der Arzneimittelforschung*, 17. Issekutz refers to A. Stoerck (1731–1803) as the pioneer researcher of this field. The *Encyclopædia Universalis* (Paris, 1989) calls Menghini's study of camphor (1755) "the first work in experimental pharmacology" (Vol. 17, p. 1,031).
70. J.M.D. Olmsted and E. Harris Olmsted, *Claude Bernard & the Experimental Method in Medicine* (New York: Abelard-Schuman, 1952): 73–80.
71. M. Leven, "Action physiologique et médicamenteuse de la caféine," *Archives de physiologie normale et pathologique* (1868): 179–86.
72. Dr. Guimaraês, "Sur l'action physiologique et hygiénique du café," *Archives de physiologie normale et pathologique* (1884): 253–54, 257–58. The author was affiliated with the Museum Laboratory in Rio de Janeiro.
73. Ibid., 252, 259, 280–82.
74. This theory of caffeine's effect on the human organism anticipates modern thinking: "Caffeine has been claimed to increase fat metabolism and to spare muscle glycogen." See Per-Olof Åstrand and Kaare Rodahl, *Textbook of Work Physiology* (New York: McGraw-Hill Book Company, 1986): 713. "Caffeine is known to stimulate the mobilisation of free fatty acids and to increase the burn-up of fat. This is significant because although carbohydrates have generally

been considered to be the primary, if not the only, fuel for muscular exercise, it is now recognised that the role of fat as a primary energy source during exercise is considerable." See Donohoe and Johnson, *Foul Play*, 35.

75. Guimaraês, "Sur l'action physiologique et hygiénique du café," 282, 285, 284.

76. Ibid., 257, 282.

77. Issekutz, *Die Geschichte der Arzneimittelforschung*, 79, 80, 101, 115; Robert Werner Schulte, "Psychologische Untersuchung eines leistungssteigernden Arzneimittels," *Die Umschau* (1927): 375.

78. Balzac, "Traité des excitants modernes," 260, 261.

79. J.-A. Fort, "Des effets physiologiques du café," *Comptes rendus de l'Académie des Sciences* 96 (1883): 794–96. The actual terms are "une excitation du *pouvoir réflexe* ou *excito-moteur*"; I have translated *aliment d'épargne* as "conserving nutrient" and *aliment de dépense* as "consuming nutrient."

80. [Charles-Édouard] Brown-Séquard, "Expérience démontrant la puissance dynamogénique chez l'homme d'un liquide extrait de testicules d'animaux," *Archives de Physiologie Normale et Pathologique* (1889): 653.

81. Quoted in J.M.D. Olmsted, *Charles-Édouard Brown-Séquard: A Nineteenth Century Neurologist and Endocrinologist* (Baltimore: The Johns Hopkins Press, 1946): 165.

82. [Charles-Édouard] Brown-Séquard, "Nouveaux faits relatifs à l'injection sous-cutanée, chez l'homme, d'un liquide extrait de testicules de mammifères," *Archives de Physiologie Normale et Pathologique* (1890): 207.

83. [Charles-Édouard] Brown-Séquard, "Du rôle physiologique et thérapeutique d'un suc extrait de testicules d'animaux d'après nombre de faits observés chez l'homme," *Archives de Physiologie Normale et Pathologique* (1889): 739, 741; "Nouvelles remarques sur le liquide testiculaire," *Comptes rendus de la Société de Biologie* (1890): 717.

84. "Animal Extracts as Therapeutic Agents," *British Medical Journal* (June 17, 1893): 1279.

85. Ch. Éloy (1893) quoted in Oskar Zoth, "Zwei ergographische Versuchsreihen über die Wirkung orchitischen Extractes," *Pflüger's Arkiv* (1896): 337. Merriley Borell has pointed out that the gap between theory and practice at this time also existed within the scientific establishment per se: "The use of organ extracts by practitioners, therefore, quickly outstripped study of these same preparations by experimentalists. The resulting tension between the clinic and the laboratory became a major feature of the early years of endocrinological research, especially with regard to the evaluation of extracts of the testes and ovaries, where particularly controversial therapeutic claims were made." See "Organotherapy and the Emergence of Reproductive Endocrinology," *Journal of the History of Biology* 18 (1985): 3–4.

86. Gustave Le Bon, "Les Recherches récentes sur la noix de Kola," *Revue Scientifique* 52 (1893): 527–31.

87. J.H., "Kola, caféine et caféine théobromée," *Revue Scientifique* (1894): 507.

88. Chibret, "A propos de la noix de Kola," *Revue Scientifique* (1894): 26. I have rendered *l'excitation génésique* as "sexually stimulated."

89. Ibid., 26–27.

90. Philippe Tissié, "Observations physiologiques concernant un record veloci-pédique," *Archive de Physiologie Normale et Pathologique* (1894): 827–30.

91. Philippe Tissié, "La fatigue chez les débiles nerveux ou 'fatigués'," *Revue Scientifique* (1896): 748.
92. Philippe Tissié, "L'entraînement physique," *Revue Scientifique* (1896): 519.
93. Philippe Tissié, "La science du geste," *Revue Scientifique* (1901): 293.
94. Tissié, "L'entraînement physique," 519; "La science du geste," 294.
95. H.G. Wells, *Tono-Bungay* (New York: New American Library, 1960): 144.
96. Olmsted, *Charles-Édouard Brown-Séquard*, 46.
97. Theodor Husemann, *Handbuch der gesammten Arzneimittellehre* (Berlin: Verlag von Julius Springer, 1883): 915, 922.
98. A (brief) exception to this rule is André Marcueil's automobile in *The Supermale*: "the machine [André's snorting auto] exhibited without modesty, one might have said with pride, its organs of propulsion." See Alfred Jarry, *Le surmâle* [1902] (Paris: Fasquelle Editeurs, 1945): 57.
99. André Lebois, *Alfred Jarry, L'Irremplaçable* (Paris: Le Cercle du Livre, 1950: 147, 150, 151.
100. Donohoe and Johnson, *Foul Play*, 3.
101. I want to emphasize that this abridged description of Jarry's tale leaves out many interesting subthemes that can be related to the science and culture of this period in France and elsewhere in Europe.
102. Michel Pierssens, "Les savoirs du surmâle," *Revue des Sciences Humaines* (1986): 134.
103. If there is a futuristic element in *The Supermale* it is the proto-Kafkaesque mating of a human protagonist with the electrified "Machine for Inspiring Love" that is endowed with a kind of human intentionality. One thinks of the execution device in Kafka's story "In the Penal Colony" (1919).
104. S. Tchiriev, "Le téléphone comme indicateur d'une excitation nerveuse," *Journal de Physiologie et de Pathologie générale* 4 (1902): 861–64; N.-E. Wedensky, "Le téléphone comme indicateur de l'excitation du nerf: A propos des objections faites par M. Tchiriev," *Journal de Physiologie et de Pathologie générale* 5 (1903): 1,042–44.
105. O. Riesser, "Über Doping und Dopingmittel," *Leibesübungen und körperliche Erziehung* (1933): 393–94.
106. Otto Riesser, "Ist medikamentöse Beeinflussung im Sport möglich?" *Die Leibesübungen* (1930): 537.
107. Hans Seel, "Medikamentöse Beeinflussung der Leibesübungen," in Wilhelm Knoll and Arno Arnold, eds., *Normale und pathologische Physiologie der Leibesübungen* (Leipzig: Verlag von Johann Ambrosius Barth, 1933): 259–60.
108. Robert Proctor, *Racial Hygiene: Medicine under the Nazis* (Cambridge, Mass.: Harvard University Press, 1988): 237–41, 46–47.
109. See, for example, Johannes Müller, *Die Leibesübungen* (Leipzig and Berlin: B.G. Teubner, 1928): 315. Müller states that "the alcohol question" has "racial hygienic significance."
110. Ferdinand Hueppe, "Sport und Reizmittel," *Berliner Klinische Wochenschrift* (1913): 551, 550, 549, 550, 551.
111. It is significant that two important publications on high-performance sports medicine that appear during this period do not even mention doping. See Arthur Mallwitz, *Körperliche Höchstleistungen mit besonderer Berücksichtigung des olympischen Sportes* (Berlin: Aus dem hygien. Institut der Kgl. Uni-

versität Berlin, 1908): 7–51; A. Albu, "Beiträge zur pathologischen Physiologie des Sports," *Zeitschrift für klinische Medizin* 78 (1913): 151–80.

112. Donohoe and Johnson, *Foul Play*, 3.

113. Albu, "Beiträge zur pathologischen Physiologie des Sports," 151–52, 180.

114. Riesser, "Über Doping and Dopingmittel," 394.

115. [K.A.] Worringen, "Doping im Sport," *Die Leibesübungen* (1926): 354.

116. Bøje, "Doping," 446.

117. Herbert Herxheimer, "Zur Wirkung von primärem Natriumphosphat auf die körperliche Leistungsfähigkeit," *Klinische Wochenschrift* (1922): 481–82.

118. Poppelreuter, "Ist die Einnahme von primärem Natriumphosphat ein Dopingmittel?," 535–36.

119. See also K.A. Worringen, "Über Arzneimittelanwendung in der sportärztlichen Praxis," 411.

120. Max Grünewald, "Einfluss der Koffeinwirkung auf Arbeitserfolg und sportliche Leistung," *Die Leibesübungen* (1928): 360.

121. R.W. Schulte, *Der Einfluss des Kaffees auf Körper und Geist* (Dresden: Verlag des Deutschen Hygiene-Museums. Deutscher Verlag für Volkswohlfahrt, 1929): 15.

122. Grünewald, "Einfluss der Koffeinwirkung auf Arbeitserfolg und sportliche Leistung," 360.

123. M. Baur, "Pharmakologische Beeinflussung der Körperleistung im Sport," *Archiv für experimentelle Pathologie und Pharmakologie* 184 (1937): 54, 59, 64.

124. Worringen, "Über Arzneimittelanwendung in der sportärztlichen Praxis," 414.

125. Riesser, "Ist medikamentöse Beeinflussung im Sport möglich?" 541.

126. G. Schönholzer, "Die Frage des Doping," *Sammlung der Referate gehalten am Sportärztlichen Zentralkurs 1937 in Bern* (Bern: Büchler & Co., 1938): 184.

127. Riesser, "Ist medikamentöse Beeinflussung im Sport möglich?" 537.

128. Rob. Werner Schulte, *Eignungs-und Leistungsprüfung im Sport* (Berlin: Verlag Guido Hackebeil A.-G., 1925): 80, 112, 266.

129. Dr. Willner, "Sport und Doping," in A. Mallwitz, ed., *Die Sportärztetagung Berlin 1924* (Munich: J.F. Lehmanns Verlag, 1925): 145, 138. The widespread use of cocaine is confirmed in Worringen, "Doping im Sport," 354.

130. Worringen, "Doping im Sport," 354.

131. Karl Ander, "Sport und Doping," *Deutsche Turn-Zeitung* (1929): 991.

132. Bøje, "Doping," 451. According to Karpovich, "since the effect of preliminary oxygen breathing wears out in 3 minutes, there is no basis for the assertion that Japanese victories in swimming were due to oxygen breathing." See "Ergogenic Aids in Work and Sports," 443.

133. Baur, "Pharmakologische Beeinflussung der Körperleistung im Sport," 60.

134. Riesser, "Über Doping und Dopingmittel," 395.

135. Janet H. Clark, "A Simple Method of Measuring the Intensity of Ultraviolet Light with Comparative Results on a Number of Physiological Reactions," *American Journal of Physiology* (1924): 200.

136. Fritz Lade, "Anwendung ultravioletter Strahlen im Training," *Die Leibesübungen* (1926): 44.

137. A. Kusserath, "Unsichtbare Strahlen im Dienste des Sportwesens," *Leibesübungen und körperliche Erziehung* (1934): 18.

138. Fritz Lickint, "Leistungssteigerung bei Leibesübungen durch Anwendung der

'künstlichen Höhensonne'?" *Münchener Medizinische Wochenschrift* (1928): 605; Karlheinz Backmund, "Ermüdung, Leistungssteigerung und künstliche Höhensonne," *Münchener Medizinische Wochenschrift* (1929): 230.

139. Karlheinz Backmund, "Sport und künstliche Höhensonne," *Die Leibesübungen* (1932): 11.

140. "Reactionary modernism is an ideal typical construct. The thinkers I am calling reactionary modernists never described themselves in precisely these terms. But this tradition consisted of a coherent and meaningful set of metaphors, familiar words, and emotionally laden expressions that had the effect of converting technology from a component of alien, Western *Zivilisation* into an organic part of German *Kultur.*" See Jeffrey Herf, *Reactionary Modernism: Technology, culture, and politics in Weimar and the Third Reich* (New York: Cambridge University Press, 1984): 1.

141. See Giselher Spitzer, *Der deutsche Naturismus* (Ahrensburg bei Hamburg: Velag Ingrid Czwalina, 1983): 14, 24, 25, 33, 36, 39. Robert Proctor has pointed out that in "the spring of 1933 the [Nazi] Ministry of the Interior announced the formation of a Healers' League of Germany (Heilpraktikerbund Deutschlands)" including "radiation therapies (*Magnetopathie und Bestrahlungsarten*)," which Proctor includes among "folk medical arts." See *Racial Hygiene*, 229.

142. Poppelreuter, "Ist die Einnahme von primärem Natriumphosphat ein Dopingmittel?" 534. Unfortunately, Poppelreuter does not say whether this refers to the 1928 Winter Games (St. Moritz) or the Summer Games (Amsterdam).

143. Dr. Hering, "Ultraviolette Strahlen für Sportzwecke," *Die Leibesübungen* (1926): 331.

144. Worringen, "Doping im Sport," 355.

145. Lickint, "Leistungssteigerung bei Leibesübungen durch Anwendung der 'künstlichen Höhensonne'?" 606.

146. Ibid., 605–6.

147. Backmund, "Ermüdung, Leistungssteigerung und künstliche Höhensonne," 233, 234.

148. Baur, "Pharmakologische Beeinflussung der Körperleistung im Sport," 61.

149. Günther Lehmann, "Arbeitsfähigkeit und Ultraviolettbestrahlung," *Forschungen und Fortschritte* (1936): 361.

150. See, for example, Hering, "Ultraviolette Strahlen für Sportzwecke," 331; Worringen, "Doping im Sport," 354.

151. Backmund, "Ermüdung, Leistungssteigerung und künstliche Höhensonne," 230.

152. Hugo Bach, "Doping im Sport," *Die Leibesübungen* (1926): 448; Lickint, "Leistungssteigerung bei Leibesübungen durch Anwendung der 'künstlichen Höhensonne'?" 607.

153. Hans Seel, "Medikamentöse Beeinflussung der Leibesübungen," in Wilhelm Knoll and Arno Arnold, eds., *Normale und pathologische Physiologie der Leibesübungen* (Leipzig: Verlag von Johann Ambrosius Barth, 1933): 262.

154. Hering, "Ultraviolette Strahlen für Sportzwecke," 331.

155. Kusserath, "Unsichtbare Strahlen im Dienste des Sportwesens," 17–18.

156. Bach, "Doping im Sport," 448.

157. See especially Proctor, *Racial Hygiene*.

158. August Bier, "Gedanken eines Arztes über die Medizin," *Münchener Mediz-inische Wochenschrift* (1926): 1362.
159. Otto Blau, "Eine neue Kraftquelle für Sportleistungen?" *Die Leibesübungen* (1930): 689.
160. A. Loewy, "Versuche über die Rückgängigmachung der Ermüdungserscheinun-gen bei Muskelarbeit," *Berliner Klinische Wochenschrift* (1910): 882.
161. Willner, "Sport und Doping," 132, 144.
162. Fred Jent, *Die neue Lehre vom Training* (Zürich: Verlag Buch und Zeitschriften A.G., 1936)
163. Schönholzer, "Die Frage des Doping," 175, 191.
164. Riesser, "Über Doping und Dopingmittel," 394.
165. W. Heubner, "Über den Begriff 'Reizstoff,'" *Klinische Wochenschrift* (1926): 3.
166. Riesser, "Ist medikamentöse Beeinflussung im Sport möglich?" 537; "Über Doping und Dopingmittel," 395. See also Poppelreuter, "Ist die Einnahme von primärem Natriumphosphat ein Dopingmittel?" 534.
167. See also Seel, "Medikamentöse Beeinflussung der Leibesübungen," 262.
168. Poppelreuter, "Ist die Einnahme von primärem Natriumphosphat ein Doping-mittel?" 536.
169. [K.A.] Worringen, "Entgegnung auf die Äußerungen von Geh. Can.-Rat Dr. Hugo Bach," *Die Leibesübungen* (1926): 448.
170. Schönholzer, "Die Frage des Doping," 186.
171. Seel, "Medikamentöse Beeinflussung der Leibesübungen," 260.
172. Worringen, "Über Arzneimittelanwendung in der sportärztlichen Praxis," 409; Alexander Hartwich, "Calcio-Coramin in der sportärztlichen Praxis," *Schweiz-erische Medizinische Wochenschhrift* (1937): 98.
173. Hartwich, "Calcio-Coramin in der sportärztlichen Praxis," 98.
174. E. Isler, "Erfahrungen mit Coramin 'Ciba' in den Schulen und Kursen der Sanitätstruppen 1928," *Schweizerische Medizinische Wochenschrift* (1929): 336–37.
175. Hartwich, "Calcio-Coramin in der sportärztlichen Praxis," 99.
176. Rudolf Staehelin, "Analeptica und Sport," *Schweizerische Medizinische Wochenschrift* (1937): 1112–13.
177. Baur, "Pharmakologische Beeinflussung der Körperleistung im Sport," 59.
178. H. Conrad, "Das Training und die medikamentöse Behandlung der Erscheinun-gen bei Übertraining," *Arzt und Sport* 12 (1936): 21–22. Reported in *Berichte über die Gesamte Physiologie und Experimentelle Pharmakologie* 99 (1937): 600.
179. Worringen, "Über Arzneimittelanwendung in der sportärztlichen Praxis," 410.
180. Bøje, "Doping," 452.
181. Riesser, "Über Doping und Dopingmittel," 395.
182. Schönholzer, "Die Frage des Doping," 174, 188.
183. Riesser, "Ist medikamentöse Beeinflussung im Sport möglich?" 541.
184. Worringen, "Doping im Sport," 354; Seel, "Medikamentöse Beeinflussung der Leibesübungen," 259.
185. Schönholzer, "Die Frage des Doping," 173.
186. Worringen, "Über Arzneimittelanwendung in der sportärztlichen Praxis," 414; Riesser, "Über Doping und Dopingmittel," 396.

187. Hartwich, "Calcio-Coramin in der sportärztlichen Praxis," 98; Seel, "Medikamentöse Beeinflussung der Leibesübungen," 260.

188. Willner, "Sport und Doping," 133; Schönholzer, "Die Frage des Doping," 174; Hartwich, "Calcio-Coramin in der sportärztlichen Praxis," 98.

189. Worringen, "Über Arzneimittelanwendung in der sportärztlichen Praxis," 408; Riesser, "Über Doping und Dopingmittel," 394.

190. Synopsis of Dr. Heitan, "Doping im Sport," *Frankfurter Zeitung*, nr., 440 (1930), in *Die Leibesübungen*, nr., 4 (1931): 111.

191. "In women, use of anabolic steroids may cause menstrual irregularities, deepening of the voice, male pattern baldness, and clitoromegaly. In adult men, priapism, alopecia, acne, oligospermia or abnormal sperm morphology may develop, as well as decreases in sperm motility and in testosterone, follicle-stimulating hormone, and luteinizing hormone levels. The effects on sperm production and motility, gonads, and skin appear to be reversible after steroid use is discontinued." See Robert E. Windsor and Daniel Dumitru, "Anabolic steroid use by athletes: How serious are the heath hazards?" *Postgraduate Medicine* 84 (1988): 47. There is now an enormous literature on the subject of anabolic steroids.

192. Hunter's readings of his experiments raise interesting questions about how scientific evidence is interpreted. "In his often cited experiments on transplantation of spurs in fowl, Hunter showed that the spur of the hen would grow to the size of a cock spur if transplanted to a cock, whereas the small spur of a young cock would not grow if transplanted to a hen (Hunter, 1794)." Given Hunter's invidious comparisons of the "powers" of male and female organisms, one might ask which is more important: the capacity of the transplanted organ to grow in a foreign medium, or the capacity of the host organism to foster growth in a transplant? See C. Barker Jórgensen, *John Hunter, A.A. Berthold, and the Origins of Endocrinology* (Odense: Odense University Press, 1971): 11.

193. Ibid., 15, 19.

194. The idea that ovarian extract was less "active" than testicular extract also appears in Oskar Zoth, "Zwei ergographische Versuchsreihen über die Wirkung orchitischen Extractes," *Pflüger's Arkiv* (1896): 336.

195. "By 1944, Kochakian found a partial dichotomy between the anabolic and androgenic effects of androstane-3 alpha, beta-diol. This increased the hope of finding compounds that were predominantly or totally anabolic. Eight years later, Eisenburg and Gordan developed a bioassay for determining the relative anabolic and androgenic components of a steroid. See Windsor and Dumitru, "Anabolic steroid use by athletes," 37.

196. Zoth, "Zwei ergographische Versuchsreihen über die Wirkung orchitischen Extractes," 338, 342, 377.

197. Fritz Pregl, "Zwei weitere ergographische Versuchsreihen über die Wirkung orchitischen Extractes," *Pflüger's Arkiv* (1896): 399.

198. See, for example, C.E. Yesalis, J.E. Wright, and J.A. Lombardo, "Anabolic-androgenic steroids: a synthesis of existing data and recommendations for future research," *Clinical Sports Medicine* 1 (1989): 117; G. Rademacher, J. Gedrat, R. Häcker, H. Buhl, "Die Beeinflussung des Adaptationsverhaltens ausgewählter Funktionssysteme von Ausdauersportlern während einer kraftbetonten Trainingsphase durch die zusätzliche Gabe von Oral-Turinabol," in R. Häcker

and H. de Marées, eds., *Hormonelle Regulation und psychophysische Belastung im Leistungssport* (Cologne: Deutscher Ärzte-Verlag, 1991): 83.

199. Oskar Zoth, "Neue Versuche (Hantelsversuche) über die Wirkung orchitischen Extractes," *Pflüger's Arkiv* (1898): 386. The Zoth-Pregl experiments retained their credibility at least as late as 1925: "Zoth and Pregl seem to have obtained definite proof, by means of ergographic records, of the stimulating action of the testicular extracts upon the muscle-nerve apparatus in man. They find that injection of such extracts not only causes an increase in the amount of muscular work which can be accomplished, but lessens the subjective fatigue sensations." See Swale Vincent, *Internal Secretion and the Ductless Glands* (New York: Physicians and Surgeons Book Company, 1925): 83. For a more recent discussion of the experiments by Zoth and Pregl see M. Tausk, "The emergence of endocrinology," in M.J. Parnham and J. Bruinvels, eds., *Haemodynamics, Hormones & Inflammation* (Amsterdam, New York, Oxford: Elsevier, 1984): 219–49. Tausk makes a surprising comment: "I doubt whether Brown-Séquard's observations were entirely due to imagination" (p. 220). Pregl eventually won the 1923 Nobel Prize for chemistry.

200. The original citation of this paper, which I have not seen, is *J. Russk. fis.-chim. Obsh.* 23 (1891): 151–55.

201. Vincent, *Internal Secretion and the Ductless Glands*, 83. Vincent comments further: "More recently [than Brown-Séquard], Poehl asserts that he has prepared a substance, *spermin* [sic], to which he assigns the formula $C_5H_{14}N_2$, which has a very beneficial effect upon the metabolism of the body. He believes that this spermin is the substance which gives to the testicular extracts prepared by Brown-Séquard their stimulating effect. He claims for this substance an extraordinary action as a physiological tonic. It is recommended that testicular preparations be employed in cases of deficiency of testicular substance, or in old age, when the testes lose their functional capacity" (p. 83).

202. Walter E. Dixon, "A Note on the Physiological Action of Poehl's Spermine," *Journal of Physiology* 25 (1899–1900): 356–63. As the above footnote indicates, the nature of spermin(e) was still unexplained in 1925.

203. I am indebted to Clark T. Sawin, M.D., for this interpretation.

204. Loewy, "Versuche über die Rückgängigmachung der Ermüdungs-erscheinungen bei Muskelarbeit," 882–84.

205. Robert E. Windsor, M.D., and Daniel Dumitru, M.D., "Anabolic steroid use by athletes," *Postgraduate Medicine* 84 (1988): 38.

206. See, for example, Herbert Herxheimer, *Grundriss der Sportmedizin* (Leipzig: Georg Thieme Verlag, 1933): 111–12; Helmut Dennig, "Über Steigerung der körperlichen Leistungen durch künstliche Veränderungen des Säurebasenhaushaltes," *Forschungen und Fortschritte* (1937): 153; Bøje, "Doping," 447–48; Horst Hellwig, "Ueber die Wirkung künstlicher Alkalisierung bei Kurz- und Mittelstreckenschwimmern" [Inaugural-Dissertation] (Berlin: Medizinische Klinik der Universität Berlin, 1940): 1–15; S. Robinson and P.M. Harmon, "The Lactic Acid Mechanism and Certain Properties of the Blood in Relation to Training," *American Journal of Physiology* 132 (1941): 757–69. The idea of a buffering strategy of potential value to athletes persists; see Per-Olof Astrand and Kaare Rodahl, *Textbook of Work Physiology: Physiological Bases of Exercise* (New York: McGraw-Hill, 1986): 325, who refer to "soda loading."

207. A. Reprew, "Das Spermin ein Oxydationsferment," *Pflüger's Arkiv* (1914): 331–32, 340, 342, 359, 360.

208. "Biochemistry and Assay of Testis Hormones," in Edgar Allen and Robert M. Yerkes, eds., *Sex and Internal Secretions* (Baltimore: The Williams & Wilkins Company, 1934): 383.

209. Casimir Funk, Benjamin Harrow, and A. Lejwa, "The Male Hormone," *American Journal of Physiology* 92 (1930): 448.

210. For a chronology of this work see M. Tausk, "Androgens and anabolic steroids," in Parnham and Bruinvels, eds., *Haemodynamics, Hormones & Inflammation*, 307–16. For a useful chronology of the crucial publications in the isolation of the male and female sex hormones see Leslie T. Morton, *A Medical Bibliography* (London: Gower, 1983): 153–56.

211. Arthur Keith, "The Differentiation of Mankind into Racial Types," *Nature* 104 (1919): 305.

212. See Häcker and de Marées, *Hormonelle Regulation*.

213. H. Lisser, "Organotherapy, Present Achievements and Future Prospects," *Endocrinology* (1925): 4. "It is important, whenever possible, to make a clean-cut distinction between true specific supplementary substitution therapy for the relief of an incretory deficiency, and the administration of a ductless gland extract for its druglike pharmaco-dynamic effect." The author is referring to the use of adrenalin against anaphylactic shock, asthma, and other disorders, and the use of pituitrin to induce labor in pregnant women.

214. See, for example, Alexander Lipschütz, *The Internal Secretions of the Sex Glands* (Cambridge: W. Heffer & Sons Ltd., 1924): 483–93.

215. David Hamilton, *The Monkey Gland Affair* (London: Chatto & Windus, 1986): 30, 59, 61.

216. Eugen Steinach, *Sex and Life: Forty Years of Biological and Medical Experiments* (New York: Viking Press, 1940): 221.

217. See the reviews by B. Romeis of Francesco Cavazzi, *Le système glandulaire et vues nouvelles en médecine* [Paris, 1930] and *On peut rajeunir* [Paris, 1930] in the *Biologisches Centralblatt* 52 (1932): 622.

218. Riesser, "Ist medikamentöse Beeinflussung im Sport möglich?" 539; Seel, "Medikamentöse Beeinflussung der Leibesübungen," 261; Baur, "Pharmakologische Beeinflussung der Körperleistung im Sport," 53–54; see also F. Meythaler and K. Wossidlo, "Über den Adrenalingehalt des peripheren menschlichen Blutes bei sportlichen Leistungen," *Klinische Wochenschrift* (1937): 658–62 [abstract in *Berichte über die gesamte Physiologie* (1937): 420].

219. Frank A. Hartman, "The Relation of the Adrenals to Muscular Activity," *Endocrinology* 6 (1922): 516. Hartman later used adrenalin therapy ("cortin") as a treatment for the generalized condition of weakness once known as "asthenia." See Frank A. Hartman and George W. Thorn, "The Effect of Cortin in Asthenia," *Proceedings of the Society for Experimental Biology and Medicine* 29 (1931–32): 48–50. I am grateful to Clark T. Sawin, M.D., for bringing this paper to my attention.

220. Bøje, "Doping," 464–65. Bøje also addresses a hormonal treatment—"a follicular product called 'Pelanin' "—for the menstruating female athlete: "In special cases among women athletes, hormone treatment has been found to be of assistance in attaining the highest level of performance. In particular, the ad-

ministration of œstrus-producing substances may delay the onset of menstruation if this should coincide with the date of the contest" (465).

221. Albrecht Bethe, "Vernachlässigte Hormone," *Die Naturwissenschaften* (1932): 180; Hans Fitting, "Die Hormone als physiologisches Reizstoffe," *Biologisches Centralblatt* (1936): 69, 70, 77, 84. Bethe concludes that "Stimulants and hormones are not one and the same thing. *Stimulant [Reizstoff] is the higher concept* (p. 180). Fitting finds no sharp distinction between hormones and vitamins (p. 69) and equates hormones with stimulants (p. 84).

222. Tausk, "Androgens and anabolic steroids," 315–16.

223. William N. Taylor, "Synthetic Anabolic-Androgenic Steroids: A Plea for Controlled Substance Status," *The Physician and Sportsmedicine* 15 (1987): 144.

224. See, for example, William N. Taylor, "Synthetic Anabolic-Androgenic Steroids: A Plea for Controlled Substance Status," *The Physician and Sportsmedicine* 15 (May 1987): 145–46.

5. The Last Frontier

1. "Schrittmacher auf dem Weg ins Grenzbereiche," *Süddeutsche Zeitung* [Munich] (March 23, 1984).

2. "Rider Taking Classical Approach," *New York Times*, (July 3, 1990).

3. Philippe Tissié, "L'éducation physique," *La Revue Scientifique* (1894): 341.

4. Gustave Le Bon, "Les Recherches récentes sur la noix de Kola," *La Revue Scientifique* (1893): 529.

5. Herbert Herxheimer, "Zur Wirkung des Alkohols auf die sportliche Leistung," *Münchener Medizinische Wochenschrift* (1922): 143, 145.

6. G. Schönholzer, "Die Frage des Doping," *Sammlung der Referate gehalten am Sportärztlichen Zentralkurs 1937 in Bern* (Bern: Dr. A. Wander A.G., 1938): 185.

7. V. Henri, "Revue générale sur le sens musculaire," *L'Année Psychologique* (1899): 419.

8. Robert Werner Schulte, *Eignungs- und Leistungsprüfung im Sport* (Berlin: Verlag Guido Hackebeil A.-G., 1925): 63.

9. Rudolf Schulze, "Steigerung der Leistung durch ethische Antriebe," in Max Brahn, ed., *Anweisungen für die psychologische Auswahl der jugendlichen Begabten* (Leipzig: Verlag der Dürr'schen Buchhandlung, 1921): 111.

10. Herxheimer, "Zur Wirkung des Alkohols auf die sportliche Leistung," 144.

11. Herbert Herxheimer, *Grundriss der Sportmedizin* (Leipzig: Georg Thieme Verlag, 1933): 115.

12. W. Caspari, "Physiologische Studien über Vegetarismus," *Pflüger's Arkiv* (1905): 585.

13. Pierre de Coubertin, "La psychologie du sport," *Revue des Deux Mondes* (1900): 176.

14. Pierre de Coubertin, *Essais de psychologie sportive* (Lausanne et Paris: Librairie Payot et Cie,1913): 92.

15. The standard work on Coubertin is John J. MacAloon, *This Great Symbol: Pierre de Coubertin and the Origins of the Modern Olympic Games* (Chicago: University of Chicago Press, 1981). On Coubertin's social theory of sport see John M. Hoberman, *Sport and Political Ideology* (Austin: University of Texas

Press, 1984): 130–34; *The Olympic Crisis: Sport, Politics, and the Moral Order* (New Rochelle, N.Y.: Aristide D. Caratzas, Publisher, 1986): 33–40.

16. Coubertin, *Essais de psychologie sportive,* 27, 32, 55.

17. Quoted in André Senay and Robert Hervet, *Monsieur de Coubertin* (Paris: Points & Contrepoints, 1960): 155.

18. Pierre de Coubertin, *Notes sur l'éducation publique* (Paris: Hachette, 1901): 213, 214.

19. Coubertin, "La psychologie du sport," 179. Here Coubertin also calls sport's tendency toward excess its "nobility" and its "poetry."

20. Karl Pearson, "On the Inheritance of the Mental and Moral Characters in Man, and its Comparison with the Inheritance of the Physical Characters," *Journal of the Anthropological Institute* (1903): 199.

21. See, for example, Joseph B. Oxendine, "Emotional arousal and motor performance," in A. Craig Fisher, ed., *Psychology of Sport: Issues & Insights* (Palo Alto: Mayfield Publishing Company, 1976): 124–35.

22. I have taken this description from Antonio Ciocco, "The Historical Background of the Modern Study of Constitution," *Bulletin of the Institute of the History of Medicine* 4 (1936): 23–38. See also W.H. Sheldon, *The Varieties of Human Physique* (New York: Harper & Brothers Publishers, 1940): 10–28.

23. Quoted in Ciocco, "The Historical Background," 24.

24. Pierre-Jean-Georges Cabanis, "Sur les habitudes morales," *Rapports du physique et moral de l'homme,* vol. 3 of *Œuvres Complètes,* (Paris, 1824): 422.

25. Ibid., 80–81.

26. Ibid., 421–22, 421.

27. Coubertin, "La psychologie de sport," 169.

28. Cabanis, *Rapports,* vol. 4 of *Œuvres Complètes,* 99.

29. For an admiring portrait of Lévy, see H. Baruk, "Le Grand Hygiéniste Michel Lévy," *Revue d'Histoire de la Médecine Hébraïque* (May 1949): 5–17.

30. Michel Lévy, *Traité d'hygiène publique et privée* (Paris: J.-B. Baillière, Librairie de l'Académie Nationale de Médecine, 1850): 64, 231, 89–90.

31. Ibid., 241, 241–42, 71.

32. On the origins of this sport, see Eric M. Macintyre, "Pedestrianism to the Trust Fund—Athletics in its Historical and Social Contexts," in J.A. Mangan and R.B. Small, eds., *Sport, Culture, Society: International historical and sociological perspectives* (London and New York: E. & F.N. Spon, 1986): 124–28.

33. Lévy, Traité, 443–44.

34. Ibid., 93.

35. Dr. Fourcault, "Tempérament," *Dictionnaire de la Conversation et de la Lecture* (Paris: Aux Comptoires de la Direction, 1858): 493–97.

36. Fourcault, "Tempérament," 494.

37. John C. Murray, "On the Nervous, Bilious, Lymphatic, and Sanguine Temperaments: Their Connection with Races in England, and their relative Longevity," *The Anthropological Review* (1870): 16, 24, 17, 20.

38. Robert Knox, *The Races of Men: A Fragment* (Philadelphia: Lea & Blanchard, 1850): 45.

39. Ibid., 47, 9.

40. L. Owen Pike, "On the Psychical Characteristics of the English People," *Memoirs of the Anthropological Society of London* 2 (1856–66): 164.

41. Ibid., 155–56, 158. See Alexander Bain, *The Sense and the Intellect* (New York: D. Appleton and Company, 1872): 73ff. Bain was Professor of Logic at the University of Aberdeen.

42. Bain, *The Sense and the Intellect*, 81, 83.

43. "Bibliographie du sens musculaire," *L'Année Psychologique* (1899): 514–57.

44. Henri, "Revue générale sur le sens musculaire," 421.

45. J.W. Jackson, "On the Racial Aspects of the Franco-Prussian War," *Journal of the Anthropological Institute* (1872): 36, 37, 32, 39.

46. John Crawfurd, "On the Physical and Mental Characteristics of the Negro," *Transactions of the Ethnological Society of London* 4 (1866): 217.

47. Quoted in Sanford B. Hunt, "The Negro as a Soldier," *The Anthropological Review* (1869): 43.

48. Cabanis, *Rapports*, vol. 3 of *Œuvres Complètes*, 420.

49. Ibid., 76–77, 198, 200.

50. Ibid., 199.

51. Bain, *The Senses and the Intellect*, 73.

52. Cabanis, *Rapports*, vol. 3 of *Œuvres Complètes*, 426, 200, 200.

53. Ibid., 200; Bain, *The Senses and the Intellect*, 335–36.

54. Alexander Bain, *The Emotions and the Will* (New York: D. Appleton and Company, 1859): 310–11.

55. Bain, *The Senses and the Intellect*, 82.

56. Cabanis, *Rapports*, vol. 3 of *Œuvres Complètes*, 200.

57. Lévy, *Traité d'hygiène*, 70.

58. N. Vaschide, "Neuro-Muscular Force: A Psychical Element in Muscular Force," *British Journal of Psychology* (1905): 317.

59. N. Vaschide and Cl. Vurpas, "Contribution expérimentale à la physiologie de la mort," *Comptes rendus de l'Académie des Sciences* (1903): 934.

60. Philippe Tissié, "L'entraînement physique," *Revue Scientifique* (1896): 518.

61. Philippe Tissié, "*L'Éducation physique et la Race* (Paris: Flammarion, 1919): 152.

62. Tissié, "L'entraînement physique," 519.

63. Tissié, *L'Éducation physique et la Race*, 148, 158; Philippe Tissié, "La science du geste," *Revue Scientifique* (1901): 295–96; Cabanis, *Rapports*, vol. 3 of *Œuvres Complètes*, 198.

64. "L'entraînement physique," 518; Philippe Tissié, "Concernant un record velocipédique," *Archives de physiologie normale et pathologique* (1894): 836. "L'entraînement est une suggestion donnée à l'état de veille. L'état psychique du coureur se rappoche beaucoup de l'état de subconscience hypnotique si favorable à l'acceptation des suggestions, surtout pendant un effort prolongé et à la suite d'une nuit passée à courir" (p. 836).

65. Tissié, "Concernant un record velocipédique," 835–37.

66. Tissié, "L'entraînement physique," 518.

67. Henri, "Revue générale sur le sens musculare," 419. The reference is to Waller, "The sense of effort: an objective study," *Brain* (1891): 179, 432. This claim takes us back to the difference between laboratory and "real-life" experience discussed above. In fact, Henri points out that Waller's conclusion had been criticized in 1893 by G.-E. Müller, who argued that the electric current did not stimulate the same muscles as those stimulated by the will. Hence Waller's experimental conclusion was invalid.

68. Warren P. Lombard, "Some of the Influences Which Affect the Power of Voluntary Muscular Contractions," *Journal of Physiology* 13 (1892): 1, 52, 57.

69. Henri, "Revue générale sur le sens musculaire," 421.

70. This is a complicated issue if only because it is clear that the sporting public *will* tolerate conventional doping practices if they are not too blatant. There seems to be a difference between a half-conscious awareness that an athlete might be doped and actually rejecting him or her as an athletic hero(ine) because doping has been confirmed. Yet it is also the case that an athlete who has clearly doped himself can remain popular with the sporting public. On this topic see Chapter 7.

71. Caspari, "Physiologische Studien über Vegetarismus," 585.

72. I have taken this from Robert A. Nye, *Masculinity and Male Codes of Honor in Modern France* (New York: Oxford University Press, 1993). See Chapter 10, "Courage."

73. Elias Auerbach, "Zur Psychologie des Mutes," *Jüdische Turnzeitung* (1905): 20–26.

74. Angelo Mosso, *Fear* (London, New York, and Bombay: Longmans, Green, and Co., 1896): 117, 276, 133.

75. Fourcault, "Tempérament," 494.

76. Tissié, *L'Education physique et la Race*, 155.

77. G. Schönholzer, "Die Frage des Doping," *Sammlung der Referate gehalten am Sportärztlichen Zentralkurs 1937 in Bern* (Bern: Büchler & Co., 1938): 189.

78. Ulfried Geuter, *Die Professionalisierung der deutschen Psychologie im Nationalsozialismus* (Frankfurt am Main: Suhrkamp Verlag, 1984): 204.

79. Alice Lee, Marie A. Lewenz, and Karl Pearson, "On the Correlation of the Mental and Physical Characters in Man," *Man* 3 (1903): 12.

80. *Die Leibesübungen* (1931:4): 111.

81. Dr. Willner, "Sport und Doping," in A. Mallwitz, ed., *Die Sportärztetagung Berlin 1924* (Munich: J.F. Lehmanns Verlag, 1925): 147.

82. Schulte, *Eignungs- und Leistungsprüfung im Sport*, 226–67.

83. José Ferrer-Hombravella, "The Psychological Doping Concept Must Be Rejected," in Gerald S. Kenyon and Tom M. Grogg, eds., *Contemporary Psychology of Sport: Proceedings of the Second International Congress of Sport Psychology* (Chicago: The Athletic Institute, 1970): 845.

84. For a recent, if brief, assessment of Kretschmer's work, see Brian W.P. Wells, *Body and Personality* (London and New York: Longman, 1983: 2–5; for an earlier and more detailed critical commentary see Donald G. Paterson, *Physique and Intellect* (New York and London: The Century Co., 1930): 232–46. See also Hans W. Jürgens and Christian Vogel, "Der Typus in der morphologischen Biologie und Anthropologie," in *Beiträge zur menschlichen Typenkunde* (Stuttgart: Ferdinand Enke Verlag, 1965): 45–72.

85. Kretschmer's brief summary of these findings is found in his *Physique and Temperament* (New York: Harcourt, Brace & Company, Inc., 1925): 34–36.

86. Ibid., 195.

87. Franz Weidenreich, *Rasse und Körperbau* (Berlin: Verlag von Julius Springer, 1927): 131.

88. Ibid., 132.

89. The brief chapter on "Constitution and Performance" that appears in the 1948 edition of *Physique and Temperament* does not appear in the original edition; what is more, this later addition deals only with mental performance—an apparent concession to a widespread interest in performance boosting he did not share. See *Körperbau und Charakter* (Berlin-Göttingen-Heidelberg: Springer-Verlag, 1948): 251–56.

90. Ernst Kretschmer and Willi Enke, *Die Persönlichkeit der Athletiker* (Leipzig: Georg Thieme Verlag, 1936): 64.

91. Kretschmer's lack of interest in sportive applications has not been emulated by all who have read him. An Austrian psychologist writing in 1954 did not hesitate to correlate the schizothymic and cyclothymic types with athletic styles."The schizothyme [soccor player] becomes the fine technician who, in the course of indefatigable training, strives for the utmost precision and achieves an artistic level of ball-handling. . . . The cyclothyme is versatile and adaptable, making up for his deficient technique with his passionate effort and astonishing tricks." See Heinz Seist, "Die psychische Eigenart der Spitzensportler," *Weiner Arkiv für Psychologie* 4 (1954): 195–96.

92. Ibid., 67; 22; 42, 46, 58, 41, 44; 60.

93. Ibid., 64.

94. Rolf Albonico, *Mensch Menschentypen: Entwicklung und Stand der Typenforschung* (Basel: Birkhäuser Verlag, 1970): 77–89.

95. Carl Krümmel, "Eignungslehre," in *Athletik: Ein Handbuch der lebenswichtigen Leibesübungen* (Munich: J.F. Lehmanns Verlag, 1930): 85, 86, 98. The German term for aptitude testing was *Eignungslehre*.

96. Ibid., 107, 109, 101. Krümmel's German in the quotation is "einen Menschen dazu zu erziehen, in einem gegebenen Augenblick über sich hinaus wachsen zu können."

97. Walther Schulz, "Sporttypus und Leistung," *Die Leibesübungen* (1932): 338.

98. Ibid., 339.

99. Geoffrey Cocks, *Psychotherapy in the Third Reich: The Göring Institute* (New York: Oxford University Press, 1985): 56.

100. Schulz, "Sporttypus und Leistung," 340, 341.

101. Walther Jaensch. "Körper-seelische Entwicklung und Leibesübungen," *Die Leibesübungen* (1932): 438.

102. Michel Lévy's portrait of the "massive constitutions of Northern Europe" are a case in point. See Lévy, *Traité d'hygiène publique et privée*, 242.

103. A proponent of racializing Kretschmer's types is Ludwig Stern-Piper, "Kretschmers psycho-physische Typen und die Rassenformen in Deutschland," *Archiv für Psychiatrie* 67 (1923): 569–99; "Zur Frage der Bedeutung der psychophysischen Typen Kretschmers," *Zeitschrift für die gesamte Neurologie und Psychiatrie* 84 (1923): 408–14. *Physique and Temperament* is not a racialistic work, and even Stern-Piper suggests (414n) that Kretschmer rejected his equating of racial and constitutional types.

104. Ferdinand Hueppe, *Hygiene der Körperübungen* (Leipzig: Verlag von S. Hirzel, 1922): 34–35, 89–106; Krümmel, *Athletik*, 102–7.

105. Hueppe, *Hygiene*, 34–35; Krümmel, *Athletik*, 105.

106. Krümmel, *Athletik*, 103, 107

107. Jokl emigrated from Germany to South Africa in the mid-1930s and eventually

settled in the United States, becoming an internationally known exercise physiologist.
108. Ernst Jokl, "Der Typ des jüdischen Sportsmannes," *Der Makkabi* 39 (1929):
4–5.
109. The best single source for this material is the *Jüdische Turnzeitung* (Berlin,
1900–1925). On the Zionist "self-criticism" of the turn-of-the-century period see
Joachim Doron, "Classic Zionism and Modern Anti-Semitism: Parallels and
Influences (1883–1914)," *Studies in Zionism* (1983): 169–204.
110. On the athletic inferiority of the Jews as seen by one of Jokl's German contemporaries, see Fritz Giese, *Geist im Sport* (Munich: Delphin Verlag, 1925): 68.
111. Paul Diepgen, "Die deutsche Medizin: Ihr Wesen und ihre Leistung," *Geist
der Zeit* (1938): 612.
112. E. Burnet Tylor, "Wild Men and Beast-Children," *The Anthropological Review*
1 (1863): 28–29.
113. Krümmel, *Athletik*, 103
114. August Bier, "Höchstleistungen durch seelische Einflüsse und durch Daseinsnotwendigkeiten," *Die Leibesübungen* (1926): 34, 34, 35, 35–36.
115. Ibid., 37.
116. Ibid., 34, 38, 35.
117. See, for example, Miroslav Vanek and Bryant J. Cratty, *Psychology and the
Superior Athlete* (London: Collier-Macmillan Limited, 1970): 118–22; A. Craig
Fisher, "Psych up, psych down, psych out: relationship of arousal to sport
performance," in A. Craig Fisher, ed., *Psychology of Sport: Issues & Insights*
(Palo Alto: Mayfield Publishing Company, 1976): 140; Angela Patmore, *Sportsmen Under Stress* (London, Melbourne, Auckland, Johannesburg: Stanley Paul,
1979): 234–35.
118. Geoffrey Cocks, *Psychotherapy in the Third Reich: The Göring Institute*, 165.
See also 72–76; 183–84.
119. Dr. Freiherrn von Schrenck-Notzing, "Eine Geburt in der Hypnose," *Zeitschrift für Hypnotismus, Suggestionstherapie, Suggestionslehre und verwandte
psychologische Forschungen* (1893): 49–52.
120. J.H. Schultz, *Das autogene Training (Konzentrative Selbstentspannung)*
(Leipzig: Georg Thieme Verlag, 1932): 1, vii, 295, 294.
121. John Hoberman, *The Olympic Crisis: Sport, Politics, and the Moral Order*, 102.
122. Schultz, *Das autogene Training*, 290, 290, 294.
123. J.H. Schultz, "Sport und Persönlichkeit," *Deutsche medizinische Wochenschrift*
(1933): 1,233, 1,233, 1,234; *Das autogene Training*, 299.
124. On the debate over trait psychology see William P. Morgan, "Sport Personol-
ogy: The Credulous-Skeptical Argument in Perspective," in William F. Straub,
ed., *Sport Psychology: An Analysis of Athlete Behavior*. (Ithaca, N.Y.: Mouvement Publications, 1978).
125. John E. Kane, "Psychological aspects of sport," in J.G.P. Williams and P.N.
Sperryn, eds., *Sport Medicine* (Baltimore: The Williams and Wilkins Company,
1976): 43–44.
126. "Die Psycho-Spiele," *Stern* (August 2, 1984), 132.
127. "The methodologic and paradigmatic themes underscoring this review have
implied that the scientific method that has characterized sport psychology until
now has lacked the rigor and impact evidenced by other exercise and sport

sciences." See Rod K. Dishman, "Contemporary Sport Psychology," *Exercise and Sport Sciences Reviews*. (1982): 152. Or: "Although potentially generalizable explanations for outcomes are suggested by many studies, the lack of uniformity in the type of subjects and sports, the performance-outcome measures employed, the psychological factors tested, and the specified procedures of the interventions make it difficult, if not impossible, to draw conclusions that are reliable and have external validity across interventions, sports, and athletes. There are few standardized principles to guide psychological aids in sports." See Rod K. Dishman, "Psychological Aids to Performance," in Richard H. Strauss, ed., *Drugs & Performance in Sport*. (Philadelphia: W.B. Saunders Company, 1987): 140. See also Rod K. Dishman, "Identity Crises in North American Sport Psychology: Academics in Professional Issues," *Journal of Sport Psychology* 5 (1983); Daniel M. Landers, "Whatever Happened to Theory Testing in Sport Psychology?" *Journal of Sport Psychology* 5 (1983): 135–51. For a good critique of the mental techniques currently popular in sports psychology see Daniel Druckman and John A. Swets, eds., *Enhancing Human Performance: Issues, Theories, and Techniques*. (Washington, D.C.: National Academy Press, 1988). "Even among sports psychologists," the president-elect of the American Association for the Advancement of Applied Sports Psychology said in 1989, "we know some things work, although we haven't done extensive research on why or how they work. Also, we know that not all mental techniques work all the time in all situations. In the end, I think people should try sports psychology, but as informed consumers. Let the buyer beware." See Janet Nelson, "Sports Psychology Becoming the Locker Room's Latest Rage," *New York Times*. (September 11, 1989), 19. I have commented on the quasi-scientific status of sport psychology in "Anthropological Consequences of Scientific Sport," presented at the Seventh Annual Meeting of the North American Society for the Sociology of Sport, Las Vegas, Nevada, October 31, 1986.

128. I have taken this list from Dishman, "Psychological Aids to Performance." There is an extensive academic literature on these techniques and a large number of handbooks for the lay reader. On two of the more widespread methods, see, for example, John M. Silva, III, "Covert Rehearsal Strategies" and Rod K. Dishman, "Stress Management Procedures," in Melvin H. Williams, ed., *Ergogenic Aids in Sport* (Champaign: Human Kinetics Publishers, 1983): 253–74; 275–20.

129. "Die schiessen wir ab," *Der Spiegel* (September 29, 1986), 231–32.

130. Silva, "Covert Rehearsal Strategies," 253.

131. Druckman and Swets, *Enhancing Human Performance*, 62. In general, mental practice has been received with cautious optimism by credible observers. "There is growing evidence from neurophysiological experiments and case studies, behavioral experiments on motor learning and control, and anecdotal self-reports by athletes that covert mental (symbolic) images or thoughts about movement are associated with the neuromuscular control of skilled-limb motion." See Dishman, "Psychological Aids to Performance," 136. See also *Enhancing Human Performance*, 61; and Daniel Goleman, "Mental Images: New Research Helps Clarify Their Role," *New York Times*, (August 12, 1986).

132. Richard M. Suinn, "Body Thinking: Psychology for Olympic Champs," *Psychology Today* (July 1976): 40–41. "Using VMBR, the Colorado State skiers practiced racing techniques, course concentration, and improving their

memorization of courses. They cut down on skiing errors by repeating the
correct actions, and they became more aggressive, the method worked" (p. 41).
Suinn goes on to point out, however, that the scientific value of his experiment
was destroyed by an unforeseen circumstance: "The team's head coach, impressed by the improvement in the VMBR group, raced them but not the skiers
from the matched control group. I was therefore unable to show as conclusively
as I would have liked that the imagery-rehearsal technique was more effective
than customary training" (pp. 41–42). This anecdote recalls a caveat from the
authors of a National Research Council report on techniques alleged to boost
human performance: "Many technique promoters appear to pay little attention
to this [research] literature, preferring an alternative route to invention: rather
than derive a procedure from appropriate scientific literature, they create techniques from personal experiences, sudden insights, or informal observation of
'what works.' " See *Enhancing Human Performance*, 9.

133. Francis Galton, *Inquiries into Human Faculty and its Development* [1883]
(London: J.M. Dent & Sons Ltd, 1928): 73, 66–67, 75–76.

134. E. J. Marey, *Movement* [*Le Mouvement*, 1894] (New York: Arno Press & The
New York Times, 1972): 139.

135. "This self-help program [SyberVision Systems] has been singled out for discussion since it is the most highly developed and influential mental practice program currently being marketed, and it purports to provide a breakthrough in
scientific understanding of how and why mental practice and imagery occurs."
See *Enhancing Human Performance*, 67. I do not mean to imply here that the
developers of the SyberVision program directly copied Marey or even knew of
his existence. As the authors I have just cited point out: "Many of the tech-
niqeus under consideration grew out of the human potential movement of the
1960s" (p. 3).

136. The 1991 address of SyberVision Systems was 7133 Kroll Center Parkway,
Pleasanton, California 94566. The programs listed in this paragraph appear in
the 1991 catalog distributed by American Airlines free of charge to its passen-
gers.

137. Quoted in *Enhancing Human Performance*, 7.

138. *Enhancing Human Performance*, 69. "Research evidence for neuromuscular
programming via holograms and Fourier transforms is elusive. Other than the
claims in the SyberVision videotapes and audiotapes, no direct scientific evidence was found that the brain acts as a holographic processor or performs
Fourier transforms. The research to which [Karl] Pribram referred us (Pribram,
Sharafat, and Beekman, 1984) discusses the possible interpretation of research
results in light of the holographic model, but the data did not provide any direct
support for the model. At the present time, therefore, the cognitive-symbolic
theory still remains the most viable explanation for mental practice effects" (p.
70).

139. Watson's theory is discussed in Robert S. Woodworth and Harold Schlosberg,
Experimental Psychology (New York-Chicago-San Francisco-Toronto: Holt,
Rinehart and Winston, 1938): 816. This idea is also related to a thesis of the late
nineteenth-century French psychologist Charles Féré, who stated that "the
energy of a movement is in proportion to the idea of that movement." The
difference is that, while Féré points to a *quantitatively* stimulating effect, the

SyberVision literature emphasizes the *qualitative* transcription of the movement from one individual to another. The Féré statement is quoted in Norman Triplett, "The Dynamogenic Factors in Pacemaking and Competition," *American Journal of Psychology* 9 (1897–98): 531. Triplett calls this phenomenon "the principle of ideomotor action" (p. 532).

140. Tissié, "Concernant un record velocipédique," 836.
141. Triplett, "The Dynamogenic Factors in Pacemaking and Competition," 515.
142. "Krefelder Psychologe: Mit Trance gegen Doping," *Frankfurter Allgemeine Zeitung*, (November 4, 1987).
143. Dishman, "Psychological Aids to Performance," 124.
144. Michio Ikai and Arthur H. Steinhaus, "Some factors modifying the expression of human strength," *Journal of Applied Physiology* 16 (1961): 157–63. This subject was "an experienced weight lifter. Somewhat skeptical of hypnosis, he set out to disprove it. In consequence, he made an exceptional effort and pulled as much as 160 lb., breaking all previous records, in his prehypnosis pulls. After three attempts extending over nearly 2 hours he was finally hypnotized. His display of strength both in the hypnotic state and under posthypnotic suggestion never fully equaled his superefforts in the control period" (p. 160). For an analysis of this study, see K.V. Baum, "Keine Rekorde in Hypnose," *Der Sportarzt* (1963): 140–45.
145. Dishman, "Psychological Aids in Sport," 124.
146. Dishman, "Psychological Aids in Sport," 132; Warren R. Johnson, "Hypnosis and muscular performance," in Fisher, *Psychology of Sport*, 172.
147. "Typen wie aus dem Panoptikum," *Der Spiegel* (July 23, 1984), 77.
148. Angela Patmore, *Sportsmen Under Stress* (London, Melbourne, Auckland, Johannesburg: Stanley Paul, 1986): 237.
149. Dishman, "Psychological Aids in Sport," 125.
150. Quoted in Hans Lenk, "Wird der Spitzensportler manipuliert?" in Helmut Acker, ed., *Rekorde aus der Retorte* (Stuttgart: Deutsche Verlags-Anstalt, 1972): 84.

6. The Myth of Communist Sports Science

1. Avery Brundage, "I Must Admit—Russian Athletes Are Great!," *Saturday Evening Post* (April 30, 1955), 37.
2. Don Canham, "Russia Will Win the 1956 Olympics," *Sports Illustrated* (October 25, 1954).
3. Jerome Bruner, Foreword to Raymond A. Bauer, *The New Man in Soviet Psychology* (Cambridge, Mass.: Harvard University Press, 1952): xxiii.
4. "Superbørn fødes i lunkent vand," *Politiken* (Copenhagen), July 10, 1983; Daniel J. Kevles, *In the Name of Eugenics: Genetics and the Uses of Human Heredity* (Berkeley and Los Angeles: University of California Press, 1986): 191. Claud Bramblett has informed me that Muller's report referred in all likelihood to experiments actually carried out at the Russian Primate Center in the Georgian city of Sukhumi, which was founded about 1917. It was widely known during the 1920s that Russian scientists were trying to impregnate female apes with human semen. The experimental animals reportedly died of hepatitis. According to a standard Soviet reference work, the Institute of Experimental

Pathology and Therapy of the Academy of Medical Sciences of the USSR in Sukhumi "has a monkey nursery." See the *Great Soviet Encyclopedia*, vol. 25 (New York: Macmillan, 1980): 218.

5. See "Frischzellen: 'Meist eine Freude erleben'," *Der Spiegel*, no. 33 (1987): 162–165.

6. Sergei Kapitza, "Antiscience Trends in the U.S.S.R.," *Scientific American* (August 1991): 32.

7. Grigori Raiport, *Red Gold: Peak Performance Techniques of the Russian and East German Olympic Victors* (Los Angeles: Jeremy P. Tarcher, 1988): xv.

8. Bauer, *The New Man in Soviet Psychology*, 49.

9. Alex Kozulin, *Psychology in Utopia: Toward a Social History of Soviet Psychology* (Cambridge, Mass.: The MIT Press, 1984): 7.

10. "In the classic case of the dog and the bell, the unconditioned reflex is the natural, inborn salivation of a dog in response to the stimulus of food. The conditioned reflex, salivation in response to a bell alone, is created by the prior repeated juxtaposition of the bell and the food." See Loren R. Graham, *Science, Philosophy, and Human Behavior in the Soviet Union* (New York: Columbia University Press, 1987): 158.

11. Ibid., 160, 161.

12. Bauer, *The New Man in Soviet Psychology*, 54.

13. Gustav Wetter, *Dialectical Materialism: A Historical and Systematic Survey of Philosophy in the Soviet Union* (New York and London: Frederick A. Praeger, 1963): 479, 475, 476.

14. Kozulin, *Psychology in Utopia*, 47.

15. This definition of Socialist Realism is, of course, both brief and simplified. Nevertheless, I believe it is a fair generalization. In addition, there are important similarities between Socialist Realism and sport as forms of "culture." See, especially, Rufus Mathewson, *The Positive Hero in Russian Literature* (Stanford: Stanford University Press, 1975).

16. Robert Edelman has pointed out to me that this idealized image of the Soviet athlete existed much more in theory than in practice.

17. "Bekhterev (1858–1927) had long before the Revolution maintained that every thought process, conscious or unconscious, expresses itself sooner or later in objectively observable behavior." See Graham, *Science, Philosophy, and Human Behavior in the Soviet Union*, 165.

18. Kozulin, *Psychology in Utopia*, 10. Not all historians of Soviet psychology, however, would agree with this interpretation.

19. Quoted in Martin S. Staum, *Cabanis: Enlightenment and Medical Philosophy in the French Revolution* (Princeton: Princeton University Press, 1980): 202, 203; Gerlof Verwey, *Psychiatry in an Anthropological and Biomedical Context* (Dordrecht/Boston/Lancaster: D. Reidel Publishing Company, 1985): 76.

20. Martin S. Staum, *Cabanis: Enlightenment and Medical Philosophy in the French Revolution* (Princeton: Princeton University Press, 1980): 202–03, 6.

21. John B. Watson, *Behaviorism* [1930] (New York: The Norton Library, 1970): xv; 42–43; 29, 33, 35. My reference to Orwell is prompted by passages like the following: "Some day we shall have hospitals devoted to helping us change our personality because we can change the personality as easily as we can change the shape of the nose, only it takes more time" (p. 302). Or: "The behaviorist

. . . would like to develop his world of people from birth on, so that their speech and their bodily behavior could equally well be exhibited freely everywhere without running afoul of group standards" (p. 303n).

22. Ibid., 269, 99, 158–59, 302, 220. V.P. Rozhin is credited with the following statement: "The materialism of Marxist logic lies primarily in the fact that thinking is regarded as the product of a physical organ of the body, namely the human brain; thought is a function of the brain." This quotation recalls similar formulations by Cabanis and Destutt de Tracy cited above. See Wetter, *Dialectical Materialism*, 520.

23. I am indebted to Clark T. Sawin, M.D., for bringing this point to my attention.

24. Watson, *Behaviorism*, 222, 26, 253–54, 166, 238, 284.

25. T.H. Pear, "The Intellectual Respectability of Muscular Skill," *British Journal of Psychology* (1922): 163, 164, 178, 180.

26. René Fuelopp-Miller, *The Mind and Face of Bolshevism* [1926] (New York: Harper Torchbooks, 1965): 24–25.

27. Kurt Johansson, *Aleksej Gastev: Proletarian Bard of the Machine Age* (Stockholm: University of Stockholm, 1983): 104, 112.

28. Richard S. Schultz and Ross A. McFarland, "Industrial Psychology in the Soviet Union," *Journal of Applied Psychology* 19 (1935): 269.

29. Johansson, *Aleksej Gastev*, 67.

30. Henry W. Morton, *Soviet Sport* (New York: Collier Books, 1963): 55.

31. Thomas P. Hughes, *American Genesis: A Century of Invention and Technological Enthusiasm 1870–1970* (New York: Penguin Books, 1989): 257.

32. Katerina Clark, "Little Heroes and Big Deeds: Literature Responds to the First Five-Year Plan," in Sheila Fitzpatrick, ed., *Cultural Revolution in Russia, 1928–1931* (Bloomington and London: Indiana University Press, 1978): 192–93.

33. Katerina Clark, "Utopian Anthropology as a Context for Stalinist Literature," in Robert C. Tucker, ed., *Stalinism: Essays in Historical Interpretation* (New York: Norton, 1977): 186.

34. Lewis H. Siegelbaum, *Stakhanovism and the Politics of Productivity in the USSR, 1935–1941* (New York: Cambridge University Press, 1988): 225.

35. Sheila Ostrander and Lynn Schroeder, *Psychic Discoveries Behind the Iron Curtain* (Englewood Cliffs, N.J.: Prentice-Hall, Inc., 1970): 390.

36. Trofim Denisovitch Lysenko (b. 1898) was a very influential (and pseudoscientific) geneticist and Stalin protégé whose career significantly retarded Soviet work in the biological sciences, especially molecular biology.

37. Wetter, *Dialectical Materialism*, 476, 477.

38. Kozulin, *Psychology in Utopia*, 4.

39. Graham, *Science, Philosophy, and Human Behavior in the Soviet Union*, 221, 225, 233, 261. As Graham points out: "The association of Soviet ideologists with humanism is not a concept for which many Western sovietologists are prepared" (p. 265).

40. See David Caute, *The Fellow-Travellers: A Postscript to the Enlightenment* (New York: Macmillan, 1973): 54.

41. Angela Patmore, *Sportsmen Under Stress* (London, Melbourne, Auckland, Johannesburg, 1979): 216, 228, 216, 199, 228.

42. Th. Valentiner, "Internationale Psychotechnische Konferenz in Moskau (8. bis 13. September 1931)," *Zeitschrift für angewandte Psychologie* 41 (1932): 188, 199.

43. John Block Friedman, *The Monstrous Races in Medieval Art and Thought* (Cambridge, Mass.: Harvard University Press, 1981): 43.

44. See, for example, "Nicht zum Singen," *Der Spiegel* (August 15, 1977): 129; "DDR: Schluck Pillen oder kehr Fabriken aus," *Der Spiegel*, n.r., 12 (1979): 194–207.

45. See Robert Jay Lifton, *The Nazi Doctors: Medical Killing and the Psychology of Genocide* (New York: Basic Books, 1986): 291.

46. "Es geht um unsere Ehre," *Der Spiegel* (August 26, 1991): 60, 62, 65.

47. Lifton, *The Nazi Doctors*, 270, 272, 277, 288, 295.

48. *Tacitus on Britain and Germany*, trans. H. Mattingly (Harmondsworth: Penguin Books, 1960): 104.

49. This figure is a predecessor of the Stakhanovite worker discussed in the previous section of this chapter. "The most characteristic epithet used for the Stakhanovite was *bogatyr'*, which places him in the tradition of fantastic Russian epic heroes who perform superhuman feats." See Clark, "Utopian Anthropology as a Context for Stalinist Literature," 186.

50. N.A. Schereschewsky, "Gigantism," *Endocrinology* 10 (1926): 17; Charles Darwin, *The Descent of Man, and Selection in Relation to Sex* [1871] (Princeton: Princeton University Press, 1981): 112.

51. J.W. Jackson, "On the Racial Aspects of the Franco-Prussian War," *Journal of the Anthropological Institute of Great Britain and Ireland* 1 (1872): 32, 39, 47.

52. Ulfried Geuter, *Die Professionalisierung der deutschen Psychologie im Nationalsozialismus* (Frankfurt am Main: Suhrkamp Verlag, 1984): 180ff.

53. See, for example, John M. Hoberman, *Sport and Political Ideology* (Austin: University of Texas Press, 1984): 201–7.

54. Willi Knecht, *Das Medaillenkollektiv* (Berlin: Verlag Gebr. Holzapfel, 1978): 59.

55. Robert Proctor, *Racial Hygiene: Medicine under the Nazis* (Cambridge, Mass.: Harvard University Press, 1988): 65.

56. Ludwig Ferdinand Clauss, *Rasse und Seele* (Munich: J.F. Lehmanns Verlag, 1933): 13, 10.

57. Artur Axmann, *Olympia der Arbeit: Arbeiterjugend im Reichsberufwettkampf* (Berlin: Junker und Dünnhaupt, 1937): 7.

58. Siegfried Moosburger, *Ideologie und Leibeserziehung im 19. und 20. Jahrhundert* (Ahrensburg bei Hamburg: Verlag Ingrid Czwalina, 1972): 159.

59. For an example of this argument in a quasi-scientific treatment of high-performance sport, see Franz Ochsenkühn, "Von der menschlichen zur sportlichen Höchstleistung," *Leibesübungen und körperliche Erziehung* (1937): 567.

60. Winfried Joch, *Politische Leibeserziehung und ihre Theorie im Nationalsozialistischen Deutschland* (Frankfurt/M.: Peter Lang, 1976): 119, 45, 48.

61. Ochsenkühn, "Von der menschlichen zur sportlichen Höchstleistung," 566.

62. Geuter, *Die Professionalisierung der deutschen Psychologie*, 204.

63. Hans Hoske, *Die menschliche Leistung als Grundlage des totalen Staates* (Leipzig: Verlag von S. Hirzel, 1936): 1, 19–20, 46, 49; 30; 2.

64. Gunther Lehmann, "Menschliche Leistung und Leistungsfähigkeit," *Forschungen und Fortschritte* (March 10, 1942): 80–81.

65. Adolf Bickel, "Die Art der Eiweissernährung als Grundlage körperlicher Leistungsfähigkeit," *Forschungen und Fortschritte* (April 20, 1942): 121.

66. Helmut Dennig, "Über Steigerung der körperlichen Leistungen durch kün-

stliche Veränderungen des Säurebasenhaushaltes," *Forschungen und Fortschritte* (April 20, 1937): 153.

67. Ochsenkühn, "Von der menschlichen zur sportlichen Höchstleistung," 567, 568.

68. Hanns Baur, "Angewandte Sportmedizin," in A. Mallwitz, ed., *Sportmedizin und Olympische Spiele 1936: Festschrift der Sportärzteschaft* (Leipzig: Georg Thieme Verlag, 1936): 13.

69. Lehmann, "Menschliche Leistung und Leistungsfähigkeit," 81.

70. Hans Peter Bleuel, *Sex and Society in Nazi Germany* (Philadelphia and New York: J.B. Lippincott Company, 1973): 161.

71. See Proctor, *Racial Hygiene*, 177–222.

72. Brigitte Berendonk, *Doping-Dokumente: Von der Forschung zum Betrug* (Berlin Heidelberg New York: Springer-Verlag, 1991): 107.

73. Havelock Ellis, "Feminism and Masculinism," in *Essays in War-Time: Further Studies in the Task of Social Hygiene* (Boston and New York: Houghton Mifflin Company, 1917): 94.

74. Ernst Günther Schenck, *Patient Hitler: Eine medizinische Biographie* (Düsseldorf: Droste Verlag, 1989): 197, 206.

75. According to Brigitte Berendonk, there have been many German reports about the alleged use of testosterone to stimulate Wehrmacht stormtroops during the Second World War. See Berendonk, *Doping-Dokumente*, 227.

76. Nicholas Wade, "Anabolic Steroids: Doctors Denounce Them, but Athletes Aren't Listening," *Science* (June 30, 1972): 1,400; Eliot Marshall, "The Drug of Champions," *Science* (October 14, 1988): 183. Wade's claim is repeated (and cited) in Herbert A. Haupt and George D. Rovere, "Anabolic Steroids: A Review of the literature," *The American Journal of Sports Medicine* 12 (1984): 469. It also appears in slightly altered form in an anonymously published "underground" steroid handbook: *Anabolic Steroids: The Competitive Edge* (C & D Enterprises, n.d.): 4.

77. Robert E. Windsor and Daniel Dumitru, "Anabolic steroid use by athletes," *Postgraduate Medicine* 84 (September 15, 1988): 41. These authors cite Wade (1972) and three other (non-German) sources.

78. "Wie schwanger ist Herr Günthör?" *Die Weltwoche* (May 10, 1990): 34.

79. Albert Q. Maisel, *The Hormone Quest* (New York: Random House, 1965): 95.

80. Quoted in Klaus Theweleit, *Male Fantasies*, vol. 1 (Minneapolis: University of Minnesota Press, 1987): 55.

81. L. Prokop, "The Struggle Against Doping and its History," *Journal of Sports Medicine & Physical Fitness* 10 (March 1970): 437; Michael Sehling, Reinhold Pollert, and Dieter Hackfort, *Doping im Sport: Medizinische, sozialwissenschaftliche und juristische Aspekte* (Munich: BLV Verlagsgesellschaft, 1989): 53.

82. Tom Donohoe and Neil Johnson, *Foul Play: Drug Abuse in Sports* (Oxford: Basil Blackwell, 1986): 41.

83. Friedrich Percyval Reck-Malleczewen, *Tagebuch eines Verzweifelten: Zeugnis einer inneren Emigration* (Frankfurt am Main und Hamburg: Fischer Bücherei, 1971): 33. The full German passage reads as follows: "Wendet es, wie ihr wollt, es gibt in diesem Zeichen kein "Als ob", kein Ausweichen in extensive Kulturen, in technische, chemische, hormonale und wie immer geartete Zaub-

erkunststücke. Sportärzte, die ich nach der vorjährigen Olympiade seligen An-
gedenkens sprach, berichteten mir, dass Amenorrhöen bei den Mädchen und
sexuelle Insuffienz bei den scheinbar so kraftstrotzenden jungen Männern
dieser sportlich hochgezüchteten Generation (keineswegs übrigens nur bei den
Leuten der Spitzenleistungen, sondern durchaus beim Durchschnitt!)
nachgerade zur Regel geworden seien" (p. 33–34). I have not used the English
translation, which omits the sentence containing the word "hormonal." See
Friedrich Percyval Reck-Malleczewen, *Diary of a Man in Despair* (New York:
Collier Books, 1972): 46.

84. I am indebted to Clark T. Sawin, M.D., for bringing this information to my
attention. The Ciba company's list of "products" included Perandren (synthetic
testosterone proprionate) by August 1936. See Edgar Allen, ed., *Sex and Internal Secretions* (Baltimore: The Williams & Wilkins Company, 939): 813. This
pioneering research on the identification of the sex hormones was heavily sub-
sidized by large pharmaceutical companies (Ciba, Organon, Schering)] See M.
Tausk, "Androgens and anabolic steroids," in M.J. Parnham and J. Bruinvels,
eds., *Haemodynamics, Hormones & Inflammation* (Amsterdam, New York, Oxford: Elsevier, 1984): 311. Ciba paid the synthesizer of methytestosterone,
Leopold Ruzicka, enough in royalties to permit him to give the city of Zurich a
museum and paintings to fill it. See Rupert F. Witzmann, *Steroids: Key to Life*
(New York: Van Nostrand Reinhold Company, 1981): 165.

85. Wilhelm Haring, "Das männliche Hodenhormon Testosteron," *Forschungen
und Fortschritte* (April 20, 1942): 122–23.

86. *Archiv der Pharmazie und Berichte der Deutschen Pharmazeutischen Gesellschaft* (1924): 538.

87. *Archiv der Pharmazie* (1926): 330.

88. *Archiv der Pharmazie* (1933): 136.

89. *Archiv der Pharmazie* (1934): 585, 588.

90. Berendonk, *Doping-Dokumente*, 29.

91. See John M. Hoberman, "The Early Development of Sports Medicine in Germany," in Jack Berryman and Roberta J. Park, eds., *Essays in the Rise and
Development of Sports Medicine* (Champaign: University of Illinois Press, 1992).

92. See Berendonk, *Doping-Dokumente*.

93. Rudolf Schulze, "Steigerung der Leistung durch ethische Antriebe," in Max
Brahn, ed., *Anweisungen für die psychologische Auswahl der jugendlichen Begabten* (Leipzig: Verlag der Dürr'schen Buchhandlung, 1921): 94, 95, 107.

94. Ibid., 94, 107, 170–71.

95. John M. Hoberman, "The Transformation of East German Sport," *Journal of
Sport History* 17 (1990): 62–68. This statement is quoted in "Festigung prinzi-
pieller Feindbilder," *Der Spiegel* (January 25, 1988): 166.

96. Schulze, "Steigerung der Leistung durch ethische Antriebe," 110, 124; 108,
111, 112, 115.

97. Ibid., 122.

98. Ibid., 123.

99. Schulze is careful to point out, however, that he is *not* suggesting that "inspirational stimuli" (*ethische Antriebe*) can cause violations of the "physical laws" of
nature. See Schulze, "Steigerung der Leistung durch ethische Antriebe," 111.

100. Clark, "Utopia Anthropology," 186. Similarly, the Maoist endorsement of high-

performance sport was rooted in a sheer belief in willpower that was an important element of Mao's charisma. See John M. Hoberman, "Sport and Social Change: The Transformation of Maoist Sport," *Sociology of Sport Journal* 4 (1987): 164.

101. I.N. Spielrein, "Zur Theorie der Psychotechnik," in Michael Erdélyi, Otto Lipmann, Isaak N. Spielrein, and William Stern, eds., *Prinzipienfragen der Psychotechnik* (Leipzig: Johann Ambrosius Barth, 1933): 49. See also William Stern and Otto Lipmann, eds., *Zeitschrift für Angewandte Psychologie* 41 (1932): 196.

102. See Wildor Hollmann and Alois Mader, "Sportmedizin in der DDR," *Sportwissenschaft* 13 (1983): 153; Peter Kühnst, *Der missbrauchte Sport: Die politische Instrumentalisierung des Sports in der SBZ und DDR 1945–1957* (Cologne: Verlag Wissenschaft und Politik, 1982): 65.

103. W. Caspari, "Nathan Zuntz zu seinem 70. Geburtstag," *Die Naturwissenschaften* (1917): 619–20.

104. See, for example, Herbert Herxheimer, *Grundriss der Sportmedizin* (Leipzig: Georg Thieme Verlag, 1933): 19–22.

105. Prof. Dr. Hans Schuster of the Research Institute for Physical Culture and Sport (FKS) was eventually awarded the National Prize of the GDR (First Class) for Science and Technology. See Berendonk, *Doping-Dokumente*, 95.

106. Kühnst, *Der missbrauchte Sport*, 65–66, 68.

107. Hollmann and Mader, "Sportmedizin in der DDR," 158, 154.

108. Rosemarie Reinwald, ed. *Sportwissenschaftliche Ergebnisse des FKS (1984–1990)* (Ahrensburg bei Hamburg: Verlag Ingrid Czwalina, 1990): 7, 13, 11; 9, 71, 105, 139; 35, 105, 149; 75, 157; 35; 151; 79, 81; 25. This volume contains several hundred abstracts (in German and English) of scientific papers produced during the period 1984–1990. The topic list I have presented is, of course, incomplete. It is worth noting that only one of these papers (p. 137) mentions "hormonal" research, and it has nothing to do with anabolic steroids, which are never referred to in this volume.

109. "Bisher war hier kein Fremder," *Der Spiegel* (January 22, 1990): 158.

110. "Aus der Druckkammer direkt zum Olympiasieg," *Frankfurter Allgemeine Zeitung* (February 12, 1990): 26. Another Olympic champion who trained in the underground chamber was the 1976 and 1980 marathon champion, Waldemar Cierpinski.

111. Hollmann and Mader, "Sportmedizin in der DDR," 156.

112. For a comparison of Oral-Turinabol and Dianabol (by East German scientists) suggesting that the former has milder side-effects, see R. Häcker, B. Bernstein, G. Rademacher, "Pharmakokinetische Vergleichsuntersuchungen von Oral-Turinabol and Dianabol mittels Radioimmunoassay," in R. Häcker and H. De Marées, eds., *Hormonelle Regulation und psychophysische Belastung im Leistungssport* (Cologne: Deutscher Ärzte-Verlag, 1991): 55–63.

113. The East German ski-jumper Hans-Georg Aschenbach, a former Olympic and world champion, described the psychosexual effects of the steroid Nandrolone (30 to 40 milligrams per day) after his defection to West Germany in 1989: "The aggressive feelings caused by the doping pills lasted for the 10 days [after discontinuing use prior to competition], but for ten nights, as well. Sometimes I could hardly stand it. These things boosted potency to the point where you

suddenly started masturbating; in the woods, just before training behind the embankment, in the bathroom and elsewhere. It sounds insane, but you simply had to do it." See "Alle DDR-Stars gedopt," *Süddeutsche Zeitung* (June 26, 1989).

114. Berendonk, *Doping-Dokumente*, 97; 114–15; 48ff., 107–8, 167–68.

115. "State Plan 14.25," termed "The Manhattan Project of Sports" by Brigitte Berendonk, was instituted in 1988. See Berendonk, *Doping-Dokumente*, 91ff.

116. Ibid., 93–94.

117. Ibid., 86, 89.

118. Ibid., 63, 213ff.

119. Ibid., 100; "Auch für Bomber-Piloten gut," *Der Spiegel* (February 18, 1991): 198.

120. "DDR braucht kleine Geheimnisse," *Süddeutsche Zeitung* (July 7, 1989).

121. "Doping aus Fürsorge," *Süddeutsche Zeitung* (February 15, 1990): 51.

122. "DDR-Forscher geben systematisches Doping zu," *Frankfurter Allgemeine Zeitung* (February 16, 1990).

123. "Menschenversuche mit neuen Dopingmitteln: Funktionäre haben Athleten gezwungen," *Frankfurter Allgemeine Zeitung* (December 5, 1990): 32.

124. "Auch für Bomber-Piloten gut," 200.

125. "Genosse Profi," *Der Spiegel* (April 13, 1987): 202; "Öffentliche Kritik an Trainer und System," *Süddeutsche Zeitung* (January 16/17, 1988); "Schelte für Schuk," *Süddeutsche Zeitung* (February 25/26, 1989).

126. "Die Perestroika und der Sport," *Süddeutsche Zeitung* (October 13/14, 1990). Robert Edelman has described this editor to me as a self-important type prone to exaggeration.

127. "Selbstkritik und Kooperation," *Süddeutsche Zeitung* (May 8, 1987).

128. "Zwölfjährige Kinder in der Sowjetunion gedopt," *Frankfurter Allgemeine Zeitung* (January 7, 1989); "Kinderdoping," *Süddeutsche Zeitung* (June 9, 1989).

129. "Steril und impotent," *Der Spiegel* (November 30, 1987): 216, 218.

130. "Glasnost und das russische Fräuleinwunder," *Süddeutsche Zeitung* (July 11/12, 1987); "Wieder menschliche Leistungen," *Süddeutsche Zeitung* (June 27, 1989).

131. "Neues Denken im Sport der UdSSR," *Süddeutsche Zeitung* (April 27, 1990).

132. "1991 World List: Women," *Track & Field News* (November 1991): 62.

133. "Glasnost mit langer Zunge," *Süddeutsche Zeitung* (May 23/24, 1987): 47. I am indebted to Robert Edelman for correcting some misinterpretations of Vlasov's political career which appear in this article.

134. "Doping mit Jugendlichen nimmt in der UdSSR zu," *Süddeutsche Zeitung* (October 11, 1990): 58; "Sport leidet unter dem neuen Devisen-Erlass; Doping ersetzt die fehlenden Lebensmittel," *Frankfurter Allgemeine Zeitung* (December 6, 1990).

135. "Es werden Wunder geschehen," *Der Spiegel* (October 7, 1991): 258. This attitude toward doping was evident in Hungary in 1985 after a Hungarian pharmacologist, Dr. Zoltan Torma, admitted giving steroids and other banned substances to Hungarian athletes—the first Eastern bloc confession of this kind. There appeared to be "tacit acceptance among Hungarian athletes and sports coaches that, without doping, Hungarian athletes cannot compete internationally against competitors who resort to unauthorized use of drugs." See Vera Rich, "Hungarian owns up," *Nature* 316 (August 8, 1985): 479.

136. "Forderung nach 'radikalen Eingriffen,' " *Frankfurter Allgemeine Zeitung* (October 9, 1986).
137. "Eine Offensive des Lächelns und Selbstbewusstseins," *Süddeutsche Zeitung* (March 20, 1986).
138. "Im Sport der DDR ist der Konflikt programmiert," *Süddeutsche Zeitung* (August 6, 1987).
139. "DDR will Vorbehalte gegen Boxen abbauen," *Süddeutsche Zeitung* (March 2, 1989).
140. "Neues Forum beklagt Medaillensucht der DDR," *Frankfurter Allgemeine Zeitung* (November 16, 1989); "Absspecken oder masten," *Süddeutsche Zeitung* (January 23, 1990).
141. "Matthes: 'Massenhysterie gegen den Leistungssport'," *Frankfurter Allgemeine Zeitung* (December 30, 1989): 23. See also "Sportler treten wegen 'Maulkorb' zurück: Uwe Ampler will die Tour de France fahren," *Frankfurter Allgemeine Zeitung* (November 20, 1989).
142. "Das Ende einer Karriere," *Frankfurter Allgemeine Zeitung* (November 20, 1989). On the sport-art equation in Marxist-Leninist societies, see John Hoberman, *The Olympic Crisis: Sport, Politics, and the Moral Order* (New Rochelle, N.Y.: Aristide D. Caratzas, Publisher, 1986): 113–16.
143. "Notizen zum DDR-Sport," *Frankfurter Allgemeine Zeitung* (January 24, 1990): 27.
144. "DDR braucht kleine Geheimnisse," *Süddeutsche Zeitung* (July 7, 1989).
145. "Doping Dokumente belasten frühere DDR-Stars," *Frankfurter Allgemeine Zeitung* (November 29, 1990).
146. Meyer klagt Munzert an, Ewald weiss von nichts," *Frankfurter Allgemeine Zeitung* (December 8, 1990); "Menschenversuche mit neuen Dopingmitteln: Funktionäre haben Athleten gezwungen," *Frankfurter Allgemeine Zeitung* (December 5, 1990): 32.

7. A Conspiracy So Vast

1. "Ich habe nichts Verbotenes getan," *Tages-Anzeiger* [Zürich] (September 29, 1987); *Track & Field News* (November 1987): 41, 58.
2. "Wie lebenslänglich," *Der Spiegel* (October 5, 1987): 218; *Track & Field News* (November 1987): 41. I have arrived at the figure of ten seconds by averaging the two figures I found in print. According to *Der Spiegel*, Gasser had improved her 1,500-meter time by eleven seconds in the course of the past year. *Track & Field News* stated that prior to running the 3:59.06 in Rome she had never run faster than about 4:08.
3. *Commission of Inquiry into the Use of Drugs and Banned Practices Intended to Increase Athletic Performance* (Ottawa: Canadian Government Publishing Centre, 1990): 85.
4. "Schuldspruch für Sandra Gasser," *Tages-Anzeiger* (October 6, 1987): 1. The Canadian report on the Ben Johnson scandal states that "the rights of athletes must be respected," but offers no procedure to ensure these rights. See *Commission of Inquiry*, 556.
5. "Ich habe nichts Verbotenes getan."
6. "Immer lächeln, auch wenn Tränen kommen," *Die Weltwoche* (October 1, 1987).

7. "Die Freundschaft ist kaputtgegangen," *Tages-Anzeiger* (January 20, 1988): 49.
8. "Sandra Gasser läuft für ihre Ehre," *Süddeutsche Zeitung* (September 6, 1989): 47.
9. "Sandra Gasser: 'Ich kam mir so klein vor,' " *Tages-Anzeiger* (January 20, 1988): 49.
10. "Aus dem Verhängnis wird ein Skandal," *Die Weltwoche* (February 4, 1988): 1. The "A" sample was supposed to contain 40 milliliters and the "B" sample 30 milliliters. In fact, these two samples contained only 20 milliliters and 15 milliliters, respectively. See "Aus dem Verhängnis wird ein Skandal," 2.
11. "Aus dem Verhängnis wird ein Skandal," 2. The two scientists were Dr. James Bäumler, 63, an early researcher in the field of doping analysis, and Dr. Werner Bernhard, 38.
12. " 'Fall Gasser': Donike macht Hoffnung," *Tages-Anzeiger* (October 13, 1987). Donike's conclusion regarding the differences between the two samples was confirmed by Dr. Wilhelm Schänzer, also of the German Sports College in Cologne, who was hired by the SLV as an independent expert. See "Aus dem Verhängnis wird ein Skandal," 1.
13. "Aus dem Verhängnis wird ein Skandal," 2.
14. "Sandra Gasser läuft für ihre Ehre."
15. "Schweizer verlangen Begründung," *Süddeutsche Zeitung* (October 1, 1987).
16. "Sandra Gasser ruft ein ziviles Gericht an," *Neue Zürcher Zeitung* (October 24/25, 1987); "Sandra Gasser vorläufig überall startberechtigt," *Tages-Anzeiger* (December 24, 1987).
17. "Sandra Gasser läuft für ihre Ehre." In the early summer of 1989, Gasser ran 1,000 meters in the world-class time of 2:33.72—a remarkable recovery of form after two years away from elite competition.
18. The *Schweizer Illustrierte*. See "Wie lebenslänglich."
19. "Hängen bleiben nur die Dummen und Unvorsichtigen," *Die Weltwoche* (February 4, 1988): 75.
20. "Wie schwanger ist Herr Günthör?" *Die Weltwoche* (May 10, 1990): 34.
21. Brigitte Berendonk, *Doping-Dokumente: Von der Forschung zum Betrug* (Berlin, Heidelberg, New York: Springer-Verlag, 1991): 187, 237, 241, 243.
22. "Hängen bleiben nur die Dummen und Unvorsichtigen," 75.
23. "Magglingen oder Der heile Körper am Ende der Welt," *Die Weltwoche* (June 29, 1989): 33.
24. "Defiant Swiss athletes's case submitted to IAAF tribunal," *The Times* [London] (January 5, 1988).
25. "Juristisches Gefecht nach dem 'Fall Gasser,' " *Neue Zürcher Zeitung* (Oct. 31/Nov. 1, 1987).
26. "Erwartetes Urteil," *Tages-Anzeiger* (January 20, 1988): 1.
27. Günther Heinze, the former general-secretary of the East German National Olympic Committee and a member of the IOC since 1981, helped to plan the IOC's first World Conference Against Doping. Dr. Manfred Höppner, the former director of the East German Sports Medical Service (SMD) who was deeply involved in doping, served for fifteen years on the IAAF Medical Commission. See "Ein Unverbesserlicher als Fehler im System," *Süddeutsche Zeitung* (December 1/2, 1990); "Es gibt kein Patentrezept," *Süddeutsche Zeitung* (December 4, 1990). For Höppner's apologia for doping—"we knew what the

Americans were doing and we wanted to stay competitive," etc.—see "Bonn fordert schnelle Untersuchung," *Süddeutsche Zeitung* (November 30, 1990).

28. See John Hoberman, *The Olympic Crisis: Sport, Politics, and the Moral Order* (New Rochelle, N.Y.: Aristide D. Caratzas, Publisher, 1986).

29. "Muskelpillen als Waffe im Klassenkampf," *Süddeutsche Zeitung* (December 5, 1990).

30. "Ewald trifft sich mit Samaranch," *Süddeutsche Zeitung* (November 12, 1991). In December 1990 Ewald actually stated that: "There was never any doping in the GDR." See "Kein Anlass zum Rücktritt," *Süddeutsche Zeitung* (December 7/8, 1990).

31. "Sandra Gasser: 'Ich kam mir so klein vor.' "

32. Nebiolo, a wealthy lawyer and investor, has retained his power in the IAAF by distributing funds to small, often Third World countries who then build their track-and-field programs and vote for Nebiolo in IAAF elections. According to *Der Spiegel*, the $20,000,000 that funded Nebiolo's International Athletic Foundation may have been a payoff from the South Korean government for Nebiolo's willingness to schedule track-and-field events during hot (and therefore unfavorable) times of day during the 1988 Seoul Olympic Games in order to accomodate the scheduling requirements of American television. He is widely held responsible for a notorious cheating incident at the 1987 world championships in Rome. An Italian long jumper, Giovanni Evangelisti, was credited with a longer jump than he actually made, and it turned out that a number of Italian officials had conspired to "win" this athlete a bronze medal without his knowledge. He subsequently returned the medal, which was later awarded to a American athlete. In addition, while president of both Fidal and the IAAF, Nebiolo presided over the awarding of an official world record to the Italian shot-putter Alessandro Andrei despite disqualifying rules violations. See "Anwalt des Schweigens," *Der Spiegel* (April 11, 1988): 214, 216.

33. "Der 'Fall Gasser' immer noch pendant," *Neue Zürcher Zeitung* (December 24/25, 1988); "Sandra Gasser ruft ein ziviles Gericht an."

34. "Aus dem Verhängnis wird ein Skandal."

35. *Proper and Improper Use of Drugs by Athletes* [Hearings before the Subcommittee to Investigate Juvenile Delinquency of the Committee on the Judiciary: United States Senate] (Washington, D.C.: U.S. Government Printing Office, 1973). These hearings were held on June 18 and July 12 and 13, 1973.

36. See, for example, Arthur Mallwitz, *Körperliche Höchstleistungen mit besonderer Berücksichtigung des olympischen Sportes* (Berlin: Aus dem hygien. Institut der Kgl. Universität, 1908). I have found no term comparable to *Höchstleistung* ("top performance") in French, English, and American texts from this period. In addition, the term "performance principle" (*Leistungsprinzip*) does not appear in other modern European languages as a colloquial term.

37. "Zwischen Schönfärberei und Schwarzmalerei," *Süddeutsche Zeitung* (July 26, 1991).

38. "Beyer fordert Doping-Freigabe," *Süddeutsche Zeitung* (August 28, 1991).

39. "Industrie lässt sich nicht von Effekten leiten," *Süddeutsche Zeitung* (October 11, 1988).

40. "Schäuble mahnt Konsequenzen an," *Süddeutsche Zeitung* (October 23, 1991).

41. "Daume und Hansen halten Sonntagsreden," *Frankfurter Allgemeine Zeitung*

(January 9, 1989). The two officials mentioned by Reichenbach were Willi Daume, president of the West German National Olympic Committee, and Hans Hansen, president of the German Sports Federation (DSB).

42. "Die meisten Zuschauer sprechen Johnson frei," *Frankfurter Allgemeine Zeitung* (January 16, 1989). Wildor Hollmann has also said that he asked Willi Daume to do away with the norms system just after the 1988 Seoul Olympic Games. See "Daume antwortet nicht," *Süddeutsche Zeitung* (December 10, 1990).

43. See, for example, "Der grosse Knall kommt," *Der Spiegel* (July 1, 1991): 160, 162. This is an interview with the former intermediate-hurdles champion Harald Schmid, appointed in 1991 to chair the Doping Commission of the German Athletics Association (DLV).

44. On the neo-Marxist critique of sport in France and West Germany see John M. Hoberman, *Sport and Political Ideology* (Austin: University of Texas Press, 1984): 232–48.

45. "Sport nicht zum Renommierfeld verkommen lassen," *Süddeutsche Zeitung* (December 1/2, 1984).

46. "Krieg der Körper," *Süddeutsche Zeitung* (August 28, 1985); 35.

47. "Grüne wollen Ausstieg aus Kinderhochleistungssport," *Frankfurter Allgemeine Zeitung* (December 12, 1988) 25.

48. "Altersgrenze gefordert," *Süddeutsche Zeitung* (September 16, 1988).

49. See, for example, *Grüne Technologie-Politik* (Stuttgart: Die Grünen Badem-Württemberg, n.d.): 11–12; *Das Programm* (Stuttgart: Die Grünen Badem-Württenberg, 1988): 64. It is worth noting that Wolfgang Schäuble, the interior minister whose role in the politics of doping is described below, has criticized the "irrationalism" of the Greens. See "Das Beste daraus machen," *Der Spiegel* (November 25, 1991): 45.

50. Harriet Ritvo, *The Animal Estate* (Cambridge, Mass.: Harvard University Press, 1987): 164.

51. "Der Sport befindet sich in einer Grenzsituation," *Süddeutsche Zeitung* (November 18, 1985): 42.

52. "Aus einer anderen Welt," *Der Spiegel* (December 24, 1990): 140. On Daume's fondness for citing classical European thinkers (Thomas Mann, Johan Huizinga, José Ortega y Gasset) see also "Oder Daume will es nicht kapieren," *Süddeutsche Zeitung* (December 17, 1990).

53. "Die Athleten nicht vorab unter Druck setzen," *Frankfurter Allgemeine Zeitung* (January 21, 1988).

54. "Until 1976 I regarded anabolic steroids as harmless," Wildor Hollmann said in 1989. See "Die meisten Zuschauer sprechen Johnson frei."

55. *Doping-Dokumente*, 18–20.

56. "Bisschen Damenbart," *Der Spiegel* (April 4, 1977): 193. Ten years later, after the death of Birgit Dressel (see Chapter 1), the Sports Committee of the Bundestag held another hearing on "Humane Possibilities in High-Performance Sport." See "Diskussion im Bundestag," *Süddeutsche Zeitung* (August 7, 1987).

57. *Doping-Dokumente*, 21.

58. Quoted in *Doping-Dokumente*, 21. As of this writing, Wolfgang Schäuble has recently appeared on the cover of *Der Spiegel* (November 25, 1991) as the leading candidate to succeed Helmut Kohl as chancellor of Germany.

59. "Weitergehende Kontrollen," *Süddeutsche Zeitung* (December 27, 1988).
60. "Kein Vertrauen in die Repräsentanten," *Süddeutsche Zeitung* (October 25, 1991).
61. "Hast wohl viel getrunken?" *Der Spiegel* (July 1, 1991): 156; *Doping-Dokumente*, 77.
62. Similarly, it was a Green member of the Swiss Federal Parliament, Dr. Lukas Fierz, who protested the firing of Dr. Hans Howald from his position as head of the Research Institute of the Swiss Sports School at Magglingen (see above). See "Magglingen oder Der Heile Körper am Ende der Welt," 33.
63. "Politiker fordern Generalangriff auf Doping," *Frankfurter Allgemeine Zeitung* (March 5, 1988).
64. "DDR-Spitzensport darf nicht zusammenbrechen," *Frankfurter Allgemeine Zeitung* (April 11, 1990).
65. "Leichtatahletik-Bundestrainer Jochen Spilker tritt zurück," *Frankfurter Allgemeine Zeitung* (December 4, 1990): 31.
66. "Sportärzte ohne Berührungsängste," *Süddeutsche Zeitung* (October 22, 1990). Brigitte Berendonk, too, has pointed out that "among all of the research institutions of the GDR, only three—and sports science institutes in particular— were accorded an unconditional right to exist by the treaty of unification." See "Müllhalde von Lug und Betrug," *Süddeutsche Zeitung* (September 17, 1991).
67. "Willige Sklaven," *Der Spiegel* (October 19, 1987): 226.
68. "Bundestag gegen Generalamnestie," *Süddeutsche Zeitung* (September 4, 1991); "Nur ein Lippenbekenntnis," *Süddeutsche Zeitung* (October 18, 1991).
69. "Bundestag gegen Generalamnestie," *Süddeutsche Zeitung* (September 4, 1991); "Die Drohung aus Bonn wird verstanden," *Süddeutsche Zeitung* (September 28/29, 1991). On the general amnesty provisions see "Das NOK sperrt Dopingsünder von Olympia aus," *Süddeutsche Zeitung* (November 18, 1991).
70. A good synopsis of this controversy is found under the title "Im Namen der Wissenschaft experimentierte auch der Westen mit Dopingmitteln," *Süddeutsche Zeitung* (October 26/27, 1991), which includes five separate articles on p. 49 of the newspaper.
71. "Das Verbotene offiziell erforscht," *Süddeutsche Zeitung* (November 2/3, 1991). It is worth noting that assisting Keul in this study was Dr. Hartmut Riedel, an important East German expert on steroids who defected to West Germany in 1987 and who has been accused by Brigitte Berendonk of "criminal" doping practices while treating East German athletes, women in particular. It is also of interest that among the authors of the 1988 paper is Dr. Manfred Donike, the world's foremost authority on methods for detecting the use of anabolic steroids by elite athletes. A second BISP-supported study, carried out during the period 1987–88, was titled "On the Effects of the Oral Administration of Testosterone Undecaoate on Regeneration Capacity." This research was directed by Dr. Heinz Liesen, a nationally known sports physician who for years has advocated the use of steroids in elite sport, and he too was assisted by Hartmut Riedel. The results of this study appear to contradict the results of the experiment directed by Joseph Keul. See "Das ist reines Doping," *Süddeutsche Zeitung* (October 26/27, 1991): 49.
72. "DSB-Dopingtests schmalbrüstig," *Süddeutsche Zeitung* (November 29, 1989): 55.

73. "Blödsinn?" *Süddeutsche Zeitung* (October 31/November 1, 1990); "Christian Schenk und die Kunst des Formulierens," *Süddeutsche Zeitung* (December 3, 1990).

74. This criticism of the decathletes' initiative was made by Dr. Manfred Steinbach, a high official (*Sportwart*) of the DLV, in an interview with the newsweekly *Der Spiegel*. See "Schicksalsstunde des Sports," *Der Spiegel* (December 10, 1990): 266. See also "Aus einer anderen Welt," 141.

75. "Hängen bleiben nur die Dummen und Unvorsichtigen," 74.

76. "Blödsinn?"

77. "Manfred Steinbach, "Sportwart des Deutschen Leichtathletik-Verbands," *Süddeutsche Zeitung* (August 11/12, 1990).

78. "Schwelt und kocht," *Der Spiegel* (September 23, 1991): 239.

79. "Bedenken gegen Dopingtests im Training," *Süddeutsche Zeitung* (November 21, 1988).

80. "Wie die Tiere," *Der Spiegel* (February 15, 1988): 214.

81. "Der grosse Knall kommt," 160.

82. "Von der Spartakiade zur Talentiade," *Süddeutsche Zeitung* (September 26, 1990).

83. "Bonn setzt auf DDR-Wissenschaftler," *Süddeutsche Zeitung* (September 28, 1990). By October 1991 East German trainers and physicians implicated in doping schemes were encountering problems. The thirty-six East German trainers hired by the DLV now faced the possibility that their contracts would be cancelled. See "Es werden Wunder geschehen," *Der Spiegel* (October 7, 1991): 255.

84. "Pillen wie das tägliche Brot," *Der Spiegel* (March 12, 1990): 216; *Doping-Dokumente*, 49, 60, 200.

85. "Auch für Bomber-Piloten gut," *Der Spiegel* (February 18, 1991): 192; *Doping-Dokumente*, 93, 103, 193.

86. "Verrat und Lüge," *Der Spiegel* (August 5, 1991): 164; *Doping-Dokumente*, 44.

87. *Doping-Dokumente*, 74, 168–69, 278.

88. "Athleten beteuern empört ihre Unschuld; Daume will eine internationale Untersuchung," *Frankfurter Allgemeine Zeitung* (November 30, 1990).

89. "Aufforderung zum Doping," *Der Spiegel* (November 13, 1989): 259.

90. In the United States, by contrast, prospective Olympic track-and-field athletes compete for three positions per event rather than against a specific norm. At the same time, these athletes must also meet the minimum performance norms of the IOC.

91. "Heuchelei um Anabolika," *Süddeutsche Zeitung* (January 5/6, 1989).

92. "Die meisten Zuschauer sprechen Johnson frei," *Frankfurter Allgemeine Zeitung* (January 16, 1989).

93. "Ärzte gegen die Normen," *Süddeutsche Zeitung* (May 12, 1989).

94. "Manfred Steinbach, Sportwart des Deutschen Leichtathletik-Verbands," *Süddeutsche Zeitung* (August 11/12, 1990).

95. "Aus einer anderen Welt," 140.

96. "DLV verzichtet auf Leistungsnormen, *Süddeutsche Zeitung* (December 7, 199).

97. "Eine fünfte Kategorie für den Sport," *Süddeutsche Zeitung* (January 10, 1989): 28.

98. "Das Kuckuckseier im Nest des DLV," *Süddeutsche Zeitung* (November 30, 1990).

99. "DDR-Forscher geben systematisches Doping zu," *Frankfurter Allgemeine Zeitung* (February 16, 1990). A comparison of the steroid-assisted Ben Johnson of 1988 and the presumably "clean" Ben Johnson of 1991 tends to confirm Buhl's estimate. Johnson ran his most famous 100-meter race in 9.79 seconds at the Seoul Olympic Games and averaged only about 10.40 seconds per race during the 1991 track-and-field season.

100. *Doping-Dokumente*, 284.

101. Ibid., 243–44. In 1982 the West German newsweekly *Der Spiegel* estimated that discus throws longer than 70 meters (229' 8") were impossible without the use of steroids. In fact, there have been relatively few throws beyond this distance, the current world record being 243 feet. The longest throw of 1991 was 227' 7". See *Track & Field News* (November 1991): 61.

102. "Ländliche Verhältnisse im Spitzensport," *Süddeutsche Zeitung* (May 8, 1985).

103. "Dopingvorwürfe auf westdeutsche Leichtathletik erweitert," *Süddeutsche Zeitung* (December 3, 1990).

104. "Der grosse Knall kommt," 162; "Ganz schnell handeln," *Der Spiegel* (December 3, 1990): 226. In September 1991 a Daimler-Benz spokesman warned the DLV that the company's patience would expire within a year at most. See "Daimler's Ultimatum," *Süddeutsche Zeitung* (September 16, 1991).

105. Arnd Krüger has informed me that Daume was at most a reserve player and that his claim to have actually played in the 1936 Olympic Games is not supported by the official Olympic program.

106. *Der Sport Brockhaus* (Wiesbaden: F.A. Brockhaus, 1977): 97.

107. *Doping-Dokumente*, 23.

108. "Das NOK sperrt Dopingsünder von Olympia aus," *Süddeutsche Zeitung* (November 18, 1991).

109. "Daume lässt 'Fall Angerer' überprüfen," *Süddeutsche Zeitung* (September 1, 1986); "Doping als das Übel aller Übel," *Süddeutsche Zeitung* (January 8, 1986); Aufforderung zum Doping," 256.

110. "Athleten beteuern empört ihre Unschuld; Daume will eine internationale Untersuchung."

111. *Doping-Dokumente*, 23; "Aus einer anderen Welt," 140.

112. *Doping-Dokumente*, 30, 20.

113. Bernhard Lüpke, "Nur siegen müssen sie selber," *Stern* 40 (August 20–26, 1987): 17. It should be noted that Lüpke, while describing Riedel as "a sought-after conversational partner," does not link this status with his doping expertise, which is never mentioned and was presumably unknown to the journalist. Brigitte Berendonk cites a report that Riedel did not mention his doping activities on the advice of Hollmann. See *Doping-Dokumente*, 35.

114. "Bewußt nicht nach Doping gefragt," *Süddeutsche Zeitung* (September 25, 1991): 63.

115. *Doping-Dokumente*, 62, 65, 83, 131, 149, 150–51, 155–57, 191, 199.

116. R. Häcker and H. de Marées, *Hormonelle Regulation und psychophysische Belastung im Leistungssport* (Cologne: Deutscher Ärzte-Verlag, 1991). For Brigitte Berendonk's critical comments on this symposium, see *Doping-Dokumente*, 289.

117. Robert Proctor, *Racial Hygiene: Medicine under the Nazis* (Cambridge, Mass.: Harvard University Press, 1988): 223.

118. See, for example, Jeffrey Herf, *Reactionary Modernism: Technology, culture, and politics in Weimar and the Third Reich* (New York: Cambridge University Press, 1984).

119. August Bier, "Gedanken eines Arztes über die Medizin," *Münchener Medizinische Wochenschrift* (April 2, 1926): 555; "Gedanken eines Arztes über die Medizin," *Münchener Medizinische Wochenschrift* (August 13, 1926): 1,362.

120. Bier, "Gedanken eines Arztes über die Medizin," *Münchener Medizinische Wochenschrift* (August 13, 1926): 1,363, 1,362.

121. Ibid., 1362.

122. Bier, "Gedaanken eines Arztes über die Medizin," *Münchener Medizinische Wochenschrift* (April 2, 1926): 555.

123. Bier, "Gedanken eines Arztes über die Medizin," *Münchener Medizinische Wochenschrift* (July 9, 1926): 1,161.

124. Bier, "Gedanken eines Arztes über die Medizin," *Münchener Medizinische Wochenschrift* (August 13, 1926): 1,360, 1,362.

125. Bier, "Gedanken eines Arztes über die Medizin," *Münchener Medizinische Wochenschrift* (April 2, 1926): 557, 558.

126. On the persistence of homeopathic medicine in Germany, see "Magier der Verdünnung," *Der Spiegel* 42 (December 19, 1988): 58–59.

127. Bier, "Gedanken eines Arztes über die Medizin," *Münchener Medizinische Wochenschrift* (August 20, 1926): 1,404; Proctor, *Racial Hygiene*, 119.

128. Bier, "Gedanken eines Arztes über die Medizin," *Münchener Medizinische Wochenschrift* (July 2, 1926): 1,103.

129. Paul Weindling, *Health, race and German politics between national unification and Nazism, 1870–1945* (Cambridge: Cambridge University Press, 1989): 170–73.

130. Bier, "Gedanken eines Arztes über die Medizin," *Münchener Medizinische Wochenschrift* (August 20, 1926): 1,404.

131. Ibid.

132. Proctor, *Racial Hygiene*, 224.

133. See, for example, Giselher Spitzer, *Der deutsche Naturismus: Idee und Entwicklung einer volkserzieherischen Bewegung im Schnittfeld von Lebensreform, Sport und Politik* (Ahrensburg bei Hamburg: Verlag Ingrid Czwalina, 1983): 62ff.

134. David Hamilton, *The Monkey Gland Affair* (London: Chatto & Windus, 1986): 44–47, 137–39.

135. W. Dernbach, "Hormone und Hormonpräparate," *Archiv der Pharmazie und Berichte der Deutschen Pharmazeutischen Gesellschaft* (1937): 426–27.

136. "Frischzellen: 'Meist eine Freude erleben'," *Der Spiegel*, no. 37 (1988): 162; "Mit Frischzellen über Stock und Stein," *Süddeutsche Zeitung* (April 10, 1990).

137. Weindling, *Health, race and German politics*, 172. Heuppe was also the founding president of the German Soccer Federation (DFB).

138. Ferdinand Hueppe, "Sport und Reizmittel," *Berliner Klinische Wochenschrift* (March 24, 1913): 550, 552.

139. Ferdinand Hueppe, *Hygiene der Körperübungen* (Leipzig: Verlag von S. Hirzel, 1922): iv.

140. Arthur Mallwitz, "Jetziger Stand des Sportarztwesens in Deutschland," in Arthur Mallwitz, ed., *Sportmedizin und olympische Spiele 1936: Festschrift der Sportärzteschaft* (Leipzig: Georg Thieme, 1936): 8–9.

141. Bruno K. Schulz, "Sport und Rasse," *Leibesüngen und körperliche Erziehung* (1939): 339–43.

142. Wilhelm Knoll, "Sportärztliche Arbeit," in Mallwitz, ed., *Sportmedizin und olympische Spiele 1936*, 10–11; Wilhelm Knoll, "Seelische Auswirkungen sportlicher Arbeit," in *Leistung und Beanspruchung* (St. Gallen: Verlag Zollikofer & Co., 1948): 197–216.

143. "Die Medizin ist Politik im grossen." Quoted in Hans Krauss, "Amtsarzt und Rassenhygiene," *Münchener Medizinische Wochenschrift* (July 22, 1927): 1238.

144. "Sportärzte-Kongress: Kritik an Muskel-Injectionen," *Frankfurter Allgemeine Zeitung* (February 1, 1988).

145. In 1989 Klümper left state service to run a private rehabilitation clinic for elite and recreational athletes. See "Klümper verlässt Staatsdienst für privates Klinik-Projekt," *Frankfurter Allgemeine Zeitung* (October 14, 1989).

146. See, for example, "Taktisch geschwiegen," *Süddeutsche Zeitung* (August 19, 1987); "Sportler wollen Klümper," *Süddeutsche Zeitung* (March 21, 1988); "Ehrenerklärung für Klümper," *Süddeutsche Zeitung* (February 11/12/ 1989).

147. "Ich mache meine eigene Medizin," *Der Spiegel* (April 1, 1991): 196, 198.

148. "Frontmann, Guru, Zielscheibe: Klümper öffnet die Tür," *Süddeutsche Zeitung* (July 19, 1988).

149. "Rosen für den Prinzen von den Heilquellen," *Der Spiegel* (February 27, 1989): 199.

150. "Frontmann, Guru, Zielscheibe: Klümper öffnet die Tür."

151. Bernhard Lüpke, "Ein Guru in der Klemme," *Stern* 39 (September 18–24, 1986): 137.

152. "Doping mit erlaubten Mitteln," *Süddeutsche Zeitung* (January 22, 1987).

153. "Wider die Doping-Mentalität der Scharlatane," *Süddeutsche Zeitung* (May 24, 1988).

154. "Siegen um jeden Preis," *Der Spiegel* (November 26, 1984): 197; Lüpke, "Ein Guru in der Klemme," 137.

155. "Wider die Doping-Mentalität der Scharlatane." In 1985 Liesen told a journalist: "We inject large amounts of vitamins and immune-system boosters to support the body's defenses." See "Zuviel Theater um Anabolika," *Süddeutsche Zeitung* (January 23, 1985).

156. "Wider die Doping-Mentalität der Schlarlatane."

157. "Siegen um jeden Preis," 195; "Zu wenig Zeit zur Regeneration," *Süddeutsche Zeitung* (November 20, 1989).

158. "Traurige Angelegenheit," *Süddeutsche Zeitung* (December 8, 1982); "Sportmedizinische Betreuung als unzureichend kritisiert," *Frankfurter Allgemeine Zeitung* (November 20, 1989).

159. "Trinken, um Leistung zu bringen," *Süddeutsche Zeitung* (June 7/8, 1986); "Frontmann, Guru, Zielscheibe,"; "Wider die Doping-Mentalität der Scharlatane"; "Doping mit erlaubten Mitteln"; "Siegen um jeden Preis," 197.

160. Otto Riesser, "Über Doping und Dopingmittel," *Leibesübungen und körperliche Erziehung* (1933):395; G. Schönholzer, "Die Frage des Doping," *Sportärztlicher Zentrallkurs 1937 in Bern* (Bern: Büchler & Co., 1938): 174, 188; Otto

Blau, "Eine neue Kraftquelle für Sportleistungen?" *Die Leibesübungen* (1930): 689.

161. In 1976 Herbert Reindell, then president of the German Association of Sports Physicians, was among several prominent sports physicians who minimized the dangers of doping. See Berendonk, *Doping-Dokumente*, 19.

162. "Doping mit erlaubten Mitteln"; "Wider die Doping-Mentalität der Scharlatane."

163. Berendonk, *Doping-Dokumente*, 19, 17.

164. Wilfried Kindermann's position on steroids is ambivalent in that he endorses what I call the "lesser harm" argument. "If we don't get strict controls," he said in 1988, "steroids will have to be taken off the doping list. If steroids are distributed, then at least we physicians will have a chance to discuss with the athletes what a responsible dosage is." See "Kontrollen in den Trainingsphasen," *Süddeutsche Zeitung* (August 11, 1988). Speaking in 1990 as the physician of the German national soccer team, Kindermann argued that codeine and ephedrin should be taken off the doping list. See "Freigabe von Dopingmitteln gefordert," *Süddeutsche Zeitung* (December 20, 1990).

165. "Zuviel Theater um Anabolika."

166. "Viel Scheinheiligkeit," *Der Spiegel* (September 8, 1986): 220; "Angerer und Wudy gedopt," *Süddeutsche Zeitung* (August 29, 1986); "Lehren aus einem Dopingfall," *Süddeutsche Zeitung* (August 30/31, 1986).

167. For a brief summary of Hollmann's career see "Wildor Hollmann und der 'Ruhestand': Mit 65 Jahren ist noch lange nicht Schluss," *Frankfurter Allgemeine Zeitung* (February 9, 1990): 31. On Hollmann's research see, for example, Wildor Hollmann, "Untersuchungen über Möglichkeiten zur Steigerung des körperlichen Leistungsvermögens von Rekruten," *Sportarzt und Sportmedizin* (1966): 582–92; "Die Beeinflussung des Leistungsverhaltens des cardipulmonalen Systems durch verschiedene Pharmaka," *Der Sportarzt* (1966): 55–58.

168. "Hochleistungssport nie mehr ohne Doping," *Süddeutsche Zeitung* (September 29/30, 1984).

169. "Der Sport ist wie ein ungepflügtes Land," *Süddeutsche Zeitung* (January 30, 1985).

170. I am indebted to Arnd Krüger for this piece of information.

171. "Doping wird wie ein Buschfeuer brennen," *Süddeutsche Zeitung* (December 20/21, 1986): 48;

172. "Eine fünfte Kategorie für den Sport," *Süddeutsche Zeitung* (January 10, 1989): 28.

173. "Sportärzte kritisieren Samaranch," *Süddeutsche Zeitung* (October 29, 1985); "Gefahren durch Flickschusterei," *Der Spiegel* (November 5, 1985): 242; "Samaranch versteht die Sorgen der Ärzte," *Süddeutsche Zeitung* (January 30, 1987):42.

174. "Typen wie aus dem Panoptikum," *Der Spiegel* (July 23, 1984): 71.

175. W. Hollmann, "Risikofaktoren in der Entwicklung des Hochleistungssports," in H. Rieckert, ed. *Sportmedizin—Kursbestimmung* [Deutscher Sportärztekongreß, Kiel, 16.–19. Oktober 1986] (Berlin: Springer-Verlag, 1987): 16.

176. "Sport ist wie ein ungepflügtes Land."

177. "Gefahren durch Flickschusterei," 242, 242, 245.

178. "Schlag ins Gesicht der Sportmedizin," *Süddeutsche Zeitung* (February 4, 1985).
179. "Gefahren durch Flickschusterei," 242.
180. "Der schwierige Weg aus der Grauzone," *Süddeutsche Zeitung* (May 18, 1987).
181. "Gefahren durch Flickschusterei," 243, 245; Berendonk, *Doping-Dokumente*, 266–69.
182. Josef-Otto Freudenreich, "Der Spritzensport," *Die Zeit* (August 5, 1988).
183. See, for example, "Auf kaltem Wege," *Der Spiegel* (November 11, 1991): 266, 268, 269.
184. "Not Enough Positives?" *Track & Field News* (December 1987): 50.
185. Robert Voy, *Drugs, Sport, and Politics* (Champaign, Ill.: Leisure Press, 1991): 108–9.
186. Berendonk, *Doping-Dokumente*, 160, 158, 241.
187. According to Wildor Hollmann: "Anabolic steroids were first used in the United States after the 1956 Melbourne Olympic Games and were brought to Europe by American athletes in conjunction with the 1960 Rome Olympic Games." See Hollmann, "Risikofaktoren," 19. My account is from Terry Todd, "Anabolic Steroids: The Gremlins of Sport," *Journal of Sport History* 14 (1987): 93–94.
188. "Ein starker Damm gegen die Dopingflut," *Süddeutsche Zeitung* (September 17/18, 1988): 48.
189. "New Drug Plan," *New York Times* (June 8, 1989).
190. On the basic science of drug testing, see Charles E. Yesalis and R. Craig Kammerer, "The Strengths and Failures of Drug Tests," *New York Times*, February 4, 1990.
191. "Deutsches Problem," *Süddeutsche Zeitung* (December 11, 1990); "Kein Anlaß zum Rücktritt," *Süddeutsche Zeitung* (December 7/8, 1990).
192. For the specifics of this case, see "Before the Doping Control Review Board in the Matter of Harry L. Reynolds" (unpublished document). For a published summary of its findings, see "Reynolds a Step Closer," *Track & Field News* (December 1991): 48.
193. "Utestengt inntil videre," *Nytt fra Norge* (September 17, 1991): 22. For a Norwegian sportswriter's critical treatment of the Norwegian federation's behavior in this case, see "Idrettsforbund på feil spor," ibid.
194. "North Korea Digs In Its Heels on Nuclear Inspections," *New York Times*, October 27, 1991.
195. "Die Doping-Kontrolleure laufen hinterher," *Süddeutsche Zeitung* (September 22/23, 1988). Howald noted that while the rate of positive drug tests at the Caracas Pan-American Games in 1983 was 8.1 percent, the comparable figure for the 1984 Los Angeles Olympic Games was a mere 0.7 percent.
196. Quoted in Shirley Hazzard, *Countenance of Truth: The United Nations and the Waldheim Case* (New York: Viking, 1990): 30.

8. Horses and Humans

1. According to Ludwig Prokop, the drugging of horses was known in ancient times among the Romans and Scythians and was very common in England as early as the sixteenth and seventeenth centuries. See "Zur Geschichte des Dopings," in Helmut Acker, ed., *Rekorde aux der Retorte: Leistungssteigerung im modernen Hochleistungssport* (Stuttgart: Deutsche Verlags-Anstalt, 1972) 23.

2. Mosso is paraphrased by a scientifically minded French army officer in 1895. See V. Legros, Préface to A. Mosso, *L'Éducation physique de la jeunesse* (Paris: Félix Alcan, 1895): xvi–xvii.

3. "Doping Racehorses," *The Pharmaceutical Journal and Pharmacist* (January 12, 1912): 23.

4. "Centaur," "Subduing Restless Horses," *The Pharmaceutical Journal* (January 12, 1907): 38. "It may be said at once that opium as a sedative or controller is absolutely unreliable in equines. In the horse the higher brain centres are less developed than in man; hence the sedative and hypnotic effects of opium are not well marked, and large doses produce excitement, restlessness, pawing, and walking round in a circle. Opium, then, is not the drug wanted to enable the horse owner to clip or shoe a vicious or restless animal."

5. "A Case of 'Gingering' Horses," *The Pharmaceutical Journal and Pharmacist* (July 12, 1913): 37; "Horse Racing Faces New Drug Problem as Steroid Use Troubles Breeders," *New York Times* (July 15, 1990): 16.

6. "Horse Drugging," *The Pharmaceutical Journal and Pharmacist* (November 1, 1913): 666.

7. "Drugs for Racehorses," *The Pharmaceutical Journal and Pharmacist* (August 1, 1914): 210.

8. According to Ludwig Prokop, the Austrian Jockey Club had invited the Russian chemist Bukowski to come to Vienna to test horses for drugs. When Bukowski refused to reveal his laboratory procedure for verifying the presence of alkaloids like heroin and cocaine, a professor at the University of Vienna, Dr. Sigmund Fränkel, developed his own saliva test for alkaloids. During 1910 and 1911 he performed tests on horses, and some owners of racehorses were penalized for these offenses. See "Zur Geschichte des Dopings," 23–24.

9. "The Doping of Racehorses," *The Pharmaceutical Journal and Pharmacist* (June 14, 1913): 609, 610.

10. William H. Brewer, "The Evolution of the American Trotting-Horse," *Nature* (April 26, 1883): 609, 610

11. Francis Galton, "The American Trotting-Horse," *Nature* (May 10, 1883): 29.

12. R. H. Thurston, "The Horse as a High Speed Engine," *Scientific American Supplement* (December 1, 1894): 15,778.

13. "Up until the 18th century roads and communications [in England] were generally poor and many of the nobility employed 'running footmen' to carry messages or race ahead to an inn to announce their arrival. . . . Some became very gifted runners and their employers often put them up for wagers against the footman of a rival. . . . However, better roads and coach services made the running footmen redundant and in order to continue in the sport they began to arrange their own matches and wagers. They now became known as 'pedestrians.'" See Eric M. Macintyre, "Pedestrianism to the Trust Fund—Athletics in its Historical and Social Contexts," in J.A. Mangan and R.B. Small, eds., *Sport, Culture, Society: International historical and sociological perspectives* (London and New York: E. and F.N. Spon, 1986): 125.

14. Francis Galton, "An Examination into the Registered Speeds of American Trotting Horses, with Remarks on their Value as Hereditary Data," *Nature* (February 3, 1898): 333. Galton also points out a specific technological development that had improved the quality of the trotting data. "The system of timing was

first put into practice more than fifty years ago, and has since been developed and improved. In 1892 a considerable change was made in the conditions by the introduction of bicycle wheels with pneumatic tyres, which produced a gain of speed, the amount of which is much discussed, but which a prevalent opinion rates at 5 seconds in the mile. Thenceforward the records are comparable on nearly equal terms" (p. 333).

15. E.J. Marey, "The Work of the Physiological Station at Paris," *Smithsonian Report* (1896): 411.

16. Thurston, "The Horse as a High Speed Engine," 15,778.

17. Theodore Andrea Cook, "The Modern Thoroughbred: His Past and Future," *The Monthly Review* 5 (November 1901): 129, 138.

18. Patrick Cunningham, "The Genetics of Thoroughbred Horses," *Scientific American* (May 1991): 92.

19. Cook, "The Modern Thoroughbred," 127, 129.

20. Ibid., 132.

21. Arthur Mallwitz, *Körperliche Höchstleistungen mit besonderer Berücksichtigung des olympischen Sportes* (Berlin: Aus dem hygien. Institut der Kgl. Universität, 1908): 35–36.

22. As of 1990 the fastest time for one and three-sixteenths miles was 1 minute 53.2 seconds, set in 1985. A straight prorating of this time yields a one-mile time of 95.3 seconds.

23. A brief comparison of the figures generated by one formula in Kennelly's table with current world records in the men's and women's 1,500-, 3,000-, 5,000-, and 10,000-meter runs shows that this is, indeed, an "approximate" law of fatigue. Kennelly predicts, for example, that as distance increases 100 percent time should increase 118 percent. The only comparison of times and distances that almost matches Kennelly's figure pertains to the women's record time for 1,500 meters (3:52.57) and the corresponding time for 3,000 meters (8:22.62), which yield an increase of 216 percent.

24. A.E. Kennelly, "An Approximate Law of Fatigue in the Speeds of Racing Animals," *Proceedings of the American Academy of Arts and Sciences* 42 (December 1906): 320.

25. Quoted in Harriet Ritvo, *The Animal Estate: The English and Other Creatures in the Victorian Age* (Cambridge, Mass.: Harvard University Press, 1987): 20.

26. N. Zuntz and C. Lehmann, "Remarks on the Chemistry of Respiration in the Horse During Rest and Work," *The Journal of Physiology* 11 (1890): 396–98.

27. F. Smith, "The Maximum Muscular Effort of the Horse," *The Journal of Physiology* 19 (1895–96): 224–26.

28. Cunningham, "The Genetics of Thoroughbred Horses," 97.

29. Lynda Birke, "Equine athletes: blood, sweat and biochemistry," *New Scientist* (May 22, 1986): 52.

30. B. Gaffney, "Estimation of genetic trend in racing performance of thoroughbred horses," *Nature* 332 (April 21, 1988): 722.

31. William G. Hill, "Why aren't horses faster?" *Nature* 322 (April 21, 1988): 678.

32. Cunningham, "The Genetics of Thoroughbred Horses," 97.

33. "Fohlen von Leihmüttern," *Süddeutsche Zeitung* (March 23, 1990): 45.

34. Cunningham, "The Genetics of Thoroughbred Horses," 97.

35. Birke, "Equine athletes," 48, 51; "Nachbrenner im Blut," *Der Spiegel* (July 21, 1986): 133.

36. Birke, "Equine athletes," 50–51. "Because blood circulation and oxygen delivery can rise linearly with exercise, a lack of oxygen is not likely to limit a horse's performance." See Cunningham, "The Genetics of Thoroughbred Horses," 98.

37. This kind of research has also been carried out on more exotic four-legged mammals. "Among the mammals, the champion endurance athlete is the antelope-like pronghorn from the North American prairies." This is the conclusion reached by scientists who "took pronghorn to the limit of their performance by running them uphill on a sloping treadmill. . . . Pronghorn seem to achieve their remarkable performance by very simple means. They have large lungs with exceptionally high diffusing capacity. Their blood has a high haemoglobin content and their cardiac output is high. Their muscles make up a larger than usual fraction of body mass and are exceptionally rich in mitochondria. The pronhorn's outstanding running capacity does not depend on any evolutionary novelty, but simply on enhancement of normal mammalian structure and physiology." See R. McNeill Alexander, "It may be better to be a wimp," *Nature* 353 (October 24, 1991): 696.

38. Cunningham, "The Genetics of Thoroughbred Horses," 98.

39. "Foals Are Getting Help Starting in Life's Race," *New York Times* (May 19, 1989).

40. Steven Crist, "A Lot at Stake for Alysheba, Forty Niner," *New York Times* (September 16, 1988).

41. Steven Crist, "Taking a Look at Lasix," *New York Times* (August 13, 1988).

42. "Geschummelt auf dem Rücken der Pferde," *Die Weltwoche* [Zürich] (November 12, 1987), "Federal indictment issued in drugging of NM racehorses," *The Dallas Morning News* (September 16, 1989); "Wenn Pferde Kaffee trinken," *Süddeutsche Zeitung* (June 20, 1989); "Wie im Krimi," *Der Spiegel* (November 7, 1986): 226, 228.

43. "Taking a Look at Lasix"; "Do Horses Need Lasix?," *New York Times* (June 3, 1990).

44. Steven Crist, "Lasix Dispute Threatens to Poison the Game," *New York Times* (May 15, 1990).

45. This study, commissioned by the Jockey Club of New York in 1988, was carried out by two scientists at the University of Pennsylvania and published in the *American Journal of Veterinary Research* in 1990.

46. "Do Horses Need Lasix?" Dr. Copelan comments as follows on the University of Pennsylvania report: "The Jockey Club study may not withstand the scrutiny of other scientists. The study did not use the classic research device of a control group, concurrent medication was not documented, water consumption was not standardized, and there was no attempt to differentiate the amount of bleeding among each of the test horses."

47. "Do Horses Need Lasix?"

48. Steven Crist, "Consulting the Evidence on Lasix," *New York Times* (May 8, 1990).

49. See, for example, "Veterinarians say deaths of racehorses not unusual," *Austin American-Statesman* (December 3, 1991): B1.

50. "An den Grenzen des Wachstums," *Frankfurter Allgemeine Zeitung* (September 2, 1991): 28.
51. Richard F. Corbisiero Jr., chairman of the New York State Racing and Wagering Board, in "Do Horses Need Lasix?"
52. "Taking a Look at Lasix."
53. "Geschummelt auf dem Rücken der Pferde."
54. Walter M. Kearns, "Testosterone Pellet Implantation in the Gelding," *Journal of the American Veterinary Medicine Association* (March 1942): 198.
55. Ibid., 200–01.
56. "Foals Are Getting Help Starting in Life's Race."
57. "Geschummelt auf dem Rücken der Pferde."
58. Steven Crist, "Handicappers to Gain A Line on Medication," *New York Times* (June 29, 1990). "For more than a decade, most racing jurisdictions have allowed the race-day use of various inflammatory drugs and diuretics, but this information did not appear in the sport's official result charts, which are prepared by the Form. Horseplayers had to keep their own records of when horses had used these drugs, and maintain files of back issues to find out if a horse used medication in a previous start. New York bettors were at a particular disadvantage when considering the prospects of out-of-town shippers, who might have been using the drugs at home but now would be denied them in New York."
59. "AHSA Sets Example Through Testing of Horses," USOC *Sportsmediscope* (February/March 1989): 12.
60. "Eisiger Empfang im WM-Hochsicherheitstrakt," *Süddeutsche Zeitung* (July 25, 1990).
61. "Wenn Pferde Kaffee trinken," *Süddeutsche Zeitung* (June 20, 1989).
62. "Der Olympiasieger will kein Denunziant sein," *Süddeutsche Zeitung* (June 12, 1989).
63. "Wie Veterinäre die Reiter im Zaum halten: Bisher dem Phantom 'Barren' nachgelaufen?" *Frankfurter Allgemeine Zeitung* (April 17, 1990).
64. "Stasi, wie Stallsicherheit," *Süddeutsche Zeitung* (February 20, 1990): 25.
65. "Schockemöhle der Tierquälerei beschuldigt," *Süddeutsche Zeitung* (July 12, 1990). The common German term for this kind of animal abuse is *Barren*.
66. "Geschummelt auf dem Rücken der Pferde."
67. "Einsam und verbittert," *Süddeutsche Zeitung* (August 2, 1990); "Neue Vorwürfe gegen Springreiter," *Süddeutsche Zeitung* (July 26, 1990); "Schmerzhaftes Urteil," *Süddeutsche Zeitung* (August 24, 1990): 38.
68. "Wie die Tiere," *Der Spiegel* (February 15, 1988): 214.
69. "Geschäfte auf dem Rücken von Roß und Reiter," *Süddeutsche Zeitung* (March 14, 1989): 43; "Schmerz gelindert, Heilung ausgesetzt," *Süddeutsche Zeitung* (March 21, 1989): 54.
70. "Helfendes Plätschern," *Der Spiegel* (March 6, 1989): 218.
71. "Abends an die Flasche," *Süddeutsche Zeitung* (August 5, 1988).
72. Bjarne Rostaing and Robert Sullivan, "Triumphs Tainted With Blood," *Sports Illustrated* (January 21, 1985): 12–17. See also Harvey G. Klein, "Blood Transfusion and Athletics," *The New England Journal of Medicine* 312 (March 28, 1985): 854–56.
73. W[ildor] Hollmann, "Risikofaktoren in der Entwicklung des Hochleistungssports," in H. Rieckert, ed., *Sportmedizin-Kursbestimmung* [Deutscher Spor-

tärztekongreß, Kiel, 16–19. Oktober 1986] (Berlin: Springer-Verlag, 1987): 16.

74. Carl Foster, "Physiologic Testing: Does It Help the Athlete?" *The Physician and Sportsmedicine* 17 (October 1989): 108, 103, 104, 104, 105, 108, 108, 109. Foster's general assessment is endorsed by the Canadian physiologist Claude Bouchard. See "Quelques réflexions sur l'avènement des biotechnologies dans le sport," in F. Landry, M. Landry, M. Yerlès, eds. *Sport . . . the Third Millennium. Proceedings of the International Symposium* [May 21–25, 1990] (Quebec City: Les Presses de l'Université Laval, 1991): 456.

75. "Doktor Faust sucht den direkten Weg," *Süddeutsche Zeitung* (February 21/22, 1987).

76. R. Häcker and A. Lehnert, "Sportliche Höchstleistung aus medizinischbiowissenschaftlicher Sicht," in R. Häcker and H. de Marées, eds., *Hormonelle Regulation und psychophysiche Belastung im Leistungssport* (Cologne: Deutscher Ärzte-Verlag, 1991): 14, 15, 17–18; D. Nicklas and A. Lehnert, "Möglichkeiten einer zielgerichteten Trainingssteuerung durch Nutzung von Ergebnissen zur hormonellen Regulation des Energiestoffwechsels," in ibid., 40–41. On the potential danger to sport posed by genetic engineering, see Bouchard, "Quelques reflexions sur l'avènement des biotechnologies dans le sport."

77. "Den Begriff neu formulieren," *Süddeutsche Zeitung* (July 27, 1987).

78. "Minister Schäuble warnt vor einer 'Doping-Hysterie,' " *Süddeutsche Zeitung* (October 21, 1989).

79. Bouchard, "Quelques réflexions sur l'avènement des biotechnologies dans le sport," 461.

80. On May 22, 1990, at a conference on "Sport . . . The Third Millennium" held in Quebec City, Bouchard claimed that five genes that account for 20 percent of the trainability of the aerobic system could already be detected in utero. The author was present and made a note of Bouchard's statement. In 1984 another investigator noted Bouchard's statement that there were as yet no genetic markers that identified sensitivity to training. See D. F. Roberts, "Genetic Determinants of Sports Performance" [1984], in Robert M. Malina and Claude Bouchard, eds., *Sport and Human Genetics,* vol. 4 of the *1984 Olympic Scientific Congress Proceedings* (Champaign: Human Kinetics Publishers, 1986): 109.

81. Roberts, "Genetic Determinants of Sports Performance," 105, 121.

82. "Gene therapy treatment to fight fatal disease," *The Guardian* [London], January 17, 1992; Patricia Kahn, "Germany's Gene Law Begins to Bite," *Science* 255 (January 31, 1992): 524–526.

83. "Olympic row over sex testing," *Nature* 353 (October 31, 1991): 784. "The technology based on polymerase chain reaction (PCR) analysis is, he says, so easy to use that sports-related genetic sex-testing may become commonplace, despite continuing scientific debate about what defines a woman and a dearth of genetic counsellors trained to explain to young female athletes what it means, for example, to have some Y chromosome motif in their genetic makeup." See "Olympic row over sex testing," *Nature* 353 (October 31, 1991): 784; see also "Der renovierte Sextest," *Süddeutsche Zeitung,* November 28, 1990; "Track Federation Urges End to Gene Test for Femaleness," *New York Times* (February 12, 1992): A1, B11; "Who Is Female? Science Can't Say," *New York Times,* February 16, 1992.

84. For a history of the eugenics movement in Great Britain and the United States,

see Daniel J. Kevles, *In the Name of Eugenics: Genetics and the Uses of Human Heredity* (Berkeley and Los Angeles: University of California Press, 1986).

85. Kevles, *In the Name of Eugenics*, 56, 62, 48.
86. John Maddox, "The case for the human genome," *Nature* 352 (July 4, 1991): 12.
87. Ibid., 11.
88. Quoted in Ronald W. Clark, *J B S: The Life and Work of J.B.S. Haldane* (New York: Coward-McCann, Inc., 1968): 65.
89. Kevles, *In the Name of Eugenics*, 126.
90. Quoted in Krishna R. Dronamraju, *Haldane: The Life and work of J B S Haldane with special reference to India* (Aberdeen: Aberdeen University Press, 1985): 105.

Index

Abderhalden, Emil, 91
Acromegaly, 49, 50
Acupuncture, 196
Adastra, 123
Adrenal steroids, 214
Adrenalin, 136, 151, 215
Advertising, dynamic-athletic body used in, 63
Africans, 46, 55–56, 118–19, 124, 167. *See also* Blacks
AHSA. *See* American Horse Show Association (AHSA)
Airplanes, 63
Albu, A., 29, 30, 59–60
Alcohol: addiction due to, 112; animal reaction to, 120; Balzac on, 113; cyclists' use of, 12, 126–27, 174; disrepute of, as stimulant, 132, 136, 156; Eskimos' reaction to, 120; fatigue caused by, 82; Herxheimer's experiments on, 156, 157; in Jarry's *The Supermale*, 130, 131; and muscle functioning, 220; for racehorses, 280; racial differences and, 120; research on, 120, 122, 262; as stimulant, 6, 113, 114, 134, 135; temperance movement and, 104; Tissié on, 95, 126–27, 128, 133
Alexeyev, Vassily, 226
Alkaline buffering, 149
Alkalosis, 212
Alma Ata, 195
Aloes, 116
Alpinists, 6, 61, 142, 155
"Alternative" therapies (Germany), 254
"Altitude training," 41–42
Alysheba, 276
Amazonian Indians, 134
American Civil War, 44
American Horse Show Association (AHSA), 281

American Indians, 34, 37, 39, 51, 55, 67, 117
Americanism, 254
Amino sugars, 260
Amphetamines, 4, 27, 214
Anabolic steroids: apologias for, 26, 245; for child-athletes, 224–25, 226, 287; debate over, 142; definition of, 146; detection method for, 100; and doping, 101; Dressel's use of, 2; early history of, 145–53; in East German sport, 19, 208–209, 285–86; epidemic use of, 266; ethics of, 26; for female athletes, 27, 225; Gasser's use of, 229–37; hazards of, 27, 93; history of, 72–76; legalization of, 3, 239; masking agents concealing, 107, 284; medical applications of, 108–109; Nazis' alleged experiments with, 208, 213–16; during 1920s and 1930s, 132; Norwegian shot-putters' use of, 267–68; Olympic athletes' use of, 266; as performance-enhancing drugs, 4; power to "masculinize," 214; and protein synthesis, 149; for racehorses, 270, 277, 279–80; research on, 109–10; self-experimentation with, 147; side effects of, 146, 147, 225; and starvation victims, 214; and "steroid deficit," 249; synthesis of, 84; as therapeutic drugs, 277–78; in West German sport, 246; and whites' perceived racial athletic inferiority, 120. *See also* Doping
Anaerobic threshold, 285
Ancient Greeks, 104–105, 166
Andaman Islanders, 45, 46, 58
Andersen, Georg, 267–68
André the Giant, 49
Angerer, Peter, 262
"Animal engine," 272